Common Symptoms of Disease in Children

The Normal Child, 8th edition 1982
Churchill Livingstone
Translated into Greek, Spanish, Japanese and Farsi

Development of the Infant and Young Child,
Normal and Abnormal, 7th edition 1980
Churchill Livingstone
Translated into Japanese, French and Polish

Lessons from Childhood: Some Aspects of the
Early Life of Unusual Men and Women with
C. M. Illingworth, 1968
Churchill Livingstone
Translated into Japanese

Babies and Young Children: Feeding,
Management and Care with C. M. Illingworth,
6th edition 1977
Churchill Livingstone

Treatment of the Child at Home: A Guide for
Family Doctors, 1971
Blackwell Scientific Publications
Translated into Greek

Basic Development Screening 3rd edition 1982
Blackwell Scientific Publications
Translated into Greek and Italian

The Child at School: A Paediatrician's
Manual for Teachers, 1975
Blackwell Scientific Publications

Common Symptoms of Disease in Children

R. S. ILLINGWORTH
MD, FRCP, DPH, DCH
Emeritus Professor of Child Health
The University of Sheffield

SEVENTH EDITION

BLACKWELL SCIENTIFIC PUBLICATIONS
OXFORD LONDON EDINBURGH
BOSTON MELBOURNE

© 1976, 1969, 1971, 1973, 1975, 1979, 1982 by
Blackwell Scientific Publications
Editorial offices:
Osney Mead, Oxford, OX2 0EL
8 John Street, London, WC1N 2ES
9 Forrest Road, Edinburgh,
    EH1 2QH
52 Beacon Street, Boston, Mass.
    02108, USA
99 Barry Street, Carlton
    Victoria 3053, Australia

First published 1967
Second edition 1969
Third edition 1971
Fourth edition 1973
Reprinted 1974
Fifth edition 1975
Sixth edition 1979
Reprinted 1980
Seventh edition 1982
Reprinted 1983

Translated into Spanish, Greek, Italian and German.

Filmset by Enset Ltd
Midsomer Norton, Bath, Avon and printed and bound in Great Britain by Billing and Sons Limited
Guildford, London, Oxford
Worcester

DISTRIBUTORS

USA
    Blackwell Mosby Book Distributors
    11830 Westline Industrial Drive
    St Louis, Missouri 63141

Canada
    Blackwell Mosby Book Distributors
    120 Melford Drive, Scarborough
    Ontario, M1B 2X4

Australia
    Blackwell Scientific Book
    Distributors
    31 Advantage Road,
    Highett, Victoria 3190

British Library
Cataloguing in Publication Data

Illingworth, Ronald S.
    Common symptoms of disease
    in children.—7th ed.
    1. Children—Diseases
    2. Semiology
    I. Title
    618.92′0072′   RJ254

ISBN 0–632–00814–8

Contents

Preface to the Seventh Edition

I have very extensively revised this edition, with many scores of additions and several new sections, including one at the end of the book entitled 'The paediatric diagnostic problem—elementary principles of diagnosis'. Numerous sections have been completely rewritten.

My aim, as before, is to guide the doctor, whether paediatrician, hospital resident or family doctor, when faced with a diagnostic problem, and as before, I have based this entirely on symptoms and have throughout provided relevant references or helpful books and articles. Throughout I have emphasised that non-disease is more common than disease, and that common conditions, including their troublesome variations, are more common than rare diseases. I have been criticized for including rare diseases—and often referring to them in several different places; I formed the impression that some reviewers had thought that the title of my book was *Symptoms of Common Diseases*. It is not: the title is *Common Symptoms of Disease*— and therefore rare diseases have to be included. The difficulty was that of deciding which of these rare diseases to include: any choice of these for inclusion would be eminently suitable for legitimate criticism. It was inevitable that some rare diseases have to be mentioned in several places, for most symptoms are the end result of a wide variety of diseases, and each disease is likely to cause many different symptoms.

I have been criticized for not including the pathology of disease. That would be irrelevant, though I have frequently tried to explain the causes of symptoms. This book is designed to cover common symptoms and to provide a guide to diagnosis: it is not an entire textbook of paediatrics. In this edition I have reduced references to special investigations which would establish a diagnosis: an entire large volume would be required to provide an adequate account of the special investigations required to establish the diagnosis for all the symptoms outlined in this book.

I have made a determined effort to rationalize the arrangement of causes of symptoms, and in so doing have faced the manifestly impossible task of arranging causes of symptoms in such a way that non-disease is mentioned before disease, common conditions before rare diseases, causes applicable to the newborn before those only relevant to the older child, and diseases of head, neck and the upper part of the body before those lower down. I have avoided nice tidy classifications which ignore these variables. I know of one book which gives albinism as the first cause of pallor: another which gives Costen's syndrome as the first cause of recurrent headaches; another which gives narcolepsy as the first cause of sleep disorders.

I have tried to keep lists of diseases as short as possible, because I think that lists are of only limited value. I know one book which lists 118 causes of unexplained fever and 112 causes of dwarfism (and another which lists 72 syndromes associated with dwarfism). Instead *I have throughout constantly drawn on my experience to emphasize the most common and important conditions with a view to avoiding the mistakes which I have seen others make or which I have made myself.*

Another difficulty was that of distinguishing symptoms from signs: they overlap. For instance, enlargement of the spleen is not normally a symptom, though it could be if it was enormous, and palpation of an enlarged spleen often causes some discomfort. I have not included it.

I repeat what I have said in each previous edition, that I should be most grateful for suggestions for improving this book.

R. S. Illingworth

Preface to the First Edition

When I was talking to my thirteen-year-old child about my attempt to write a book concerning the common symptoms of disease in children, mentioning the difficulties which I was encountering, and the fact that no one, to my knowledge, has attempted it, she said 'Isn't that all the more reason why you should do it?' I replied that it may well be that the reason why others have not done it is the fact that they have more sense than to try.

I have attempted to write a précis of the common symptoms of disease in children because I felt that the family doctor, when faced with a symptom in a child whom he is examining, would find it useful when in difficulty to refer quickly to conditions which have to be considered. The textbooks, general or specialist, for the most part do not deal with symptoms. For instance, I referred to a large textbook of otorhinolaryngology for information about stridor, but the word was not in the index. It is likely to take a family doctor a long time to find a textbook which discusses the very common cyanotic or apnoeic attacks of the newborn. The great majority of the symptoms which I have discussed in this book are not, in fact, mentioned in the index of the majority of textbooks, and many of the symptoms are not mentioned in the index of any of them. This is not intended to be a criticism of textbooks. Discussion of symptoms would have greatly lengthened them, and inevitably have caused repetition.

In consequence I have discussed about a hundred common symptoms of disease in childhood. I have made no attempt to provide a complete list of all the possible causes of a symptom, but I have tried to pick out the important causes, making it clear which I think are the most common ones, and which I consider to be rare.

Though classifications are useful for memorizing, and though they look neat and tidy, I have avoided them almost completely, because of their inherent weakness in not giving the common conditions first.

Where a symptom may be psychological or organic I have included it, but where a symptom is entirely psychological I have omitted it, because I have discussed psychological problems in my books *The*

Normal Child in His First Five Years* and *The Child at School*.† I have, however, included a section concerning psychological manifestations of organic disease, and the somatic manifestations of psychological symptoms.

The book is confined to the subject of diagnosis. I have named common investigations which need to be carried out in order to elucidate the problem—but again have made no effort to name them all. (In a recent article on jaundice in the newborn, the author listed 75 special investigations which should be carried out.) I have not described the normal values of the investigations, nor the methods of performing them: but I have named the investigations in order that the family doctor would know some of the tests which are necessary to establish the diagnosis, and would then know when to refer the child to a special centre for study. I thought, furthermore, that knowledge of the necessary tests would help him in his talks with the parents. I have made a special point of emphasizing the conditions which do require such special investigation.

There is inevitably a certain overlap between signs and symptoms and I have allowed myself a little licence in interpreting the word 'symptoms'. For instance, I have included a short section on enlargement of the spleen. Admittedly an adult experiences discomfort when his spleen is felt. My reason for including it, however, was the frequency of splenic enlargement in children and therefore its importance in the diagnosis of so many different diseases.

I have assumed that the family doctor has basic medical knowledge. I have also had to assume that the family doctor does not want or need profound knowledge on any subject. My notes may well, therefore, be criticized for being superficial. They are deliberately made so, because I did not feel that the family doctor would want more. But I have throughout assumed that having looked through a section of this book to read about a particular symptom, he would then refer to one of the recognized textbooks for more information. To this end I have listed principal sources of further knowledge. For instance, as a general source of information on a paediatric problem I have recommended Nelson's *Textbook of Pediatrics*.

---

*The Normal Child, Eighth Edition, 1982, London, Churchill.
†*The Child at School: a Paediatrician's Manual for Teachers* (1975). Blackwell Scientific Publications, Oxford.

In my opinion no one should attempt to make a diagnosis in a sick child without knowing what drugs he has already received. The side effects of drugs are so frequent and far reaching, and the number of drugs taken, whether prescribed by a doctor or otherwise, is so great, that it is essential to know what medicines have been given. I have mentioned the side effects of drugs in the relevant sections, and summarized them in a special section.

At the risk of repetition, I have inserted a brief section about commonly held misbeliefs in paediatric diagnosis—including such a misbelief as the idea that convulsions are caused by teething. I am aware of the fact that there is a small amount of repetition in different sections. I decided to retain this for the convenience of the reader.

I hope that family doctors will find this book useful in General Practice. I believe that students will find this book useful for the purposes of revision. It would not serve as a basic textbook for them, but I believe that it would be useful in conjunction with one of the standard textbooks.

It is certain that many will think of causes of which I have not thought, or of symptoms which should have been included. I should greatly welcome comments and suggestions so that the book can be improved if another edition is required.

I wish to thank my friends Dr Peter Wyon, Family Doctor, of Thirsk, Yorks, Dr Frank Harris, Lecturer in Child Health, the University of Sheffield, and my wife, Dr Cynthia Illingworth, for reading every word of the script and for their most useful criticisms: and to my secretaries, Miss D. Bain, Miss J. Grundy and Mrs D. Ackroyd, for typing the drafts of this book.

Failure to Thrive

All those who are concerned with the care of children are repeatedly faced with the problem of the child who refuses to gain weight in the approved manner. It is surprisingly difficult to obtain a composite picture of this problem in the standard texts. In this chapter I have attempted to put together the main conditions which have to be considered when a child's weight gain is below the average. In the first place one must decide whether or not there is anything wrong with the child.

All children are different. Some are small and some are big, some are thin and some are fat. Though nutrition has much to do with this, it is not true to say that nutrition is the only factor. Many factors are unknown. It is difficult and usually impossible to draw the line between normal and abnormal. A child may be pounds below the average in weight, and inches below the average in height, and yet be normal. It is far more important that the child should be full of energy, free from lassitude and abounding in *joie de vivre,* than that he should be average in weight and height. It is much more healthy to be below the average weight than above it. All that one can say is that the further away from the average is the child's weight and height, the less likely it is to be 'normal'.

When a child is smaller than average, his appetite is likely to be correspondingly less than that of others, so that the parents become worried and try to persuade him to eat. The inevitable result is food refusal—termed by mothers 'poor appetite'.

Mothers are often worried about the normal slowing down of weight gain in the second half of the first year. This is associated with a reduction in appetite, which may cause food forcing and so food refusal. Children take all they need if given a chance and it is never necessary to try to make them eat. A well child's poor appetite is almost always due to food forcing.

Normal physical growth and variations

Tables 1 and 2 show the average weight of boys and girls in the first 10 years.

1

Failure to thrive

Table 1. Average weight of boys and girls

Boys

Age in years	CENTILES 10		CENTILES 50		CENTILES 90	
	lb	kg	lb	kg	lb	kg
0	6·17	2·8	7·72	3·5	9·04	4·1
0·25	11·05	5·01	13·07	5·93	15·41	6·99
0·5	14·99	6·8	17·42	7·9	20·28	9·2
0·75	17·59	7·98	20·28	9·2	23·43	10·63
1·0	19·40	8·8	22·49	10·2	25·79	11·7
2	24·25	11·0	28·0	12·7	32·19	14·6
3	28·00	12·7	32·41	14·7	37·26	16·9
4	31·52	14·3	36·60	16·6	42·11	19·1
5	34·61	15·7	40·72	18·5	47·4	21·5
6	38·14	17·3	45·20	20·5	52·91	24·0
7	41·89	19·0	49·82	22·6	59·29	26·9
8	46·03	20·9	55·11	25·0	66·13	30·0
9	50·48	22·9	60·62	27·5	73·63	33·4
10	55·56	25·2	66·68	30·3	82·23	37·3

Girls

Age in years	CENTILES 10		CENTILES 50		CENTILES 90	
	lb.	kg	lb	kg	lb	kg
0	6·28	2·85	7·50	3·4	8·71	3·95
0·25	10·6	4·81	12·26	5·56	14·13	6·41
0·5	14·2	6·44	15·21	6·9	18·72	8·49
0·75	16·71	7·58	19·22	8·72	22·09	10·02
1·0	18·52	8·4	21·38	9·7	24·69	11·2
2	22·93	10·4	26·89	12·2	31·09	14·1
3	27·11	12·3	31·52	14·3	36·15	16·4
4	31·09	14·1	35·93	16·3	41·44	18·8
5	35·05	15·9	40·34	18·3	47·17	21·4
6	38·8	17·6	44·97	20·4	53·79	24·4
7	42·33	19·2	49·82	22·6	61·07	27·7
8	46·29	21·0	55·34	25·1	68·78	31·2
9	50·7	23·0	61·07	27·7	78·04	35·4
10	55·34	25·1	68·56	31·1	90·39	41·0

Table 2. Average height of boys and girls

Boys

Age in years	CENTILES 10		CENTILES 50		CENTILES 90	
	in	cm	in	cm	in	cm
0	20·2	51·4	21·3	54·0	22·3	56·6
1	28·7	72·8	30·0	76·3	31·4	79·7
2	32·6	82·7	34·2	86·9	35·9	91·1
3	35·1	89·3	37·1	94·2	39·0	99·1
4	37·8	96·1	40·0	101·6	42·1	107·1
5	40·2	102·2	42·6	108·3	45·0	114·4
6	42·5	108·0	45·1	114·6	47·7	121·2
7	44·7	113·5	47·4	120·5	50·2	127·5
8	46·8	118·8	49·7	126·2	52·6	133·5
9	48·8	124·0	51·8	131·6	54·8	139·3
10	50·7	128·8	53·9	136·8	57·0	144·8

Girls

Age in years	CENTILES 10		CENTILES 50		CENTILES 90	
	in	cm	in	cm	in	cm
0	19·8	50·4	20·9	53·0	21·9	55·9
1	27·9	70·8	29·2	74·2	30·6	77·7
2	32·0	81·3	33·7	85·6	35·4	89·8
3	34·7	88·1	36·6	93·0	38·5	97·9
4	37·4	94·9	39·5	100·4	41·7	105·9
5	39·8	101·1	42·4	107·2	44·6	113·2
6	42·0	106·8	44·5	113·4	47·2	120·0
7	44·2	112·4	47·0	119·3	49·7	126·3
8	46·3	117·6	49·2	125·0	52·1	132·4
9	48·4	122·9	51·4	130·6	54·4	138·3
10	50·5	128·3	53·7	136·4	56·9	144·5

Tanner JM, Whitehouse RH, Takaishi M (1966). Standard from birth to maturity for height, weight, height velocity and weight velocity. *Arch. Dis. Child.*, **41**, 613.

Failure to thrive

Mothers are liable to be worried if a child is smaller than usual. After the first year it may be useful to attempt to predict the child's eventual height. Prediction can be only approximate because of the many variables, but it may help a parent's understanding and allay anxiety. Table 3, based on the work of Tanner, shows the percentage of eventual height reached at various ages. An example of the value of such a table is as follows. A child of three years was referred because of her small size, being 34 inches (86 cm) high. Her mother was 5 feet (150

Table 3. Height in childhood in relation to expected adult height

Expected adult height	5 ft	150 cm	5 ft 6 in	165 cm	6 ft	180 cm
Height of boys Age in years	in	cm	in	cm	in	cm
1	25·8	65·5	28·3	72·0	30·9	78·6
2	29·4	74·7	32·1	81·7	35.3	89·6
3	31·8	80·8	35·1	89·2	38·1	97·0
4	34·4	87·3	37·8	96·1	41·2	104·7
5	36·6	93·0	40·3	102·3	43·9	111·6
6	38·7	98·4	42·7	108·4	46·6	118·4
7	40·7	103·5	44·8	113·9	48·9	124·2
8	42·6	108·2	46·9	119·0	51·1	129·9
9	44·6	113·2	49·0	124·4	53·4	135·7
10	46·2	117·4	50·8	129·1	55·5	140·9
Height in girls Age in years	in	cm	in	cm	in	cm
1	27·0	68·5	28·3	72·0	32·4	82·2
2	31·1	79·2	34·3	87·1	37·4	95·0
3	33·9	86·0	37·2	94·5	40·6	103·1
4	36·5	92·8	40·2	102·1	43·9	111·4
5	39·0	99·1	43·0	109·1	46·9	119·0
6	41·3	104·8	45·4	115·3	49·6	125·9
7	43·5	110·5	47·8	121·5	52·2	132·6
8	45·6	115·7	50·1	127·3	54·6	138·8
9	47·6	120·9	52·2	133·0	57·1	145·1
10	49·5	125·7	54·4	138·3	59·4	150·9

As a rough guide, the height on the second birthday is half the expected adult height. Calculated from Tanner, *et al.* (1966). Example—7-year-old girl, height 43·5 inches. Probably eventual height is 5 feet.

cm) tall and was relieved to hear that the girl could be expected to reach a similar height.

When an apparently well child is unusually small for his age, one should consider the following factors:

1   Genetics. When a parent is unusually small, not only in height and weight but in physical build, the child may be correspondingly small. Furthermore, there is often a familial pattern of growth, such as a tendency for slower than usual growth in the early months.

2   Low birth weight. The smaller the child is at birth, particularly if he was small for dates, the smaller he is likely to be in later years. Conversely, the larger he is at birth, the larger he is likely to be in later years. It seems that growth in utero is some indication of his later growth potential (Black, Brown & Thomas 1977). Defective growth in utero can be caused by maternal malnutrition, placental insufficiency, placental malaria, drugs taken by the mother (nicotine, alcohol, methotrexate, propranolol etc.) and other factors.

3   Socio-economic factors. Socio-economic factors, together with genetic factors and low birth weight, explain the great majority of cases of unusually slow physical growth, and these should always be considered before special investigations are requested. Intensive investigations are unlikely to be productive when the history and examination do not suggest organic disease (Mitchell, Gorrell & Greenberg 1980).

4   Defective physical growth from previous disease, now cured.

Experimental work on animals has shown that if growth is retarded in early life, the growth remains defective later in spite of adequate nutrition. Many human infants who suffered major surgical procedures in the early weeks, and who were excessively small in weight in that period, are small in later years (Eid 1971). The longer the growth retardation persists before the cause is corrected, the greater is the subsequent growth deficit. Umansky & Hauck (1962) showed that children operated on for ligation of a patent ductus arteriosus, and who were far below the average in size at the time of the operation, did not usually catch up to the average height after the ligation. Only 20 per cent of 444 children showed a marked post-operative acceleration of growth in height. It seems that there is a 'critical period' in physical growth, after which a normal diet will not restore the child to an average size.

Classification of causes of failure to thrive
    Defective intake
        Breast feeding—insufficiency of milk
        Artificial feeding
            Inadequate quantity for preterm baby
            Fear of overfeeding
            Incorrectly prepared food
        Emotional deprivation: prolonged crying: non-accidental injury
        Vitamin deficiency on synthetic diets
        Chronic infection e.g. urinary tract, tuberculosis
        Protein calorie malnutrition
    Defective absorption
        Fat, carbohydrate, protein
        Hirschsprung's disease
        Allergy to cow's milk
    Increased loss
        Excessive perspiration. Overclothing. Inadequate fluid intake in hot climate
        Diarrhoea, vomiting
    Rare errors of metabolism e.g. renal acidosis, hypercalcaemia, nephrogenic diabetes insipidus, adrenocortical hyperplasia, hypophosphatasia, Bartter's syndrome, De Toni-Fanconi syndrome
    Organ diseases, involving the brain, heart, chest, kidney, pancreas
        Mental deficiency, cerebral tumour, subdural effusion
        Congenital heart disease
        Severe asthma, bronchiectasis
        Renal or hepatic insufficiency
        Diabetes mellitus
    Miscellaneous—chromosome abnormality. Fetal alcohol syndrome

Defective intake

A breast fed baby is more likely to suffer from underfeeding than an artificially fed baby, because the mother cannot know how much milk she has without weighing him. Mothers think that the leaking of milk from the breast (lactorrhoea) signifies that there is an abundance of milk, though it signifies nothing more than the draught reflex, or the unusually easy escape of milk from the breast. Many doctors think that if a baby is contented he must be obtaining sufficient milk from the breast. This is far from the truth. Many young babies are content to starve and do not cry, even though receiving a totally inadequate amount of milk.

The most accurate way of establishing the diagnosis of defective intake by a breast fed baby is the test feed—weighing the baby before and after every feed in the day, expressing milk fully after each feed and measuring it, and then adding up the total. If expression is not carried out, the result is seriously misleading, for all that one is then measuring is the milk which the baby has taken from the breast, but not the milk available in the breast. If a baby sucks badly or is drowsy or irritable or if the nipple is a difficult one for him, he may not obtain the available milk.

A small preterm baby may fail to gain weight on human milk, but thrive on skimmed cow's milk. A common cause of the failure of a preterm baby to gain weight is inadequate intake: it is often forgotten that whereas a full term baby usually needs 2½ ounces of milk per pound per day (150 ml per kg), a preterm baby after two weeks usually needs 3 ounces per lb per day (188 ml per kg) and 4 ounces per lb per day (250 ml per kg) after four weeks: but overfeeding may cause vomiting and loss of weight.

A bottle fed baby may be underfed either because of starvation, or because of errors in the constitution of the feeds. When investigating the method of feeding, one asks how much milk powder and water the mother is putting into each feed, and how many feeds she is giving per day. It is futile to accept a mother's statement that she is giving the baby 'five ounces of Cow and Gate' at each feed. She may be making the feed up far too dilute, so that the baby is underfed. Sometimes mothers wrongly ascribe their baby's loose stools, wind or other symptoms to *overfeeding*, reduce the feeds and cause underfeeding. After early infancy underfeeding may be due to parental food fads or ignorance.

When a baby is seriously underweight, one commonly finds that the quantity which the mother states that she is giving is adequate, but that when the baby is admitted to the ward he is ravenously hungry, has a far bigger than average weight gain, and has been half starved. I have known such babies gain as much as 25 ounces a week (709 g) when given as much as they want. *It is important to accept with scepticism the mother's story of the quantity given. When a child is failing to thrive, and no obvious cause can be found, one should suspect underfeeding, whatever the mother says.* This must be eliminated before one embarks on complex laboratory investigations.

An important cause of defective intake of food is *emotional deprivation*. One often sees older babies who refuse to gain weight in hospital, in the absence of evidence of disease. They gain weight normally when the mother is admitted to the hospital to be with the child, or when she takes him home. An important cause of failure to thrive is excessive crying. There are many possible causes of this (pp. 98, 261). Continual crying not only uses up energy, but also leads to loss of fluid through the lungs and so to defective weight gain. It may tire the baby, so that when food is offered he does not take it well.

Child abuse, (non-accidental injury), is an example of severe emotional deprivation. It may take the form of emotional cruelty, deliberate starvation, the deprivation of fluid, physical trauma (broken bones, bruises, subdural haematoma, the infliction of burns, injury to the mouth or viscera), or the administration of poison, salt or overdose of drugs. As child abuse is almost always denied by the parents, diagnosis can be difficult. Factors which should arouse suspicion are repeated injuries, complaints about the child's bad behaviour or constant crying, delay in seeking advice, an implausible story which does not fit the clinical findings, previous injury, including a history of injury to siblings, burns or poisonings, frequent attendances at the hospital, or failure to thrive. Risk factors include low birth weight, nursing in an intensive care unit causing separation of mother and baby, poverty, unemployment, bad social conditions, or maternal illness. Any fracture under the age of two years should arouse the suspicion of child abuse: and signs suggesting it include bruises around the neck or in places not normally involved in the usual falls, small round cigarette burns, a torn alveolar frenum, haemorrhages in the optic fundus, bruises of different ages and evidence of old fractures as indicated by a skeletal survey. Radiological changes may indicate that the date of the fracture could not correspond with the mother's story. Emotional deprivation may cause functional pituitary growth hormone deficiency with polydipsia, abdominal distension and dwarfism (Raynes & Rudd 1973).

Cronic infection. Acute infections, even when frequent, do not usually cause defective weight gain, because children have a compensatory increase of appetite after a febrile illness and make up lost ground, but a severe chronic infection such as bronchiectasis or urinary tract infection may well cause defective weight gain.

Congenital cytomegalovirus or toxoplasma infection may lead to failure to thrive. There may be hepatosplenomegaly and purpura with retinal changes. Chronic malaria, ancylostomiasis or tuberculosis in developing countries may cause defective growth partly because of associated defective intake.

Mann, Wilson & Clayton (1965) described *deficiency states in infants on synthetic foods* (e.g. low phenylalanine for phenylketonuria, low lactose for galactosaemia, low sodium and low calcium). The children failed to thrive and developed sores around the external nares, fissured lips, lesions at the outer canthus of the eyes, angular stomatitis and psoriasiform lesions on the buttocks. They responded immediately to Ketovite tablets and syrup. Beriberi occurs especially in breast-fed babies, often at the age of 2 or 3 months. There may be vomiting, abdominal distension, and later head retraction, rigidity, fits, loss of weight, failure to thrive and diarrhoea.

Protein calorie malnutrition, manifestations of which are often precipitated by infection, is of importance in many developing countries.

Defective absorption

When considering the cause of failure to thrive due to defective absorption, we must think of defective absorption of fat, carbohydrate and protein.

Defective absorption of fat (steatorrhoea)

There are many causes of steatorrhoea. In an analysis of 266 cases of steatorrhoea in children. Charlotte Anderson found that 52 per cent were due to fibrocystic disease of the pancreas, 35 per cent to coeliac disease, and 13 per cent to other causes, of which the main ones were giardiasis, chronic intestinal infection, anomalies of the alimentary tract, and certain diseases of the liver and pancreas.

The commonest cause of steatorrhoea is *fibrocystic disease of the pancreas*. It occurs in approximately one in every 2400 children. There are four main modes of presentation—meconium ileus in the newborn baby, failure to thrive, steatorrhoea, and chronic or recurrent chest disease. Meconium ileus (p. 65) presents as intestinal obstruction in the newborn. Failure to thrive is seen at any age in young children from infancy onwards. Bulky, offensive or loose stools may be noticed by the mother at any stage, but this is relatively unusual. In many cases of coeliac disease or fibrocystic disease of the pancreas, the mother has not noticed anything unusual about the stools. One should always investigate for fibrocystic disease when a child has chronic pulmonary infection such as bronchiectasis or persistent radiological abnormality in the lung such as pulmonary collapse. Two other signs may draw attention to the possibility of fibrocystic disease—unexplained generalized oedema or prolapse of the rectum: there are other causes of both of these conditions, but both are sometimes early features of steatorrhoea and in particular fibrocystic disease of the pancreas. Cirrhosis of the liver is sometimes a feature. In some atypical cases the sweat chloride may be within normal limits (Huff, Huang & Arey 1979).

Coeliac disease is the second most common cause of steatorrhoea. The majority of cases are due to sensitivity to gluten, but a few may be due to milk allergy. There may be associated carbohydrate intolerance which confuses the diagnosis because it may be responsible for an unsatisfactory response to exclusion of gluten (Gracey & Burke 1973).

The symptoms of coeliac disease commence when cereals are introduced into the diet, so that the age of onset is variable. The usual initial symptom is vomiting. Other symptoms are undue irritability, loss of appetite and failure to thrive. In an advanced case there is wasting of the buttocks with a protuberant abdomen (as in other forms of steatorrhoea). The appetite in coeliac disease tends to be poor, while that in fibrocystic disease tends to be unusually good, but in the absence of chronic pulmonary infection one cannot distinguish the two conditions on clinical grounds. It is most important that the diagnosis should be properly established by laboratory means: it is bad practice to rely on the response to treatment, because once one has embarked on the special diet it is difficult to discontinue it because of fear of harming the baby. In severe cases six to eight weeks may elapse before improvement occurs.

Steatorrhoea may result from *chronic intestinal infection,* particularly *giardiasis* or *salmonella*. Though rare in England, giardiasis is common in many developing countries. Some feel that giardiasis is secondary to other conditions, and not the principal cause of the steatorrhoea.

Certain *congenital anomalies of the alimentary tract* may cause steatorrhoea. They include *malrotation, stenosis, gastrocolic fistula, intestinal lymphangiectasia and intestinal reduplication* (Leslie & Matheson 1965). *Crohn's disease* (regional ileitis) may cause failure to thrive due to defective absorption of protein and fat. There may be no other symptom or sign pointing to that condition (Sobel *et al.* 1962). Common symptoms are abdominal pain, fever, diarrhoea, weight loss or defective growth. Less common are arthritis, anorectal disease including fistula or erythema nodosum (O'Donoghue & Dawson 1977).

There is an association of steatorrhoea with *pancreatic insufficiency and chronic neutropenia.*

Steatorrhoea may be found in cases of *carbohydrate intolerance, protein-losing enteropathy, tuberculosis of the mesentery, biliary atresia, cirrhosis of the liver and ulcerative colitis.* It is found in the rare abetalipoproteinaemia in which there is ataxia, absence of betalipoproteins in the serum, reduced serum lipoids and a crenated appearance of the red cells (acanthocytosis). Retinal changes occur in the later stages. There is a rare form of familial steatorrhoea with mental retardation and calcification of the basal ganglia (Cockel *et al.* 1973). A cause which is rare in childhood is Whipple's disease, in which there is steatorrhoea, polyarthralgia, fever, weight loss and lymphadenopathy. Steatorrhoea may be a feature of acquired agammaglobulinaemia.

Steatorrhoea may result from the administration of certain *drugs*—kanamycin, mercaptopurine, methotrexate, neomycin and P.A.S.

Carbohydrate intolerance and malabsorption

Carbohydrate intolerance may be primary (genetic) or secondary to coeliac disease, fibrocystic disease of the pancreas, sprue, gastroenteritis or giardiasis. It should be seriously considered whenever one is faced with the problem of a child with failure to thrive and loose stools. The stools are tested for reducing substances by the Clinitest, and if that is positive, the sugar is identified by paper chromatography. Only the fluid part of freshly collected stools should be tested, and the child should have been on a normal diet.

Lactose intolerance presents usually with diarrhoea, vomiting, lactosuria and failure to thrive. Symptoms begin as soon as the baby is put to the breast. The child promptly improves when lactose is excluded from the diet.

In *alactasia* there is diarrhoea due to unabsorbed disaccharides, because of defective absorption of lactose. The child improves when sucrose is given and lactose is excluded. The Clinitest on the stools is positive.

Maltose or *sucrose intolerance* are rather less common. Diarrhoea and failure to thrive are the usual features.

In *fructosaemia and fructose intolerance* there is vomiting, failure to thrive, lassitude, perspiration, trembling, palpitation and fits, with hepatic enlargement and sometimes jaundice. Some of the symptoms are the result of hypoglycaemia. The symptoms begin when the child eats sugar, sweets, fruit, honey or certain vegetables. There are no symptoms when the baby is breast feeding. There may be albumin and fructose in the urine and abnormal aminoaciduria. There may be a particular aversion to sweet food. Older children experience vomiting and abdominal pain 20 or 30 minutes after eating sugar-containing substances. These is usually no diarrhoea. The symptom of fits on eating sugar suggests the diagnosis. The Clinitest on the stools is positive.

Amylase deficiency is associated with diarrhoea.

Galactosaemia usually presents in the newborn baby with vomiting, purpura, weight loss and jaundice with hepatic enlargement as soon as he receives breast milk. Cataracts and mental deficiency soon develop. Galactose is found in the urine. The Clinitest or Benedict test is positive. The Clinistix may also be positive, because the damaged renal tubule allows glucose to leak through.

Udani *et al.* (1972) described a high calorie form of malnutrition due to *carbohydrate deficiency*: there was polyuria, failure to thrive, abdominal distension, irritability, constipation, and an excessive appetite. The polyuria was thought to be due to the high solute load.

Defective protein absorption

This may be due to chronic diarrhoea from any cause, such as ulcerative colitis. It may be due to deficiency of trypsinogen (Townes 1965); this presents with oedema due to hypoproteinaemia. Enterokinase deficiency is associated with hypoproteinaemia and oedema.

The so-called exudative enteropathy is a condition in which there is generalised oedema due to protein loss in the stools. It may result from ulcerative colitis, regional ileitis or other conditions.

Silverman *et al.* (1971) listed 21 causes of protein-losing enteropathy in their list of 70 diseases causing malabsorption. I have purposely listed only a few. There is no satisfactory test for protein malabsorption.

Allergy to cow's milk

Otherwise unexplained failure to thrive may be due to *allergy to cow's milk* (Hill 1979, Jakobsson & Lindberg 1979, Wood 1980). Other symptoms are diverse: they include skin reaction—urticaria, angioneurotic oedema and other rashes, anaphylaxis; respiratory symptoms—wheezing, stridor, cough and unexplained crying; and alimentary symptoms—abdominal pain, diarrhoea, vomiting, colic and colitis, and blood in the stools. Sometimes the presenting symptom is a failure to recover fully after gastroenteritis. There may be secondary lactose intolerance. The clinical diagnosis may be confused by additional sensitivity to egg or soya, and by the fact that the symptoms may develop 24 hours or more after challenge.

Hirschsprung's disease

Defective absorption and failure to thrive may result from Hirschsprung's disease. There will be a history of severe constipation from birth, often with abdominal distension, and a story that no stool was passed in the first 24 to 36 hours. On the other hand the symptom of constipation may not be impressive, and the diagnosis may be missed because of attacks of severe diarrhoea and vomiting. These suggest enterocolitis, when in fact the cause is Hirschsprung's disease. On rectal examination it is found that the rectum is empty. Swenson *et al.* (1973) analyzed 501 cases. Ninety-four per cent had not passed meconium in the first 24 hours; 94 per cent were constipated: 87 per cent had abdominal distension; 64 per cent had vomited; 26 per cent had diarrhoea; 3 per cent presented with perforation in the newborn period. It may be associated with mongolism.

A closely similar condition, neuronal intestinal dysplasia, presenting with similar symptoms, and diagnosed only by enzyme and histological examination of a biopsy specimen from the rectosigmoid, was described by Schärli (1981).

Increased loss of nutriments and fluid

Excess loss of fluid in perspiration may result from *over-clothing or an excessively hot environment*. It leads to constipation and failure to gain weight adequately. In hot climates I have seen infants who were given quantities of fluid suitable for the British climate, but unsuitable for the country in question. They were being given 2½ ounces per lb (150 ml per kg) per day, which is the usual quantity needed in England, but insufficient in a country such as Egypt, where there is a greater fluid loss through perspiration. The loss of fluid through the lungs resulting from excessive crying has already been mentioned.

Chronic vomiting or diarrhoea will prevent an adequate weight gain.

Some metabolic causes of
failure to thrive (rare)

When a baby or toddler who is failing to thrive in spite of adequate food intake is found to be grossly constipated, one should think of one of the conditions associated with polyuria, notably renal acidosis, hypercalcaemia and particularly in a boy, nephrogenic diabetes insipidus.

Renal tubular acidosis is an uncommon but important condition of infancy. It is important because appropriate treatment will enable the baby to gain weight normally, and failure to diagnose it is likely to lead to the child's death. It is manifested by vomiting and failure to thrive, often with polyuria. It is due to failure of the renal tubules to reabsorb bicarbonate.

Idiopathic hypercalcaemia presents with similar symptoms. There is polyuria with resulting constipation. In severe cases there is a characteristic facies and a systolic cardiac murmur. The diagnosis is made by estimation of the serum calcium, though this level usually falls to normal after infancy. Proper treatment may prevent mental deterioration and should enable the child to thrive normally.

Nephrogenic diabetes insipidus is another condition with symptoms like those of renal acidosis. The diagnosis can usually be established by the finding of a high serum sodium, a high urea nitrogen and a fixed low specific gravity in the urine. Tests are needed to distinguish it from diabetes insipidus due to pituitary deficiency, and investigation in hospital is essential.

Adrenocortical hyperplasia with salt loss may cause vomiting, diarrhoea and failure to thrive. The diagnosis would be suggested when a girl is found to have a large clitoris or a boy has a large penis—though the enlargement of the penis may not be obvious. The presence of hypospadias in an infant who is not thriving would suggest the likelihood that the child is a girl with virilization due to adrenocortical hyperplasia. Pigmentation of the nipples and scrotum is a useful sign in affected boys. The buccal smear should establish the nuclear sex. It is urgent to make the diagnosis, for many affected babies die in early infancy without the diagnosis being made, whereas they would have survived with proper treatment.

Hypophosphatasia. Children with this rare condition fail to thrive, have rickets, other bone deficiencies, and sometimes vomiting, constipation and convulsions.

In the *De Toni-Fanconi syndrome* there may be polyuria, abnormal aminoaciduria, glycosuria and rickets. For *Bartter's syndrome* see p. 291.

Organ disease involving the brain, heart, chest, kidney, liver or pancreas

A variety of diseases of the brain, heart, chest, kidney, liver and pancreas may be responsible for the failure of the infant to thrive. *Certain brain diseases,* other than mental deficiency, are associated with defective physical growth. *Mentally defective children,* especially when they also have cerebral palsy, are commonly malnourished, partly because they are unable to chew until much later than a normal child. As a result they have to be fed on semi-liquid feeds, and defective intake of necessary foodstuffs may result. It is easy to miss the age at which they learn to chew, and if they are not given solids at the time when they have recently learnt to chew, they will be diffident about taking them later, refusing them or vomiting. This depends on the so-called 'sensitive' or 'critical period' (Illingworth & Lister 1964). Defective physical growth in mentally defective children may be due to the underlying brain defect.

A *craniopharyngeal cyst* may cause defective physical growth. I have seen children with this condition who presented with defective weight gain and no other symptoms. Ophthalmoscopic examination may point to the diagnosis. The finding of unilateral optic atrophy or of papilloedema would point to the need for further investigation, including an X-ray of the skull for ballooning of the sella or calcification.

Other *neoplasms in the region of the hypothalamus and third ventricle, including the diencephalic syndrome,* are associated with failure to thrive (Addy & Hudson 1972). Affected children are emaciated, notably alert, and have a normal or increased appetite. The onset is usually in the first year. Growth is at first accelerated, but loss of weight then follows. There may be signs of autonomic disturbance, such as profuse sweating, and there may be nystagmus. There are usually no abnormal neurological signs and there is no papilloedema. The important feature in many is a high C.S.F. protein.

A *chronic subdural effusion* may be associated with failure to thrive. This could be explained by vomiting, reduced appetite or non-accidental injury.

Congenital heart disease, such as a patent ductus arteriosus, atrial or ventricular septal defect, or Fallot's tetralogy, is usually associated with stunting of growth. The reasons for this are not altogether clear. I have seen several examples of severe food refusal resulting from food forcing, which in turn resulted from the parents' anxiety about slow weight gain and smallness of size. It is important that the cause of the stunting of growth should be recognized, partly because it may be remedied surgically, and partly because the parents may then avoid food forcing.

Bronchiectasis, asthma and other chronic pulmonary conditions are likely to be associated with defective weight gain. Most children with severe asthma are small in height and below the average weight. This is aggravated by prolonged corticosteroid treatment. Tuberculosis in England is now a rare cause of failure to thrive.

Renal insufficiency should be remembered when an infant or child is not thriving. It may be due to congenital renal fibrosis, polycystic kidneys, hydronephrosis or chronic pyelonephritis. The importance of the specific gravity is commonly forgotten. A fixed low specific gravity suggests renal insufficiency or other cause of polyuria. The blood pressure should be recorded.

It should not be difficult to diagnose *cirrhosis of the liver,* a rare cause of failure to thrive. One cause of cirrhosis of the liver is fibrocystic disease of the pancreas. Other causes include hepatolenticular degeneration, diagnosed largely by the estimation of serum copper oxidase, tyrosinosis, which is associated with renal tubular defects and rickets, and alpha-1-antitrypsin deficiency.

Diabetes mellitus will be readily eliminated by examination of the urine. Fibrocystic disease of the pancreas is discussed elsewhere (see particularly pp. 9–10).

Miscellaneous conditions

A variety of *chromosomal abnormalities* and the rubella syndrome are associated with failure to thrive. The *fetal alcohol syndrome* (Hanson 1977), due to maternal alcoholism in pregnancy, is characterized by a typical facies, with a flat bridge of nose, an upturned nose, maxillary hypoplasia, prominent forehead, short small palpebral fissures, small eyes, facial hirsutism, sometimes cleft palate, restricted joint movements, congenital heart disease, tremors and mental subnormality, with defective physical growth.

Conclusion

Provided that the family doctor has satisfied himself that the unduly small infant or small child is not small merely because he takes after one of his parents, or because he was an unusually small baby at birth, and that the problem is not merely one of defective intake, he should have the problem investigated by an expert. The problem of failure to thrive is one of the most difficult and yet one of the most common problems facing the paediatric physician. It is important to make the diagnosis in order that the appropriate treatment can be given. Failure to do so may mean that the child will not survive or that his growth will remain permanently defective.

References

Addy DP, Hudson FP. Diencephalic syndrome of infantile emaciation. *Arch Dis Child* 1972; **47:** 338.

Anderson C, Burke V. *Paediatric gastroenterology*. Oxford: Blackwell Scientific Publications, 1975.

Black B, Brown C, Thomas J. A follow up study of 58 preschool children less than 1500g birth weight. *Austr Paediatr J* 1977; **13:** 265.

Cockel R, Hill EE, *et al.* Familial steatorrhoea with calcification of the basal ganglia and mental retardation. *Q J Med* 1973; **42:** 441.

Eid EE. A follow up study of physical growth following failure to thrive with special reference to a critical period in the first year of life. *Acta Paediatr Scand* 1971; **60:** 39.

Gracey M, Burke V. Sugar-induced diarrhoea in children. *Arch Dis Child* 1973; **48:** 331.

Hanson JW. Alcohol and the fetus. *Br J Hosp Med* 1977; **18:** 126.

Hill DJ, Cow's milk allergy—fact or fiction. *Records of the Adelaide Children's Hospital* 1979.

Hill DJ, Davidson GP, *et al.* The spectrum of cow's milk allergy in childhoood. *Acta Paediatr Scand* 1979; **68:** 847.

Huff DS, Huang NN, Arey JB. Atypical cystic fibrosis of the pancreas with normal levels of sweat chloride and minimal pancreatic lesions. *J Pediatr* 1979; **94:** 237.

Illingworth RS, Lister J. The critical or sensitive period with special reference to certain feeding problems in infants and children. *J Pediatr* 1964; **65:** 839.

Jakobsson I, Lindberg T. A prospective study of cow's milk protein intolerance in Swedish infants. *Acta Paediatr Scand* 1979; **68:** 853.

Leslie JWM, Matheson WJ. Failure to thrive in early infancy due to abnormalities of rotation of the mid-gut. *Clin Pediatr Phila* 1965; **4:** 681.

Mann TP, Wilson M, Clayton BE. A deficiency state arising in infants on synthetic foods. *Arch Dis Child* 1965; **40:** 364.

Mitchell WG, Gorrell RW, Greenberg RA. Failure to thrive: a study in a primary care setting. *Pediatrics* 1980; **65:** 971.

O'Donoghue DP, Dawson AM. Crohn's disease in childhood. *Arch Dis Child* 1977; **52:** 613.

Raynes PHW, Rudd BT. Emotional deprivation in three siblings associated with functional pituitary growth hormone deficiency. *Australian Paediatr J* 1973; **9:** 79.

Schärli AF, Meier-Ruge W. Localised and disseminated forms of neuronal intestinal dysplasia mimicking Hirschsprung's disease. *J Pediatr Surg* 1981; **16:** 164

Silverman A, Roy CC, Cozzetto FJ. *Pediatric clinical gastroenterology*. St Louis: Mosby, 1971.

Sobel EH, Silverman FL, Lee CM. Regional ileitis without symptoms. *Am J Dis Child* 1962; **103:** 575.

Swenson O, Sherman JO, Fisher JH. Diagnosis of congenital megacolon. An analysis of 501 patients. *J Pediatr Surg* 1973; **8:** 587.

Tanner JM, Whitehouse RH, Takaishi M. Standard from birth to maturity for height, weight, height velocity and weight velocity. *Arch Dis Child* 1966; **41:** 613.

Townes FL. Trypsinogen deficiency disease. *J Pediatr* 1965; **66:** 275.

Udani PM, Parekh UC, *et al.* Carbohydrate malnutrition (Carbohydrate deprivation syndrome). *Indian Pediatrics* 1972; **9:** 311.

Umansky R, Hauck AJ. Factors in growth of children and patent ductus arteriosus. *Pediatrics* 1962; **30:** 540.

Wilson JF, Lahey ME, Heiner DC. Studies on iron metabolism. Further observations on cow's milk induced gastrointestinal bleeding in infants with iron deficiency anaemia. *J Pediatr* 1974; **84:** 335.

Wood CBS. The recognition and management of milk intolerance. *J Mat and Child Health* 1980; **5:** 214.

Shortness of stature

Only a minority of examples of unusual smallness of stature is due to organic disease. The commonest causes are *genetic* or *racial* (e.g. Pygmies), *low birth weight* and *socio-economic*. A *low birth weight* especially if the child was small for dates, is a major cause of smallness in later childhood: *mixed social factors* are of similar importance; in a Newcastle study (Parkin 1976), of 82 children whose height was below the third centile, 84 per cent had no organic disease; the factors were low birth weight, smallness of parents, low IQ, low social class and large size of family. One third had suffered emotional deprivation. In developing countries gross *malnutrition,* commonly associated with infection, is a major factor. Most of the causes of 'failure to thrive' discussed in the previous section are likely to lead to smallness of stature. Reviews of the subject include those of Langer (1969), who lists 112 causes, Smith (1976), Vines (1976) and Zachmann (1977).

Other causes of unusual shortness of stature

Chromosomal conditions especially the trisomies

Turner's syndrome in girls is diagnosed in infancy by the finding of oedema of the lower limbs, often with webbing of the neck, pigmented naevi, coarctation of the aorta, a low hair line at the back of the neck, cubitus valgus and a short fourth metacarpal. Later there is small stature and absence of secondary sexual characteristics. It is easy to diagnose cubitus valgus when it is non-existent. Usually when the upper arms are fully extended and touching, the forearms cannot without difficulty be brought parallel, whereas they can in Turner's syndrome (and some normal people). The short fourth metacarpal is demonstrated by placing a ruler or firm card across the outer knuckles: normally the ruler will not touch all three knuckles. If there is a short fourth metacarpal, the card touches the third and fifth metacarpals, acting as a bridge over the fourth. There are variants of Turner's syndrome which in the older child are less easy to diagnose; the height may be normal or increased and the appearance of the child may be normal, apart from the absence of breast enlargement. When a young girl is unusually small in height and there is no obvious disease, Turner's syndrome is a possibility to be considered even if the mother is also unusually small: nevertheless, the most likely explanation of a girl's unusually small height, when the mother is small, is merely the familial factor.

The *Ullrich-Noonan* syndrome (Nora *et al.* 1974), closely resembles Turner's syndrome. It is an autosomal dominant condition, with congenital heart disease, short stature, undescended testes, a low hair line, cubitus valgus, webbing of the neck, naevi, lymphoedema and facial anomalies. Whereas in Turner's syndrome the commonest cardiovascular defect is coarctation of the aorta, in the Noonan syndrome pulmonary stenosis with or without an atrial septal defect is more common. Chromosomal findings are normal.

Several workers have described chromosomal changes in the *Prader-Willi syndrome* (Ledbetter *et al.* 1981), characterised by a low birth weight, sucking difficulties in early infancy, undescended testes, hypoplastic scrotum or labia, hypotonia in the early months, and obesity developing by the second or third year. There is smallness of hands, feet and penis, dwarfism, and sometimes diabetes in later years (Stephenson 1980).

Drugs

Fetal growth is retarded by heavy smoking and alcoholism and certain other drugs taken during pregnancy. *Neuro-stimulant* drugs taken by the child, notably methylphenidate or amphetamines, reduce his growth in height. (Safer, Allan & Barr 1972). Corticosteroid drugs taken over a long period of time cause severe stunting of growth.

Skeletal disease

Scores of these are associated with dwarfism. Warkany's book lists 72 of them. They include various forms of *rickets, achondroplasia* and *punctate epiphyseal dysplasia*. *Achondroplasia* should be readily diagnosed by the shortness of the humerus and femur, with a large head and depressed bridge of nose. When the child puts his hands down by his side, they do not reach as far as those of a normal child. There are several rare allied conditions. One is *punctate epiphyseal dysplasia,* commonly due to the mother taking warfarin during pregnancy; there is a cataract, the appearance of achondroplasia, limited extension of some joints and characteristic X-ray changes.

Trauma to the epiphyses of a growing child will retard growth.

Endocrine disorders

Hypopituitarism is rare in children. The child is usually dwarfed but of normal proportions. An X-ray of skull may show evidence of a craniopharyngioma. *Growth hormone deficiency* may be genetic or due to a craniopharyngioma, or damage to the hypothalamus or emotional deprivation. Isolated growth hormone deficiency occurs in *Aarskog's syndrome* (Kodama *et al.* 1981), a short stature, genital anomalies and unusual facies sometimes with hypertelorism.

A child with *thyroid deficiency* is small due to delayed skeletal maturation. He retains the infantile proportions of a larger upper than lower segment (pubis to heel). One should think of this condition when a child stops growing before puberty. When an older child develops thyroid deficiency the facies may not be characteristic at least for several months.

Pseudo-hypoparathyroidism is a rare condition in which there is shortness of stature, short fingers and often mental subnormality or fits. The middle finger may be shorter than the index finger.

For *Cushing's syndrome* see p. 27.

Inadequately treated *diabetes mellitus* may be associated with defective physical growth.

Other metabolic diseases.

These include storage diseases, mucopolysaccharidoses and inadequately controlled phenylketonuria.

For obesity with short stature, see p. 26.

References

Kodama M, Fujimoto S, *et al.* Aarskog's syndrome. *Eur J Pediatr* 1981; **135**: 273.
Langer LO. Short stature. *Clin Pediatr* 1969; **8**: 142.
Ledbetter DH *et al.* Deletions of chromosome 15 as a cause of the Prader-Willi Syndrome. *N Engl J Med* 1981; **304**: 325.
Nora JJ, Nora AH, *et al.* The Ullrich-Noonan syndrome. *Am J Dis Child* 1974; **127**: 48.
Parkin JM. Short stature. *Br Med J* 1976; **2**: 1139.
Safer D, Allen R, Barr E. Depression of growth in hyperactive children on stimulant drugs. *N Engl J Med* 1972; **287**: 217.
Smith DW. Compendium on shortness of stature *J Pediatr* 1976; **70**: 463–519.
Stephenson JBP. Prader-Willi Syndrome: neonatal presentation and later development. *Dev Med Child Neurol* 1980; **22**: 792.
Vines RH. The short child, causes, investigation, treatment. *Drugs* 1976; **11**: 135.
Warkany J. *Congenital malformations.* Chicago: Year Book Publications, 1971.
Zachmann M. In: Paediatrics and growth, ed. Barltrop D. London: Unigate. Paediatric Workshop. Fellowship in Postgraduate Medicine, 1977.

Loss of Weight

When a child loses weight, other than in the course of an acute infection, one always feels concern. There are many possible causes, some of them serious.

In considering a mother's complaint that her child has lost weight, the first essential is to determine the evidence for her statement. Usually she has no figures to support her claim, but she may say that the child's clothes no longer fit because they are now too big for him. The child may have been weighed on different scales—perhaps one time in clothes and another time without—and the mother had not thought of the possibility that the scales were inaccurate. When the weight of a baby is to be compared one day with that at another, it is essential that it should be recorded on each occasion at the same time in relation to feeds. It would not be profitable to weigh the baby before a feed one day and to compare this with his weight after a feed on another day.

Loss of weight, other than that during an ordinary acute infection such as gastroenteritis, may be due to any of the following conditions, amongst others:

> Overheating (in the case of a baby)
> Emotional causes. Child abuse. Anorexia nervosa
> Conditions causing persistent vomiting
> Conditions causing diarrhoea
> Conditions associated with polyuria
>> Diabetes mellitus
>> Diabetes insipidus (rare)
>> Hypercalcaemia (rare)
>> Renal acidosis (rare)
>> Renal failure (rare)
> Malabsorption
>> Fats (steatorrhoea)
>> Carbohydrates (intolerance)
>> Protein
>> Hirschsprung's disease
>> Beriberi in the tropics
> Regional ileitis (Crohn's disease)
> Infections
>> Urinary tract
>> Tuberculosis
>> Partial collapse of the lung
>> Other
> Asthma
> Drugs
> Rare—thyrotoxicosis, Addison's disease, malignant disease, muscular dystrophy, lipodystrophy

In the section 'Failure to thrive' it was stated that an infant separated from his mother may fail to gain weight or may lose weight. Worries about home or school may cause an older child to lose weight. I have seen anorexia nervosa in older children who have been teased on account of obesity.

Persistent vomiting, such as that due to hiatus hernia, or *persistent diarrhoea*, as in ulcerative colitis, may cause loss of weight.

A useful test which should always be carried out when there is unexplained loss of weight is estimation of the specific gravity of the urine. A fixed low specific gravity would lead to investigation for one of the causes of *polyuria*, such as renal failure, nephrogenic diabetes insipidus or hypercalcaemia. Diabetes mellitus must be eliminated by testing the urine for reducing substances. The other causes of polyuria have been described in the section entitled 'Failure to thrive'.

Loss of weight may be due to *malabsorption*, including fibrocystic disease of the pancreas and coeliac disease. In the case of carbohydrate intolerance there is usually some diarrhoea. For Crohn's disease see p. 11.

A chronic *urinary tract infection* may present as loss of weight with lassitude. No examination of a child who has lost weight is complete without microscopy and culture of a clean specimen of urine. In the same way no examination would be complete without a tuberculin test unless the child has previously been given BCG.

Lassitude and loss of weight following what appeared to be a simple upper respiratory tract infection may be due to *partial collapse of the lung*. This may be suspected because of physical signs, but an X-ray is needed for confirmation.

Most children with *severe asthma* are underweight and some lose weight.

Certain *drugs* may cause loss of weight. When one institutes treatment for cretinism with thyroxine, some loss of weight is common. It is said that loss of weight may be a side effect of sulthiame or a stimulant drug given for overactivity.

Thyrotoxicosis and *Addison's disease* are rare in children, but the signs are the same as those in adults and can hardly be missed.

Malignant disease, whether cerebral, intra-thoracic, intra-abdominal or elsewhere, may be the cause of loss of weight.

There is general muscle wasting in the later stages of *muscular dystrophy*.

Generalized *lipodystrophy* is a rare cause of loss of weight. The child will be well, and it can be seen that the appearance of emaciation and the weight loss are due to loss of fatty tissue only.

Conclusion

Loss of weight is one of the important symptoms of childhood which demands full investigation, except where the cause is obvious, such as gastroenteritis or diabetes mellitus. Hospital laboratory facilities are usually necessary for the elucidation of this symptom.

Excessive Height

The following are the usual causes of excessive height:
  Heredity
  Rare—
    Cerebral gigantism
    Additional Y chromosome, Klinefelter's syndrome
    Marfan's syndrome, homocystinuria
    Eosinophilic adenoma of the piruitary
The commonest reason for excessive height is genetic—the child taking after one of his parents. Obese children are usually tall for their age (until the epiphyses fuse). Children with sexual precocity or adrenocortical hyperplasia are tall for their age.

Cerebral gigantism is rare. It is associated with mental deficiency, an odd face (often hypertelorism), antimongoloid slant of the eyes, prognathism and fits.

An additional Y chromosome is often associated with tallness and perhaps a tendency to delinquency.

Marfan's syndrome of arachnodactyly, dislocation of the lens and congenital heart disease is assocated with excessive height.

Reference

Ott JE, Robinson A. Cerebral gigantism. *Am J Dis Child* 1969; **117**: 357.
Sotos JF, Cutler EA. Cerebral gigantism. *Am J Dis Child* 1977; **131**: 625.

Obesity

The commonest type of obesity is the so-called *simple obesity*—a misnomer, because the cause of obesity is far from simple (*JAMA* 1970). Basically this is due to an imbalance between intake and output, the child eating more than he needs. Most fat children have developed the sweet-eating habit, and are commonly to be seen eating potato crisps, lollipops and ice creams, taking large quantities of sugar in their drinks and frequent glasses of orange squash. Part of the answer to problems of obesity may lie in the metabolism of brown fat (British Medical Journal 1981). Genetic factors and sibling rivalry are also relevant.

Mothers argue that the children are so big that they need a lot to fill them; and that they have a 'marvellous appetite'. There are often important emotional factors which cause overeating. Obesity in the early weeks, shown by Eid (1970), to be related to obesity in later years may be due to the premature administration of cereals: but not all fat children become fat adults.

Obesity may develop because of inactivity—as in prolonged bed rest, the Werdnig–Hoffmann syndrome, muscular dystrophy in its later stages, mongolism or severe cerebral palsy of the spastic, not athetoid type, especially around puberty. It may be responsible for severe respiratory symptoms (the Pickwickian syndrome, Cayler *et al.* 1961). A rare cause of obesity is the *adenoma of the islet cells of the pancreas* causing hypoglycaemia and hunger.

Most fat children are tall for their age because of secondary adrenocortical overactivity, but their epiphyses fuse prematurely so that most of them are ultimately small.

Clonazepam and sodium valproate may increase the appetite and cause excessive weight gain.

If a fat child is small for his age, the following rare conditions should be considered:

Cushing's syndrome.
Prader-Willi syndrome (p. 20).
Turner's syndrome (p. 19).
Thyroid deficiency (p. 21).

Pituitary syndromes.

Prolonged corticosteroid therapy.

In *Cushing's syndrome* there is a characteristic distribution of fat, involving mainly the trunk (buffalo hump) and face, with relatively normal limbs: a phlethoric face with red cheeks, a deep voice, hypertrichosis, purple striae and often hypertension. The presence of striae in a fat child should not lead one to diagnose Cushing's disease, for striae occur normally in fat children.

The *pituitary syndromes* are extremely rare, Frölich's syndrome is so rare that I have not yet seen a case. It consists of obesity dwarfism, hypogonadism, optic atrophy, headache, polyuria and glycosuria, due to a cyst in the region of the pituitary. The apparent smallness of the penis should not lead one to the erroneous diagnosis of Fröhlich's syndrome: the penis is buried in the fatty tissue and looks smaller than it really is. The Laurence-Moon-Biedl syndrome consists of obesity, polydactyly, retinitis pigmentosa, mental subnormality and hypogonadism.

Not all small fat children fall into the above categories: the relatively small height cannot always be explained.

References

British Medical Journal. Metabolic obesity? Leading article 1981; **1**: 172.

Cayler GC, Mays J, Riley HD. Cardiorespiratory syndrome of obesity (Pickwickian syndrome) in children. *Pediatrics* 1961; **27**: 237.

Eid EE. Follow up study of physical growth of children who had experienced excessive weight gain in the first six months of life. *Br Med J* 1970; **2**: 74.

Journal of the American Medical Association. Obesity: a continuing enigma. Leading article. 1970; **211**: 492.

Unexplained Fever

In this section I shall refer to the problem of prolonged temperature elevation whose cause has not been determined by taking the history and examining the child—there being no abnormal physical signs apart from the fever and the appearance of illness. It is assumed that the physical examination has included the inspection of the eardrum for otitis media. The problem is a fairly common one, and it is one which may be extremely difficult to solve even with the fullest laboratory assistance.

Petersdorf & Beeson (1961) suggested that pyrexia of unknown origin should be defined as fever for at least three weeks, exceeding 38·3°C on several occasions, defying diagnosis after a week of intensive investigation. Most cases prove to be atypical manifestations of common diseases rather than exotic conditions (Jacoby & Swartz 1973). When faced with a child with pyrexia of unknown origin, common conditions are more likely than rare ones. Pizzo *et al.* (1975) in a study of 100 such children in Boston, found that 52 per cent had infection, 20 per cent collagen vascular diseases and 6 per cent neoplasms. They found that in 18 per cent of their cases the temperature eventually settled to normal without a diagnosis having been made: a similar observation was made by Sheon & Van Ommen (1963).

The following conditions should be considered, not necessarily in the order of likelihood

    Normal variation

    Dehydration and overheating. Polyuria.

    Malingering

    Absorption of blood. The effect of trauma and surgical procedures. C.N.S. haemorrhage

    Infections

    Rheumatoid arthritis (pre-arthritic stage)

    The effect of drugs and poisons

    Post-operative—retained surgical swab

Rare causes:

    Collagen diseases

    Reticuloses and malignant disease

    Sarcoid

    Mucocutaneous lymph node disease

    Alimentary conditions

      ulcerative colitis

      regional ileitis (p. 11)

    Liver disease

    Subdural effusion

    Ectodermal dysplasia

Caffey's disease
Agammaglobulinaemia
Familial dysautonomia

Normal variations

Excitement or exertion may cause a slight rise of temperature. The temperature should not be taken immediately after a hot drink. An occasional child has a slight persistent elevation of the temperature, or a daily elevation up to 38°C, without any discoverable disease. The elevation of temperature is usually discovered after some childhood infectious disease or tonsillitis. The child appears to be well and is symptom-free. Exhaustive tests fail to reveal any abnormality. Eventually the parent is advised to stop taking the temperature, and on follow-up study the child remains well. These cases are always worrying and have to be investigated and followed up with the greatest of care, but one never feels confident in concluding that there is no disease. One would be especially uncertain if the child, in addition to the elevation of temperature, does not feel well, energetic and free from lassitude, or if his weight gain is not satisfactory. A good non-specific test which helps, and one which is easily carried out in the doctor's surgery, is the ESR. A normal figure does not exclude disease but it does make it less likely. A raised figure means that disease is almost certainly present and must be looked for.

A rectal temperature is commonly a little higher than that in the mouth. The rectal temperature depends on the depth to which the thermometer is inserted. Those interested should read the monograph written by Talbot many years ago (Talbot 1931).

Dehydration

The so-called *dehydration fever of the newborn* consists of a sudden rise of temperature a day or two after birth. It is thought to be due to loss of fluid. The temperature rapidly settles when boiled water or other fluid is given.

A baby may develop a rise of temperature if overheated. The most striking example of this occurred during a ward round. A baby was well when I saw him, but an hour later had a temperature of 41°C and was severely dehydrated, because his crib had been in contact with a radiator. The dehydration was such that he had to be given an immediate intravenous infusion.

Because of the absence of sweat glands, the temperature may rise in infants with *ectodermal dysplasia* when overheated. In the congenital anhydrotic type of ectodermal dysplasia, the child seems to be normal at birth. Later there is a dry skin, unexplained fever, sparse hair, delayed or absent dentition or widely-spaced incisors and conical canines, often with a saddle-shaped nose and frontal bossing. In the dominant hydrotic form there are dystrophic nails, hyperkeratosis of the palms and soles, absent or sparse hair at birth, and later hypertrichosis and pigmentation.

A rise of temperature may result from other conditions causing dehydration, apart fom the ordinary infections. These include *nephrogenic diabetes insipidus* and *idiopathic hypercalcaemia.*

A rise in temperature due to the *absorption of blood* is short lived, and should not cause confusion for more than a day or two. Fever may occur in C.N.S. haemorrhage.

Malingering

I have seen serious diagnostic difficulties from malingering in childhood. A raised temperature with a normal pulse rate may arouse the suspicion of malingering. A ten-year-old girl was referred from another hospital on account of high swinging fever of some weeks' duration. She had been extensively investigated and no cause had been found. The suddenness of the rise of temperature and the fact that the girl was well when the temperature was markedly raised suggested the diagnosis of malingering. When a nurse turned her back the girl rapidly rubbed the bulb of the thermometer with her bedclothes. Vigorous rubbing of the bulb of the thermometer will raise the mercury from 36° to 40°C in some five seconds. It takes longer to raise the temperature to that point by placing it in contact with the average hot water bottle. Vigorous shaking of the inverted thermometer may have a similar result. When in doubt, the urine temperature may be a guide to the diagnosis of malingering.

Urinary tract infection

The most common cause of fever in a child without abnormal physical signs is a urinary tract infection. There are usually no symptoms referable to the urinary system, and it is not usual to find either loin tenderness or albumin in the urine. The absence of infection in a specimen of urine does not absolutely exclude infection. The flow of urine from a pyonephrosis may be blocked, the urine examined having come from the other kidney.

Other infections

Tuberculosis can be eliminated by a tuberculin test, though when a child has miliary or meningeal tuberculosis the tuberculin test may be negative on account of anergy, as it may be in measles or severe malnutrition. On ophthalmoscopic examination choroidal tubercles can be found in over 60 per cent of children with miliary tuberculosis. An X-ray of the chest would clinch the diagnosis. Meningeal tuberculosis would be confirmed by lumbar puncture. In all other forms of tuberculosis the tuberculin test would be positive except when there is anergy due to measles, malnutrition or an overwhelming infection.

In *typhoid and paratyphoid fever* there is almost always enlargement of the spleen, and there are usually rose spots on the abdomen.

Brucellosis is rarely seen in Britain. It is usually accompanied by fever and an enlarged spleen.

Roseola infantum can cause confusion for three or four days. The child has a high temperature without abnormal physical signs, and then the temperature subsides as the erythematous rash develops.

An occasional child may have a raised temperature throughout the incubation period of *measles*. In many other children there is a high temperature for five or six days, in association with an infection of the upper respiratory tract, before the measles rash appears. Koplik's spots can be seen in the buccal mucosa during the pre-eruptive phase.

Infectious mononucleosis (glandular fever) may occasionally present with fever but without other abnormal signs, though there is usually enlargement of the spleen and often lymph node enlargement.

Acute toxoplasmosis and acute cytomegalovirus infection resemble glandular fever. Both may be associated with lymphadenopathy, hepatosplenomegaly, thrombocytopenia, choroidoretinitis, fever and jaundice, with atypical mononuclear cells in the blood film.

Toxocara canis or catis infection may give no abnormal signs apart from fever. There may be fever, polyarthritis, hepatomegaly, jaundice, rash, epididymitis, fits and abdominal pains. There is usually an eosinophilia.

Meningococcal septicaemia may present as fever of unknown origin. It is essential to look carefully for petechial haemorrhages, particularly on the conjunctival surfaces of the eyelids. A joint effusion in conjunction with petechiae would suggest the diagnosis and a blood culture would confirm it.

Certain *closed-off abscesses* may give rise to fever without physical signs, at least for a time. They include particularly the subphrenic or perinephric abscess, a pulmonary abscess or an abscess in a silent area of the brain. The pulmonary abscess can be seen in an X-ray of the chest, but the others may present difficulty. Continued fever following an attack of abdominal pain should suggest the possibility of a subphrenic abscess following the perforation of an appendix. An X-ray may show gas under the diaphragm. A perinephric abscess may present considerable difficulties. It may be preceded by trauma or a staphylococcal skin infection. There are likely to be rigors, and there may be pain on the affected side, with pain on flexing the spine. There are not usually urinary symptoms. An X-ray may show a bulging psoas shadow. There is usually intermittent but not continuous pyuria.

A cerebral abscess is usually associated with headache and often with neck stiffness. There is often but not always papilloedema, but there may be no localizing neurological signs. The diagnosis would be suspected if there had been a neighbouring focus of infection, as in the ear or scalp, or if there were bronchiectasis or congenital heart disease. It would be confirmed by lumbar puncture, echogram, electroencephalograms, scanning and air studies. A cerebral abscess may persist undiagnosed for some weeks. In the case of all these abscesses, with the occasional exception of the cerebral abscess, the white cell count is likely to show a polymorphonuclear leucocytosis, and the erythrocyte sedimentation rate (ESR) would probably be raised. After a surgical operation *a retained swab* should be considered.

A low-grade *osteitis* may cause considerable difficulty in diagnosis. The possibility must be remembered in any child with prolonged low-grade fever and signs of an infection. The routine examination of a child with unexplained fever must include palpation of all the bones for local tenderness, and if there is a suspicion of tenderness (or if there is local pain), an X-ray should be taken. I have known a low-grade osteitis persist for many months before localizing signs developed. A raised ESR and a polymorphonuclear leucocytosis should suggest the possibility but there may be leucopenia.

A child with unexplained fever without abnormal physical signs may have a low grade *septicaemia*. If there is a heart murmur, the possibility of subacute bacterial endocarditis should be remembered. There is not necessarily a history of previous heart disease. In a London study (Lowes *et al.* 1980) of 60 patients with bacterial endocarditis, 21 had a history of rheumatic fever, 13 of congenital heart disease, but 18 had no previous heart trouble. A particularly careful search for petechiae should be made, and the urine should be examined for excess of red cells in the deposit. In cases of *hydrocephalus* treated with a Spitz-Holter valve, colonization of the valve is a common occurrence, causing septicaemia.

An *apical tooth infection* may cause difficulty in diagnosis. We have seen several examples of such infection in children receiving corticosteroids. The infection was painless and there were no local signs pointing to the root of the tooth. When a child or adult has an unexplained fever (or lassitude), the teeth should be examined. If any tooth is known to be dead, or to have a root filling, an X-ray of the tooth should be taken.

When children have lived in countries in which amoebic infections occur, an *amoebic abscess of liver* should be considered. There may (or may not be) obvious liver enlargement. There is a polymorphonuclear leucocytosis. Screening may show decreased movement of the diaphragm on the affected side. Sigmoidoscopy may show amoebic ulcers and amoebae may be found in the stools.

Subclinical hepatitis may cause unexplained fever. A history of exposure to infection together with liver function tests may lead to the correct diagnosis.

Other infections include mycoses, psittacosis, and after holidays in certain countries, malaria, leishmaniasis etc.

Rheumatoid arthritis is an important cause of prolonged or recurrent unexplained fever (see also p. 247). Schaller & Wedgwood (1972) found that episodes of fever occurred in 26 per cent of their cases of rheumatoid arthritis, and that in 10 per cent prolonged fever preceded joint symptoms.

Drugs

The so-called drug fever, which occurs especially with sulphonamides, but occasionally with other antibiotics, including rifampicin,
may cause considerable difficulty in diagnosis. The temperature falls
by crisis when the drug is withdrawn. Lipsky & Hirschmann (1981)
wrote that the fever may be a pharmacological action, the effect of the
drug on thermoregulation, a local complication of parenteral
administration, or unexplained. It probably has an immunological
basis. The fever usually begins after seven to ten days of treatment.
Other drugs may sometimes cause elevation of temperature. They
include acetazolamide, amphetamines, azathioprine, carbamazepine,
cephalosporins, colistin, erythromycin, ethambutol, meprobamate,
methimazole, nitrofurantoin, nortriptyline, P.A.S. penicillamine,
phenytoin, potassium iodide, streptokinase and thiouracil. Certain
drugs in an overdose may cause a rise of temperature. They include
antihistamines, drugs of the atropine group, haloperidol, indomethacin, isoniazid and mono-amine oxidase inhibitors. Methicillin
may cause rigors.

The reticuloses and collagen diseases

Systemic lupus erythematosus, dermatomyositis and periarteritis
nodosa must be considered when there is unexplained fever.

Systemic lupus may present with fever, a butterfly rash on the face,
arthralgia and thrombocytopenic purpura (Jacobs 1963). There may be
polyserositis, hepatosplenomegaly, enlarged lymph nodes, hypertension and albuminuria. Other symptoms include fever, weight loss
and abdominal pain. There may be puncta on the palms and finger-
tips. It may follow the use of a variety of drugs, including antibiotics
(especially sulphonamides), anticoagulants, anti-arrhythmic drugs
(e.g. propranolol), antiepileptics, anti-inflammatory drugs, analgesics, chlorpromazine, gold, isoniazid, methyldopa, P.A.S.,
penicillamine, reserpine and thiouracil.

Periarteritis nodosa can present with unexplained fever (Roberts &
Fetterman 1963) often with cough, conjunctivitis, abdominal and limb
pains, and arthralgia—sometimes resembling rheumatoid arthritis.
There is sometimes oedema of hands and feet. One should palpate the
skin of the whole body for nodules, which consist of aneurysmal

dilatations of the vessel walls. There is often albuminuria and leucocytosis with eosinophilia.

In *Hodgkin's disease and the reticuloses,* splenic enlargement is usually present. Unless there is obvious lymph node enlargement, permitting biopsy, the diagnosis can be difficult. There is often a hypoplastic anaemia, sometimes with considerable leucocytosis. Sometimes a bone marrow examination reveals the nature of the condition. Fever is common in leukaemia, but is less common in Hodgkin's disease. It occurs in 20 per cent of children with Wilms's tumour at some stage. *Sarcoidosis* (p. 248) may cause unexplained fever. *Chronic granulomatous disease* (p. (p. 315) is a rare cause.

The rare *Mucocutaneous lymph node (Kasawaki) syndrome* (Neches & Young 1979, Kangilaski 1981), commonly under the age of five is characterised by prolonged fever, lymph node enlargement, conjunctivitis, sore throat, stomatitis, and oedema, erythema or desquamation of the hands and feet. There are commonly myocarditis, coronary aneurysms, aseptic meningitis and arthralgia. There are no specific tests for it.

Alimentary conditions

Ulcerative colitis may be associated with fever, but the presence of diarrhoea with blood and mucus in the stools usually points to the diagnosis. *Regional ileitis* can cause fever with failure to thrive for some weeks before alimentary symptoms develop (p. 11).

Liver disease

Cirrhosis of the liver, malignant tumours and other conditions of the liver including subclinical hepatitis may be associated with fever.

Miscellaneous

A *subdural effusion* in an infant may be accompanied by fever. The fontanelle may be bulging and there are likely to be retinal haemorrhages.

Caffey's disease in the newborn baby may be manifested by unexplained fever for 3 or 4 weeks before the characteristic swelling of the jaw and perhaps tender swellings of the tibiae, due to periostitis, become obvious.

Agammaglobulinaemia and *Riley's syndrome* of *familial dysautonomia* may be associated with unexplained fever (p. 41).

References

Jacobs JC. Systemic lupus erythematosus in childhood. *Pediatrics* 1963; **32**:257.

Jacoby GA, Swartz MN. Fever of undetermined origin. *N Engl J Med* 1973; **289**: 1407.

Kangilaski J. Kawasaki disease. *JAMA* 1981; **246**: 819.

Lipsky BA, Hirschmann JV. Drug fever. *JAMA* 1981; **245**: 851.

Lowes JA *et al*. Ten years of infective endocarditis at St Bartholomew's Hospital. Analysis of clinical features and treatment in relation to prognosis and mortality. *Lancet* 1980; **1**: 133.

Neches WH, Young LW. Mucocutaneous lymph node syndrome. *Am J Dis Child* 1979: **133**: 1233 & 1244.

Petersdorf RG. Beeson PB. Fever of unexplained origin; report on 100 cases. *Medicine (Baltimore)* 1961; **40**: 1.

Pizzo PA, Smith DH, Lovejoy FH. Prolonged fever in children: review of 100 cases. *Pediatrics* 1975; **55**: 468.

Roberts FB, Fetterman GH. Polyarteritis nodosa in infancy. *J Pediatr* 1963; **63**: 519.

Schaller J, Wedgwood RJ. Juvenile rheumatoid arthritis: a review. *Pediatrics* 1972; **50**: 940.

Sheon RP, Van Ommen RA. Fever of obscure origin. *Am J Med* 1963; **34**: 486.

Talbot F. Skin temperatures in children. *Am J Dis Child* 1931; **42**: 965.

Hyperpyrexia

McCarthy & Dolan (1976) in a study of 93 children, found that the causes in order, were pneumonia (16), otitis media (16), meningitis (13), septicaemia (7), pharyngitis (3), dehydration (3), cellulitis (1), unknown 34. They emphasized the high incidence of meningitis in their cases.

Malignant hyperpyrexia during anaesthesia is associated with a number of myopathies. There is usually fever, generalized muscle rigidity and severe metabolic acidosis, especially on exposure to halothane. The creatine phosphokinase is usually high (Moulds & Denborough 1974).

Hyperpyrexia may occur in the newborn baby as a result of *adrenal or intraventricular haemorrhage*. In older infants and children it may result from *infections of the central nervous system*, including bulbar poliomyelitis, in *heat stroke* and in *salicylate poisoning*. The drug Dantrolene, used to relieve spasticity, and tricyclic anti-depressants may cause hyperpyrexia.

References

Kaplan AM, Bergeson PS, Gregg SA, Curless RG. Malignant hyperthermia associated with myopathy and normal muscle enzymes. *J Pediatr* 1977; **91:** 431.
McCarthy PL, Dolan TF. Hyperpyrexia in children. *Am J Dis Child* 1976; **130:** 849.
Moulds RFW, Denborough MA. Biochemical basis of malignant hyperpyrexia. *Br Med J* 1974; **2:** 241 & 245.

Hypothermia

Hypothermia in an infant, apart from chilling, may be due to a serious infection, such as septicaemia. Other causes are hypothyroidism, malnutrition (especially kwashiorkor), hypoglycaemia, and drugs— phenothiazines and chlormethiazole.

Lassitude

It is common to hear the complaint that a child seems to be constantly tired or lacking in energy. In this section only chronic lassitude will be discussed. Lassitude of acute onset is likely to be due to an infection, such as measles or tonsillitis. It may be an early symptom of *diabetes mellitus*.

The following are conditions which have to be considered when there is chronic lassitude or lack of energy:

Developmental feature: puberty
Familial feature
Insufficient sleep
Malnutrition
Psychological factors, including personality, depression and insecurity, school phobia, overventilation
Hypoglycaemia
Anaemia
Infection
Low-grade infection, such as pyelonephritis, tuberculosis
Persistent haemolytic streptococcal throat infection, or early rheumatic fever
Apical tooth infection
Infectious mononucleosis
Chronic hepatitis
Partial collapse of the lung
Rheumatoid arthritis
Effect of drugs
Rare
Myasthenia gravis
Dermatomyositis, systemic lupus
Muscular dystrophy, motor neurone disease
Gilbert's disease (p. 120)
Congenital or acquired heart disease
Bacterial endocarditis, chronic obstruction of the airway. Gross obesity
Renal failure
Endocrine—hypothyroidism, hyperthyroidism, Cushing's syndrome, Addison's disease

Apparent lack of energy may be a *developmental feature*. It is common for a child of two to five or so to show little inclination to play outside and to seem to become tired too easily.

Many mothers become worried when the boy or girl at *puberty* seems to have no energy after having been constantly 'on the go' only a year or two previously. This is a common feature of early puberty. Nevertheless, it is the doctor's responsibility to see that there is not one of the other causes, such as tuberculosis, anaemia or a urinary tract infection

Many children are thought to be lacking in energy and easily tired when the problem is entirely a matter of their *personality*, which is usually a familial feature. Some children prefer to read books rather than to play active games out of doors: some prefer their own company and that of their family to that of children in the street. Sometimes children are afraid of going out to play or are worried about so doing, because they are teased by others or are being bullied. A child may seem to his mother to be tired and lacking in energy when he is well and fit but worried about home or school, or feeling insecure. It may also be a feature of boredom.

After infancy lassitude may be due to *insufficient sleep*. Children may go to bed too late or stay awake for a long time, usually as a result of parental mismanagement.

A child may refuse to play with others and therefore prefer to stay indoors because he is a *'clumsy'* child (p. 190), and cannot keep up with other children. His mother may think that he is tired or lacking in energy. For overventilation see p. 137.

One must never conclude that a child's lassitude is entirely psychological until one has eliminated organic disease, because organic disease may cause behaviour problems. As in the case of unexplained fever, a useful non-specific test is the ESR. If it is normal it does not eliminate organic disease, but if it is raised it makes organic disease almost (not quite) certain. Lassitude, pallor and irritability before meals may be due to *hypoglycaemia*.

Low-grade anaemia is an important organic cause of lack of energy and easy fatigability. If there is any doubt a haemoglobin estimation should be performed.

A common cause of undue fatigue and vague unwellness is a chronic *urinary tract infection*. It is essential to eliminate a tuberculous infection by performing a tuberculin test.

One commonly sees children who are well until they develop acute tonsillitis, and are then tired and lacking in energy for three or four weeks or more. This may be due to a *persistent haemolytic streptococcal infection*, or may represent the onset of an attack of rheumatic fever. It is worth while taking a throat swab and carrying out a therapeutic test with oral penicillin for ten days, provided that other causes have been eliminated.

Whenever there is unexplained fatigue (or unexplained fever), an *apical tooth infection* should be considered, especially if it is known that there is a dead tooth. An X-ray examination is required.

Another infection not infrequently seen in a children's hospital out-patient department is *partial collapse of the lung.* The child presents with lassitude and perhaps a slight cough, following a respiratory infection without known pneumonia. The clinical signs may suggest the diagnosis, but an X-ray of the chest is required to establish it.

Rheumatoid arthritis may present as easy fatigability and sometimes with unexplained fever for weeks or months before eventually arthritis become manifest (p. 247).

Drugs may give rise to the complaint of lassitude. This may be due to drowsiness or to muscle weakness. Muscle weakness may be a side effect of amitriptyline, beta-blockers, carbenoxolone, chloroquine, clonazepam, diuretics, ethosuximide, nalidixic acid, piperazine or streptomycin. Corticosteroids may cause weakness through a form of myopathy.

Rare causes of the symptom of lassitude include *myasthenia gravis, dermatomyositis, Gilbert's disease, muscular dystrophy,* and *subacute bacterial endocarditis.*

Myasthenia gravis is rare in childhood. The symptoms become more marked towards the end of the day. The first symptom may be ptosis. The child may find it tiring to climb stairs or to walk. There is no atrophy of muscle. The therapeutic test with neostigmine is valuable confirmatory evidence.

Dermatomyositis may present as fatigue, muscle pain, fever, weight loss and weakness, especially in the legs. The child is miserable and the muscles may feel stiff. There may be a facial rash with a violaceous hue, periorbital oedema and characteristic 'cigarette paper' lesions on the knuckles, elbows and knees, with telangiectasia around the nail bed, sometimes with oedema of hands and feet. The skin tends to become bound to the underlying tissues at the joints. It occurs at any age including infancy. It is more common in girls than boys. There is commonly a raised creatine phosphokinase. For *systemic lupus* see p. 34.

Muscular dystrophy may present as easy fatigability. The child cannot walk far, and in the Duchenne type finds it difficult to get up stairs. The serum creatine phosphokinase will help to establish the diagnosis when there is doubt. I saw a girl who had been attending a child guidance clinic for two years for so-called hysteria, the main symptom being lassitude. A glance at the tongue, which showed wasting and fasciculation, immediately made the diagnosis of motor neurone disease.

Gilbert's disease is rare. It consists of a mild low-grade persistent jaundice. *Congenital or acquired heart disease, subacute bacterial endocarditis, chronic obstruction of the airway* (due to gross enlargement of tonsils), *gross obesity* and *chronic renal failure* are other rare causes of chronic lassitude.

Reference

Bitnun S, Daeschner CW, *et al*. Dermatomyositis. *J Pediatr* 1964; **64**: 100.

Excessive Sweating

Excessive sweating in the absence of fever is rarely due to disease. It may be due to *over-clothing*; even in cold weather I have seen babies with sweat rashes and even 'prickly heat'.

Sweating around the head is a common symptom in normal children. The cause is ill-understood: it used to be ascribed to rickets. Sweating hands are often a feature of normal children and adults.

Excessive sweating is only very rarely due to tuberculosis; to put it another way, night sweats are not a feature of childhood tuberculosis.

For unexplained fever, see p. 27.

In the newborn, excessive sweating may result from the withdrawal from the mother's drugs of addiction. In later infancy mercury poisoning, as in Pink disease (now virtually eliminated) may cause excessive sweating. Drugs which may cause it include amitriptyline, amphetamine, antihistamines, ephedrine, haloperidol, imipramine, methylphenidate, pethidine and phenothiazines. Thyroxine overdose in the treatment of hypothyroidism may cause the symptom. *Thyrotoxicosis* may be associated with excessive sweating:

Excessive sweating is one of the symptoms of *Riley's syndrome* of familial dysautonomia in Jewish children (rare) (Freedman 1966). The child does not shed tears. He sweats excessively, has a blotchy rash and exhibits hypotonia and areflexia. There is a characteristic smooth tongue without the normal papillae. The affected newborn baby usually has difficulty in sucking and swallowing, has poor muscle tone, and an absent or poor Moro reflex. The condition is usually associated with mental subnormality. Other features are ataxia, recurrent pneumonia, attacks of vomiting, nasal speech and fits. Riley's syndrome is a genetic condition with an error of catecholamine metabolism.

Attacks of excessive sweating may be associated with the following conditions.

1 Vasomotor disturbance, such as fainting, especially if there is anaemia, or if there were recumbency due to illness.

2 Pain (such as abdominal colic).

3 Hypoglycaemia (rare).

4 Rarely—phaeochromocytoma, neuroblastoma, diencephalic syndrome.

If there are unexplained attacks of excessive sweating not associated with fainting, one should consider *hypoglycaemia, phaeochromocytoma* or *neuroblastoma* (Voorhess 1966). Hypoglycaemia is diagnosed in the first place by a fasting blood sugar. Phaeochromocytoma causes attacks of headache, sweating, fits, pallor, polydipsia, vomiting and lassitude, polyuria, anxiety, tremors, postural hypotension, and often but not always elevation of the blood pressure. It can be confused with thyrotoxicosis or diabetes mellitus.

References

Freedman AR. Familial dysautonomia. *Clin Pediatr (Phila)* 1966; **5**: 265.
Voorhess ML. Functioning neural tumours. *Pediatr Clin North Am* 1966; **13**: 3.

Enlargement of the Lymph Nodes

The important causes of enlargement of the lymph nodes in children are the following:

Infection

Local—throat infection, scalp or other infections (e.g. perineal or perianal in the case of inguinal nodes)

Primary tuberculosis

B.C.G.

Cat scratch fever

General—eczema with secondary infection rubella (mainly occipital, but may be other nodes), infectious mononucleosis, toxoplasmosis, toxocara, cytomegalovirus, tuberculosis, syphilis, brucellosis, tularaemia

Serum sickness

Immunological diseases: hypergammaglobulinaemia with giant lymphoid hyperplasia and an immune deficiency state with thrombocytopenia, intermittent fever and haemolytic anaemia (Vaughan VC *et al.*, 1979)

Rheumatoid arthritis

Mucocutaneous lymph node syndrome (p. 35)

Leukaemia

Reticuloses and neoplasms, histiocytosis X.

Drugs

The commonest cause of enlargement of the lymph nodes is *infection*. Those in the neck are enlarged if there is infection in the throat, in the skin of the face, the skin behind the ear or the scalp. When there is no other obvious source of infection, one must examine the scalp for sore places in association with pediculosis or other infection. Regional lymph nodes may be enlarged as a result of a small and apparently insignificant skin lesion due to primary tuberculosis. Black and Chapman (1964) described children with cervical adenitis due to organisms which resembled the tubercle bacillus. Many similar cases have been described in different parts of the world.

In the case of enlargement of the axillary lymph nodes, the cause may lie in *BCG vaccination.*

Almost all persons have palpable inguinal lymph nodes. They are commonly said to be enlarged when they are normal. It is easy to forget to examine the perianal region when the nodes are enlarged. Most children with *generalized eczema* have enlarged lymph nodes— probably as a result of secondary infection from scratching.

Cat scratch fever is due to a virus infection. Ten to thirty days after infection there is malaise, fever and enlargement of the lymph nodes draining the infected area. Keratitis and encephalitis have sometimes occurred as complications.

In *infectious mononucleosis* there is not necessarily enlargement of the nodes. In most children only the cervical ones are involved. There are clinical conditions which closely resemble infectious mononucleosis but in which the usual tests for that infection are persistently negative. *Toxoplasmosis and cytomegalovirus infection* give a similar picture, and can be diagnosed by serological tests. *Tuberculosis* may cause general lymph node involvement. Generalized lymph node enlargement may occur in *serum sickness.*

Rheumatoid arthritis may be associated with lymphadenopathy and hepatosplenomegaly (Still's disease).

For the mucocutaneous lymph node syndrome see p. 35.

Generalized lymph node enlargement may occur in *leukaemia, reticuloses* and allied conditions.

Histiocytosis X (which includes Hand–Schüller–Christian disease, Letterer–Siwe disease) may include generalized lymphadenopathy, hepatosplenomegaly, rash, bone and pulmonary lesions. *Sarcoidosis* may cause generalized lymphadenopathy, parotitis, uveitis, rash, bone and pulmonary lesions. For *chronic granulomatous disease* see p. 315.

Various *drugs* may cause lymphadenopathy. They include carbamazepine, cephaloridine, iron dextran, meprobamate, P.A.S., phensuximide, phenylbutazone, primidone, sulphadimidine and troxidone. Phenytoin may cause not only lymphadenopathy but also hepatosplenomegaly.

Reference

Black RG, Chapman S. Cervical adenitis in children due to human and unclassified mycobacteria. *Pediatrics* 1964; **33**: 887.

Vaughan VC, *et al.* (eds) *Nelson textbook of pediatrics,* 11th edn. Philadelphia: Saunders, 1979.

Swelling of the Face

Swelling of the face may be due to the following causes:

Trauma

Generalized oedema

Acute infection—such as cellulitis, erysipelas, sinus thrombosis, sinusitis, osteitis, dental abscess. Osteitis should always be considered whenever there is acute inflammation over bone

Naevoid and lymphangiomatous conditions

Lymphadenitis, especially preauricular

Paratoid swelling

Caffey's infantile cortical hyperostosis

A swelling in the region of the *parotid gland* is often wrongly ascribed to parotitis, when it is due to enlargement of the preauricular lymph nodes; and in addition, mumps is often incorrectly diagnosed when there is swelling of cervical or submaxillary lymph nodes.

Much the commonest cause of acute parotitis is mumps: but it can be due to other viruses, such as parainfluenza and coxsackie and to pyogenic organisms (Yamauchi & Vollman 1979, David & O'Connell 1970).

Recurrent parotitis is a mysterious condition of uncertain cause. (Wilson *et al.* 1980, Katzen & du Plessis 1964, Maynard 1965). Theories include infection, allergy, autoimmune disease, stricture of Stensen's duct—possibly by trauma, sialectasis, inspissated mucus or calculus. It can occur at any age from the newborn period onwards, and attacks frequently cease by puberty. The parotitis may or may not be painful, and many involve one side on one occasion and the other at another time. The attacks last from an hour or so to a few weeks, but averaging three to seven days. Sometimes there is slight residual swelling of the gland between attacks. In the attacks the duct orifice may be red and sometimes pus can be expressed.

Parotid swelling due to *sarcoid* is commonly associated with uveitis.

Sjögren's syndrome (rare) may present as recurrent parotid swelling (Chudwin *et al*. 1981); it is associated with collagen diseases, xerostomia, keratoconjunctivitis sicca and enlargement of salivary glands. In the *Mikulicz syndrome* there is idiopathic bilateral painless enlargement of the parotid and lachrymal glands, often with dry mouth and eyes; it may be associated with leukaemia or lymphosarcoma.

Swelling of the parotid gland may be caused by clonazepam, iodides, isoprenaline or phenylbutazone.

References

Chudwin DS, *et al*. Spectrum of Sjögren's syndrome in children. *J Pediatr* 1981; **98**: 213.

David RB, O'Connell EJ. Suppurative parotitis in children. *Am J Dis Child.* 1970; **119**: 332.

Katzen M, du Plessis DJ. Recurrent parotitis in children. *South African Med J* 1964; **38**: 122.

Maynard JD. Recurrent parotid enlargement. *Br J Surg* 1965; **52**: 784.

Wilson WR, Eavey RD, Lang DW. Recurrent parotitis during childhood. *Clin Pediatr* 1980; **19**: 235.

Yamauchi T, Vollman EC. Epidemic parotitis due to parainfluenza 3 virus. *Pediatr Res* 1979; **13**: 394.

Anaemia and Pallor

Many children are treated for anaemia in family practice when there is no anaemia at all. The child may be pale because he has been indoors a great deal, is tired, or has an infection, or because he has a pale complexion, taking after a parent in that respect. The sudden development of pallor may be due to a wide variety of illness. Attacks of pallor and a shock-like appearance, occurring every few minutes, may be due to *intussusception,* even though there is no pain or vomiting (p. 105). In milk degrees of anaemia it is impossible to be certain of the diagnosis without a haemoglobin estimation.

Many are unaware of the normal levels of haemoglobin at different ages. The following are normal figures in grammes per cent (O'Brien & Pearson 1971).

	Mean	Range
Cord blood	17·1	13·7–20·5
7 days	18·8	14·6–23·0
20 days	15·9	11·3–20·5
45 days	12·7	9·5–15·9
75 days	11·4	9·6–13·2
120 days	11·9	9·9–13·9
1 year	12·2	10·0–13·0
5 years	12·5	12–13
10 years	13·5	13–14
Older	15	14–16

The normal range in the young baby depends on the birth weight. A drop from 16·0 g at birth to 8·0 at 6 weeks is normal for a 1·5 kg low-birth-weight baby, but not at 2 weeks, and is not normal for a full term baby.

In the newborn baby, the usual cause of anaemia at birth is haemolysis due to blood group incompatibility; but it could be due to bleeding from a placental vessel, feto-maternal transfusion, or in the case of twins, to bleeding of one twin into the other. An important cause is bleeding from the umbilical cord, and on the second to about the fifth day, the most likely cause is blood loss due to haemorrhagic disease of the newborn. Anaemia may arise in the first days as the result of infection.

In later infancy the most likely cause is prematurity. It is the commonest cause of anaemia between six and 12 months of age. Another cause is severe anaemia in the mother in the latter part of pregnancy. From ten months onwards nutritional anaemia is the most common, due to a poor diet.

A simple classification of the causes of anaemia is as follows:

Blood loss

Nutritional defects

Infection

Haemolysis

Defective red cell production and other serious blood diseases.

There is some overlapping between these groups.

Anaemia due to blood loss

Bleeding from placental vessels, or into the placental
    circulation
Bleeding of one twin into the other
Bleeding from the umbilical cord
Haemorrhagic disease of the newborn
    Melaena. Haematemesis
Extensive cephalhaematoma
Nose bleeds
Bleeding from the alimentary tract
    Aspirin and other drugs
    Hookworms (in the tropics)
    Meckel's diverticulum (p. 86)
    Ulcerative colitis (p. 84)
    Rectal polyp (p. 87)
    Milk allergy
    Telangiectasia (rare, p. 328)
    Reduplication of intestine (rare, pp. 11, 114)
Bleeding from the urinary tract
Blood diseases—haemophilia, etc.
Trauma

Bleeding from placental vessels, etc. This is the second most common
cause of anaemia at birth, the most common being haemolytic disease
of the newborn. It is due to rupture of the cord, anomalous placental
vessels, damage to the placenta by instruments or separation of the
placenta. Transplacental haemorrhage may also occur; this consists of
bleeding into the maternal circulation. The child is pale and the pallor
persists in spite of normal respirations and the administration of
oxygen. The child's pulse is rapid, while the child with pallor due to
anoxia has a slow pulse. If the haemoglobin is below 9 grammes per
cent, transfusion is urgent.

Bleeding of one twin into the other (Rausen *et al.* 1965). One twin
is born plethoric, the other anaemic. Both twins may need treatment,
the plethoric one needing a replacement transfusion, replacing some
blood by plasma, and the other needing the administration of blood.

Bleeding from the umbilical cord. Bleeding from the umbilical cord is
usually due to contraction of the cord, leaving the ligature slack.

Serious bleeding may occur and an urgent transfusion may be required.

Haemorrhagic disease of the newborn. (British Medical Journal 1977). When a newborn baby in the first three or four days vomits blood or passes blood per rectum, it is essential to determine whether it is the mother's blood, swallowed during delivery or from her nipple, or the baby's blood, because if it is the baby's blood, the appropriate treatment must be given (usually Vitamin K) and a careful watch must be kept in order to determine whether a transfusion is necessary. The material should be filtered, and to 5 parts of the supernatant fluid one adds 1 part of 0·25 N (1 per cent) NaOH. If the colour changes to yellow, it is the mother's blood, and if it remains pink, it is the baby's blood, because the fetal haemoglobin is more resistant to alkali. This condition is a matter of urgency. It is a tragedy to allow an infant to die from melaena neonatorum when his life could readily have been saved by a transfusion.

It is rare for bleeding into a *cephalhaematoma* to be excessive. If it does occur, it should suggest a blood disease such as haemophilia. It is common for haemophilia to occur without a family history of that condition.

A subaponeurotic haemorrhage causes a more diffuse swelling, for the cephalhaematoma, being subperiosteal, is confined by the sutures.

Oesophageal varices are likely to be found only in cases of cirrhosis of the liver or hypersplenism.

Hiatus hernia is an important cause of bleeding. The diagnosis should be suspected when an infant or child has a long history of vomiting, with occasional traces of blood in the vomitus. The diagnosis may be established by a barium swallow and faecal occult blood test.

Aspirin may cause gastric bleeding, and if given frequently, may cause severe anaemia. The bleeding occurs largely as a result of direct irritation of gastric mucosa by particles of aspirin, and it may also be due to hypoprothrombinaemia or thrombocytopenia. Various *other drugs* may cause gastrointestinal haemorrhage. They include acetazolamide, antimetabolites, chlortetracycline, indomethacin, methotrexate and thiazides.

Hookworm infection is an important cause of anaemia due to blood loss in tropical countries or in immigrants from those countries. The diagnosis is made by the finding of ova in the stools.

Meckel's diverticulum, reduplication of the intestine, ulcerative colitis and rectal polyp are discussed elsewhere. For other causes of blood in the stool, see p. 85.

Wilson *et al.* (1974) found that 17 of 34 infants with iron deficiency anaemia had occult blood loss due to whole cow's milk. The bleeding ceased when they received soya bean milk.

Haematuria. Prolonged haematuria may follow an attack of acute nephritis. I have seen severe anaemia develop from this cause.

Haemolysis

> Haemolytic disease of the newborn
> > Blood group incompatibility, including ABO incompatibility
> Acholuric jaundice; spherocytosis; elliptocytosis
> Hereditary nonspherocytic haemolytic anaemia (rare)
> Sickle-cell anaemia, haemoglobinopathies
> Glucose-6-phosphate dehydrogenase deficiency (rare in Britain)
> Pyruvate kinase deficiency (rare)
> Autoimmune haemolytic anaemia (rare)
> Drugs
> Infections
> Acute haemolytic anaemia of unknown origin (rare)
> Disseminated intravascular coagulation
> Wilson's disease (hepatolenticular degeneration)
> Haemolytic uraemic syndrome
> Periarteritis and disseminated lupus
> Solvent sniffing

This list is by no means complete, but it does include the more important conditions.

The most common cause of anaemia on the first day of life is *haemolytic disease,* and this is almost certainly the diagnosis if in addition there is jaundice. The possibility of prenatal blood loss must be remembered. *As treatment may be urgently needed, it is vital that an exact diagnosis should be established immediately, with the help of the Blood Transfusion Laboratory or other laboratory service.*

Acholuric jaundice. A family history of acholuric jaundice or unexplained anaemia should alert one to the diagnosis. The spleen is almost always enlarged. There is a rare hereditary nonspherocytic haemolytic anaemia.

Sickle-cell anaemia. There are several types of sickle-cell anaemia, all associated with an abnormal haemoglobin. The sickle-cell trait is found in nine per cent of American Negroes, in parts of India and in 45 per cent of some African tribes. It is a chronic debilitating disease with symptoms of anaemia, thromboses in various organs or limbs and consequent pain and fever. There may be haemolytic or aplastic crises, often precipitated by infections. No coloured child should be treated for iron deficiency anaemia without sickle-cell anaemia being considered. If there is no response to iron in four weeks, full laboratory investigation for sickling and other conditions should be carried out.

Thalassaemia (Cooley's anaemia) is a related condition with abnormally shaped red cells, occurring in the Mediterranean area or in those originating from that region. It is found in parts of India, Bangladesh and Sri Lanka. In mild forms there is a mild persistent anaemia; in severe forms there is progressive severe anaemia with gross splenomegaly unless repeated transfusions are given. A characteristic facies develops owing to the thickening of the bones of the face and skull. Thalassaemia may be associated with the sickle cell trait.

Glucose-6-phosphate dehydrogenase deficiency occurs in some millions of persons including Greeks, Cypriots, Turks, Chinese, Indians, Saudi Arabians, Filipinos and Jews from Iran and Iraq. It leads to haemolysis particularly when certain drugs are administered, notably antimalarial drugs, B.A.L., diphenhydramine, naphthalene, nitrofurantoin, phenacetin, salicylates, sulphonamides and vitamin K. Haemolysis may also occur if broad beans are eaten, and favism is due to deficiency of this enzyme. There may be haemolysis with some infections, such as infective hepatitis or glandular fever. *Pyruvate kinase deficiency* is a rare enzyme deficiency associated with haemolysis.

Autoimmune haemolytic anaemia. This occurs in association with a variety of unrelated conditions, including virus infections (herpes, infective hepatitis), pyelonephritis, disseminated lupus erythematosus, periarteritis nodosa and dermatomyositis. The Coombs' test is positive.

Drugs may cause haemolysis, apart from glucose-6-phosphate dehydrogenase deficiency. They include antimalarials, cephaloridine, chloramphenicol, cyclophosphamide, mefenamic acid, nalidixic acid, nitrofurantoin, P.A.S., penicillin, phenacetin, quinine, rifampicin, sulphonamides, troxidone and vitamin K.

The haemolytic uraemic syndrome is a mysterious condition in which the child develops haemolytic anaemia, fever, abdominal pain, jaundice and signs of renal failure, often with thrombocytopenic purpura. There is commonly a mild gastroenteritis or upper respiratory tract infection, followed in two to five days by acute symptoms—vomiting, abdominal pain, oliguria or anuria, oedema, convulsions and intestinal haemorrhages. There may be hepatosplenomegaly. In the urine there are red cells, casts and albumin. Outbreaks have occurred in certain areas, and a virus cause has been suspected. The diagnosis depends on the demonstration of haemolysis, thrombocytopenia and renal failure, with characteristic burr cells (odd-shaped cells) in the blood smear. The condition is more common in the first four years, especially the first year. The mortality is high (40 per cent). Recovery follows in others after four to eight weeks. The condition may be the same as thrombotic thrombocytopenic purpura. Disseminated intravascular coagulation is manifested by haemorrhage state, haemolytic anaemia and thrombosis, commonly in association with severe systematic disease.

Haemolysis may occur in *mycoplasma* infection.

Nutritional anaemia

> Prolonged breast feeding
> Poor diet; mental deficiency
> Anaemia of prematurity
> Rickets
> Scurvy
> Steatorrhoea

By far the commonest cause of anaemia in a child after about nine months of age is *nutritional anaemia*. This may be due to a poor diet with inadequate protein and iron content, and an excess of milk and carbohydrate. It occurs in tropical countries as a result of prolonged breast feeding. One must not be deterred by a mother's claim that the child is receiving a good mixed diet; such a history is frequent, but there is no doubt that the child has not been receiving an appropriate diet. Mentally defective children (including those with cerebral palsy) are liable to develop anaemia because of the difficulty which they experience in chewing and therefore in taking solid foods. They have to be maintained on thickened feeds, and nutritional anaemia or avitaminoses may develop.

The anaemia of prematurity is not strictly a nutritional anaemia, but it is convenient to include it here. If small premature infants are not given additional iron they are likely to become anaemic, especially after the age of six months.

Nutritional rickets is itself associated with a hypochromic anaemia. The diagnosis can be made in severe cases by the finding of the markedly thickened epiphysis of the radius and ulna at the wrist, but the diagnosis must be confirmed by X-ray of the wrist, along with estimation of the plasma calcium, phosphorus and alkaline phosphatase.

Scurvy is now rarely seen, but is more likely to occur in defective children who are unable to chew and cannot take an ordinary mixed diet. The diagnosis is suggested by spongy bleeding gums, anaemia and severe pain in a leg due to subperiosteal haemorrhages.

The anaemia of *steatorrhoea* is due to malabsorption, and so must be included under the heading of nutritional anaemia.

Defective red cell production

> Infections
> Drugs
> Lead poisoning
> Hypoplastic and aplastic anaemia
> Megaloblastic anaemia
> Thyroid deficiency
> Miscellaneous
>> Malignant disease
>> Leukaemia
>> Liver disease
>> Bone disease
>> Uraemia
>> Lipoid storage disease (rare)
>> Letterer Siwe disease (rare)

Infections. When a three or four weeks old baby gradually becomes anaemic, the cause may be a low-grade infection. The umbilicus must be examined for infection, and a blood culture should be performed if there is doubt. In older infants and children, a low-grade infection, such as pyelonephritis, may cause a persistent mild anaemia.

Drugs. Numerous drugs are capable of causing anaemia. (Huguley 1966). They include antiepileptic drugs, antihistamines, antimitotics, antithyroid drugs, carbenicillin, cephalexin, chloramphenicol, chlorothiazide, chloroquine, cycloserine, gold, griseofulvin, imipramine, indomethacin, lincomycin, mefenamic acid, mepacrine, meprobamate, methicillin, P.A.S., phenacetin, phenothiazines, phenylbutazone, pyrimethamine, quinidine, quinine, ristocetin, salicylates, streptomycin, sulphonamides, tetracycline, thiaben-dazole, and trimethoprim. Over 400 drugs or chemicals are known to cause blood dyscrasias. It follows that when a child presents with anaemia, one should ask in detail about all drugs taken in the previous few months. Various poisons, such as cleaning agents, paints, paint removers, lacquers and hydrocarbons may cause anaemia, often hypoplastic in type.

Lead poisoning in some areas, especially in low social classes, is an important cause of anaemia, especially where there is pica. It is commonly acquired by eating paint which is flaking off window-sills and other objects. Manifestations include abdominal pain, encephalopathy, headache, vomiting, anorexia, incoordination and weight loss. In severe cases there may be peripheral neuritis. Stippling of the red cells is unreliable. An X-ray may show increased density at the end of long bones, but the diagnosis is established by blood lead estimation.

Hypoplastic and aplastic anaemia may remain unexplained after the fullest investigation, but it may be due to drugs and poisons, including lead, infections or exposure to irradiation. One form of hypoplastic anaemia (*Fanconi's syndrome*) is associated with skeletal deformities (notably an absent radius), skin pigmentation, hypogenitalism, dwarfism, microcephaly and webbed neck. In some cases there is an arrest in the maturation of the red cell for no discoverable reason, leading commonly to severe anaemia between the age of two and eighteen months. Many cases of 'hypoplastic' or 'aplastic' anaemia prove eventually to be due to leukaemia.

Megaloblastic anaemia may be due to steatorrhoea, pernicious anaemia, liver disease, drugs (anticonvulsants, nitrofurantoin), leukaemia and tapeworms. It may be caused by chronic infection in a malnourished child.

Cretinism may be associated with anaemia which responds to treatment with thyroxine.

A variety of other conditions cause anaemia, of which the most common is *malignant disease*, including leukaemia. Certain *bone diseases*, especially osteopetrosis, are associated with anaemia. *Renal failure* is usually accompanied by anaemia.

Conclusion

Anaemia in the newborn period is an acute emergency, requiring immediate hospital investigation and treatment.

Many children are treated with iron for a non-existent anaemia—and many other children, especially coloured ones, have an anaemia which is not diagnosed, and so do not receive treatment.

Iron deficiency is the commonest cause of anaemia after the newborn period, but the diagnosis should only be made with the help of a blood count. If there is not a good rise of haemoglobin after treating a child with ferrous sulphate for a month, and if one can be sure that he really took the iron, the child should be properly investigated by a hospital laboratory.

References

See p. 59.

Purpura

As the causes of purpura differ in the newborn baby from those in older children, the subject will be discussed in relation to the child's age.

The newborn

Petechial haemorrhages over the face and forehead are normal, and retinal haemorrhages can be found in about 20 per cent of all newborn babies, except those born by Caesarian section, and in 50 per cent of those born by vacuum extraction (Baum & Bulpitt 1970).

Neonatal purpura may be due to drugs taken by the mother during pregnancy; they include anticoagulants, antiepileptics, chloroquine, quinine, salicylates and thiazide diuretics. It is sometimes the result of maternal drug addiction.

Other causes include *rubella* in early pregnancy, maternal *cytomegalovirus* or *toxoplasmosis* infection, *immune-mediated thrombocytopenia* (maternal anti-platelet antibodies) (Scott 1966), *congenital leukaemia* and *ABO incompatibility*.

Rare causes in the newborn include *septicaemia, renal vein thrombosis, generalized herpes, the Fanconi (absent radius) syndrome* and *galactosaemia*. Disseminated intravascular coagulation is a possible cause especially if the baby were of low birth weight, was hypoxic, acidotic, hypothermic, infected or had rhesus incompatibility. (Chesterman 1980). When a baby has a large *cavernous haemangioma* he may have thrombocytopenic purpura.

Purpura after the newborn period

The common causes of purpura after the newborn period are as follows:

Trauma (e.g. child abuse)
Henoch-Schönlein or anaphylactoid purpura
Idiopathic thrombocytopenic purpura
Leukaemia
Petechiae after a convulsion
The effect of drugs

Less common causes are:

Aplastic anaemia
Haemolytic uraemic syndrome
Uraemia
Meningococcal septicaemia and other
severe infections
Common infectious diseases
Haemophilia and allied diseases
Scurvy
Hereditary telangiectasia (rare)
Purpura with eczema (Wiskott-Aldrich syndrome—rare)

Disseminated lupus erythematosus (rare)
Ehlers-Danlos syndrome (rare)

Henoch Schönlein purpura is more common in boys than girls. It occurs particularly around the age of five or six years. Preceding haemolytic streptococcal infection is not usually a factor. There are commonly petechiae on the extensor surface of the limbs and around the buttocks, frequently associated with urticaria, effusion into joints and with abdominal pain and often bleeding from the bowel. The face is usually spared except in infants. Nephritis with haematuria complicates the condition in about 40 per cent of cases. *Special investigations give entirely negative results*—an important diagnostic feature. The platelet count, bleeding and clotting time and capillary fragility tests are all normal. Provided that the diagnosis is correct, there is probably no indication for hospital treatment, as no specific treatment is available, but it would be unwise to keep at home an early case complicated by nephritis, because complications of nephritis (such as hypertensive encephalopathy) have to be treated in hospital. It would be a disaster to diagnose Henoch-Schönlein purpura when the child in fact had meningococcal septicaemia.

Thrombocytopenic purpura is by far the commonest type of purpura in children after the Henoch-Schönlein type (Baldini 1966). The child having been previously well is found to have bruises in various parts of the body without history of injury. It is more common between the age of three and seven than at other ages. The limbs are always involved, and there is commonly bleeding from the bowel, vagina or urinary tract. The course may be acute, lasting for three or four weeks, but it may last for many months. It is important to note that the spleen is not usually palpable; an enlarged spleen would strongly suggest some other diagnosis, such as leukaemia. The capillary fragility test is positive; the blood pressure cuff is inflated to a point halfway between the systolic and diastolic pressures, and the pressure is maintained for eight minutes. In a ring 1·5 cm in diameter 2·5 cm below the crease of the elbow the number of petechiae are counted half a minute after removal of the cuff. The test is positive if more than 20 are found. The diagnosis is confirmed in the laboratory by the prolonged bleeding time, thrombocytopenia and a normal blood film. It has to be distinguished above all from leukaemia by the blood film and bone marrow examination. A child with suspected thrombocytopenic purpura should be referred to a specialist for laboratory investigation, because other conditions may be confused with it and only eliminated by laboratory means. For instance, purpura may be due to meningococcal septicaemia, and a mistaken diagnosis would be likely to lead to the child's death.

Purpura may be due to *drugs*. Those causing thrombocytopenia include acetazolamide, actinomycin D, antiepileptic drugs, antihistamines, atropine, carbenicillin, cephalexin, chlordiazepoxide, chlorothiazide, chlorpheniramine, corticosteroids, digoxin, indomethacin, iodides, meprobamate, methimazole, novobiocin, P.A.S., penicillamine, penicillin, phenylbutazone, quinidine, quinine, rifampicin, salicylates, sedormid, sulphadimidine, tolbutamide and trimethoprim. Numerous *poisons* affect the blood; they include paints, lacquers, paint removers and cleaning agents. In parts of Africa there is an unexplained thrombocytopenic purpura (called Onyalai) with 'blood blisters' in the mouth: it may be due to an ingestant or infection.

Purpura may be due to *hypoplastic or aplastic anaemia, Wiskott-Aldrich syndrome* of eczema, purpura and recurrent infections, *disseminated lupus erythematosus* and the *haemolytic uraemic syndrome* (p. 52).

The possibility of *uraemia* should be remembered in an ill child with unexplained purpura at any age, including infancy. The blood pressure will be raised, and this part of the examination should not be forgotten.

Petechiae or ecchymoses are commonly found in *meningococcal septicaemia* (p. 32).

Purpura may occur in combination with *rubella, measles, chickenpox, scarlet fever or diphtheria*. Purpura may follow *rubella* one to ten days after the onset of the rash.

A few petechiae may result from *whooping cough* or follow a *major convulsion*.

Bruising may be a feature of *haemophilia, Christmas disease*, and other bleeding disorders. A full laboratory investigation is essential. In *Von Willebrand's disease* there are epistaxes and bleeding from the gums and gastrointestinal tract. The bleeding time is prolonged, but the clotting time and platelet count are normal. The diagnosis is made by capillary microscopy and other means.

Purpura occurs in *hereditary telangiectasia,* in which telangiectases can be seen on the face, on the fingers and in the nasal or buccal mucosa, and in the *Ehlers–Danlos syndrome* in which there are overextensible joints and a hyperelastic skin.

References

Baldini M. Idiopathic thrombocytopenic purpura. *N Eng J Med* 1966; **274:** 1245, 1301, 1360.

Baum JD, Bulpitt CJ. Retinal and conjunctival haemorrhage in the newborn. *Arch Dis Child* 1970; **45:** 344.

Brit Med J Leading article: Bleeding in the newborn. 1977: **2:** 915.

Chesterman CN. Disseminated intravascular coagulation and related disorders. *Medicine UK* 1980; **No 28:** 1428.

Huguley CM. Hematological reactions (drugs). *JAMA* 1966; **196:** 408.

O'Brien RT, Pearson HA. Physiological anaemias of the newborn infant. *J Pediatr* 1971; **79:** 132.

Rausen AR, Seki M, Strauss L. Twin transfusion syndrome. *J Pediatr* 1965; **66:** 613.

Scott JS. Immunological diseases and pregnancy. *Brit Med J* 1966; **1:** 1559.

Wilson JF, Lahey ME, Heiner DC. Studies on iron metabolism. Further observations on cow's milk induced gastrointestinal bleeding in infants with iron deficiency anaemia. *J Pediatr* 1974; **84:** 335.

Poor Appetite

When a newborn baby goes off his food, the most likely cause is an infection, such as a urinary tract infection, otitis media or meningitis. Cold injury or developing kernicterus are other causes—the latter only if there has been hyperbilirubinaemia.

I have discussed the problem of a poor appetite in detail elsewhere (Illingworth 1982). By far the commonest cause of a poor appetite, other than that due to an acute infection, is *food forcing*. This consists of feeding the child with a spoon, often by force, persuading him to eat more, offering him bribes if he will finish his dinner, threatening punishment if he does not eat, smacking him for not eating, allowing him to choose exactly what he would like to eat, allowing him to eat snacks at any time he likes between meals, and using various methods of distraction, so that when his attention is distracted some food can be put in by spoon.

Food forcing is itself due to a variety of causes, the chief of which are probably the following:

Excessive anxiety about the child's nutrition and weight

Dawdling with food—the child giving the impression that he
has no appetite

Failure to realise that because of his small build (which is
usually a familial feature, or related to his low birth
weight) he has a smaller than average food requirement

The mother may confuse the average weight with the normal
weight—thinking that if the child is below the average weight, he
must have something wrong with him. She does not realize that all
children are different and that a child may be pounds below the
average weight and yet be normal. Many mothers are concerned
because the child's appetite is less in the second six months of his life
than in the first six months. Mothers should be told how the weight
gain falls off as the child grows older-averaging 7 oz per week (198 g)
in the first three months, 5.3 oz per week (150 g) from four to six
months, 3½ oz per week (99 g) from seven to nine months, and 2½
oz per week (71 g) from ten to twelve months.

When babies are beginning to feed themselves, from nine to about
18 months, they characteristically dawdle with their food, playing
with it, patting it with the back of the spoon, and giving the
impression that they are not hungry. The mother then becomes
worried and tries to make them eat.

Well children vary in their appetite. There are little eaters and big
eaters. In general the active wiry child eats less than the fat placid one.
Efforts to make little eaters eat more always lead to the opposite of the
effect desired.

The mother's anxiety about her child's appetite is bound up with
many other factors. The problem is more common in an only child or
in a child born many years after the previous one. It is more common
when the parents are elderly and cannot have another child.

When food forcing occurs, food refusal results from the two main
reasons. The child resists because of his normal negativism which is a
feature from nine months to three years. In addition he becomes
conditioned against food because whenever food is presented to him
it is associated with unpleasantness, forcing methods and often
punishment, so that he develops a real dislike for food.

Certain drugs may reduce the appetite—apart from amphetamine
and the appetite suppressants. They include aminophylline,
amitriptyline, antimetabolites, carbamazepine, chlordiazepoxide,

ephedrine, ethionamide, ethosuximide, indomethacin methotrexate, methylphenidate, penicillamine, phenytoin, sodium valproate, sulphasalazine and Vitamin A or D excess.

If in addition to a poor appetite, the child does not appear well, one must look for organic causes, such as chronic urinary tract infection, coeliac disease or other cause of 'failure to thrive' (p. 1).

Reference

Illingworth RS. *The normal child.* 8th ed. London: Churchill Livingstone, 1982.

Pica (dirt eating)

Pica, or dirt eating, occurs particularly in the first four or five years. It is more prevalent in the lower social classes than in the upper ones. It is more common in mentally defective children than in those of normal intelligence, partly because mentally defective children continue to take objects to the mouth long after the normal child has ceased to do so.

It has been thought by some that pica was associated with iron deficiency anaemia, but the association is often coincidental—iron deficiency anaemia and pica both being related to the low social class and to malnutrition. There is commonly a family history of pica, so that the child may have merely followed the example of others.

The danger of pica is the risk of infection, ingestion of worms and lead poisoning. In all cases the haemoglobin and blood lead should be determined.

References

Crosby WH. Food, pica and iron deficiency. *Arch Int Med* 1971; **127**: 960.
Lourie RS. *Clin Proc, Children's Hosp of Columbia* 1965; **21**: 193.

Nausea

Apart from the nausea which usually precedes vomiting, nausea is not a common symptom of childhood. The usual causes are:

> Psychogenic, including attention seeking and distaste for school. Unpleasant sights or smells
> Morning nausea
> Dislike for certain foods
> Fatty foods
> Vasomotor disturbance—posture, anaemia
> Infective hepatitis
> Urinary tract infection
> Cerebral tumour
> Drugs

Nausea in the morning when *getting ready for school* may or may not signify the child's preference for staying at home. It is not always easy to be sure, because some children and adults feel nausea in the morning—and have little breakfast. One needs to ask whether the morning nausea is as frequent in the weekends and holidays as it is in term time. Nausea may represent an attention-seeking device—when a mother expresses anxiety over the child's various symptoms.

Nausea on *changing posture* occurs in some older children. It is a vasomotor disturbance and is more common when there is anaemia.

Subclinical infective hepatitis may cause nausea and lassitude. Liver function tests will help if the urine examination for bile does not reveal the diagnosis.

Urinary tract infection may show itself by vague unwellness and nausea.

It is a mistake to assume that the vomiting due to a *cerebral tumour* is not accompanied by nausea.

Numerous *drugs* may cause a feeling of nausea. They include amitriptyline, carbamazepine, cephaloridine, clonidine, chlordiazepoxide, diazepam, niclosamide, penicillamine, phenytoin, primidone, sodium valproate, sulphasalazine and many others.

To establish the diagnosis a full physical examination is necessary, including culture of the urine in order to eliminate a urinary tract infection.

Vomiting

It is probable that all children vomit, at least sometimes: but some vomit more readily than others. Almost all normal babies bring some milk up after feeds. Either it wells up into the mouth, or else vomited material shoots out with a belch of wind. The difficulty lies in deciding whether vomiting can be disregarded as being within the range of normality, or whether it is necessary to investigate to determine if disease is present.

The causes of vomiting are legion, and it would not be profitable to attempt to give a complete list. Hence the discussion to follow is inevitably and intentionally incomplete; but I have tried to include the most important causes. For convenience I have related the discussion to three age periods—the newborn infant, the infant after the newborn period, and the child after infancy. There will be some overlapping between these three groupings.

The newborn infant

The following causes of vomiting may be important:

Normal possetting

Sucking and swallowing difficulties (p. 166)

Infections. Meningitis. Septicaemia

Intracranial—oedema, haemorrhage, kernicterus

Obstruction—oesphagus, duodenum, small intestine

Vascular ring, meconium plug or ileus

Lactobezoar

Chalasia (p. 42)

Perforation of stomach or pharynx

Renal insufficiency, urethral obstruction.

Metabolic disorders (rare)—phenylketonuria, galactosaemia, carbohydrate intolerance, hypervalinaemia, adreno-cortical hyperplasia.

Drugs

It is common for the normal newborn baby to bring some milk up after feeds. When the vomiting is frequent one has to consider the possibility of organic disease. When only small amounts come up after

63

feeds and the child is well, taking the feeds normally and gaining weight (after the first two or three days), disease is unlikely. It has been suggested, on what evidence I am not sure, that much vomiting in the newborn period is due to irritation of the stomach by amniotic contents, meconium or blood swallowed during delivery. Since all babies in utero constantly swallow amniotic fluid, it seems unlikely that amniotic fluid would cause vomiting after birth. It is at least true to say that some newborn babies vomit fairly frequently in the first few days after birth, sometimes causing anxiety, and then settle down without further trouble and without treatment.

Amongst organic causes of significant vomiting in the newborn period, the commonest are probably *obstruction* and *infection*. It is particularly important that if there is obstruction in one part of the alimentary tract (e.g. an imperforate anus) there is a considerable risk that there will be another anomaly of the alimentary tract elsewhere (e.g. tracheo-oesophageal fistula, duodenal stenosis).

The features which would make one seriously consider organic disease are as follows:

1 Hydramnios.

2 Persistent vomiting, as distinct from occasional vomiting.

3 The presence of bile in the vomit (green vomitus). This would suggest obstruction below the ampulla of Vater, but green vomitus may occur when there is a serious infection or birth injury. *Green vomitus should be regarded as being due to intestinal obstruction until proved otherwise.* Green vomitus should be distinguished from yellow colostrum or from vomitus containing meconium.

4 Drowsiness, failure to suck well, failure to demand feeds.

5 Abdominal distension. This suggests obstruction in the lower part of the intestinal tract. There is commonly no distension in the presence of high intestinal obstruction.

6 Failure to gain weight or loss of weight.

7 Dehydration.

8 Fever. This may be due to dehydration or infection.

9 Failure to pass meconium in the first 24 hours. This suggests meconium ileus, Hirschsprung's disease or intestinal obstruction. The passage of a stool in the first 24 hours does not, however, exclude obstruction.

10 Visible peristalsis from right to left, suggesting obstruction in the jejunum, ileum or colon.

11 The presence of a palpable mass—meconium ileus, enlarged kidneys, reduplication of the intestine or a palpable bladder.

12 The presence of a bulging fontanelle, suggesting cerebral oedema or an intracranial haemorrhage.

These and other conditions will now be discussed in more detail.

Obstruction in the alimentary tract

Hirschsprung's disease is perhaps the commonest cause of intestinal obstruction in the newborn (Fraser & Wilkinson 1967).

Atresia of the oesophagus is suggested when the infant's mother had hydramnios. In such a case it is the practice to pass a catheter down the infant's oesophagus immediately after birth, in order to make sure that there is no atresia, and until that has been done a feed must not be given. If there is atresia, the catheter commonly meets an obstruction four inches (10 cm) from the lips. The lower end of the catheter may coil itself in the blind upper pouch of the oesophagus, and one may be misled unless an X-ray photograph is taken. Atresia is suspected when the infant's mouth is overflowing with mucus and saliva. It will be suspected when a baby chokes and vomits on being given his first feed, or vomits nothing but mucus between feeds. The diagnosis of atresia is usually confirmed by a straight X-ray (without lipiodol).

According to Ducharme *et al.* (1971) *perforation of the pharynx* in the newborn causes symptoms identical with those of oesophageal atresia. It may be impossible to pass a nasogastric tube in either condition, and radiological studies are confusing. A *vascular ring* will be considered if there is stridor, usually inspiratory and expiratory, commonly with vomiting. *Chalasia of the oesophagus,* or lax cardio-oesophageal sphincter, is an unusual cause of vomiting in the newborn period (p. 72).

Duodenal stenosis would be suspected when a baby vomits repeatedly without abdominal distension. Bile will be present in the vomitus only when the obstruction is below the ampulla. Duodenal stenosis or atresia may be a feature in mongols.

A *meconium plug* consists of greyish brown inspissated material which precedes the passage of normal meconium. The plug may sometimes be expelled after digital examination of the rectum.

Meconium ileus may be suspected when meconium is not passed in the first 24 hours. Multiple masses may sometimes be felt in the distended abdomen. As it is usually a manifestation of fibrocystic disease of the pancreas, there may be a history of that condition in a sibling. It is more likely to occur in low birth weight infants. Signs are mainly abdominal distension, abdominal mass, vomiting, diarrhoea and sometimes signs of gastric perforation.

Intestinal atresia may be associated with other congenital abnormalities of the alimentary tract, such as oesophageal atresia or imperforate anus. The symptoms and signs are persistent vomiting with bile in the vomitus, abdominal distension, often visible peristalsis and constipation. Vomiting tends to occur later and to be less profuse when the obstruction is in the lower part of the alimentary tract, but distension is more marked. Obstruction may be caused by malrotation or volvulus. Vomiting, blood in the stool and abdominal distension may follow perforation of the colon after a replacement transfusion (p. 114). Obstruction a few days after birth may result from *inspissated milk (lactobezoar),* usually resulting from milk being insufficiently diluted (Schreiner *et al.* 1979).

Ganglion-blocking drugs given in pregnancy to the mother for hypertension may be followed by ileus in the newborn baby for the first week or two.

A second serious cause of vomiting in the newborn period is an *infection.* This may be septicaemia, resulting from an infected umbilicus, urinary tract infection, meningitis or gastroenteritis. *Meningitis in the young baby is commonly manifested by drowsiness, loss of appetite, vomiting and sometimes by fits. There may or may not be a bulging fontanelle. There is commonly no neck stiffness or other sign of meningism. The unexplained drowsiness and illness without other discoverable cause demands a lumbar puncture in order to exclude pyogenic meningitis. The diagnosis of this condition is a matter of great urgency. Delay in instituting treatment is likely to be fatal or to lead to serious permanent sequelae, such as mental deficiency.*

In a serious infection the vomited material may be green, as it is when there is intestinal obstruction.

Vomiting may be an important symptom of *cerebral oedema or of an intracranial haemorrhage, such as a subdural haematoma.* The signs are often bulging of the fontanelle and wide separation of the sutures. The child may have an abnormal high-pitched cry and be unduly drowsy or irritable—with an exaggerated startle reflex and even twitching, frank convulsions or cyanotic attacks. The Moro reflex may be exaggerated or absent. There may be retinal haemorrhages—though it must be remembered that small haemorrhages may be found in normal newborn babies. Vomited material may be green. Depression of the respiratory centre as a result of increased intracranial pressure may cause atelectasis, so that respiratory symptoms may outweigh the cerebral ones.

The diagnosis of a *subdural effusion* must be made by subdural tap. Failure to diagnose a subdural effusion causes serious brain damage and progressive hydrocephalus.

Kernicterus is now very rare because it can nearly always be prevented by replacement transfusion when the serum bilirubin reaches a dangerous level, but sometimes it occurs in a fulminating septicaemia, causing a very rapid rise of serum bilirubin, with possibly unavoidable brain damage. Symptoms usually commence about the fifth to the ninth day, and consist of vomiting, loss of appetite, arching of the back, spasticity, rolling of the eyes and sometimes convulsions. There may be a peculiar pronation of the wrist.

Renal causes of vomiting include *hydronephrosis* from *urethral obstruction*. A useful pointer to the diagnosis would be a distended bladder with a poor urinary stream—or failure to pass urine.

Metabolic causes of vomiting include phenylketonuria, galactosaemia, lactose or fructose intolerance and adrenocortical hyperplasia. Vomiting due to these causes may occur in the newborn period, but is usually later. The diagnosis of *phenylketonuria* has to be suspected when a sibling has the disease; phenylpyruvic acid does not usually appear in the urine in the early days, and the diagnosis should be made within a few days of birth by estimation of the serum phenylalanine and tyrosine.

Infancy after the newborn period

The following causes should be considered:

> Non-organic
>> Normal possetting. Food coming up with wind
>> Incorrect feeds
>> Overfeeding (premature babies only)
>> Careless handling after feeds
>> Rumination
>> Giving solids before the baby can chew. Food forcing

Delay in giving solids
Crying causing vomiting
Travel sickness
Migraine
Allergy
Organic
Infection—otitis media, gastroenteritis, whooping cough, winter vomiting disease etc.
Intracranial
Obstruction
Peptic ulcer
Coeliac disease
Appendicitis
Metabolic diseases. Diabetes
Rare—uraemia, phenylketonuria, galactosaemia, carbohydrate intolerance, ketotic hypoglycaemia, adrenocortical hyperplasia, Reye's syndrome
Drugs and poisons

Probably all normal infants bring some milk up after feeds, but some bring up more than others, or bring it up more frequently. The difficulty in such cases lies in deciding whether the vomiting is within normal limits or not, and so whether it is desirable to investigate for organic disease.

The first feature which guides one is the weight gain. If there is a story of vomiting over a prolonged period, and the child's weight in relation to his birth weight is average or above average, one is less likely to miss organic disease than if he is underweight. The child may be an average weight because he was previously overweight before the vomiting began. One is frequently asked to see an infant who is said to have vomited the whole of every feed every day for some weeks, and who is above the average weight for the age. One then knows that the mother, in her anxiety or desire to impress, is exaggerating. It would not be safe to assume that organic disease in such a case could be absolutely excluded, for he might have a hiatus hernia. Organic disease is more likely if the child is underweight.

Another feature of importance would be the presence of blood in the vomitus, for that would suggest *hiatus hernia* or *reflux* due to chalasia of the oesophagus (p. 72).

By far the commonest non-organic cause of vomiting is *excessive wind*. In a breast fed baby this is due to the baby sucking too long on the breast, or sucking on an empty breast so that he swallows air. Sometimes a breast fed baby swallows air as a result of gulping milk rapidly. He does this not because he is 'greedy', but because the milk is flowing out of the breast rapidly—usually at the first feed in the morning, when the breast is distended. The young baby commonly does not bring his lips tightly round the nipple and sucks in air at the angle of the mouth. In a bottle fed baby the almost invariable cause of excessive wind is the presence of too small a hole in the teat. A bottle feed should not take more than 10 or 15 minutes. I am repeatedly told by mothers of 'windy' babies that the feeds take 45 to 60 minutes. All that time the baby is swallowing air. A baby may swallow an excess of air if he is allowed to suck when the teat has flattened as a result of a vacuum having been created in the bottle. For the same reason the baby may suffer from wind if he is left to suck on a bottle which has been propped up on a pillow. Two babies were referred to me on account of excessive wind because the mother in each case had filled the bottle with sago pudding and expected the baby to be able to suck it through the teat.

Theoretically the baby may be sick as a result of wrong food. In fact this is rare in my experience, though one must always ask a mother not just how much milk the baby is being given, but how much milk powder and water is being given at each feed. I have seen some impressive mistakes. It is a regrettable fact that many doctors and nurses, when faced with a baby who cries, vomits, or has other symptoms, still advise mothers to change from one dried food to another in order to find one which 'suits' the baby. The differences between the dried milks are so trivial that *it is never necessary to change from one dried milk to another,* except in the case of the rare metabolic diseases such as hypercalcaemia or carbohydrate intolerance. Yet I have seen hundreds of babies who have been tried on one dried milk after another in an effort to find one which 'suits' the baby—when his symptoms were due to something different, such as congenital pyloric stenosis.

Some would say that *overfeeding* is an important cause of vomiting.

Careless handling of the baby after a feed may cause milk to be brought up. This applies particularly to the premature baby in which the cardio-oesophageal sphincter is lax. If his nappy is changed after a feed, and the buttocks and therefore lower part of the body are elevated, milk may be brought up.

Rumination is an unusual non-organic cause of vomiting (*British Medical Journal* 1979, Fleisher 1979). The baby, usually between three months and a year, but sometimes older, seems to try to get the milk up, pushes his abdomen in and out, arches his back, and eventually brings it up, with apparent satisfaction. He may appear almost to gargle with it, the milk disappearing and reappearing in his throat. There may be associated sucking movements in the lips and cheeks. His action stops when watched or when he is actively interested in something. It is commonly ascribed to emotional deprivation, but it is wise to eliminate a hiatus hernia, by radiological examination, for these conditions are commonly associated with rumination, making it easier for the baby to regurgitate.

A baby is likely to vomit if *given solids before he can chew.* Most babies begin to chew at six or seven months; they can be given thickened feeds before then, but not solids. A retarded child is later than the normal child in beginning to chew, and so is liable to vomit from this cause. If a child is not given solids at a time when he has recently become able to chew, he is likely to refuse solids and to vomit them. This probably depends on the sensitive or critical period (Illingworth & Lister, 1964).

Some infants may develop a strong *dislike for certain foods,* and vomit them if the mother insists on giving these foods. Some mothers force their infants to take certain foods which are thought to be good for them, or try to compel them to take more than they need, with the result that they vomit.

Some infants have an unfortunate way of vomiting if they are *left to cry* for any length of time. This may be due to the baby air-swallowing when crying, or to his putting his thumb or finger into the back of the throat.

Travel sickness may begin in young infants five or six months of age.

Migraine begins as vomiting. It may first appear in infancy (p. 92).

Allergy to cow's milk is a rare cause of vomiting (p. 13).

Vomiting is *not* due to teething.

An *organic cause* for vomiting would be suspected if the child suddenly began to vomit after being previously well; if he were ill or febrile in addition to vomiting; if there were other symptoms; if he had an inadequate weight gain or lost weight; or if there were blood in the vomitus.

When a previously well infant becomes ill and vomits, the possible causes are numerous. The most likely is an *infection*. These include otitis media, gastroenteritis, urinary tract infection, whooping cough, 'winter vomiting' and meningitis. Otitis media is suspected when an infant has a cold or has just recovered from one, and is readily diagnosed by the auriscope. Gastroenteritis may cause some difficulty in the diagnosis for a few hours, in that vomiting may precede diarrhoea. A history of diarrhoea in another member of the family makes the diagnosis easier. For necrotizing enterocolitis, see p. 83.

Whooping cough is an important cause of vomiting (p. 140).

The term *'winter vomiting'* disease is not a good one, for it occurs in summer and winter. This is a virus infection, due commonly to the orbivirus, rotavirus or calicivirus. It has been well described in a report by the College of Practitioners, in which 1300 cases were recorded by 106 family doctors. It is highly infectious, with an incubation period of one to three days. Haworth *et al.* (1956) found a pleocytosis in the cerebrospinal fluid of all three children in whom a lumbar puncture was carried out, and suggested that a neurotropic virus might be responsible. Normally the only symptom is vomiting, nearly always in the night. Diarrhoea, if it occurs at all, is most unusual. The child is afebrile and is well until he suddenly vomits without previous nausea and without warning. The vomiting may recur.

Congenital pyloric stenosis occurs in one in 150 boys and one in 775 girls. There is genetic factor. The onset of vomiting is nearly always between three and six weeks of age, though rarely it can begin in the newborn period. If vomiting begins after the age of ten weeks, it is exceedingly unlikely to be due to pyloric stenosis: in about one per cent vomiting is delayed until the third month. The essential feature is projectile vomiting immediately after or during a feed. There is one big vomit and almost the whole feed comes up. If the baby is merely bringing small quantities up at intervals between one feed and the next, e.g., an hour or two after a feed, pyloric stenosis can be almost excluded. Rarely a child may have one big vomit immediately after or during a feed, and bring small quantities up for an hour or two, like a normal baby frequently does; but this is an unusual picture. There is no bile in the vomitus, but there is occasionally some blood. Jaundice is a rare feature. The vomiting begins with one feed and may then occur in every subsequent feed or not until the next day. It rapidly becomes more frequent, so that in two or three days the baby is

Vomiting

vomiting at almost every feed. As a result of the vomiting the baby becomes constipated and dehydrated. Peristaltic waves may be seen crossing from left to right in the upper abdomen. The expert will feel a pyloric tumour which comes and goes and is commonly of the size of a pea, slightly to the right of the umbilicus and usually a little above. He feels the baby during a feed. If the stomach is distended when he is about to begin, he will wash the stomach out first, because it is often impossible to feel a tumour when the stomach is distended.

Owing to the infrequency with which pyloric stenosis is seen in general practice, the family doctor should not rely on his ability to feel the tumour. He should suspect the diagnosis and ask the paediatrician to express an opinion on examination. The diagnosis is established by feeling the tumour. X-ray examination is nearly always unnecessary. There is no place for a therapeutic test of atropine methyl nitrate, for the correct treatment is surgical. The majority of babies with congenital pyloric stenosis seen in hospital have been tried on one dried food after another to find one which suits the baby.

Pylorospasm in my opinion is probably a non-existent condition in infants, though some will disagree. I can certainly say that I have never recognised a case, or seen a case thought by someone else to be pylorospasm and which did not appear to me to be incorrectly diagnosed. I have seen no evidence that such a condition exists. I usually find that babies thought to have this condition are suffering from excessive wind, congenital pyloric stenosis or are merely normal 'possetters'.

Chalasia of the oesophagus and hiatus hernia should be suspected if there is blood in the vomitus. If this is the case, a barium swallow X-ray should be performed. I would certainly have this done if a vomiting baby were also anaemic, because of the possibility of a hiatus hernia, of if there were much vomiting or loss of weight. One has also to be guided by the degree of the mother's anxiety. Sometimes a really anxious mother is not reassured until an X-ray examination has been performed. One has to balance this against the irradiation which a barium swallow involves.

Gastro-oesophageal reflux with or without hiatus hernia is an important cause of vomiting (Weissbluth 1981). The vomiting is commonly effortless, but may be projectile. Theoretically it should be more prominent when the child is lying down rather than sitting upright, but this is unreliable. When asked to see a persistent vomiter, one always asks whether there is blood in the vomitus, for that immediately suggests oesophagitis from reflux. The vomiting may lead to failure to thrive. In about 12 per cent of cases there are pulmonary complications consisting of cough and patchy consolidation. Rarely in the young infant the regurgitation may lead to apnoeic episodes. Gastro-oesophageal reflux is sometimes a feature of children who are mentally subnormal or have cerebral palsy (Cadman *et al.* 1978, Sondheimer & Morris 1979). The association of reflux with torticollis or opisthotonos is described on page 259 (Kinsbourne 1964).

The possibility of a *tracheo-oesophageal fistula* should be considered if there is persistent unexplained vomiting, especially if there has been another anomaly of the alimentary tract, such as an imperforate anus. The diagnosis, if not made by X-ray, may be made by the passage of a stomach tube, with the proximal end of the tube under water: when the tube is slowly withdrawn up the oesophagus, bubbles reveal a fistula.

Peptic ulcers can occur at any age. Johnson and colleagues (1980) described 16 under the age of 11 weeks; 9 of them presented with recurrent vomiting and 7 with bleeding or perforation.

Coeliac disease (p. 10) may present as vomiting when gluten-containing foods are introduced.

Appendicitis can occur at any age (p. 102). In infancy it commonly presents as an abdominal mass, peritonitis and diarrhoea.

Metabolic diseases which may present with vomiting include diabetes mellitus, Reye's syndrome and a variety of rare diseases.

Reye's syndrome affects infants and young children. (Starko *et al.* 1980). After a mild respiratory infection, there is often the sudden onset of vomiting, encephalopathy, irritability and coma, with hepatic dysfunction. The cause is unknown, but it may be a virus infection.

Ketotic hypoglycaemia may present as vomiting and fits. It is more common in low birth weight infants.

Drugs and Poisons. Innumerable drugs may cause vomiting. Poisoning should always be considered when a previously well child begins to vomit without discoverable cause. It must be remembered that the possibility of poisoning may be stoutly denied by a parent, and in that case it may be a form of *non-accidental injury.*

Vomiting after infancy

Non-organic causes

Vomiting because of psychological factors is common in children. These causes may be grouped as follows:

1 Excitement. Some children may vomit as the result of excitement, such as the prospect of going to a party.

2 Fear or anxiety. Anxiety about going to school, or about leaving home, may cause vomiting in school-age children in the morning before departure for school.

3 Suggestion and imitation. Vomiting may be suggested by anxious parents on a car journey. Vomiting may result from the child seeing another child vomit.

4 Attention-seeking device. Vomiting may occur as an attention-seeking device if the child sees that sickness causes consternation and anxiety.

5 Insertion of a finger into the throat. Some small children make themselves sick, probably accidentally, by insertion of a finger into the throat—sometimes when the throat is sore as a result of tonsillitis.

6 Migraine. Though it may be argued that migraine is an example of organic disease, emotional factors may precipitate attacks. Migraine, also termed in children the periodic syndrome, is described elsewhere.

7 Travel sickness.

Organic causes are suggested if the vomiting is of sudden onset, or if the child between attacks of vomiting is not well and is lacking in energy—though these symptoms may be psychological in origin. They are certainly suggested if there is loss of weight. The periodic syndrome can be confused with other conditions such as recurrent volvulus, herniation of the stomach through the diaphragm, ketotic hypoglycaemia, or recurrent urinary tract infection; and even if a child is known to suffer from migraine, he may also develop a different condition such as acute appendicitis, which also causes abdominal pain and vomiting.

Organic causes including the following:

Infection, especially tonsillitis or otitis media
Meningitis
Winter vomiting disease

Appendicitis, mesenteric lymphadenitis
Intestinal obstruction
Torsion of the testis (p. 297)
Poisons and drugs

As in the younger child, the commonest organic cause of vomiting is *an infection*—such as otitis media, tonsillitis, pyelonephritis, whooping cough, gastroenteritis or the winter vomiting disease. Meningitis is another possible cause, but in the case of the older child signs of meningism are usually but not invariably present.

Unexplained vomiting may be due to *drugs or poisons.* Innumerable medicines cause vomiting. They include anthelmintics, antibiotics, antidepressants, antiepileptic drugs, antihistamines, antimitotic drugs, morphia, pethidine, salicylates, tranquillisers and other drugs.

Vomiting may be a symptom of *lead poisoning*.

References

Br Med J Six month old persistent vomiters. Leading article 1979; **2**: 459.

Cadman D, Richards J, Feldman W. Gastro-esophageal reflux in severely retarded children. *Dev Med Child Neurol* 1978; **20**: 95.

College of Practitioners. Epidemic winter vomiting. Symposium by the epidemic observation unit of the college of general practitioners. *Research News Letter No. 8* (no date).

Ducharme JC, Bertrand R, Debie J. Perforation of the pharynx in the newborn. A condition mimicking oesophageal atresia. *Can Med Ass J* 1971; **104**: 785.

Fleisher DR. Infant rumination syndrome. *Am J Dis Child* 1979; **133**: 266.

Fraser GC, Wilkinson AW. Neonatal Hirschsprung's disease. *Br Med J* 1967; **2**: 7.

Haworth JC, Tyrell DAJ, Whitehead JEM. Winter vomiting disease with meningeal involvement. *Lancet* 1956; **2**: 1152.

Illingworth RS, Lister J. The critical or sensitive period, with special reference to certain feeding problems in infants and children. *J Pediatr* 1964; **65**: 839.

Johnson D, L'Heureux P, Thompson P. Peptic ulcer disease in early infancy: clinical presentations and roentgenographic features. *Acta Paediatr Scand* 1980; **69**: 753.

Kinsbourne M. Hiatus hernia with contortion of the neck. *Lancet* 1964; **1**: 1058.

Schreiner *et al.* Increased incidence of lactobezoars in low birth weight infants. *Am J Dis Child* 1979; **133**: 936.

Sondheimer JM, Morris BA. Gastro-oesophageal reflux among severely retarded children. *J Pediatr* 1979; **94**: 710.

Starko KM, Ray CG, *et al.* Reye's syndrome and salicylate use. *Pediatrics* 1980; **66**: 859.

Weissbluth M. Gastro-esophageal reflux. *Clin Pediatr* 1981; **20**: 7.

Haematemesis

Before accepting the diagnosis of haematemesis, one must be sure that what was thought to be altered blood was not chocolate. When a child brings blood up from the stomach, the following are the conditions to consider first:

In a newborn infant
 Swallowed blood during delivery
 Swallowed blood from the mother's nipple
 Haemorrhagic disease of the newborn
 Drugs taken in pregnancy—anti-coagulants, diuretics, salicylates (rare cause)

Infancy after the newborn period
 Hiatus hernia
 Chalasia of the oesophagus
 Blood diseases
 Congenital pyloric stenosis

After infancy
 Hiatus hernia
 Severe retching for any reason
 Nose bleeds
 Acute tonsillitis
 Oesophageal varices
 Peptic ulcer (especially when on corticosteroids)
 Intestinal obstruction (altered blood)
 Blood diseases
 Uraemia
 Poisons (corrosive substances, ferrous sulphate overdose); drugs

Rare causes
 Enterogenous cyst
 Disseminated intravascular coagulation
 Tyrosinosis (p. 116)
 Gaucher's disease (p. 116)
 Hypernatraemia
 Zollinger-Ellison syndrome
 Curling's ulcer (burns)
 Polycystic disease of the liver and kidney

Foreign body in oesophagus

C.N.S. injury

When a newborn in his first three or four days vomits blood, one needs to know whether it is the baby's or the mother's blood. He may have swallowed the mother's blood during delivery, or blood from the mother's cracked nipple. The two are readily distinguished by the chemical test described on p. 49: if it is the baby's blood, the most likely cause is haemorrhagic disease of the newborn, commonly due to hypoprothrombinaemia. In this case he requires treatment, and a careful watch must be kept to ensure that the blood loss is not such that a transfusion is necessary.

After the newborn period, blood-streaked vomitus is most commonly caused by *hiatus hernia* or *chalasia*. It is unusual in *pyloric stenosis*.

At any age haematemesis may be a feature of *blood diseases*.

Severe retching may lead to streaking of vomitus with blood.

Other causes of blood in the vomitus of a child are *blood swallowed after a nose bleed or from acute tonsillitis*—presumably as a result of rupture of a blood vessel in the acutely inflamed nose or throat.

Oesophageal varices only occur in association with *cirrhosis of the liver, portal hypertension or hypersplenism*.

In *portal hypertension* there may be a history of omphalitis, hepatitis, exchange transfusion by an umbilical vein catheter, or umbilical sepsis. It may be the result of cirrhosis of the liver or an abnormal vascular arrangement.

Aspirin may cause bleeding from the stomach. Salicylates in an overdosage may cause bleeding by hypoprothrombinaemia or thrombocytopenia. Haematemesis may result from an overdose of aminophylline. The possibility of *poisoning* by a corrosive substance or other material (such as ferrous sulphate), or boric acid poisoning, must be remembered.

Peptic ulceration may occur in children, though it is a rare cause of haematemesis. The possibility should be remembered when a child receiving corticosteroids complains of abdominal pain.

The Zollinger-Ellison syndrome is more common in boys; it consists of peptic ulceration with a non-beta-cell islet tumour of the pancreas or liver (Buchta & Kaplan 1971). The symptoms include abdominal pain, vomiting, haematemesis, diarrhoea and melaena.

Altered blood in the vomitus is a feature of *intestinal obstruction*.

References

Buchta RM, Kaplan JM. Zollinger-Ellison syndrome in a nine-year-old child: a
    case report and review of this entity in childhood. *Pediatrics* 1971; **47**: 594.
Rosenblud ML. Zollinger-Ellison syndrome in children. *Amer J Med Sci* 1967;
    254: 884.

Constipation

The causes of constipation include the following: those without
disease are the commonest.

> Non-disease
>> Breast fed babies—normal infrequent stools (not true
>> constipation). Rarely—excess of fatty foods, cream etc.
>> taken by lactating woman
>> Bottle fed—insufficient sugar or fluid in the feed. Undiluted
>> cow's milk
>> Toilet training errors
>> Unexplained normal variations
>> Drugs—chronic use of laxatives etc.
> Disease
>> Obstruction: imperforate anus, meconium plug, Hirsch-
>> sprung's disease, anorectal stenosis, ectopic anus
>> Severe vomiting
>> Polyuria (see p. 291)
>> Severe hypotonia. Congenital absence of abdominal muscles
>> (Prune-belly syndrome)
>> Hypothyroidism
>> Lead poisoning

Non-disease

Normal fully breast fed infants may have very infrequent stools,
maybe one every five days or so. The stools are loose—the same as
those of breast fed babies who have frequent stools—maybe several a

day. Very rarely, if a mother mistakenly takes a gross excess of protein and fat, a breast fed baby's stools may be firmer and pultaceous.

Occasional bottle fed babies, with no evidence of disease, pass hard stools. This may occur if the baby is given insufficient fluid, especially in a hot climate, or is perspiring excessively, because of over-clothing. If a baby in the first four months or so is given undiluted cow's milk, constipation may result. If he finds it painful to pass a stool because it is hard or because there is an anal fissure, he may withhold stools and become even more constipated.

Constipation after about 9 months of age may be due to *unwise toilet training*—compelling the child to sit on the pottie against his will. The baby becomes conditioned against using the pottie and troublesome constipation results. But not all constipation can be explained by errors of toilet training (Davidson *et al.* 1963)—though it is customary for child psychologists to blame a mother for it. There are differences in intestinal fluid absorption and rates of peristalsis. It may be found that gut hormones—such as the vasoactive intestinal polypeptides—may play a part. Dietary or genetic factors may be relevant.

Various *drugs* may cause constipation. They include amitriptyline, chlordiazepoxide, imipramine and vincristine. Prolonged use of laxatives may cause constipation.

Constipation with disease

An *imperforate anus* will not long pass unnoticed, but *anorectal stenosis* may escape detection for a long time until someone performs a rectal examination. Sometimes a history of the child passing stools shaped like expelled toothpaste may point to the diagnosis. An *anterior ectopic anus* was described by Leape & Ramenofsky (1978) as a common cause of constipation.

Ninety per cent of infants pass meconium in the first 24 hours. Delay in passing meconium (e.g. until after 36 hours) strongly suggests Hirschsprung's disease (Fraser & Wilkinson 1967) but it could be due to a meconium plug which can be released by insertion of a finger into the rectum (Ellis & Chatworthy 1966). Hirschsprung's disease may affect only a terminal ultra-short segment (Clayden & Lawson 1976). Constipation may be caused by other forms of intestinal obstruction.

Vomiting for any cause, such as congenital pyloric stenosis, leads to constipation. Constipation may be due to any of the causes of polyuria, such as renal acidosis, hypercalcaemia or nephrogenic diabetes insipidus. If a child is being investigated for 'failure to thrive' the history of gross constipation, with palpable faecal masses in the abdomen, strongly suggests one of the metabolic causes of polyuria.

Rare causes include hypotonia, the prune-belly syndrome, thyroid deficiency, diabetes or lead poisoning.

Anything which causes vomiting, such as *excessive possetting* or *pyloric stenosis,* will cause constipation.

Coeliac disease may present as constipation.

References

See p. 81.

Encopresis and Faecal Incontinence

Soiling, faecal incontinence or encopresis is usually associated with constipation, and is especially common in mentally retarded children (Levine 1975, Bentley 1978). It occurs in otherwise normal children most commonly at the age of six to eight years; it is more common in boys. The mother's complaint is usually that the boy has diarrhoea with soiling, or that he just soils. On rectal examination it is found that the rectum is loaded with a huge mass of faeces. The 'diarrhoea' is due to liquid material leaking round the edge of the faecal mass. There may be associated urinary incontinence especially if the soiling is not due to constipation. In about a third there is a history of early bowel-training difficulties. About half the affected children have never controlled the bowel, and have acquired the encopresis, usually after an emotional disturbance such as the birth of a sibling, starting school , or separation from the mother. The constipation is occasionally due to ultra-short segment Hirschsprung's disease, causing failure of the anus to relax. Soiling without constipation is a more troublesome behaviour problem due to emotional disturbance and insecurity. It is commonly associated with urinary incontinence.

Faecal incontinence may be due to a gross neurological abnormality such as a *meningomyelocele or lipoma* involving the spinal cord.

References

Bentley JFR. Faecal soiling and achalasia. *Arch Dis Child* 1978; **53**: 185.

Clayden GS, Lawson JON. Investigation and management of longstanding chronic constipation in childhood. *Arch Dis Child* 1976; **51**: 918.

Davidson M, Kugler MM, Bauer CH. Diagnosis and management in children with severe and protracted constipation and obstipation. *J Pediatr* 1963; **62**: 261.

Ellis D, Chatworthy HW. The meconium plug revisited. *J Pediatr Surg* 1966; **1**: 54.

Fraser GC, Wilkinson AW. Neonatal Hirschsprung's disease. *Br Med J* 1967; **2**: 7.

Leape LL, Ramenofsky ML. Anterior ectopic anus, a common cause of constipation in children. *J Pediatr Surg* 1978; **13**: 627.

Levine MM. Children with encopresis: a descriptive analysis. *Pediatrics* 1975; **56**: 412.

Diarrhoea

Many infants and children are said by their mothers to have diarrhoea when in fact their stools are normal.

Fully breast fed babies always have loose stools, unless they have Hirschsprung's disease. Their stools are explosive, contain curd (in the early weeks), and may be bright green in colour. They may be frequent, as many as 24 stools in the 24 hours. Fully breast fed babies virtually never suffer from gastroenteritis.

The so-called *starvation stools* may be confused with diarrhoea. These are loose green frequent small stools, containing little faecal matter. They are due to gross deficiency of food intake. It is a disaster if further restriction of food occurs on the grounds that the child has gastroenteritis or is being overfed. I doubt whether *overfeeding* causes diarrhoea. Many infants are said to be suffering from overfeeding when the correct diagnosis is underfeeding.

Many older children are referred to the paediatrician on account of chronic diarrhoea and on examination it is found that they are up to the average in weight. If the mother is asked to bring sample stools on a subsequent occasion, it is found that they are normal. It is important to see the stools if there are reasons for doubting the mother's story.

It is vital to remember that *diarrhoea is never due to teething.*

Causes

Excess of sugar in infant's feeds

Phototherapy

Toddler's diarrhoea ('Irritable colon')

Psychogenic

Infections, including entercolitis, septicaemia, malaria and
 other tropical diseases

Important surgical or semisurgical conditions

  Hirschsprung's disease

  Appendicitis, intussusception, peritonitis.

  Malrotation

  Ulcerative colitis, regional ileitis, polyposis

  Tumours—lymphoma, carcinoid, catecholamine-secreting
   neural tumours

Malabsorption—fat, carbohydrate, protein. Intestinal lymphangiectasia

Cow's milk allergy

Immune deficiency

Rare endocrine diseases

  Thyrotoxicosis

  Hypoparathyroidism

  Zollinger–Ellison syndrome (p. 77)

  Adrenogenital hyperplasia or insufficiency

Miscellaneous rare disease

  Congenital chloride diarrhoea

  Acrodermatitis enteropathica (p. 326)

  Wiskott–Aldrich syndrome (p. 58)

Drugs

Excess of sugar in the feeds of a bottle fed baby is a common cause of
diarrhoea

Phototherapy for neonatal jaundice is sometimes followed by
diarrhoea, possible as a result of temporary intestinal lactase
deficiency (Bakken 1977).

Toddler's diarrhoea—termed by some the 'Irritable Colon
Syndrome'—is common in well thriving toddlers aged one to three.
Davidson & Wasserman (1966) described 186 children with it. These
children have a normal weight gain: dietary alteration and medicines
have little effect, though Cohen *et al* (1979) found that some respond

to an *increase* of fat in the diet. There is no evidence of malabsorption or infection. It is said that some have raised prostaglandin levels, and some have increased specific enzyme activity for adenyl cyclase (Walker-Smith 1980, Dodge 1981).

Psychogenic diarrhoea occurs in older children—often as an indication of distaste for school. Diarrhoea with soiling of the pants after infancy is commonly due to constipation, often of psychological origin (p. 78).

The commonest cause of acute diarrhoea is *infection*. Gastroenteritis is usually due to contamination of food, but it may be due to respiratory tract organisms, pathogenic *E. coli* and a variety of viruses. It occurs in association with otitis media or urinary tract infection. It may be caused by *Yersinia* which also causes abdominal pain, vomiting, fever, mesenteric adenitis and occasionally polyarthritis and erythema nodosum (Rodgers & Karn 1975), or *campylobacter,* (which also causes abdominal pain and melaena (Butzler *et al* 1973). Diarrhoea is sometimes a symptom in *neonatal septicaemia.*

Necrotizing enterocolitis affects especially low-birth-weight babies fed on cow's milk, especially when given hyperosmolar feeds, or when there was anoxia, respiratory distress syndrome, apnoeic attacks or an exchange transfusion (Brown & Sweet 1978, Santulli *et al* 1975). The features are bile-stained vomiting, abdominal distension, diarrhoea often with blood in the stool and sometimes perforation or terminal jaundice.

Pseudomembranous enterocolitis (Pittman 1979) is precipitated by antimicrobial drugs, in particular lincomycin, clindamycin and ampicillin, but sometimes by penicillin, cotrimoxazole, cephalosporins, chloramphenicol or metronidazole: the organism commonly found is clostridium difficile.

Other important infective causes of diarrhoea include dysentery and salmonella, and in developing countries giardiasis, bilharzia, trichuriasis, amoebiasis and malaria. Giardiasis is associated with steatorrhoea, diarrhoea, abdominal distension or abdominal pain (Burke 1975).

Hirschsprung's disease may present in the newborn baby with diarrhoea, thus confusing the diagnosis.

Acute appendicitis which can occur at any age, including infancy, may be associated with diarrhoea, especially when there is peritonitis, or when the appendix is pelvic, retrocaecal or retroileal; (p. 102) and intussusception may be accompanied by diarrhoea (p. 105).

Ulcerative colitis may begin in early infancy as intermittent attacks of diarrhoea, in the first place without blood or mucus in the stool. Later blood and mucus appear, sometimes with weight loss, defective physical growth, fever, clubbing of the fingers, arthritis, anaemia, stomatitis and enlargement of the liver. *Granulomatous colitis* is similar (Kerolitz *et al* 1968).

The catecholamine-secreting *neural tumours,* especially the ganglioneuroma, may cause chronic diarrhoea (Voorhess 1966), possibly through vasoactive intestinal polypeptides (Long *et al* 1981).

For *malabsorption syndromes* see p. 9. Gastroenteritis or prolonged starvation may cause secondary lactase deficiency and so chronic diarrhoea.

Carbohydrate intolerance may be simulated by intolerance to lactulose in baby milks (Hendrickse *et al* 1977). Symptoms ascribed to allergy to cow's milk may be related to lactose intolerance. (Harrison *et al* 1976).

For *cow's milk allergy* see page 13.

Congenital chloride diarrhoea (Holmberg *et al* 1977) is an autosomal recessive condition. There is often a history of hydramnios and a family history of the same complaint. There is persistent diarrhoea, failure to thrive, abdominal distension, hypochloraemia, hyponatraemia and high faecal chlorides. Sometimes the cause of protracted diarrhoea eludes full investigation (Larcher *et al* 1977).

For acrodermatitis enteropathica see page 326.

Numerous *drugs* cause diarrhoea apart from those causing pseudomembranous colitis. Penicillin and ampicillin by mouth very commonly cause diarrhoea. Other drugs include antimetabolites, antirheumatic drugs, bephenium, carbamazepine, dichlorophen, ergotamine, fenfluramine, griseofulvin, iron, nalidixic acid, niclosamide, P.A.S., phenothiazine, rifampicin, sodium fusidate, thiabendazole, thyroxin overdose and viprynium.

References

Bakken AF. Temporary intestinal lactase deficiency in light treated jaundiced infants. *Acta Paediatr Scand* 1977; **66:** 91.

Brown EG, Sweet AY. Preventing necrotizing entercolitis in neonates. *JAMA* 1978; **240:** 2452.

Burke JA. Giardiasis in childhood. *Am J Dis Child* 1975; **129**: 1304.

Butzler JP *et al.* Related Vibrio in stools. *J Pediatr* 1973; **82**: 493.

Cohen SA *et al.* Nonspecific diarrhoea. *Pediatrics* 1979; **64**:402.

Davidson M, Wasserman R. The irritable colon of childhood (Chronic non-specific diarrhoea) *J Pediatr* 1966; **69**:1027.

Dodge JA *et al.* Toddler diarrhoea and prostaglandins. *Arch Dis Child* 1981; **56**: 705.

Harrison M, Kilby A *et al.* Cow's milk intolerance; a possible association with gastroenteritis, lactose intolerance and 1 g A deficiency. *Br Med J* 1976; **2**: 1501.

Hendrickse R, Woolridge M, Russell A. Lactulose in baby milks causing diarrhoea, simulating lactose intolerance. *Br Med J* 1977; **1**: 1194.

Holmberg C, Perheentupa J *et al.* Congenital chloride diarrhoea. *Arch Dis Child* 1977; **52**: 255.

Kerolitz BI, Gritetz D, Kopel FB. Granulomatous colitis in children: Study of 25 cases and comparison with ulcerative colitis. *Pediatrics* 1968; **42**: 446.

Larcher VF, Shepherd R *et al.* Protracted diarrhoea in infancy. *Arch Dis Child* 1977; **52**: 597.

Long RD *et al.* Clinicopathological study of pancreatic and ganglioneuro-blastoma tumours secreting vasoactive intestinal polypeptide (vipomas). *Br Med J* 1981; **1**: 1767.

Pittman FE. Antibiotic associated colitis, an update. *Adverse Drug Reaction Bulletin* 1979; **No. 75**: 268.

Rodgers B, Karn G. Yersinia enterocolitis. *J Pediatr Surg* 1975; **10**: 497.

Santulli TV, Schnullinger JN *et al.* Acute necrotizing enterocolitis in infancy. *Pediatrics* 1975; **55**:376.

Voorhess MK. Functioning neural tumours. *Pediatr Clin North Am* 1966; **13**: 3.

Walker-Smith JA. Toddler's diarrhoea. *Arch Dis Child* 1980; **55**: 329.

Blood in the Stool

When a newborn baby passes blood in the stool or vomits blood one determines whether it is the mother's blood or his own (p. 49).

Blood in the stool of an infant may be due to *injury by a rectal thermometer*. It is unwise to take the temperature by this route unless it is thought essential. Blood in the stool of an ill newborn baby may be due to *mesenteric thrombosis* or *perforation of the intestine.* The baby will be collapsed, pale and have abdominal distension. Another cause is *necrotizing enterocolitis.*

If the stool is lined with blood, the source is commonly low in the tract. When there is red blood in a baby's stool, the source may be fairly high, while red blood in the stool of an older child would suggest a low source.

After the newborn period the commonest causes are *constipation or dysentery*.

Blood may sometimes be found in the stool after *bleeding from the nose* or from *acute tonsillitis*. Bleeding resulting from aspirin is likely to be detected only by chemical tests.

Salmonella and dysentery infections are common causes, as is intussusception. In some countries ulcerative colitis is common. All the other causes listed are rare; they include

> Hiatus hernia, gastro-oesophageal reflux, oesophageal varices
> Peptic ulcer, congenital pyloric stenosis
> Meckel's diverticulum
> Duplication of intestine
> Haemangioma or telangiectasia of intestine, polypi, tumours
> Mesenteric thrombosis
> Volvulus, intussusception
> Infections—salmonella, dysentery, enterocolitis, rectal candidiasis
> Ulcerative colitis, Crohn's disease, granulomatous disease
> Fissure in ano, fistula, piles, rectal prolapse
> Foreign body in rectum
> Blood diseases, haemolytic uraemic syndrome, uraemia, disseminated intravascular coagulation, Wiskott-Aldrich syndrome (p. 58)
> Cow's milk allergy
> Severe hypernatraemia
> Tyrosinosis (p. 116)
> Developing coountries—amoebiasis, ancylostoma, bilharzia, trichuriasis
> Non-specific ulceration of the ileum

The quantity of blood in the stool when there is a *hiatus hernia* is small, and unlikely to be detected by any but chemical tests. Blood arising from *oesophageal varices* is more likely to be vomited, but some is likely to pass into the stomach and intestines.

Bleeding from *congenital pyloric stenosis* or a *peptic ulcer* may occur, but is unusual.

When there is bleeding from a *Meckel's diverticulum*, there is usually little pain. The blood passed is usually dark red (Rutherford 1966). The diagnosis is established by laparotomy. There is an association between Meckel's diverticulum and Turner's syndrome.

Duplication of the intestine may cause considerable blood loss. The diagnosis is usually made by a barium study, but sometimes by laparotomy.

A *haemangioma of the intestine* may cause bleeding from the bowel (Nader & Margolin 1966). Blood loss may result from *intestinal telangiectasia*, and the face should be examined for evidence of that condition. It is sometimes associated with blue naevi (blue bleb syndrome), and the skin should be searched for this (Rook *et al.* 1979). It is also associated with Turner's syndrome.

Rectal polyp, or polypi higher in the alimentary tract, may cause considerable bleeding. Rectal polypi can only occasionally be felt by the finger. They are usually found by proctoscopy or sigmoidoscopy. Higher polypi are found by means of a barium enema or laparotomy. A survey of 50 cases (Toccalino *et al.*, 1973) showed that all had rectal bleeding and seven had abdominal pain. There was a single polyp in 46 of the children, who were mostly aged two to six years. The polyps were mostly situated 10 cm from the anus. Diagnosis was by rectosigmoidoscopy.

Profuse bleeding from the bowel may occur in the various *blood diseases*, such as thrombocytopenia, allergic purpura or leukaemia. It also occurs in *uraemia*, and in the early stage of the *haemolytic uraemic syndrome* (p. 52). It occurs in severe *hypernatraemia* (as in accidental addition of salt to an infant's feeds), and in *disseminated intravascular coagulation*.

Ancylostoma and *trichuriasis* are important causes of blood loss from the bowel in many developing countries. Diarrhoea with blood in the stool may be due to *bilharzia* or *amoebiasis*. It may arise from *non-specific ulceration of the ileum* (Sunaryo *et al.*).

It is often impossible to determine the cause of blood in the stool, even after the fullest investigation.

References

Nader PR, Margolin F. Hemangioma causing gastrointestinal bleeding. *Am J Dis Child* 1966; **111:** 215.

Rook A, Wilkinson DS, Ebling FJG. *Textbook of dermatology* Oxford: Blackwell Scientific Publications, 1979.

Rutherford RB. Meckel's diverticulum; a review of 148 paediatric patients with
    special reference to the pattern of bleeding and to mesodiverticular bands.
    Surgery 1966; **59:** 618.
Sunaryo FP *et al.* Primary non-specific ileal ulceration as a cause of massive
    rectal bleeding. *Pediatrics* 1981; **68:** 247.
Toccalino G, Guastavino E *et al.* Juvenile polyps of th rectum and colon. *Acta
    Paediatr Scand* 1973; **62:** 337.

The Colour of the Stools

The following are the principal colour changes in stools.
    Black
        Meconium
        Altered blood
        Iron, bismuth, lead
        Possibly liquorice
        Charcoal
        Eating earth or coal
    Abnormally pale
        Obstructive jaundice, including infective hepatitis
        Steatorrhoea
        Aluminium hydroxide
        The periodic syndrome. Stools are often pale in the attacks
    Green
        Breast feeding. It is normal for the stools of fully breast fed
            babies to be bright green in colour at times. They may be
            green when passed, or become green on standing
        Diarrhoea
    Red
        Blood
        Viprynium (for threadworms)
        Red gelatin desserts
        Serratia marcescens
    Pink
        Diazepam syrup
The non-pathogenic organism *Serratia marcescens* may produce an
alarming red colour in the baby's nappy.

Pain—General Comments

When we attempt to assess the significance and severity of pain or what we think is pain, we have to face the difficulty of assessing someone else's pain. In fact we can only assess it by inference.

The infant shows that he has pain by crying. There are many causes of crying other than pain, and many an infant is thought to have pain when he has no such thing. The fact that he draws his legs up and cries does not mean that he has pain, for babies usually 'draw up their legs' when they cry for any reason. I have had numerous babies referred to me on account of 'acute indigestion' and 'terrible wind', which was supposed to be the reason for the cries in the night, when the crying was due entirely to the usual causes of sleep problems—mainly bad habit formation and parental anxiety. Infants may rub their ears when they have earache, or roll their head or hold it when thy have a headache, but infants rub the ear, roll the head or hold the head when they have no pain there at all. It may be difficult to decide whether the infant has pain or not. Severe pain causes a child to emit high-pitched screams. The cry of pain is different from that of fatigue, boredom, loneliness or other causes. The pain is not severe if the crying stops as soon as he is picked up.

When the child is old enough to express his feelings in words, it is easier to decide whether he really feels pain. Even so, one has to assess the severity of his pain not by what he says, or even entirely on what the mother says about the pain, but by associated signs. For instance, a pain is not likely to be severe if it does not stop him playing, if it does not stop him eating, if it does not keep him awake, or if there is no change in his colour. A severe pain usually makes the child cry, though some children are more stoical than others. A severe abdominal pain is likely to make him double up. *It is always profitable to ask the mother whether she would know that he had the pain if he did not tell her. If she would not know, the pain is not severe.*

We have to assess the child's pain not only by the presence or absence of associated signs, but by our assessment of the mother's personality. The question of whether or not the child is taken to the doctor on account of his pain depends on the parental threshold for anxiety. Some loving mothers will take the child to the doctor if he has the most trivial and short-lasting pain; others take the child to the doctor only when the pain is severe and frequent. Some mothers aggravate a child's pain by displaying anxiety about it, by rubbing his abdomen, petting him and giving him pleasant warm drinks, so that he complains all the more as an attention-seeking device. In order to assess a child's pain, one has to assess the family pattern of behaviour as a whole and to determine whether other members of the family have similar pains. This is not merely because migraine or peptic ulcer commonly has a hereditary basis; it is because a child may imitate his parents, consciously or unconsciously, or fear that he has the same symptoms. If his father frequently complains about his gastric symptoms, or had had to go to hospital on their account, or if the mother is seen to have incapacitating attacks of migraine, it would not be surprising if the child also experienced pains, not necessarily due directly to peptic ulcer or migraine. When talking to a child about pain, it is important to ask whether any of his friends have a similar pain. The answer is frequently in the affirmative.

A child may experience pain (particularly in the head or abdomen) as a result of worries and anxieties about school. He may be in difficulty with a particular subject such as arithmetic, or he may be worried by a teacher's loud voice or threats of punishment. He may be worried because of bullying or because of teasing about his clothes, appearance or obesity. He may experience the pain when he is getting ready to go to school. He is not necessarily malingering; he is not pretending: he may really experience the pain, though it is entirely psychological in origin.

Pain may be suggested by an anxious mother. A few minutes after I had talked to a mother about her boy's abdominal pain, telling her that I had found no disease to explain it, she was overheard saying to the boy, 'Of course you have pain in your tummy, darling, haven't you?' He had.

Diagnostic errors may result from referred pain. Familiar examples are the following:

Site of pain	*Source of pain*
Abdomen	Chest
Shoulder tip	Spleen (e.g. rupture), gall bladder
Ear, face	Molar tooth
Wrist, shoulder	Elbow (e.g. pulled elbow)
Knee	Hip

When a child (or adult) suffers two fractures to a limb, as in a road traffic accident, pain may be localised to the site of one fracture, so that the other fracture may be missed.

Headache

Headache is a common symptom in childhood. Oster and Nielsen (1972) found that 20·6 per cent of 2178 school children experienced headaches.

In no more than five per cent of children referred to hospital on account of headache is an organic cause discovered, but because of the ever-present possibility of a serious organic cause every child presenting with a headache demands careful history taking and a full general and neurological examination, including ophthalmoscopy. If a child is completely well between the attacks, he is much less likely to have serious organic disease than if there were a complaint of lassitude, loss of appetite, loss of weight or the development of clumsiness of movement; all these symptoms would strongly suggest a serious organic disease.

The following are the main conditions which should be considered:

Psychological factors
Physical environmental factors
   a stuffy room
   lack of fresh air
   climatic conditions (e.g., thunder)
Hunger
Infection
Migraine
Epilepsy
Head injury
Benign intracranial hypertension
Intracranial causes
Osteitis
Nephritis
Hypertension

Effect of drugs
Earache or toothache
Eye strain (rare). Glaucoma (rare)
Antrum infection (rare)
Basilar impression syndrome (rare)
Phaeochromocytoma (rare)

A variety of *psychological factors* are associated with headaches. They include worry and anxiety about school work, about an unkind teacher or about bullying. There is the well-known 'headache of convenience' which may bring about a happy release from the arithmetic class. A headache may well become an attention-seeking device if excessive anxiety is shown about it. For the combination of headaches and growing pains, see p. 242.

Simple factors such as *hunger, a stuffy room, lack of fresh air and exercise, an impending thunderstorm,* may be important and common causes of headache. It may be due to hunger and hypoglycaemia.

Any infection may be accompanied at its outset by a headache and by non-specific aches and pains. Amongst less obvious infective causes of headaches or general lassitude is an apical tooth infection.

Migraine is a common symptom of childhood. I do not think that one can draw a clear-cut line between migraine and other headaches, though for research purposes, such as the assessment of a drug, one would define migraine as typically a unilateral headache with vomiting, preceded by visual aurae and having a hereditary basis; but the pain is by no means always unilateral. A comprehensive review of childhood migraine, running into 147 pages, was written by Bille (1962).

Symptoms of migraine commonly begin in early childhood. Vomiting attacks which recur and which later turn out to be due to migraine may begin as early as six months of age. In at least a third of all children with migraine, symptoms begin before the fourth year. Selby and Lance (1960) found that 30 per cent of their 500 cases of migraine began before the age of ten. One in five also had travel sickness.

Migraine may manifest itself in childhood by any combination of the following symptoms—headache, vomiting, abdominal pain or fever, sometimes associated with the passage of pale stools (Brown 1977). This group of symptoms is commonly termed the 'periodic syndrome'. It used to be termed 'cyclical vomiting' or 'acidosis attacks' until it was realized that the acidosis was the result of the attacks, and not their cause. There may be premonitory visual, auditory, sensory or mental symptoms, the commonest visual aura consisting of fortification figures. There may be aphasia, blurring of vision or paraesthesiae in the limbs. Sometimes these symptoms occur without a headache. It is said that a convulsion can occur during the premonitory phase. The headache is commonly described as unilateral and frontal, and some would not accept the diagnosis of migraine otherwise; but I disagree with this rigid view of migraine. Selby & Lance, in their analysis of 500 cases of migraine, found that 38 per cent had hemicrania alone (and that in 21 per cent the headache was always on the same side), 23 per cent had hemicrania and general headache, and 38 per cent had pain all over the head. It is interesting to note that there was no difference with regard to the incidence and nature of associated phenomena between those with hemicrania and those with general headache. The attacks may last an hour or two, or two or three days. They commonly last a few hours, and are relieved by sleep.

In *basilar artery migraine* there may be loss of consciousness, vertigo, ataxia, diplopia, dysarthria, hemiplegia, paraesthesiae in the hands and feet, usually but not always with a headache. It is more common in girls and usually begins before the fourth year. The attacks clear completely (Golden & French 1975).

Attacks may be caused by certain foodstuffs, especially mono-amine-containing foods (cheese, containing tyramine, chocolate, containing phenylethylamine) and other substances. Headache and shivering may result from monosodium glutamate intolerance in children: the glutamate is an additive to numerous prepared foods (Reif-Lehrer 1975). Attacks may also be precipitated by emotional disturbances, fatigue, menstruation, hypoglycaemia (hunger), bright lights, loud noise, long car journeys and infections.

The initial symptoms are associated with vasoconstriction of the intracranial arteries, leading to the visual and other symptoms, with marked pallor, followed by dilatation of the vessels with the development of a headache which is commonly throbbing in character. Later there may be suffusion of the face and conjunctivae and even a haematoma.

Bille and others considered that children who suffer from migraine are more likely to be shy, anxious, sensitive and more vulnerable to frustration than controls; their parents tend to be more perfectionist, rigid, ambitious and efficient than others. The diagnosis is not always easy. It is difficult or impossible to distinguish many cases of migraine from 'tension' headaches.

The nature of the headache is of some value in diagnosis. An occipital headache is more likely than a frontal one to be due to an organic lesion, though a supratentorial tumour commonly causes a frontal headache. The headache of increased intracranial pressure is liable to be affected by change of posture; it is worse on rising in the morning, on stooping or on straining. It is often a dull, throbbing or bursting pain, while a headache of nervous origin is more likely to consist of a feeling of pressure; but the headache of migraine may be of a throbbing nature.

Apart from ophthalmoscopic examination, which can never be omitted from the examination of a child with headache, one must remember to auscultate the skull, because that might lead to the diagnosis of an intracranial vascular anomaly. When an infant is being examined because of the possibility of a cerebral tumour, the skull should be percussed. A 'cracked pot sound' may be elicited if there is increased intracranial tension. One may also be able to detect undue separation of the cranial sutures.

There are no pathognomonic signs of migraine. Apparently typical attacks of migraine may be due to an intracranial aneurysm. One is particularly concerned about this possibility when a child has neurological signs in the attacks—such as aphasia, paraesthesiae or weakness of a limb. It is essential to include ophthalmoscopy in one's examination, together with a blood pressure estimation to exclude hypertension. It is a matter of experienced clinical judgment to decide at what stage further investigation is required. The necessary investigation would include an EMI scan and possibly in addition a carotid angiography, a procedure not without risk, for up to one per cent subjected to this investigation develop a hemiplegia. An ophthalmologist referred a 12-year-old girl to me on account of migraine, having found that she had no abnormality on examination of the eyes. The history was typical of migraine and there was a family history of the same complaint. There were no abnormal physical signs, but there was considerable psychological instability. I discussed the diagnosis with the parents, telling them that the girl had migraine. Three days later, on an excursion to the seaside, the girl slowly and imperceptibly lapsed into unconsciousness. A carotid angiogram did not show an abnormality, but a vertebral angiogram showed an aneurysm of the vertebral artery. Cerebral tumours can for a time give a picture identical with that of migraine.

There is an important danger in the diagnosis of recurrent attacks of migraine. A child may have several attacks of migraine, and then unfortunately develop pyogenic meningitis with similar symptoms. The true diagnosis may then be missed.

There are occasions when it is necessary to distinguish migraine from *epilepsy*. The latter condition may manifest itself by sudden attacks of severe headache of instantaneous onset lasting for a few minutes followed by sleep, but without convulsive phenomena. Many children go to sleep in an attack of migraine. It has already been stated that during the phase of vasoconstriction in the intracranial vessels, a convulsion may occur. The aura of migraine may lead to the wrong diagnosis of epilepsy—though an aura is definitely unusual in childhood epilepsy. When in doubt an electroencephalogram should be carried out, though an EEG is often normal in epilepsy of grand mal type and so may not help. One is then justified in carrying out the therapeutic test of giving phenytoin in full dosage; it should stop the attacks if they are epileptic in origin.

In 90 per cent of cases of migraine there is a family history of the same complaint, though headaches in adults are common, whether or not their children have migraine. If there is anything about the story of the child's attacks which raises a doubt in my mind about the diagnosis, I would be more doubtful if there were no history of migraine in the parents.

Follow-up studies following *head injuries* have shown how rarely head injury in children is followed by sequelae—except in the case of severe head injury with laceration of the brain. The ordinary mild concussion, so common in children, is most unlikely to be followed by headaches in subsequent weeks and months, and if they do occur, they are much more likely to be related to heredity or environmental and personality factors than to the injury. In the same way emotional sequelae of head injuries are more likely to be related to previous personality traits and subsequent environmental factors than to a structural defect resulting from the injury (Otto, 1960). Nevertheless, when one sees any child complaining of headache following a head injury, one must examine the optic fundi for papilloedema, indicating increased intracranial pressure, and one should have an X-ray of the skull to exclude a fracture, and possibly an echogram or E.M.I. scan for a subdural effusion or tumour. In an infant one palpates the sutures for abnormal separation, the fontanelle for bulging, and takes serial measurements of the skull circumference.

Rose and Matson (1967) reviewed the condition of *benign intracranial hypertension,* describing 23 cases. There was a sudden onset of headache with sixth nerve palsy and papilloedema without loss of consciousness. The C.S.F. was normal. In some cases there was a preceding respiratory infection, otitis media or head injury. Recovery was complete. The condition may be caused by ampicillin, corticosteroids, nalidixic acid, nitrofurantoin and tetracyclines.

Other intracranial causes of headache include tumour, abscess, arteriovenous malformations, poliomyelitis, encephalitis and meningitis. Normal optic discs, though not excluding a space occupying lesion, help to make such a lesion unlikely. Osteitis of the skull would be obvious on simple examination.

Nephritis and *hypertension* are possible causes of headache. It follows that the examination cannot be complete without examination of the urine for nephritis and pyelonephritis, and without recording the blood pressure. Hypertension has been precipitated by prolonged use of ephedrine nose drops (Saken *et al* 1979).

Pain from an *ear* or a *tooth* may cause a headache.

Eyestrain is a most unlikely cause of headache, unless the symptom of eyestrain is obvious. If the child cannot see his book without bringing his eyes very close to it, or if he cannot read what is written on the blackboard, then his eyes should be tested. Ophthalmoscopic examination is a routine part of the examination of any child with a headache. If the fundi are normal, and in the absence of any symptom pointing to the eyes, the child's visit to the eye specialist is most unlikely to be profitable. *Glaucoma* is a rare cause.

A chronic antrum infection is most unlikely to be a cause of recurrent headaches, particularly in the first 7 or 8 years. I have never seen a child with headache due to a chronic infection of the antrum. In any case, chronic antrum infection can be diagnosed with reasonable certainty on clinical grounds. There will be a history of a continuous purulent nasal discharge between colds, or of a continual postnasal discharge, visible on examination of the throat, and causing the usual symptoms, such as cough on lying down and constant clearing of the throat. An X-ray of the antrum will confirm the diagnosis. In my experience children with a chronic infection are not more likely to suffer from headaches than any other child. It is true that an acute antrum infection may cause a headache.

A variety of drugs may cause headaches: they include acetazolamide, amitriptyline, antihistamines, carbamazepine, chlorpromazine, diazepam, ephedrine, ethambutol, |ethosuximide, fenfluramine, griseofulvin, indomethacin, isoniazid, methylphenidate, nalidixic acid, niclosamide, nitrofurantoin, phenytoin, sodium valproate, rifampicin, sulphasalazine, sulphonamides, sulthiame, tetracycline, thiabendazole, trimethoprim, troxidone and vincristine.

Lead poisoning may cause headaches. The *basilar impression syndrome* causes persistent occipital headache. There is a short neck, lower cranial nerve palsy, nystagmus, ataxia or spasticity. It is due to a congenital abnormality of the upper cervical spine and base of the skull. It may be associated with the Klippel-Feil syndrome.

References

Bille B. Migraine in school children. *Acta Paediatr Uppsala* 1962; **51**: Suppl. 136.

Brown JK. Migraine and migraine equivalents. *Dev Med Child Neurol* 1977; **19**: 683.

Golden GS, French JH. Basilar artery migraine in young children. *Pediatrics* 1975; **56**: 722.

Oster J, Nielsen A. Growing pains. *Acta Paediatr Scand* 1972; **61**: 329.

Otto U. Postconcussion syndrome. *Acta paedopsychiatrica* 1960; **1**: 6.

Rief-Lehrer L. Monosodium glutamate intolerance in children. *N. Eng J Med* 1975; **293**: 1204.

Rigg CA. Migraine. *Clinc Proc Children's Hospital National Medical Centre* 1979; **53**: 3.

Rose A, Matson DD. Benign intracranial hypertension in children. *Pediatrics* 1967; **39**: 227.

Saken R, Kates GL, Miller K. Drug induced hypertension in infancy. *J Pediatr* 1979; **95**: 1077.

Selby G, Lance JW. Observation on 500 cases of migraine and allied vascular headaches. *J. Neurol Neurosurg Psychiat* 1960; **23**: 23.

Abdominal Pain

Acute abdominal pain

General comments

Joseph Brennemann, famous Chicago paediatrician, wrote 'After 40 years of extensive experience I still approach the acutely painful abdomen of a child with much apprehension and a greater feeling of uncertainty than any other domain of childhood'.

The history

A detailed history is an essential step in the diagnosis. In the first place one needs to know how long the child has had the pain, asking in particular whether he ever had it before the date mentioned, and whether he was well before that date.

One next needs to know whether the pain is continuous or intermittent. If it is intermittent, one needs to know how frequent the attacks are, how long they last, and whether they are becoming more or less frequent. One frequently finds that the pain is infrequent—for example once in three or four months, and that when it occurs it only lasts for a minute or two. This is important, because one has to try to assess the significance of the complaint. In the case of an acute abdominal pain, it is usually true to say that a pain which comes and goes is unlikely to be due to appendicitis, the pain of which is more often continuous.

One needs to know where the pain is. Most of the non-organic recurrent abdominal pains of childhood are localized vaguely in the umbilical region. Apley (1975) remarked that the further the pain is localized away from the umbilicus, the more likely is there to be an underlying organic disorder. I would feel that when a child complains of pain in one part of the body one day and a different part on another, and there is no constant localization, organic disease is less likely than when the pain is always localized to one area. An obvious exception to this is the pain of acute appendicitis, which may begin in the umbilical region and settle in the right iliac fossa.

The severity of the pain has to be assessed. Zachary (1965) suggested that one should ask the child 'whether it is different from ordinary tummy-ache'. Apley found that a quarter of the children with recurrent abdominal pain without organic disease suffered from severe pain. He wrote that the truly severe pain, causing the child to thresh and writhe in agony, is hardly ever organic in origin. Whether the pain is continuous or intermittent, one must determine whether the pain is getting better or worse. One pays more attention to a pain which is becoming worse.

The nature of the pain may be helpful in diagnosis. A stabbing pain, feeling as if needles are being pushed in, may be pleural or peritoneal in origin. A pain which regularly comes and goes, lasting for a minute or two, with corresponding free intervals, suggests an alimentary origin.

The mode of onset may be important. A pain of instantaneous onset lasting a few minutes only and followed by sleep may be due to epilepsy. The duration of the pain is important. *An attack of abdominal pain lasting more than three hours should be regarded as an abdominal emergency until proved otherwise.*
It may be useful to ask what brings the pain on, what relieves it and what makes it worse. A pleural pain (and sometimes a peritoneal pain) is worse on breathing or coughing.

It is vital to enquire about associated symptoms. An associated headache may point to migraine, though headache may be a symptom of fever. Associated diarrhoea suggests an alimentary origin. Associated urinary symptoms suggest a lesion of the urinary tract. In the case of acute abdominal pain, associated vomiting should indicate the need for great caution in the diagnosis, for it may well point to a condition for which surgical treatment will be needed. When the pain is due to an acute surgical condition, it usually precedes other symptoms, such as vomiting.

Finally one must assess the family as a whole. One must know whether other members of the family have abdominal pains. One must assess the personality of the parents, noting whether they are tense, anxious, worried or placid characters, for this will help one to establish the diagnosis.

The examination

When a child presents with abdominal pain, the whole child must be examined, if for no other reason but the fact that many extra-abdominal conditions cause pain in the abdomen.

Many a small child steadfastly refuses to lie down when asked to do so, and determined efforts to get him to lie down will inevitably lead to tears, so that it becomes impossible to examine the abdomen adequately. It is reasonably satisfactory to examine the child's abdomen when he is standing or kneeling. Sometimes it is impossible to get the child to relax, and in that case, if accurate examination is vital, he should be given a sedative. Even if the child is crying, increased vigour of crying may help to localize the site of pain and tenderness.

Medical students commonly make the mistake of keeping the eyes on the abdomen when palpating it. I commonly tell them that omphaloscopy does not help in establishing the diagnosis. It is essential to watch the child's face in order to detect signs of abdominal tenderness. Another common mistake is to examine the abdomen when the head is elevated on two or more pillows. Unless the head is flat on the bed, or only slightly elevated on a low pillow (which is often preferable), it may be impossible to detect splenic enlargement.

Tenderness over the descending colon is not of importance. There may be only deep tenderness when an inflamed appendix is retro-caecal. Rectal examination is essential for any child with acute abdominal pain. One notes particularly whether there is more tenderness or heat on one side than on the other. Inspection of the scrotum and hernial orifices must not be omitted.

Auscultation of the abdomen may contribute to the diagnosis of ileus, the absence of peristaltic sounds being the important feature of that condition.

The diagnosis

The following are the main conditions which should be considered:
    Infantile colic
    Dietary indiscretion
    Pain from vomiting, coughing or diarrhoea

Pain referred from the chest—lobar pneumonia, pleurisy, pleurodynia

Pain referred from the spine (rare)

Alimentary tract—appendicitis, intussusception, obstruction, strangulated hernia, volvulus

　Rare—Crohn's disease, Meckel's diverticulum

Mesenteric lymphadenitis

Peritonitis

Pancreas—fibrocystic disease, diabetic acidosis, hypo-glycaemia

　Rare—acute pancreatitis, pancreatic pseudocyst,

　Zollinger-Ellison syndrome (p. 77)

Liver—infective hepatitis

Gall bladder (rare)

Kidney—acute nephritis, calculus, Wilms' tumour, urinary tract infection.

Testis—torsion

Ovary (rare): twisted pedicle, ruptured cyst

Blood diseases—anaphylactoid purpura, sickle-cell crises, haemophilia

Infections—infectious mononucleosis, rheumatic fever

　Tropics—malaria, round worm, strongyloides, bilharzia, trichuriasis

Collagen diseases (rare)

Porphyria (rare before puberty)

Drugs—lead poisoning

Trauma

Infantile colic

The term 'colic' is a term wrongly applied by many to any infant who cries more than usual: it is not a diagnosis. Often it is due to excessive wind—if the baby is breast fed due to sucking too long on the breast or sucking on an empty breast, and if he is bottle fed almost always due to the feed taking too long because the hole in the teat is too small.

　Evening colic, also called *three months colic* because it usually ceases by three months of age, affects well thriving babies, breast or bottle fed, largely confined to the evenings between about 6.0 p.m. and

10.0 p.m., and therefore with a characteristic circadian rhythm. Occasionally it occurs at other parts of the day, and is then more likely to be confused with other causes of crying (see p. 261). The pain may be mild, merely causing the child to be restless in the evenings, or severe, with rhythmical screaming attacks, lasting a few minutes at a time, alternating with equally long quiet periods in which he almost goes to sleep, before another attack starts. The attacks are clearly intestinal in origin, from their rhythmical timing; and in the attacks loud borborygmi can often be heard. The child obtains some relief in the prone position or on passing flatus per rectum. The attacks are prevented by the anticholinergic drug dicyclomine hydrochloride before the evening feed. It is possible that the pain is due to wind becoming locked in a loop of bowel. I guess that it may be shown to be related to prostaglandin metabolism or to the action or deficiency of a gut hormone.

Colicky pain in infants may sometimes be due to *allergy to cow's milk* (p. 13): in the case of breast fed babies it has been ascribed to cow's milk taken by the mother (Jacobsson & Lindberg 1978). A trial of soya milk for a bottle fed baby may be worthwhile but, according to Crook, (1980), a baby may be allergic to that too.

A strange not uncommon error of diagnosis is that of infantile colic when the attacks are typical of infantile spasms (p. 215).

Pain from vomiting, diarrhoea, or coughing. Any child with severe vomiting or coughing may experience some abdominal pain.

Lobar pneumonia and pleurisy. Referred pain from pleurisy with or without pneumonia is a common source of confusion in a child with acute abdominal pain. The finding of reduced air entry at one base, possibly with a slight alteration in the character of the breath sounds, or in the so-called indux crepitations, should indicate lobar pneumonia. An X-ray of the chest confirms the diagnosis. Pleural friction may be heard if there is pneumonia and pleurisy. *Epidemic pleurodynia* (Bornholm disease) may give rise to severe abdominal pain.

Abdominal pain may be a complaint when a child has *tonsillitis* or other respiratory tract infection, including measles. Sometimes this may be due to mesenteric lymphadenitis (below).

Appendicitis

The symptoms and signs of appendicitis are so well known that I do not propose to describe them here. Instead I shall draw attention to the common sources of error in diagnosis. In an excellent paper, Jackson of Newcastle (1963) described many of these sources of confusion. These are as follows:

1 The appendix is not always in the 'typical' position. Of Jackson's 313 cases in childhood, the appendix was in the typical site in 32 per cent, retrocaecal in 27 per cent, pelvic in 23 per cent, and elsewhere (retroileal, subhepatic, splenic, or left iliac fossa) in 11 per cent. When the appendix is retrocaecal there may be no abdominal tenderness.

2 In only 30 per cent of cases the pain begins in the periumbilical confined to the central area, in 25 per cent it is confined to the right iliac fossa, whereas in the remaining 25 per cent it is situated elsewhere in the abdomen.

3 Though the pain of appendicitis is usually continuous from the onset, it is occasionally intermittent. It was intermittent throughout in 12 per cent of Jackson's cases, and in a further 22 per cent it was intermittent first and continuous later.

4 The pain may be milk or even absent. In four of Jackson's 313 cases there was no complaint of pain at all. Mildness of the pain may lead to delay in diagnosis.

5 There is not always vomiting.

6 There may be urinary symptoms and signs, particularly in children in whom the appendix is in the pelvis. About 12 per cent experience some dysuria. There may be an excess of white blood cells in the urine.

7 Instead of the usual constipation there may be diarrhoea. About ten per cent experience this symptom, which may cause serious confusion in the diagnosis. Diarrhoea is especially liable to occur in the infant or very young child, or when the appendix is pelvic, retrocaecal or retroileal.

8 Though the temperature is not usually high, above five per cent have a temperature of over 39°C.

9 Appendicitis is rare under the age of three (though it can occur in early infancy), and when it does occur the diagnosis may be missed. Howard Williams of Melbourne (1947) described 42 cases in this age group. He found that 50 per cent presented with an abdominal mass due to perforation; 37 per cent presented with general peritonitis; 20 per cent had diarrhoea; and eight per cent had dysuria. The symptoms

were fever, vomiting, fretfulness and diarrhoea. Another Australian, Auldist (1967), reviewed 203 cases of appendicitis under the age of five years. He found anorexia in 99 per cent, vomiting in 94 per cent, pain in 93 per cent, fever in 68 per cent, respiratory symptoms in 31 per cent, and diarrhoea and constipation each in 26 per cent. In 38 per cent there was a palpable mass in the right iliac fossa. Shaul (1981), writing about the diagnosis of acute appendicitis in the newborn, stated that while the usual symptoms were irritability, vomiting and abdominal distension, often with excess of white cells in the urine, an important feature in some infants was oedema of the abdominal wall, often localized to the right flank, sometimes with erythema.

10 Previous attacks of abdominal pain. In about one in every ten cases of acute appendicitis, there is a history of previous attacks of pain. Recurrent attacks of abdominal pain favour the diagnosis of a non-organic cause though a child may have had a history of recurrent abdominal pain followed on this occasion by a different pain with fever due to appendicitis.

11 Appendicitis may coexist with other conditions, notably acute tonsillitis, but also with pneumonia, urinary tract infection or even gastroenteritis.

Acute peritonitis should be considered when a child is acutely ill with abdominal pain and fever, and generalized rigidity is found on abdominal examination. The commonest cause of peritonitis is a perforated appendix, but the peritonitis may be due to the pneumococcus or other pyogenic organism. Holgersen and Stanley-Brown (1971), analysing 100 cases of acute appendicitis with perforation, found that vomiting, fever and abdominal pain were the main symptoms, but in 40 per cent there was an unlocalized abdominal pain, and in five per cent there was no pain at all. In one child the pain was confined to the testis. Four had had previous abdominal pain. The white cell count was not helpful in infancy, eight infants having a white cell count of less than 10,000. In 28 there was albuminuria, in nine haematuria, and in 16 acetonuria. There was a significant increase of white cells in the urine of 24 children.

Mesenteric lymphadenitis. This may be difficult to distinguish from acute appendicitis. It is said that a shifting of the point of maximum tenderness on turning the patient on his side is in favour of mesenteric adenitis. It is not a reliable sign. The temperature tends to be higher in mesenteric adenitis than in appendicitis, but it is not always so. There may be a tonsillitis in either case. There is usually more true rigidity over the right iliac fossa in a child with acute appendicitis. When there is doubt, and this is not infrequent, one will establish the diagnosis by laparotomy. Mesenteric adenitis may be due to Yersinia, adenovirus, coxsackie or influenza B infection (Prince 1979, Kerr *et al* 1975).

Intussusception

The common age at which intussusception occurs is five to nine months. It is unusual after the first two years. It is said to be more common in babies who are above the average weight and who are artificially fed. Intussusception should be strongly suspected when an infant becomes suddenly ill with abdominal pain, vomiting and pallor. The most common initial symptom is pain, and vomiting usually follows shortly after. The onset may be so sudden that the mother may be able to state the exact time at which the pain started. The pain is commonly rhythmical in character, coming and going. The child characteristically becomes pale in each spasm. He rapidly becomes ill, goes off his food, becomes pale and collapsed. In some cases there may be no pain at all, the only sign being sudden collapse with pallor and shock. These sudden attacks of pallor have led to the incorrect diagnosis of fits. Ein & Minor (1976) found that there was no pain in 56 (13 per cent) of 422 cases of intussusception seen in Toronto. The colic commonly lasts for two or three minutes, recurring very 15 to 20 minutes. After three or four attacks the child is likely to be pale and drowsy. Intussusception should be suspected if attacks of colic persist for over two hours. The passage of blood in the stool is not usually an early symptom. A history of previous attacks of abdominal pain is a point in favour of the diagnosis.

On examination in an early case there may be a palpable mass in the right upper quadrant of the abdomen; later there may be a tumour to the left of the midline. The mass is best felt during a spasm of pain. It is most often felt in the right hypochondrium but may be felt anywhere along the line of the colon. When in doubt and the child is crying, one palpates the abdomen after a sedative has been given. Even when one cannot feel a mass, there may be guarding over the upper part of the right rectus muscle. On rectal examination the rectum is empty; there may be blood on the finger stall.

Snares in diagnosis include the fact that some children pass a stool in the first 24 hours after the onset of symptoms, so that intestinal obstruction is not suspected: there may be diarrhoea at the onset: there may be no blood in the stool, at least in the early stages: there may be no vomiting for 6 to 12 hours: there is often an elevation of temperature, and there is often a history of preceding upper respiratory tract infection: there may be a polymorphonuclear leucocytosis: and most difficult of all, there may be no pain, the child presenting with unexplained shock and pallor of sudden onset.

Chronic intussusception may present with a history of days or weeks of abdominal pain, vomiting, constipation and the presence of blood and mucus in the stools. The diagnosis of ulcerative colitis or salmonella infection could easily be made in error.

The clinical diagnosis is confirmed by a straight X-ray of the abdomen, followed, if necessary, by a barium enema.

Amongst other causes of intestinal obstruction, Janik & Ein 1979 have described *intermittent volvulus* secondary to a non-fixed but normally rotated intestine: they described it as 'not rare'.

Meckel's diverticulitis may cause pain in the right iliac fossa. A previous history of blood in the stool, or the presence of blood in the stool in the present attack, would suggest the diagnosis.

Crohn's disease (regional ileitis) is an important though rare cause of abdominal pain, often leading to unnecessary appendicectomy (p. 11).

Other causes

Children with *fibrocystic disease of the pancreas* may experience attacks of abdominal pain, sometimes as a result of faecal impaction. Abdominal pain is an important symptom of *diabetic acidosis* or hypoglycaemia.

Acute pancreatitis is usually due to mumps (Dodge, 1976). Three or four days after the swelling of the parotid gland there is vomiting, peri-umbilical pain, shock and then diarrhoea. There may be fever, bulky stools and polyuria.

Pancreatitis may also be due to other virus infections, injury, fibrocystic disease of the pancreas, choledochal cyst, gallstones, hypercalcaemia, hyperlipoproteinaemia, malnutrition and drugs (Buntain *et al* 1978).

Reimann (1976) described *chronic relapsing pancreatitis,* with abnormal pancreatic function in attacks only: it is a genetic condition, usually beginning in infancy or childhood, the child being well between attacks.

A *pancreatic pseudocyst* may develop about a month after injury in a cycle accident. The symptoms are abdominal pain, vomiting, fever and an abdominal mass (Wool & Goldring 1967). The serum amylase is usually but not always raised (Jordan & Ament 1978). The pancreatic pseudocyst may be the result of non-accidental injury (Pena & Medovy 1973, Dahman & Stephens 1981).

Various *drugs* cause pancreatitis, particularly prednisolone (Lendrum 1981). Others include azathioprine, chlorothiazide, frusemide, immunosuppressants, indomethacin, isoniazid, paracetamol, salicylates, sulphonamides, sodium valproate and tetracycline.

Infective hepatitis. Some children at the onset of infective hepatitis experience pain in the right upper quadrant of the abdomen. The diagnosis should be established by the presence of bilirubin in the urine and icterus.

Cholecystitis is rare in children (Andrassy *et al* 1976). It is accompanied by pain in the right upper quadrant of the abdomen, vomiting, fever and abdominal distension. It is difficult to distinguish from intestinal obstruction or a high retrocaecal appendicitis.

Gallstones, though rare, especially in the absence of acholuric jaundice, do occur in childhood, usually, but not always, with a family history of gall bladder trouble.

A child at the onset of *acute nephritis* may experience pain in the abdomen, leading to a diagnosis of appendicitis. The diagnosis should be established by examination of the urine for albumin, red cells, granular and cellular casts.

Renal colic is an unusual cause of abdominal pain in children. It may result from sulphonamide crystalluria or from prolonged recumbency.

Abdominal pain only rarely results from *urinary tract infection.*

Pain from *torsion of the testis* may be referred to the abdomen. Chapman & Walton (1972) described 85 cases of torsion of the testis and 16 of torsion of the hydatid of Morgagni, including 6 cases in the first year. In 38 there had been previous attacks. The most common error of diagnosis is *epididymitis*: this would be extremely rare in the absence of a chronic urinary infection, but it can be caused by Haemophilus influenzae (Chesney *et al* 1978).

An *ovarian cyst,* rupture of a *follicular* cyst or *twisted ovarian pedicle* may cause lower abdominal pain with shock and vomiting.

For *anaphylactoid purpura,* a common cause of acute abdominal pain, see p. 57. Rarely the pain may precede the development of purpura.

Infections are an important cause of abdominal pain, and include any which cause diarrhoea. *Acute rheumatic fever* may present with severe pain in the right iliac fossa.

Sickle-cell anaemia crises in coloured children may cause severe abdominal pain. The diagnosis is made by the haematologist. The pain may be accompanied by rigidity of the abdominal wall, pains in the legs, arthritis, flank pain or convulsions. Jaundice usually follows in two or three days.

Glandular fever and acute infectious lymphocytosis may be associated with abdominal pain.

Pain may be precipitated in *porphyria* by sulphonamides or barbiturates. There may be a history of vomiting and colicky abdominal pain, sometimes with photosensitivity, exposure to sunlight causing a vesicular or bullous eruption. There may be hypertrichosis, limb pains and tenderness of muscles, and red coloured urine when sulphonamides or barbiturates are given.

Drugs which may cause abdominal pain include amitriptyline, azathioprine, carbamazepine, cephalosporins, chlordiazepoxide, corticosteroids, dichlorophen, ergotamine, erythromycin, ethionamide, gentian violet, imipramine, iodides, iron, lincomycin, methotrexate, niclosamide, nystatin, P.A.S., phenytoin, piperazine, primidone, rifampicin, tetracycline, thioridazine, trimethoprim, troxidone, vincristine and viprynium.

Lead poisoning is a possible cause of abdominal pain.

Conclusion

The diagnosis of the cause of acute abdominal pain in a child may be a matter of the greatest difficulty. It is certainly a matter of the utmost importance, and many tragedies are caused by over-confidence, which so often involves delay in the diagnosis of some condition which could readily have been cured by prompt surgical treatment. It follows that there should be no hesitation in calling in expert advice when one is faced with the problem of a child with acute abdominal pain.

Recurrent abdominal pain

When faced with a child suffering from recurrent abdominal pain, the following conditions should be considered.

Psychological factors
Periodic syndrome
Hydronephrosis
Peptic ulcer
Abdominal epilepsy
Abdominal allergy
Sickle-cell anaemia
Lactose intolerance
Constipation
Worm infestation
Lead poisoning
Periodic peritonitis
Chronic relapsing pancreatitis
Hereditary angioneurotic oedema.

Psychological factors

In his monograph on *The Child with Abdominal Pains* Apley described a study of 1000 school children in Bristol. The incidence of abdominal pains was 12·3 per cent in girls and 9·5 per cent in boys. In 92 per cent of children referred for recurrent abdominal pain, no organic cause could be found after full investigation. In half of the affected children, there was another member of the family who suffered from pains. Two out of three had associated vomiting, one out of two had pallor in the attacks, and one out of five had headaches. One out of four went to sleep after the attack. Various comparisons were made between affected children and controls. The incidence of appendicectomy was 17 times greater than in controls and headaches were three times more frequent. The incidence of convulsions, however, was three times greater in controls than in the children with abdominal pains. There was a much greater incidence of headaches, nervous breakdowns and other nervous symptoms in the family of affected children than in the family of controls. With regard to intelligence, there was no difference between the affected children and controls. The pain was umbilical in two-thirds; it consisted usually of a dull ache, and in a quarter it was severe. It occurred in the day or night, and occasionally in holidays. The duration and frequency varied considerably from child to child. Of 30 children followed up eight to 12 years later, nine were symptom-free and three had migraine. The *periodic syndrome* or migraine (p. 92) is a common cause of recurrent abdominal pain, commonly with fever, vomiting or pale stools.

In a study of 6000 Buckinghamshire school children, it was found that up to the age of 10 years four per cent had recurrent abdominal pain, at the age of 12 to 13 years 15 per cent had it and from 14 to 15 years 25 per cent had it (Shepherd *et al.* 1971). In a study of 117 children with recurrent abdominal pain in Israel, organic disease was found in 10 per cent (Versano *et al* 1977). But I suspect that, as in the case of evening colic and toddlers' diarrhoea, a physiological basis will be found in time (e.g. related to prostaglandins or gut hormones) (Marx 1979, Lancet 1980, Lucas & Mitchell 1980).

Complaints of pain may be an attention-seeking device. If the mother expresses anxiety about the child's complaints, rubs his abdomen, gives him sweets, medicine or a warm drink and makes him lie down, the pain is likely to recur.

A child may complain of pain in imitation of one of his parents, who is constantly complaining of his pains. He may feel worried about his parents' symptom and express his anxiety by feeling the same pain as that of his parent. Pains may be due to worry and anxiety—worries about bullying at school, fear of a teacher or dislike of being teased.

Hydronephrosis can cause troublesome abdominal pain. The pain is by no means always localized to the loins. It is frequently impossible to palpate the kidney and the urine may be normal on examination. Even if there is a pyonephrosis, the flow of urine from the affected kidney may be blocked, so that the urine examined is normal. One can never entirely eliminate hydronephrosis as a cause of abdominal pain without a pyelogram. Abdominal pains in children are common, and one wants to avoid pyelography where possible for three important reasons: it is unpleasant for the child; it involves a fairly considerable degree of irradiation; the child has to be deprived of fluid before the procedure and the hyperosmolar injection may cause dehydration; and there is a small risk of dangerous iodine sensitivity. One has to use one's judgment, therefore, in deciding whether an intravenous pyelogram is needed. The further danger of a retrograde pyelogram is the introduction of infection by instrumentation. Even if one finds a double renal element as a result of the pyelography, one cannot be sure whether the pain is related to the renal anomaly or not.

There are widely differing views as to the frequency of *peptic ulceration* in children. Some regard it as common while some think that it is rare. Many adults with proved peptic ulcer date the onset of abdominal symptoms to childhood. The symptoms in a child are more vague and indefinite than they are in an adult. The diagnosis can be made by the finding of occult blood in the stools and by a barium meal examination. The latter involves irradiation and one has to use one's judgment in deciding whether to have it done or not.

Abdomimal epilepsy is a possible cause of recurrent abdominal pain (Douglas & White 1971). In order to make the diagnosis one must obtain a history that the attacks are of sudden onset, last a few minutes only and are followed by sleep. An electroencephalogram may confirm the diagnosis, but the EEG is frequently normal in epilepsy of grand mal type. The therapeutic test of phenytoin in full dosage is perhaps a more reliable method of establishing the diagnosis.

Though some would say that *allergy* is a common cause of abdominal pain, I have seen few children for whom I found this diagnosis satisfactory (Crook 1980). Nevertheless, one should ask whether any particular food causes the child's pain. One may then try to prevent the pain by elimination diets. So-called *milk allergy* may prove to be *lactose or sucrose intolerance* (Liebman 1979, Barr *et al* 1979). Liebman found lactose intolerance in 11 of 38 children with recurrent abdominal pain.

Constipation is commonly blamed for abdominal pain in children. Unless there is impaction of faeces causing intestinal obstruction, I am doubtful whether constipation ever causes abdominal pain in children. Children with gross constipation, often with soiling, rarely suffer from abdominal pain as a result, but a child may have pain on passing a hard stool. If they do not have pain, it seems unlikely that children with a much less degree of constipation would have pain either. Davidson (1971) ascribed many recurrent abdominal pains to hypertonus of the colon with excessive drying of the stool and therefore constipation.

Worm infestation with ascaris may cause pain. It is probably rare in Britain. Unless *threadworms* block the appendix, I find it difficult to believe that they would cause pain. I cannot imagine the mechanism whereby minute threads, averaging a few millimetres in length and lying loosely in the intestine would cause abdominal pain. Reimann (1976) described three genetic causes of recurrent abdominal pain; periodic peritonitis, occurring especially in Jews, Armenians, Turks and Arabs, sometimes with pleurisy; hereditary angioneurotic oedema (p. 301) and chronic relapsing pancreatitis.

Unknown causes. Usually there is no discoverable cause of recurrent abdominal pain in otherwise well children.

References

Andrassy RJ *et al.* Gall bladder disease in children and adolescents. *Am J Surgery* 1976; **132:** 19.

Apley J. *The child with abdominal pains.* Oxford: Blackwell Scientific Publications, 1975.

Auldist AW. Appendicitis in patients under five years of age. *Austr Paed J* 1967; **3:** 144.

Barr RG, Levine MD, Watkins JB. Recurrent abdominal pain of childhood due to lactose intolerance. *N Engl J Med* 1979; **30:** 1449.

Buntain WL, Wood JB, Woolley MM. Pancreatitis in childhood. *J Pediatr Surg* 1978; **13:** 143.

Chapman RH, Walton AJ. Torsion of the testis and its appendages. *Br Med J* 1972; **1:** 164.

Chesney PJ, Saari T, Mueller G. Acute epididymo-orchitis due to haemophilus influenzae Type B. *J Pediatr* 1978; **92:** 685.

Crook WG. Recurrent abdominal pain. *Am J Dis Child* 1980; **134:** 326.

Dahman B, Stephens CA. Pseudocyst of the pancreas after blunt abdominal trauma in children. *J Pediatr Surg.* 1981; **16:** 17.

Davidson M. Recurrent abdominal pain. *Am J Dis Child* 1971; **121:** 179.

Dodge JA. *Topics in pediatric gastroenterology.* London: Pitman Medical, 1976.

Douglas EF, White PT. Abdominal epilepsy—a reappraisal. *J Pediatr* 1971; **78:** 59.

Ein SH, Stephens CA. Intussusception. *J Pediatr Surg* 1971; **6:** 16.

Ein SH, Minor A. The painless intussusception. *J Pediatr Surg* 1976; **11:** 563.

Holgersen LO, Stanley-Brown EG. Acute appendicitis with perforation. *Am J Dis Child* 1971; **122:** 288.

Jackson RH. Parents, family doctors and acute appendicitis in childhood. *Br Med J* 1963; **2:** 277.

Jacobsson I, Lindberg T. Cow's milk as a cause of infantile colic. *Lancet* 1978; **2:** 437.

Janik JS, Ein SH. Normal intestinal rotation with non fixation: a cause of chronic abdominal pain. *J Pediatr Surg* 1979; **14:** 670.

Jordan SC, Ament ME. Pancreatitis in children and adolescents. *J Pediatr* 1978; **92:** 211.

Kerr AA, Downham MAP *et al.* Influenza B causing abdominal symptoms in children. *Lancet* 1975; **1:** 291.

Lancet Leading Article. (Re prostaglandins) Primary dysmenorrhoea. 1980; **1:** 800.

Lendrum R. Drugs and the pancreas. *Adverse Drug Reaction Bulletin* 1981; No. 90: 328.

Liebman WM. Recurrent abdominal pain in children. Lactose and sucrose intolerance. *Pediatrics* 1979; **64:** 43.

Lucas A, Mitchell MD. Prostaglandins in human milk. *Arch Dis Child* 1980; **55:** 950.

Marx JL. Dysmenorrhea: basic research leads to a rational theory. *Science* 1979; **205:** 175–6.

Pena SDJ, Medovy H. Child abuse and traumatic pseudocyst of the pancreas. *J Pediatr* 1973; **83:** 1026.

Prince RL. Evidence for an aetiological role for adenovirus type 7 in the mesenteric adenitis syndrome. *Med J Austr* 1979; **2:** 56.

Reimann HA. Three periodic diseases as causes of recurrent abdominal pain in childhood. *Arch Dis Child* 1976; **51:** 244.

Shaul WL. Clues to the early diagnosis of neonatal appendicitis *J Pediatr* 1981; **98:** 473.

Shepherd M, Oppenheim B, Mitchell S. *Child behaviour and mental health.* London: Univ. of London Press, 1971.

Versano I, Zeidel A, Matoth Y. Recurrent abdominal pain in children. *Paediatrician* 1977; **6:** 90.

Williams H. Appendicitis in the young child. *Br Med J* 1947; **2:** 730.

Wool G, Goldring D. Pseudocyst of the pancreas. *J Pediatr* 1967; **70:** 586.

Zachary RB. Diagnosis of the acute abdomen in childhood. *Br Med J* 1965; **1:** 635.

Abdominal Distension

Non-disease

Abdominal distension is not necessarily due to disease. Infants swallow large quantities of air during a feed—usually in the case of breast-feeding due to sucking too long on the breast or sucking on an empty breast, usually in the case of the bottle fed baby due to the hole in the teat being too small so that sucking is prolonged. Babies swallow air when crying for a prolonged period, with resulting abdominal distension.

Many toddlers are thought to have a big abdomen when they are normal. If there is lordosis the abdomen may appear to be unduly large. One occasionally sees marked distension as a result of severe constipation (without Hirschsprung's disease). A fat child may have a large abdomen.

For reasons which are not clear, a child suffering severe emotional deprivation (non-accidental injury) may have an unusually large abdomen (p. 8).

Neonatal abdominal distension

The most important organic causes of abdominal distension in the very young infant are as follows:

> Intestinal obstruction, meconium ileus or plug, lactobezoar
> Perforation of alimentary, biliary or urinary tract
> Congenital heart disease
> Tracheo-oesophageal fistula, forcing air into the stomach
> Hirschsprung's disease
> Tumours and cysts, especially renal tumours
> Infection—septicaemia, peritonitis, necrotizing enterocolitis
> Congenital nephrotic syndrome (rare)
> Urethral obstruction: distended bladder
> Drug—chloramphenicol

Rupture of the stomach of the newborn baby leads to abdominal distension, respiratory distress, vomiting and melaena, commonly on about the third day. On auscultation no bowel sounds can be heard. Oedema of the abdominal wall suggests peritonitis. Even in newborn infants, *appendicitis* may occur, usually with perforation. The symptoms are vomiting, abdominal distension and shock. *Perforation of the colon* of a newborn baby suggests Hirschsprung's disease or meconium peritonitis. Colonic perforation may follow an exchange transfusion. (Hardy *et al* 1972). Four to 15 hours after the transfusion the child becomes poorly, develops abdominal distension and vomits, and there is usually blood in the stool. On auscultation no bowel sounds are heard.

Perforation of the rectum by a rectal thermometer is a well-known hazard.

Intestinal duplication or duplication cysts may cause considerable swelling of the abdomen. The cysts are often mobile and may reach a considerable size. There may be abdominal pain and rectal bleeding. A ladder pattern of visible peristalsis indicates obstruction.

Infections may cause abdominal distension. When a newborn baby develops septicaemia, in addition to distension of the abdomen there is often vomiting, diarrhoea, jaundice, lethargy, respiratory distress and apnoeic attacks. It may be due to gram negative bacteria or group B streptococci. For necrotizing enterocolitis see p. 83.

When there is *urethral obstruction* (due to urethral valves, etc.) there may be gross enlargement of the bladder. The diagnosis, suspected on account of the fact that the swelling involves the lower abdomen more than the upper part, is confirmed by observation of the stream of urine and by running an opaque substance into the bladder and inverting the baby, so that the material will run into the patulous ureters. There may be perforation of the urinary tract when obstruction is severe, with ascites; neonatal ascites should be regarded as due to obstructive uropathy until proved otherwise. It can be due to congenital heart disease, nephrosis, congenital cirrhosis, congenital cytomegalovirus infection, peritonitis due to meconium or syphilis. The ascites can also be chylous, as a result of malformation of the lymphatic system, rupture of a mesenteric cyst, neoplasm, trauma or obstruction of the lymphatic system: often the cause cannot be determined.

Chloramphenicol in an overdose in the newborn period causes abdominal distension, cyanosis, shock and other manifestations of the 'grey syndrome'.

Abdominal distension subsequent to the newborn period

The causes after the newborn period include the following:

Aerophagy

Intestine—obstruction, ileus, perforation, duplication, cysts, Hirschsprung's disease

Omentum and mesentery—cysts, mesenteric thrombosis

Peritoneum—peritonitis, malignant disease

Ascites—diseases involving the heart—(congestive failure)

Pericardium (constrictive pericarditis)

Kidney (acute nephritis, nephrotic syndrome)

Liver (cirrhosis, portal hypertension)

Pancreas (chronic pancreatitis)

Inferior vena cava—thrombosis, other obstruction

Lymphatic obstruction: congenital: chylous ascites: trauma: tuberculosis: Hodgkin's disease

Hypoproteinaemia: beriberi

Liver—cyst, tumour, storage diseases, tyrosinosis, subcapsular haematoma choledochal cyst, perforation of bile ducts

Kidney—tumour, hydronephrosis, polycystic disease, renal vein thrombosis

Adrenal—neuroblastoma, haemorrhage

Spleen—leukaemia, haematoma

Pancreatic cyst (p. 107)

Ovary—cyst

Vagina—hydrocolpos

Uterus—pregnancy

Sacrococcygeal teratoma, dermoid, anterior meningocele

Hypokalaemia

Carbohydrate or fat malabsorption

Aerophagy sometimes occurs in older children (Gauderer *et al.*).

Tyrosinosis presents in early infancy with failure to thrive, fever, diarrhoea, vomiting, hepatomegaly and abdominal distension. There may be melaena, haematemesis, haematuria and jaundice, with glycosuria and generalized aminoaciduria.

Gaucher's disease occurs in two forms—acute infantile, with moderate hepatosplenomegaly and bulbar palsy, ending fatally by the age of two to six years, and the chronic form, with early abdominal enlargement, splenomegaly rather than hepatomegaly and bone pain.

Drugs which may cause abdominal distension include diphenoxylate and indomethacin.

References

Corkery JJ, Dubowitz V. *et al.* Colonic perforation after exchange transufsion. *Br Med J* 1968; **4**: 345.

Gauderer *et al.* Pathological childhood aerophagia: a recognizable clinical entity. *J Pediatr Surg* 1981; **16**: 301.

Gwinn JL, Lee FA. Rupture of the stomach in the newborn infant. *Am J Dis Child* 1970; **119**: 257.

Hardy JD, Savage TR, Shirodaria C. Intestinal perforation following exchange transfusion. *Am J Dis Child* 1972; **124**: 136.

Koop CE. Abdominal mass in the newborn infant. *N Engl J Med* 1973; **289**: 569.

Wolfson JJ. Rectal perforation in infants by thermometer. *Am J Dis Child* 1966; **111**: 197.

Jaundice

Jaundice in infancy

The following statements can be made with little fear of contradiction:

1 The diagnosis of the cause of prolonged jaundice in a young infant is commonly one of great difficulty.

2 Jaundice on the first day of life must be considered to be due to haemolytic disease until proved otherwise.

3 Physiological jaundice is not seen in the first 24 hours. With rare exceptions, jaundice after the first week in a full-term baby is not physiological and must be investigated

4 In physiological jaundice, including breast milk jaundice, the urine and stools are a normal colour. There is no bilirubin in the urine and the stools contain normal bile pigments.

5 Pale-coloured stools with a dark urine containing bilirubin signify an obstructive element. The commonest cause is neonatal hepatitis. Laboratory tests cannot at present distinguish this from congenital obliteration of the bile ducts.

6 In the newborn period, infection is an important cause of jaundice (e.g. septicaemia), particularly when the jaundice begins after the fourth day. The bilirubin is partly direct and partly indirect, so that the stools may be pale.

7 It is essential that every effort be made to establish the correct diagnosis because some of the conditions demand urgent treatment.

The diagnosis

Jaundice must be distinguished from the yellow colour of the skin caused by *carotinaemia*. This is due to the lipochrome carotene, present predominantly in carrots, but also in other yellow vegetables, including yellow corn, and in greens, in which the yellow is obscured by chlorophyll (Lascari 1980). Yellow staining of the skin is usually due to an excess of carrots in the diet of a lactating mother, or an excess of pureed carrots in the baby's diet. Carotinaemia is also associated with *hypothyroidism, diabetes mellitus* and the *nephrotic syndrome*.

A similar condition in *lycopenaemia*, in which the skin is an orange-yellow colour, usually due to a large amount of tomatoes in the diet. Lycopene is an isomer of beta-carotene, and is the colouring matter in tomatoes (and tomato juice), beetroots and rosehips. Both pigments are present in commercial infant foods.

The skin is stained yellow by *mepacrine.*

In all the above cases jaundice is eliminated by the absence of yellow pigment in the sclera.

The baby's skin may be yellow as a result of meconium staining in *postmaturity* and the *placental dysfunction syndrome.*

Drugs taken by the mother during pregnancy may be a factor in neonatal jaundice. They include sedatives and tranquillisers (diazepam, phenothiazines), salicylates, sulphonamides and excess of Vitamin K.

For corticosteroids and oxytocin see p. 119.

At the risk of some oversimplification, one can state that there are four main groups of causes of jaundice in the infant and young child. More than one of these causes may be operative at the same time. They are as follows:

1 *Deficiency of the enzyme glucuronyl transferase.* Bilirubin is fat soluble, and before it can be excreted by the liver into bile or excreted in the urine, it must be converted into a water soluble form by conjugation with glucuronic acid. In the absence of glucuronyl transferase this indirectly reacting pigment ('unconjugated') accumulates in the plasma and may damage the nervous system.

The following are the conditions in which deficiency of the enzyme glucuronyl transferase plays a part:

> Jaundice following severe anoxia
>
> Hypothyroidism
>
> Breast milk jaundice
>
> Drugs given to the mother or newborn
>
> Rare causes—Maternal diabetes
>> Congenital pyloric stenosis
>> Crigler-Najjar syndrome
>> Gilbert's syndrome
>> Galactosaemia
>> Adrenocortical hyperplasia
>> Fructose intolerance
>> Hirschsprung's disease

Physiological jaundice is due to a combination of immaturity of the liver with consequent transferase deficiency, and the breakdown of red cells immediately after birth. The jaundice of prematurity, whose basis is the same, is more severe than that of the mature baby, because of greater immaturity of the enzyme system. Severe anxoia during delivery or cold injury after delivery tends to increase the jaundice.

Physiological jaundice is not seen in the first 24 hours. In a full-term baby it begins at the end of the second day and lasts for two or three days. It rarely lasts into the second week. If jaundice lasts into the second week in a full-term baby, the cause should be sought elsewhere.

The jaundice of a premature baby begins later, is more severe and lasts longer. One would not expect physiological jaundice in a premature baby in the first 48 hours. Physiological jaundice reaches its maximum about the fifth or sixth day (depending on the degree of immaturity), and in the smallest ones may last up to the 18th day. When food is withheld for 48 to 72 hours after birth, the jaundice is increased. It is reduced by early feeding. Physiological jaundice is sometimes prolonged in hypothyroidism because of deficiency of the transferase enzyme.

Breast milk jaundice, for unknown reasons, has become common. The jaundice clears as soon as breast feeding is discontinued and returns when it is restarted. It appears to be harmless, and has not caused kernicterus; there is no need to take the baby off the breast, and the jaundice disappears after a short time without treatment. The theory that it was due to an abnormal steroid in breast milk has been discarded—and the later theory, that it was related to lipoprotein lipase, found no support with Greek workers (Constantopoulos *et al* 1980). It may, in some way as yet unknown, be due to delayed maturation or inhibition of glycuronyl transferase (Poland 1981).

It is possible that *corticosteroids* given to the mother during pregnancy may increase the depth of jaundice in the baby by inhibition of the transferase system. Novobiocin given to the mother or baby may act in the same way. Oxytocin, given to start labour, increases the fetal bilirubin, probably by interfering with the glucuronyl transferase. Buchan (1979) suggested that the oxytocin raised the infant's serum bilirubin by increasing the breakdown of red cells. Wood *et al* (1979), on the other hand, suggested that the apparent increase in the incidence of neonatal jaundice was more related to factors in breast milk or to epidural anaesthesia.

The *Crigler-Najjar syndrome* is a rare recessive condition in which there is a deficiency of transferase. Extrapyramidal rigidity develops in a few weeks and persists. The picture is similar to that of kernicterus. There is no evidence of haemolysis or of obstruction. The bilirubin is unconjugated.

Gilbert's disease is a much less serious congenital disease due to deficiency of the same enzyme. Mild jaundice with lassitude persists throughout life. It is non-haemolytic, and more common in males. It is inherited as an autosomal dominant. The bilirubin is unconjugated.

Occasionally infants with *congenital pyloric stenosis* have jaundice with a raised serum bilirubin of indirect type (Nakai & Margaretten, 1962). The explanation of this is unknown, but Bleicher *et al* 1979 suggested that it was due to inhibition of glucuronyl transferase by hypergastrinaemia.

The jaundice of *galactosaemia* may be due to delayed development of transferase or a toxic damage to the liver cells. When milk is given, the child goes off his food, vomits, loses weight, becomes jaundiced, and his liver and spleen enlarge.

Jaundice is sometimes an early feature of *adrenocortical hyperplasia* and of *fructose intolerance.*

It will be noted that in none of the above conditions is there bile in the urine, and in all of them the stools are of normal colour. In none of them is there haemolysis. The serum bilirubin is of the indirect or unconjugated variety.

2 *Increased bilirubin production —mainly due to haemolysis.* The main conditions are as follows:

> Congenital haemolytic disease (Rhesus or ABO incompatibility: more rarely Kell, Kidd, or Duffy group)
> Hereditary spherocytosis or acholuric jaundice. Thalassaemia. Sickle-cell anaemia
> Drugs—vitamin K, neomycin, camphor, sulphonamides
> Infections—septicaemia, syphilis, Weil's disease
> Absorption of blood from a large cephalhaematoma or other haemorrhage
> Glucose-6-phosphate dehydrogenase deficiency (p. 51)
> Rarely pyruvate kinase deficiency

Jaundice on the first day must be regarded as *haemolytic disease* due to blood group incompatibility until proved otherwise. It is essential that a child with jaundice on the first day should be referred immediately to hospital for investigation and treatment, which may well consist of a replacement transfusion. Failure to do so without delay may lead to the death of the child or to kernicterus which is either lethal or crippling for life.

Though haemolytic disease due to rhesus incompatibility does not occur in the first pregnancy unless there has been a previous incompatible transfusion, that due to ABO incompatibility may occur in the first pregnancy, and it cannot be anticipated by tests during pregnancy. In this case the mother is usually Group O and the baby Group A, but the baby may be Group B. Rarely the mother is Group A and the infant Group B, or vice versa. The Coombs test in the infant with ABO incompatibility is commonly negative.

The diagnosis of *congenital spherocytosis or acholuric jaundice* is readily established by the family history of that complaint, together with examination of the child's blood for spherocytes, reticulocytosis and abnormal red cell fragility.

Vitamin K in an overdose increases the level of jaundice by three possible mechanisms—haemolysis, a toxic action on the liver or by competing for conjugating enzymes. It should be remembered that if the mother is given large doses of vitamin K during delivery it is likely to affect the baby.

If nappies have been stored in *camphor balls,* the baby may absorb the camphor and develop haemolytic anaemia. Neomycin may cause some degree of haemolysis.

Infections cause jaundice partly by haemolysis and partly by a toxic action on the liver which may interfere with the transferase system (Rooney *et al* 1971). The serum bilirubin is mostly unconjugated (indirect) but partly conjugated (direct). Jaundice appearing rapidly after the fourth day in a full-term infant should always be considered as infective in origin until proved otherwise: it may cause kernicterus. The relevant infections include septicaemia and syphilis. Sometimes the jaundice is the only manifestation of a urinary tract or other bacterial infection. The diagnosis of septicaemia would be strongly suggested by a moist umbilicus and would be confirmed by blood culture. An important cause is group B streptococcal infection from the mother's vagina. The diagnosis of syphilis would be suspected if there were a history of inadequately treated syphilis in the mother and stigmata in the child. It would be confirmed by serological examination, remembering that in a newborn infant a false negative Wassermann reaction may be obtained for 4 to 12 weeks, and that a false positive may be found for a similar period. If the titre of the baby's blood is higher than that of the mother, or if the titre is rising, treatment should be instituted.

If a *cephalhaematoma* is a large one, the absorption of blood may lead to a rise in the serum bilirubin.

3 *Interference with protein binding.* Sulphonamides, flucloxacillin and caffeine and sodium benzoate may increase the jaundice of a newborn baby by competing with bilirubin for protein binding and displacing bilirubin into the tissues (Hanefeld & Ballowitz 1976). These drugs should therefore be avoided.

4 *Obstructive jaundice.* The following are the main causes in the newborn infant:

> Neonatal hepatitis due to maternal rubella, coxsackie virus, adenovirus, herpes, listeriosis, toxoplasmosis, cytomegalovirus, syphilis
> Biliary atresia
> Inspissated bile, fibrocystic disease of the pancreas
> Urinary tract infection
> Rare
>> Choledochal cyst
>> Gallstones
>> Dubin-Johnson syndrome
>> Alpha 1 antitrypsin deficiency
>> Tyrosinosis
>> Galactosaemia
>> Fructose intolerance (p. 12)
>> Glyogen storage disease type IV
>> Gaucher's disease
>> Mucopolysaccharidosis
>> Porphyria
>> Drugs

Neonatal hepatitis is a somewhat mysterious condition of uncertain aetiology. It has occurred in two or three children of the same family. In some, the rubella virus has been isolated. It may be the end result of several conditions such as serum hepatitis in the mother. The relationship of neonatal hepatitis to biliary atresia is uncertain.

Jaundice due to neonatal hepatitis may be present at birth or appear during the first week or two. It is of varying duration and may last for several months before clearing.

There are no certain means of distinguishing neonatal hepatitis from *biliary atresia*. An American paper on neonatal jaundice described 73 liver function tests recommended for this age period. Even a liver biopsy may not provide a definite answer. It is important to determine whether there is any obstructive lesion of the biliary tract which can be corrected by surgery: only a small number of cases can be corrected, but one must give the child the benefit of the doubt. This can be determined by limited laparotomy with a cholangiogram after injecting dye into the gallbladder and biopsy of a specimen of liver. If nothing is or can be done for an infant with biliary atresia, he continues to have severe jaundice with biliary cirrhosis and dies in a few months, or rarely a few years. The diagnosis is made by serological methods.

Hepatitis due to *toxoplasmosis or cytomegalovirus* is rare, but that due to maternal rubella is relatively common. The diagnosis is made by serological methods.

Alpha₁ - antitrypsin deficiency may cause hyperbilirubinaemia following physiological jaundice; or the jaundice may not develop for three or four months. It usually lasts two or three months, after which the child is well, but enlargement of the liver remains, cirrhosis developing in later childhood (Lancet 1977).

Jaundice may be the only obvious symptom of *urinary tract infection*. The bilirubin is partly direct and partly indirect (Seeler & Hahn 1969). The jaundice develops commonly between the 8th and 56th day, mostly in boys and is usually associated with an *E. coli* infection.

Obstructive jaundice may occasionally develop in infants suffering from haemolytic anaemia due to *blood group incompatibility*. This has been ascribed to inspissated bile blocking the bile duct. It is rare, but there have been instances in which the jaundice has cleared after the duct has been washed through at laparotomy.

A choledochal cyst is a rare cause of obstructive jaundice. The chief signs are jaundice and a palpable mass (Harris & Kahler 1978).

The *Dubin-Johnson syndrome* is a rare type of chronic jaundice with bile in the urine, due to an inability of the hepatic cells to excrete conjugated bilirubin. The bilirubin is partly direct and partly indirect.

It is an autosomal dominant condition, and is probably the same as the Rotor syndrome.

In *tyrosinosis* the phenistix test is positive. In galactosaemia the clinitest is positive, but the clinistix is negative.

Jaundice after infancy

1 *Obstruction*

By far the commonest cause of jaundice after infancy is *infective hepatitis*. There will be bile in the urine and the stools will be clay coloured. It could also be due to serum hepatitis, if the child has had a transfusion, or has been given injections with a contaminated needle.

Toxic hepatitis can be caused by scores of *drugs* (Sherlock, 1964). These include antibiotics, drugs such as acetazolamide, amitriptyline, ampicillin, amphetamine, anabolic steroids, antimetabolites, carbamazepine, cephalexin, chloramphenicol, chloroquine, clonidine, cotrimoxazole, dioctyl sulphosuccinate, erythromycin estolate, ethambutol, ethionamide, ethosuximide, gold, griseofulvin, haloperidol, halothane, ibuprofen, imipramine, indomethacin, iron, isoniazid, kanamycin, lincomycin, methimazole, methotrexate, nalidixic acid, neomycin, nitrofurantoin, novobiocin, oleandomycin, oxyphenisatin (dulcolax), paracetamol, P.A.S., penicillin, phenacetin, pheneturide, phenothiazines, phenytoin, pyrazinamide, quinine, rifampicin, streptomycin, sulphonamides, testosterone, tetracycline, thiouracil, troxidone, vancomycin and vincristine. It can also be caused by a wide variety of poisons, such as phosphorus, iron, arsenic, bismuth or fungi. Obstructive jaundice has been traced to a chlorinated hydrocarbon in breast milk (Bagnell & Ellenberger 1977).

In the tropics, *malaria* and *bilharzia* cause jaundice. Ingestion of certain poisons or moulds (alpha toxins) may be relevant.

Jaundice could be caused by *solvent sniffing*.

Cirrhosis of the liver in its late stages causes jaundice as in adults. Valman *et al* (1971) described four children with prolonged obstructive jaundice and *fibrocystic disease of the pancreas*—possibly because of increased density of bile. Rare causes to consider include Wilson's disease (p. 205), tyrosinosis and Niemann-Pick disease.

Weil's disease (leptospirosis) is a rare cause of jaundice. It is characterised by jaundice, fever, leucocytosis, albuminuria and haemorrhages. It is diagnosed by agglutination tests, isolation of the spirochaete in the blood or inoculation of a guinea-pig.

Infectious mononucleosis is on rare occasions complicated by jaundice.

2 Haemolytic

In jaundice due to haemolysis the urine does not contain bile and the stools are of a normal colour. The causes are congenital spherocytosis (acholuric jaundice), sickle-cell anaemia and thalassaemia, and acquired (autoimmune) haemolytic anaemia.

References

Bagnell PC, Ellenberger HA. Obstructive jaundice due to a chlorinated hydrocarbon in breast milk. *Can Med Ass J* 1977; **117**: 1047.

Bleicher MA, Reiner MA, *et al.* Extraordinary hyperbilirubinaemia in a neonate with hypertrophic pyloric stenosis. *J Pediatr Surg* 1979; **14**: 527

Buchan PC. Pathogenesis of neonatal hyperbilirubinaemia after induction of labour with oxytocin. *Br Med J* 1979; **2**: 1255.

Constantopoulos A, Messaratakis J, Matsaniotis N. Breast milk jaundice: the role of lipoprotein lipase and the free fatty acids. *Europ J Pediatr* 1980; **134**: 35.

Hanefeld F, Ballowitz L. Flucloxacillin and bilirubin binding. *Lancet* 1976; **1**: 433.

Harris VJ, Kahler J. Choledochal cyst: delayed diagnosis in a jaundiced infant. *Pediatrics* 1978; **62**: 235.

Lancet. Childhood liver disease with alpha 1 antitrypsin deficiency. *Leading article* 1977; **1**: 82.

Lascari AD, Carotinemia. *Clin Pediatr* 1980; **20**: 25.

Nakai H, Margaretten W. Protracted jaundice associated with hypertrohic pyloric stenosis. *Pediatrics* 1962; **29**: 198.

Poland RL. Breast milk jaundice. *J Pediatr* 1981; **99**: 86.

Rooney JC, Hill DJ, Danks DM. Jaundice associated with bacterial infection in the newborn. *Am J Dis Child* 1971; **122**: 39.

Seeler RA, Hahn K. Jaundice in urinary tract infection in infancy. *Am J Dis Child* 1969; **118**: 553.

Sherlock S. Jaundice due to drugs. *Proc Roy Soc Med* 1964; **57**: 881.

Valman HP, France NE, Wallis PG. Prolonged neonatal jaundice in cystic fibrosis. *Arch Dis Child* 1971; **46;** 805.

Wood B, Culley P, *et al.* Factors effecting neonatal jaundice. *Arch Dis Child* 1979; **54**: 111.

Persistent Cyanosis

Peripheral cyanosis is a normal feature of newborn infants. The limbs are cyanosed, while the face and trunk are a normal pink. The cyanosis lasts a few days only.

Causes of *persistent generalized cyanosis* in an infant include the following:

Congenital heart disease
Severe chest disease (acute only). Respiratory distress syndrome.
Cerebral oedema or haemorrhage
Methaemoglobinaemia (rare)
  (i) Congenital
  (ii) Absorption of aniline from laundry marks on clothes
  (iii) Other poisons—acetanilide, dinitrophenol, nitrites, phenazopyridine, potassium perchlorate
  (iv) Phenytoin taken by breast-feeding mother
Sulphaemoglobinaemia (rare)

Congenital heart disease is the most common cause of persistent cyanosis in an infant. In the newborn period, the usual causes are complete transposition of the great vessels or cor triloculare. Other causes are a truncus arteriosus or tricuspid atresia. In the first two of these there may be no cardiac murmur. After the newborn period the usual lesion is Fallot's tetralogy. It can also be due to a right to left shunt when there is a patent ductus arteriosus with coarctation of the aorta proximal to the ductus. Other causes are a hypoplastic left heart, isolated pulmonary stenosis or atresia, tricuspid atresia and a persistent truncus. The diagnosis is established by the usual investigations—X-ray of the chest for heart shape and size, ECG, cardiac catheterization and angiocardiography. The rather non-specific condition termed *fibroelastosis* may also cause persistent cyanosis with heart failure.

Severe chest disease is an unlikely cause of persistent cyanosis in a baby, except in an acute illness such as the respiratory distress syndrome or atelectasis.

A baby may rapidly develop respiratory distress, bronchitis, cyanosis and intercostal retraction after the accidental *inhalation of talcum powder* (British Medical Journal 1969).

Persistent generalized cyanosis in association with dyspnoea is likely to be due to *atelectasis,* or possibly *pneumothorax, mediastinal or lobar emphysema* or a large *diaphragmatic hernia.* Atelectasis may itself be due to a *cerebral haemorrhage.* One must not forget to palpate the anterior fontanelle and the sutures for evidence of increased intracranial pressure.

Methaemoglobinaemia may be congenital, or it may result from the absorption of aniline from laundry marks which have been applied *after* the nappies or clothes have been boiled. If they are applied before boiling, absorption does not occur. Methaemoglobinaemia has occurred in rural areas as a result of the presence of *nitrates* in well water used for making up the feeds (British Medical Journal 1966). They have been used as fertilisers in the fields, and have percolated into the water. A variety of other rather unlikely poisons may cause the condition. When a lactating mother takes phenytoin, the baby may be cyanosed as a result.

Babies may develop cyanosis and methaemoglobinaemia as a result of eating spinach, especially if they are also given the water in which it was boiled. It is due to nitrates in the spinach. It has apparently resulted from taking carrot juice (Keating *et al.* 1973).

Cyanosis may result from polycythaemia or nitrofurantoin.

Sulphaemoglobinaemia is a rare congenital metabolic disorder.

In the older age group the likely causes of persistent cyanosis are *congenital heart disease, pulmonary hypertension* or *pulmonary fibrosis.*

References

British Medical Journal. Annotation. Spinach, a risk to babies. 1966; **1**: 250. 250.

British Medical Journal. Accidental inhalation of talcum powder. 1969; **4**: 5.

Keating JP. *et al.* Infantile methaemoglobinaemia caused by carrot juice. *N Engl J Med* 1973; **288**: 824.

Cyanotic (Apnoeic) Attacks in the Newborn

Everyone who looks after newborn babies is conversant with cyanotic attacks ('apnoeic attacks'). A baby, usually in his first few days, but sometimes a little later, is found to be ashen grey in colour and not breathing. The condition is far more common in the preterm baby than in the full-term one, and the smaller the preterm baby the more common are apnoeic attacks. These attacks are particularly common during feeds because of milk entering the trachea.

The causes of apnoeic attacks may be grouped as follows:

Depression of the respiratory centre
    Anoxia
    Prematurity
    Analgesic or anaesthetic drugs during labour
    Cerebral oedema or haemorrhage; brain defects
    Meningitis or septicaemia
    Respiratory distress syndrome

Obstruction of the airway
    Aspiration of meconium
    Vomited material inhaled
    Milk entering the trachea
    Thick mucus, etc.
    Nasal obstruction, including choanal atresia
    Laryngeal obstruction

Convulsions
    Hypocalcaemia (tetany)
    Hypoglycaemia
    Hypernatraemia, hyponatraemia
    Tetanus
    Infections
    Cerebral oedema, haemorrhages, defects
Primary alveolar hypoventilation (rare)

In a study in Sheffield, we found that congenital heart disease was a rare cause of apnoeic attacks.

Depression or immaturity of the respiratory centre is an important cause of cyanotic attacks, probably mainly be anoxia (Kattwinkel 1977, Kelly & Shannon 1979). Attacks are sometimes precipitated by a sudden stimulus, such as a suction catheter. In small preterm babies phasic respiration, including Cheyne-Stokes breathing, is a normal finding: some cyanotic attacks are due to failure to restart breathing after the normal brief apnoeic stage. It has been suggested that there is sometimes a connection between apnoeic attacks and a rise of temperature in the incubator (Sinclair 1970). After the newborn period cyanotic attacks may be a feature of congenital heart disease, especially Fallot's tetralogy (Sulayman & Thilenius 1981).When a one or two week old baby who has been previously well develops apnoeic attacks, pyogenic meningitis must be remembered as a possible cause.

Obstruction of the airway is a major cause of apnoeic attacks. Nasal obstruction may cause apnoeic attacks because the newborn baby does not usually open his mouth to breathe when the nose is blocked. Choanal atresia is rare but of the utmost importance, in that the correct treatment is easy to apply and lifesaving (Holbolth *et al* 1967). It is due to a web or membrane behind the palate. If it is complete, the child gasps for breath or has apnoeic attacks, but his distress is immediately relieved by crying or by the insertion of an oral airway pending elective surgery.

Many apnoeic attacks are *convulsions*.The newborn infant does not have major convulsions. He may twitch and he may have apnoeic attacks. Convulsions are an important and frequent cause of apnoeic attacks. The causes of neonatal convulsions are discussed on p. 209. In that section the importance of diagnosing and therefore treating one of the main causes of convulsions in the newborn, namely hypoglycaemia, is emphasized. Apnoeic attacks may be due to *primary alveolar hypoventilation* ('Ondine's curse') (Taitz & Redman 1971), in which there is shallow breathing, often with apnoeic attacks, with chronic respiratory acidosis—probably due to failure of the central mechanism of respiration.

References

Holbolth N, Buchman G, Sandberg LE. Congenital choanal atresia. *Acta Paediatr Scand* 1967; **56:** 286.

Kattwinkel J. Neonatal apnea: pathogenesis and therapy. *J Pediatr* 1977; **90:** 342.

Kelly DH, Shannon DC. Periodic breathing in infants with near miss sudden infant death syndrome. *Pediatrics* 1979; **63:** 355.

Sinclair JS. The premature baby who forgets to breathe. *N Engl J Med* 1970; **282:** 508.

Sulayman RF, Thilenius OG. Complications of heart disease in children. Congestive heart failure, cyanotic spells and infective endocarditis. *Paediatrician* 1981; **10:** 99.

Taitz LS, Redman CWG. Ondine's curse with recovery. *Proc Roy Soc Med* 1971; **64:** 58.

Dyspnoea in the Newborn

The following conditions should be considered:
- Choanal atresia
- Respiratory distress syndrome
- Group B streptococcus infection
- Massive aspiration of amniotic fluid or meconium
- Intrauterine pneumonia
- Wilson-Mikity syndrome
- Bronchopulmonary dysplasia
- Atelectasis
- Cerebral anoxia or haemorrhage
- Mediastinal or lobar emphysema
- Pneumothorax, air cyst
- Chylothorax, congenital pulmonary lymphangiectasia (rare)
- Pancreatic pseudocyst (rare)
- Fibrocystic disease of the pancreas
- Tracheo-oesphageal fistula
- Diaphragmatic hernia or paralysis
- Anaemia
- Heart failure
- Vascular ring
- Thoracic dysplasia
- Histiocytosis X (rare)

Fore gut duplication (rare)

Inhalation of talc (p. 126)

For a comprehensive discussion of this difficult subject, the reader is referred to the book by Schaffer and Avery.

The most common cause of dyspnoea in the newborn baby is the *respiratory distress syndrome* ('hyaline membrane syndrome') (Brice & Walker 1977). This occurs under three main circumstances—when the baby is born prematurely, is born by Caesarian section or is born by a diabetic mother. It is more common in boys than girls. Within the first hour of birth there is a rising respiration rate. The baby begins to make a grunting sound on expiration. There is indrawing of the lower part of the chest and sternum and there may be some cyanosis or cyanotic attacks. On examination there may be râles in the chest and dullness on percussion or signs of emphysema. There may be signs of heart failure with peripheral circulatory failure, cyanosis and muffled heart sounds. The X-ray of the chest shows a characteristic picture. Persistent pulmonary emphysema may follow the respiratory distress syndrome (Stocker & Madewell 1977). The respiratory distress syndrome is thought to be different from the 'transient tachypnoea of the newborn', which occurs especially after Caesarian section: but the differentiating features are not clear. The respiratory distress syndrome can be confused with most of the conditions below.

Transient tachypnoea of the newborn was described by Halliday *et al* (1981) as being usually benign, with little respiratory distress, but sometimes associated with generalized myocardial failure, pulmonary hypertension or right left shunt.

Massive aspiration of amniotic fluid or meconium (Milner 1980). This occurs particularly in post-mature babies and in babies delivered by forceps or breech, and after prolonged labour, placental insufficiency or prolapse of the cord, or a cord which has been tightly knotted or tightly round the neck. The child may be shocked as a result of anoxia, and soon after birth, usually within three or four hours, he becomes dyspnoeic. There may be associated signs of brain injury, such as a high-pitched cry or an absent or exaggerated Moro reflex. There may be complicating atelectasis, emphysema, pneumothorax or pneumonia.

Intrauterine pneumonia may follow prolonged rupture of the membranes. The initial symptoms are non-specific. The child is ill at birth, shows little inclination to suck, and may vomit. The temperature is subnormal or raised. There are rapid often grunting respirations, usually without cough. The abdomen may be distended. It has to be distinguished from *staphylococcal pneumonia,* which develops later. The onset is usually insidious, the child becoming ill and toxic in appearance. He may develop an empyema or pyopneumothorax.

The *Wilson-Mikity syndrome* (Wilson & Mikity 1960) is a condition of uncertain aetiology, mainly in low birth weight babies with no known prenatal factors. The symptoms begin a week or two after birth, sometimes after the respiratory distress syndrome. There is an insidious onset of cyanosis, wheezing and cough with rapid respirations, worsening in the next three or four weeks. It may last for several months before recovery.

Bronchopulmonary dysplasia, with cyanosis and dyspnoea, follows the treatment of respiratory distress by prolonged mechanical ventilation. It occurred in 21 per cent of 299 infants ventilated for the respiratory distress syndrome (Edwards *et al* 1977).

Atelectasis may be associated with persistent cyanosis and feeble respiratory movements. The apex beat is deflected towards the affected side. Agenesis of the lung causes dullness and decreased breath sounds on the affected side with gross mediastinal displacement to the same side. It can be difficult to be sure that the respiratory symptoms are not due to cerebral oedema or haemorrhage.

Mediastinal emphysema and pneumothorax are associated with dyspnoea, rapid shallow respirations and cyanosis. The chest may appear to be over-distended, and in the case of pneumothorax there will be decreased movement on one side, with displacement of the trachea and apex beat to the opposite side. In either case there will be hyperresonance over the affected area, and in the case of mediastinal emphysema there may be a characteristic crunching sound with each heart beat (Hamman's sign). A large air-containing cyst cannot be distinguished clinically from pneumothorax.

A *Group B streptococcal infection* can mimic the respiratory distress syndrome. It occurs especially when there has been premature rupture of the membranes and causes respiratory symptoms with shock in the first 24 hours. (Ablow *et al* 1976).

Obstructive emphysema presents especially a week or two after birth, with increasing respiratory distress, tachypnoea, retraction of the chest with bulging on one side and sometimes an expiratory wheeze (Williams & Phelan 1975).

According to Chernick & Reed (1970), a pneumothorax is more common in the newborn than at any other age. There is usually a history of fetal distress or difficult delivery, often with aspiration of meconium, followed by resuscitation; it may complicate the respiratory distress syndrome or pneumonia. They wrote that pleural effusion may be a manifestation of hydrops or Turner's syndrome or follow pneumonia. The most common cause of a pleural effusion in a neonate is the chylothorax (Sweet 1977).

Mallard *et al* (1977) described the spread of a *pancreatic pseudocyst* bulging into the mediastinum, with resulting respiratory distress.

A *tracheo-oesophageal fistula* will cause dyspnoea if the diagnosis is delayed until after feeds are given, with resultant regurgitation or entry of milk into the trachea.

Diaphragmatic hernia is an acute emergency if the hernia is large. There is commonly cyanosis and dyspnoea from birth, though these may develop later. The chest may be overfilled while the abdomen may be flat. There is resonance or dullness.

Paralysis of the diaphragm is most commonly associated with Erb's palsy. Respirations are rapid and there are decreased respiratory movements on the affected side with decreased sounds at the base.

Severe anaemia and *heart failure* are important though rare causes of dyspnoea, requiring immediate treatment (Lees 1969). The symptoms of heart failure include feeding difficulties, rapid respirations and oedema. It may be caused by myocarditis, congenital heart disease, fibroelastosis, glycogen storage disease, heart block, paroxysmal tachycardia, respiratory distress syndrome and septicaemia.

Oberklaid *et al.* 1977 described the syndrome of *asphyxiating thoracic dysplasia*, consisting of dyspnoea, small chest, short ribs and limbs and dwarfism, closely resembling the Ellis-van Creveld syndrome in which there is also frequently polydactyly, abnormal nails, dental cysts and congenital heart disease. They distinguished this from bone diseases with a small chest. Hull & Barnes (1972) noted that most of the children with a small chest had chondrodystrophia: they listed *achondroplasia, thanatophoric* and *diastrophic dwarfism* as causes.

Histiocytosis X may cause a pneumo-mediastinum any time in the first year (Sweet 1977).

A *vascular ring* may cause dyspnoea and stridor with cyanosis during feeding.

The features of the various conditions may be summarized as follows (modified from Schaffer):

> Severe dyspnoea immediately after birth—suggesting a major malformation
>
> Violent respiratory efforts with no air entry—laryngeal atresia, choanal atresia
>
> Early dyspnoea—respiratory distress syndrome, diaphragmatic hernia, massive aspiration, intrauterine pneumonia, group B streptococcus infection
>
> Sudden dyspnoea after a few hours—pneumothorax, atelectasis
>
> Overfull chest—lobar emphysema, pneumothorax, diaphragmatic hernia
>
> Asymmetrical chest—diaphragmatic hernia, diaphragmatic paralysis, pneumothorax air-containing cyst, lobar emphysema, pulmonary agenesis
>
> Hyperresonance—lobar emphysema, pneumothorax, air-containing cyst
>
> Local dullness—atelectasis, tumour, diaphragmatic hernia
>
> Wheeze—vascular ring, unilobular emphysema, mediastinal tumour
>
> Stridor—see p. 146
>
> Grunting respirations—respiratory distress syndrome, pneumonia

References

Ablow RC. *et al.* A comparison of early onset group B streptococcal neonatal infection and the respiratory distress syndrome of the newborn. *N Engl J Med* 1976; **294**: 65.

Brice JEH, Walker CHM. Changing pattern of respiratory distress in newborn. *Lancet* 1977; **2**: 752.

Chernick V, Reed MH. Pneumothorax and chylothorax in the neonatal period. *J Pediatr* 1970; **76**: 624.

Edwards DK, Dyer WM, Northway WH. Twelve years experience with bronchopulmonary dysplasia. *Pediatrics* 1977; **59**: 839.

Halliday HL, McClure G, McCreid M. Transient tachypnoea of the newborn: two distinct entities? *Arch Dis Child* 1981; **56**: 322.

Hull D, Barnes ND. Children with small chests. *Arch Dis Child* 1972; **47**: 12.

Lees MH. Heart failure in the newborn infant. *J Pediatr* 1969; **75**: 139.

Mallard RE, Stilwell CA. *et al.* Mediastinal pancreatic pseudocyst in infancy. *J Pediatr* 1977; **91**: 445.

Milner AD. Bronchopulmonary dysplasia. *Arch Dis Child* 1980; **55**: 661.

Oberklaid F, Danks DM. *et al.* Asphyxiating thoracic dysplasia: clinical, radiological and pathological information on 10 patients. *Arch Dis Child* 1977; **52**: 758.

Schaffer AJ, Avery ME. *Disease in the newborn.* Philadelphia: Saunders, 1977.

Stocker JT, Madewell JE. Persistent interstitial pulmonary emphysema: another complication of the respiratory distress syndrome. *Pediatrics* 1977; **59**: 847.

Sweet EM. Causes of delayed respiratory distress in infancy *Proc Roy Soc Med* 1977; **70**: 863.

Williams H, Phelan PD. *Respiratory illness in children* Oxford: Blackwell Scientific Publications, 1975.

Wilson MG, Mikity VG. A new form of respiratory disease in premature infants. *Am J Dis Child* 1960; **99**: 489.

Dyspnoea after the newborn period

Acute dyspnoea may be due to the following:

    Foreign body causing acute stridor (p. 140, 151)

    Pulmonary—pneumonia, asthma, asthmatic bronchitis, pneumothorax, mediastinal or obstructive emphysema, massive collapse of the lung, large air-containing cyst, pleural effusion

    Inhalation of smoke in a fire

    Cardiovascular—heart failure, paroxysmal tachycardia, congenital heart disease

Of these conditions, those most likely to be missed are foreign body, pneumothorax or paroxysmal tachycardia.

Mellins & Park (1975) wrote that acute dyspnoea after exposure to smoke in a burning building is due to thermal burn of the airway, irritant gases (e.g. from burning plastic) or carbon monoxide.

Chronic dyspnoea may be due to the following conditions:

    Chest conditions

    Asthma

Unrecognised pleural effusion
Obstructive emphysema
Large air-containing cyst, pneumothorax, massive collapse
of lung
Pulmonary agenesis
Pulmonary fibrosis, cor pulmonale, aspergillosis, farmer's
lung
Diaphragmatic hernia
Mediastinal mass
Alpha$_1$-antitrypsin deficiency (rare) (p. 123)
Heart conditions
Congenital or rheumatic disease
Adherent pericardium (rare)
Severe chest deformity
Anaemia
Obesity
Abdominal conditions—ascites
Renal failure
Overventilation
Drugs

It is one of the characteristic features of *asthma* that exertion causes wheezing and therefore dyspnoea. In severe cases the emphysema causes dyspnoea on exertion.

One has seen children referred for breathlessness with an un-recognised *pleural effusion or large diaphragmatic hernia.*

Obstructive emphysema, due to a tuberculous lymph node, a foreign body or other lesion, may cause symptoms and signs similar to those of a large air-containing cyst or pneumothorax.

Serious progressive dyspnoea results from *pulmonary fibrosis* and especially from *fibrocystic disease of the pancreas.* A common end result of fibrocystic disease of the pancreas or extensive bronchiectasis is cor pulmonale with severe dyspnoea. Another cause of severe extensive fibrosis is the *Hamman-Rich syndrome* (Pepys 1965). The Hamman-Rich syndrome consists of diffuse interstitial fibrosis of the lungs, and leads to progressive dyspnoea and death. The diagnosis is made by X-ray. *Pulmonary aspergillosis* should be considered when there is asthma and eosinophilia. *Farmer's lung* is associated with the in-halation of the dust of mouldy vegetable material: it is associated with malaise, fever, febrile aches and pains and dyspnoea. Various *drugs* may cause respiratory symptoms (Davies 1976). *Pulmonary eosino-philia* may be due to aspirin, imipramine, isoniazid, methotrexate, nitrofurantoin, P.A.S., penicillin, streptomycin and sulphonamides; there are fever, cough and dyspnoea, with lung changes on X-ray. Pulmonary fibrosis can be a side effect of cyclophosphamide, methotrexate, nitrofurantoin, sulphonamides or vincristine.

Alpha $_1$-antitrypsin deficiency may present as unexplained dyspnoea.

Congenital heart disease, and especially pulmonary stenosis (with or without Fallot's tetralogy), is perhaps the commonest cause of chronic breathlessness in the first three or four years. After the age of four or five, severe rheumatic carditis is a possible but unusual cause of chronic breathlessness. An *adherent pericardium* is another possible cause.

Severe chest deformity, such as that associated with kyphosis or severe degrees of funnel chest, may cause breathlessness. Severe anaemia or ascites are other causes. Renal failure with uraemia or hypertension are possibilities.

Dyspnoea may be a side effect of *rifampicin.*

References

Davies P Drug induced respiratory disease. *Medicine U.K.* 1976; **22:** 1074.

Mellins RP, Park S. Respiratory complications of smoke inhalation in victims of fire. *J Pediatr* 1975; **87:** 1.

Pepys J. Hypersensitivity reactions in relation to pulmonary fibrosis. *La Medicina del Lavoro* 1965; **56:** 451 (in English).

Williams H, Phelan PD. *Respiratory illness in children.* Oxford: Blackwell Scientific Publications, 1975.

Overventilation

The causes of overventilation are mainly the following:

      Psychogenic overventilation
      Hypernatraemic dehydration
      Diabetic acidosis
      Uraemia
      Reye's syndrome (p. 73)
      Drugs

Enzer & Walker (1967) reviewed 44 cases of overventilation in children, Joorabchi (1977) 50 cases, and Herman and colleagues (1981) described 38 aged eight or younger: those figures suggest that the condition is not rare. The symptoms were episodes of chest pains (tightness or stabbing pains), head, limb or abdominal pains, breathlessness, paraesthesiae, vertigo, dry mouth, choking feelings, palpitations, weakness, blurred vision or confusion. The overbreathing was not always a prominent feature. These symptoms all occurred in attacks or episodes, and were rarely persistent: they were thought to portend psychological symptoms in later years.

Overventilation is an important symptom in hypernatraemic dehydration of infancy. Diabetic acidosis is readily diagnosed by the smell of acetone in the breath and the finding of glycosuria.

Drugs which cause overventilation are acetazolamide, aminophylline, salicylates or sulthiame. Salicylate poisoning is of especial importance because of its frequency, and it must be considered however firmly the parents deny that their child could have had access to drugs—because they do not wish to admit to carelessness, or because they deny that they have deliberately given the drugs (as a form of non-accidental injury), or because they genuinely do not believe that the child could have taken the drug (Pickering 1964). It is important that delayed action preparations of salicylates may cause toxic symptoms later than other preparations (and a correspondingly later rise in the level of serum salicylates).

References

Enzer NB, Walker PA. Hyperventilation syndrome in childhood. A review of 44 cases. *J Pediatr* 1967; **70:** 521.

Herman SP, Stickler GB, Lucas AR. Hyperventilation syndrome in children and adolescents: long term follow up. *Pediatrics* 1981; **67:** 183.

Joorabchi B. Expressions of the hyperventilation syndrome in childhood. *Clin Pediatr* 1977; **16:** 1110.

Mowat AD. Encephalopathy and fatty degeneration of viscera. Reye's syndrome. *Arch Dis Child* 1973; **48:** 411.

Pickering D. Salicylate poisoning. The diagnosis when its possibility is denied by the parents. *Acta Paediatr Uppsala* 1964; **53:** 501.

Cough

The important conditions to consider include the following:

Acute respiratory infections
Asthma and asthmatic bronchitis
Measles
Whooping cough
Foreign body in the bronchus

Chronic cough

Habit or tic
Smoking by child or parents
Postnasal discharge: sequel of a cold
Adenoids
Antrum infection
Whooping cough
Bronchitis and asthma
Fibrocystic disease of the pancreas
Partial collapse of the lung
Small tracheo-oesophageal fistual (in an infant)
Overspill from chalasia of the oesophagus or hiatus hernia

Other congenital anomalies—laryngeal stenosis, cyst, angioma, neurofibroma: tracheomalacia or tracheal obstruction: bronchomalacia: sequestrated lobe.

Bronchiectasis
Foreign body in the bronchus
Tuberculosis
Allergy
Congenital heart disease
Immunological deficiency (rare)
Psittacosis (rare)
Deficiency of alpha $_1$-antitrypsin (rare)

Acute cough

Cough is an unusual symptom in the newborn. There is usually little or no cough when the infant has the respiratory distress syndrome, atelectasis or pneumonia. Cough with choking in a newborn infant

139

may be due to *tracheo-oesophageal* fistual or oesophageal atresia, congenital laryngeal cleft or perforation of the pharynx. After the newborn period, the principal cause of cough is a respiratory infection. A cold may be followed by laryngitis, tracheitis, bronchitis or pneumonia. In some children, colds are followed by asthmatic bronchitis (p. 144), or true asthma. An acute attack of cough with dyspnoea may be due to the *accidental inhalation of talc*. Most recurrent coughs are due to asthma or viral bronchitis.

A pneumonia-like illness may occur in *sickle-cell disease.*

An acute respiratory infection may be the initial sign of *measles*. In this case Koplik's spots will be found in the buccal mucosa.

Cough is *not* due to teething, and one cannot visualize any mechanism whereby the eruption of a tooth through the periosteum would cause a cough. Neither is cough due to an 'enlarged thymus'.

An infant may have no immunity from *whooping cough* at birth and may therefore develop the infection from the newborn period onwards. A cough which is worse at night and which repeatedly makes the child sick should be regarded as whooping cough until proved otherwise. The typical whoop may not be heard if the attack is a mild one or has been modified by partial immunization or in a young infant, and it may not be heard for a week or two after the onset. The whoop is not specific for pertussis. A whoop may be heard in another condition in which there is inspissated mucus which the child has difficulty in bringing up—namely *fibrocystic disease of the pancreas.* Whooping cough may be caused not only by Bordetella pertussis, parapertussis or bronchiseptica, but by several viruses.

In an uncomplicated whooping cough there are no abnormal physical signs on auscultation, but there will be signs if there is a serious complication such as bronchopneumonia or extensive collapse of the lung. The cough may persist for several weeks, or improve after a time and then apparently relapse.

The possibility of a *foreign body* in the bronchus must be remembered, especially when there is a history of the sudden onset of a severe cough. This may be followed by a silent period and then by fever, cough and signs of infection in the obstructed lung. There may be a history of a child eating peanuts or playing with small objects which could have been inhaled. Whenever a child presents with a cough of sudden onset, without a preceding cold, or with collapse of a lobe of the lung, the diagnosis of a foreign body in the bronchus must be eliminated. In a review of 230 cases of inhaled foreign bodies, 46·5 per cent of all foreign bodies were nuts (Pyman, 1971). There is often a delay in the onset of signs and symptoms. One hundred and six of the children presented only with a wheeze without a cough. In a review of 200 cases, Blazer and colleagues (1980) reported that in 24 children there was no history of inhaling a foreign body. They emphasized that dyspnoea and stridor suggested laryngeal obstruction, while cough, wheezing or recurrent intractable pneumonia suggested a foreign body in the bronchus. The removal of one foreign body did not exclude the presence of another one. Peanuts frequently fragment.

Chronic cough

A cough may be due to a *habit, tic, or attention-seeking device* (Williams 1975). It may be to *school phobia*(Weinberg 1980). Cough may be due to smoking: and recent studies have shown that children whose parents smoke suffer more bronchitis than children of non-smokers (Colley *et al* 1974): the children of mothers who smoked during pregnancy suffer more from bronchitis in their first year than do children of mothers who did not smoke in pregnancy (Harlap & Davies 1974, Rantakillio 1978). A common and troublesome cause of cough in a young child is a *postnasal* discharge. The usual cause of this is a cold. The child has little or no cough when up and about, but coughs continually as soon as he lies down. The postnasal discharge can be seen on inspection of the throat. The child may be helped by sleeping in the prone position.

Adenoids or antrum infection may cause a cough by the same mechanism. If a child has a postnasal obstruction and a postnasal discharge, with nasal speech and recurrent otitis media, the likely diagnosis is adenoids. If the ear, nose and throat specialist is unable to obtain a good view of the postnasal space in a young child, a lateral X-ray of the nasopharynx will show a pad of adenoids. If there is a chronic antrum infection there will almost certainly be a history of a persistent purulent nasal discharge between colds, or of a postnasal discharge with cough. There may be an allergic basis. The diagnosis is confirmed by an X-ray.

Fibrocystic disease of the pancreas is discussed on p. 9. The diagnosis should be suspected when a child has a persistent or frequently recurring cough with pulmonary infections, except when the cough immediately follows an ordinary cold.

When a child has an acute respiratory infection and fails to make the usual recovery, feeling tired and off colour, the cough continuing, one suspects a *partial collapse of the lung.* There may be râles localized to one base, or even bronchovesicular breathing. Sometimes there are no definite signs, but the X-ray establishes the diagnosis.

When a young infant regularly coughs during feeds, the possibility of a *small tracheo-oesophageal fistula* has to be considered.

When an infant regurgitates a great deal and also has a cough, the cause could be *chalasia of the oesophagus or hiatus hernia,* with inhalation of some regurgitated material into the lung (Christie *et al.* 1978). The presenting symptom may be a chronic cough, and it may be only on direct questioning that the history of regurgitation is obtained.

Other congenital malformations include bronchomalacia, a sequestrated lobe or a bronchial cyst (Mellis 1979), laryngeal or tracheal stenosis, cysts or angioma.

Bronchiectasis is now rarely seen in British children. It would be suspected if the child had a persistent productive cough with clubbing of the fingers and an antrum infection. It may be due to an underlying congenital abnormality, or it may result from an adenovirus infection following measles. The diagnosis would be established by an X-ray and bronchogram.

A chronic cough following an acute onset could be due to a *foreign body* in the bronchus.

Pulmonary tuberculosis is an unusual cause of cough in England. In primary tuberculosis without complicating bronchial obstruction, a cough is not to be expected. The diagnosis would be made on the history of exposure to an adult with tuberculosis (even if the tuberculosis were said to be healed), a positive tuberculin test, and X-ray of the chest, and if necessary the culture of tubercle bacilli from stomach washings.

Cough may be due to *congenital heart disease,* especially when there is a left to right shunt, or to *deficiency of alpha $_1$-antitrypsin* (p. 123), in which there are dyspnoea, chronic antrum and respiratory infections, emphysema and sometimes hepatosplenomegaly with jaundice.

Psittacosis is usually a respiratory illness or atypical pneumonia diagnosed by serological means.

Frequent severe respiratory illnesses should arouse the suspicion of an *immunological deficiency,* especially if there were also recurrent skin infections.

References

Blazer S, Naveh Y, Friedman A. Foreign body in the airway. A review of 200 cases. *Am J Dis Child 1980;* **134:** 68.

Christie DL, O'Grady LR, Mack D.V. Incompetent lower oesophageal sphincter and gastro-oesophageal reflux in recurrent acute pulmonary disease in infancy and childhood. *J Pediatr* 1978; **93:** 23.

Colley JRC, Holland WW, Corkhill RT. Influence of passive smoking and parental phlegm on pneumonia and bronchitis in early childhood. *Lancet* 1974; **2:** 1031.

Harlap S, Davies AM. Smoking in pregnancy and child development. *Br Med J* 1974; **2:** 610.

Mellis CM. Evaluation and treatment of chronic cough in children. *Pediatr Clin North Am* 1979; **26:** 553.

Pyman C. Inhaled foreign bodies in childhood. A review of 230 cases. *Med J Austr* 1971; **1:** 62.

Rantakillio P. Relationship of maternal smoking to morbidity and mortality of the child up to the age of five. *Acta Paediatr Scand* 1978; **67:** 621.

Weinberg EG. Honking: psychogenic cough tic in children. *S African Med J* 1980; **57:** 198.

Williams HE. Chronic and recurrent cough. *Austr Paediatr J* 1975; **11:** 1.

Wheezing

Wheezing is an extremely common symptom in childhood. It is commonly confused with 'ruttling'. Ruttling, heard readily without a stethoscope, is due to air bubbling through fluid in the trachea or bronchi: on auscultation coarse râles are heard. A wheeze is due to narrowing of the airway with the production of high-pitched rhonchi. In the young infant the wheeze is due largely to oedema of the mucosa: it is only later when the smooth muscle has developed further, that bronchial spasm develops. A wheeze usually signifies asthma or asthmatic bronchitis (Phelan 1972). In the first year, however, persistent 'ruttling' is commonly an early sign of asthma.

Later high-pitched râles develop and gradually, as the infant gets older, there is a transition to rhonchi. In an older child a ruttle is usually a sign of bronchitis but not asthma.

The causes of wheezing are as follows:

>Asthma and asthmatic bronchitis
>>Allergy to cow's milk protein
>>Effect of drugs and food additives
>Acute bronchiolitis
>Foreign body
>Inhalation of hot smoke (e.g. in a burning house)
>Alpha₁-antitrypsin deficiency (p. 123)
>Tracheal or bronchial obstruction
>>Tracheomalacia, bronchomalacia
>>Tracheal web, stenosis, tumour
>>Tuberculosis and mediastinal lymph nodes
>>Vascular ring or congenital heart disease
>>Mediastinal cyst
>>Fibrocystic disease of the pancreas

Asthmatic bronchitis and asthma. In the first five or perhaps six years many children respond to a cold by wheezing (Horn *et al* 1979, Henderson *et al* 1979, Cohen 1979). One to three days after the development of a typical cold the child becomes dyspnoeic and wheezes, and the attack is clinically indistinguishable from asthma. If the child only wheezes after a cold, and never at any other time, and did not have eczema, the prognosis is good, in that by the age of five or six he is likely to cease to respond to colds by wheezing, while others are likely to continue to have attacks for many years. Asthmatic bronchitis may be a mild form of asthma, the cold having lowered the threshold for the allergen to cause bronchial oedema or spasm (*British Medical Journal* 1973, Delaney 1976) but Butler & Peckham (1978) claimed that the aetiological factors are different in the two conditions: in asthmatic bronchitis there is a lower incidence of eczema and hay fever in the family, but a higher incidence of migraine and sore throats in the child. It is significant that between attacks of asthmatic bronchitis there is no wheezing on exertion: the usual cause is the rhinovirus or respiratory syncytial virue. After the age of five the common organism concerned is the mycoplasma.

Asthma is often precipitated by infections, almost always viral, but the child also wheezes at times when he has not just had a cold, and particularly on exertion or on psychological stress. (The three components of asthma are allergy, infection and psychological stress.) The findings of eosinophilia in the sputum or nasal secretions helps to establish a diagnosis if in doubt.

Asthma may be caused by cow's milk protein, aspirin or pro-pranolol or other beta-blockers. Children who react to aspirin in this way often have nasal polypi; half an hour or so after taking the aspirin there may be a profuse nasal discharge, vomiting, diarrhoea and wheezing; similar reactions can occur with indomethacin or ibu-profen. It is not strictly an allergic reaction. Tartrazine, used as a colouring agent in over 100 drugs, as well as in orange squash and other foodstuffs, may cause wheezing, urticaria or angioneurotic oedema. Wheezing may also be caused by poisoning by organophosphorus insecticides, by disodium cromoglycate (if not given in the form which is combined with isoprenaline) and by cephalosporins, erythromycin, ethionamide, lipiodol, neomycin, penicillin, rifampicin, streptomycin, tetracycline, vaccines and Vitamin K. Parental smoking is a factor in the aetiology of wheezing in children.

Bronchiolitis is predominantly a disease of infancy, especially of the first six months. It is usually due to the respiratory syncytial virus. The attack begins insidiously with a cold and in a day or two the child becomes severely dyspnoeic and often cyanosed. Respirations are rapid, and there are subcostal retraction, inspiratory crepitations and an expiratory wheeze. The inspiratory phase is short and expiration is prolonged. The temperature is usually but not always raised. Bronchiolitis in infancy is commonly followed by asthma in later years.

Wheezing may rarely be caused by a *foreign body* in the bronchus.

Wheezing is sometimes a symptom of *congenital heart disease* or of a vascular ring. *Tuberculosis* is an important cause of wheezing in countries in which the infection is prevalent. *Fibrocystic disease of the pancreas* may be associated with wheezing, and one can readily forget its possibility in a child with obvious asthma.

Wheezing has to be distinguished from laryngotracheobronchitis, (p. 151) and the distinction can be difficult.

Richards (1974) listed 94 conditions which should be distinguished from asthma: but in my opinion the list above is sufficient for practical purposes.

References

British Medical Journal. Analgesics and asthma. Leading Article. 1973; **3:** 419.

Butler N, Peckham C. A national study of asthma in childhood. *J Epidemiol and Comm Health.* 1978; **32:** 79.

Cohen SR. Asthmatic Bronchitis. *Children's Hospital Nat Med Center* 1979; **35:** 353.

Delaney JC. Response of patients with asthma and aspirin idiosyncracy to tartrazine. *Practitioner.* 1976; **217:** 285.

Henderson FW *et al*. The etiologic and epidemiologic spectrum of bronchiolitis in pediatric practice. *J Pediatr* 1979; **95:** 183.

Horn MEC, Reed SE, Taylor P. Role of viruses and bacteria in acute wheezy bronchitis in childhood. *Arch Dis Child* 1979; **54:** 587.

Phelan PD. Wheezing in childhood. *Austr Paediatr J* 1972; **8:** 167.

Richards W. *Differential diagnosis of childhood asthma*. Chicago: Year Book Publishers, 1974; **4:** 3.

Stridor

In order to consider the diagnosis it is necessary to distinguish chronic stridor from acute stridor. The commonest cause of chronic stridor in the very young infant is congenital laryngeal stridor. The usual cause of acute stridor in infants and young children is an acute infection, especially laryngotracheitis.

Chronic stridor

The following are the main causes to consider:
> Supraglottic causes
>> Congenital laryngeal stridor
>> Micrognathia. Macroglossia
>> Mongolism
>> Gross enlargement of tonsils and adenoids
>> Lingual, aryepiglottic, thyroglossic or laryngeal cysts (rare)
>> Supraglottic webs (rare)

Glottic causes

Laryngeal web, polyp, papilloma

Vocal cord paralysis

Hydrocephalus

Foreign body

Dislocation of the cricothyroid or cricoarytenoid articulations

Infraglottic causes

Congenital subglottic stenosis

Tracheal obstruction or stenosis, haemangioma, neurofibroma

Tracheomalacia

Vascular ring

Mediastinal tumour or thyroid (rare)

Foreign body

Acute stridor

Epiglottitis, laryngotracheobronchitis (croup)

Trauma, corrosive, smoke

Foreign body

Diphtheria, rabies

Retropharyngeal abscess

Laryngeal spasm, tetany

Angioneurotic oedema, allergy to cow's milk protein

Chronic stridor

The elucidation of the cause of stridor dating from birth can be a matter of considerable difficulty. It may also be a matter of great importance to the child, for some of the conditions which cause stridor may be fatal without surgical intervention. The danger of superadded upper respiratory tract infections may be considerable, and it is said by some that these children are more than usually prone to them. Hence it is important that the correct diagnosis should be known (Pracy 1965, Quinn-Bogard & Potsic 1977).

The first and most important observation which must be made in order to consider the diagnosis consists of the timing of the stridor. Stridor may be inspiratory or expiratory or both. *A purely inspiratory stridor is less likely to be of serious import than one which is both inspiratory and expiratory, or expiratory alone. On the other hand a purely inspiratory stridor can be due to a serious condition demanding surgical treatment.* It follows that whatever the timing of the stridor, an accurate diagnosis should be established. Stridor which is entirely inspiratory is usually of supraglottic origin. Stridor which is entirely expiratory usually arises from the trachea (Holinger & Johnston, 1955).

The second observation which must be made is the estimation of the quality of the voice. If there is hoarseness or weakness of the voice, the glottis must be involved. Severe stridor with dyspnoea, but with a normal voice, may be subglottic or tracheal in origin. Stridor with a muffled cry is likely to arise from pharyngeal or supraglottic lesions. Inspiratory stridor with an abnormal cry may be due to weakness of the recurrent laryngeal nerve or to a laryngeal web or cyst.

A high-pitched stridor persisting through inspiration or expiration usually implies severe glottic obstruction. A low-pitched stridor usually points to a supraglottic cause.

Stridor with a deep barking or 'brassy' cough usually points to tracheal obstruction.

Hyperextension of the neck sometimes occurs when there is a *retropharyngeal abscess or obstruction of the trachea.*

Feeding difficulties sometimes occur with *congenital laryngeal stridor* or a *vascular ring.*

Supraglottic causes

Supraglottic causes of stridor consist mainly of *congenital laryngeal stridor* (laryngomalacia) which is by far the commonest cause of stridor in infants. Other causes include *laryngeal or lingual cysts, supraglottic webs and micrognathia.*

Congenital laryngeal stridor, the commonest cause of stridor in infants, has also been termed laryngomalacia. It dates from shortly after birth, usually after the first week or two, and tends to get worse until the age of three to six months. There is usually no change between the age of six and 12 months, and thereafter it usually decreases, disappearing by 18 to 24 months; but according to Smith & Cooper (1981) the symptoms may last considerably longer, with persistent inspiratory obstruction in later childhood.

It is important to accept that so-called benign congenital laryngeal stridor, though usually benign, is not always so. It is due to abnormal collapse of the supraglottic tissues in inspiration. The epiglottis may be elongated or abnormally curved, or the arytenoepiglottic folds may be redundant. The stridor is mainly inspiratory, but is sometimes partly expiratory (Phelan *et al.* 1971). Phonation is normal. The voice and cry are unaffected. It is commonly intermittent, disappearing during rest and sleep, but much increased by crying. It is reduced in the prone position and increased when the child lies supine. The stridor is of all degrees of severity, from the most trivial to the severe. In any but the trivial degrees, there is indrawing of the lower part of the chest on inspiration.

For reasons which are not altogether clear, infants with congenital laryngeal stridor are more liable to have feeding difficulties, such as regurgitation and choking on feeding, than are normal children. I have seen alarming cyanotic attacks in children with this condition.

All patients with inspiratory stridor should be investigated: 90 per cent will prove to have congenital laryngeal stridor, but others will have a variety of conditions including haemangioma, neurofibroma or cleft larynx.

The micrognathic infant is liable to have inspiratory stridor, probably because the hypoplasia of the mandible permits the base of the tongue to displace the epiglottis. *Macroglossia,* seen in cretinism and other conditions, may have the same effect.

Stridor is fairly common in *mongols*. The reason is not altogether clear. In some cases seen by me lateral X-rays of the airway have demonstrated an unexplained thickening of the tissues between the vertebral column and the airway.

When a child is older, stridor, worse when he is lying on his back, may be due to *gross enlargement of the tonsils and adenoids*. The obstruction may be so severe that it leads to cor pulmonale.

Inspiratory stridor may be due to a *thyroglossal cyst* at the base of the tongue, a *lingual thyroid* or a *dermoid cyst*. The epiglottis is pressed backwards and downwards, with the result that there is inspiratory stridor, a muffled cry and usually feeding difficulties. The condition can be demonstrated in a lateral X-ray of the airway.

A *supraglottic web* causes a marked inspiratory stridor, a subdued cry, hoarseness and chest retraction. *Laryngeal cysts* have the same effect.

Glottic lesions

Glottic lesions include in particular *laryngeal webs, polypi* and *papillomata*. A laryngeal web is a serious condition and the treatment is difficult. The stridor is usually but not always inspiratory only, and occurs in all positions when the child is awake or asleep. The voice is usually abnormal and the cry weak. The diagnosis is made by laryngoscopy.

Paralysis of both vocal cords is seen in children with *hydrocephalus*, as a result of stretching of the vagi in the Arnold-Chiari malformation; though hydrocephalic infants are liable to have stridor due to other but undetermined causes. When there is *bilateral cord paralysis*, there is marked inspiratory stridor, chest retraction, a hoarse voice, weak cry and choking in feeds.

Stridor may be due to *birth injury*, involving damage to the recurrent laryngeal nerve, or dislocation of the cricothyroid or cricoarytenoid articulations. In either case there is hoarseness. In either case the diagnosis would be made by laryngoscopy.

Subglottic causes

Stridor due to subglottic causes is more likely to develop only after a few weeks. *Subglottic causes* of stridor include in particular the *haemangioma* and *congenital subglottic stenosis*. The haemangioma causes serious obstruction, inspiratory or expiratory stridor or both, sometimes with a croupy or brassy cough. In only three of six cases described by Williams and his colleagues (1969) was there a subcutaneous naevus to provide a clue to the diagnosis. I have seen a case due to a *subglottic neurofibroma*. The stridor is usually inspiratory, and the cry is usually weak, but not hoarse. The diagnosis should be made by laryngoscopy and lateral X-ray.

Tracheal causes of stridor include *tracheal stenosis, tracheal cysts* and *tracheomalacia*—a condition in which there is an absence of or a defect in the cartilaginous rings. The stridor is commonly expiratory only.

An important cause of stridor is the *vascular ring*, in which there is a double aorta or an abnormally placed subclavian artery. The presenting symptom is either regurgitation of food with cyanotic attacks or stridor. The stridor is commonly both inspiratory and expiratory, but may be either inspiratory only or expiratory only. It usually occurs in sleep as well as at rest. There is often opisthotonos, and flexion of the neck increases the dyspnoea. The cough in infants with a vascular ring is sometimes brassy or bitonal. There is unlikely to be a cardiac murmur on auscultation, or other abnormal physical signs on examination of the heart and chest. The diagnosis is made in the first place by exclusion of other cause by laryngoscopy and lateral X-ray of the airway. Some regard bronchoscopy as dangerous to these infants.

A *mediastinal tumour*, such as a thyroid, is a rare cause of stridor, but an enlarged thymus is not a cause.

Acute stridor

Stridor of acute origin, commonly termed *croup*, is usually due to laryngeal involvement in an acute upper respiratory tract infection by the respiratory syncytial or other viruses. There are other causes such as epiglottitis, laryngeal oedema resulting from traumatic instrumentation, or a foreign body. Diphtheria is now hardly seen in the United Kingdom. Rabies is a possible cause.

Laryngotracheobronchitis may be associated with a stridor which is inspiratory at first, and then both inspiratory and expiratory. There is indrawing of the lower part of the chest in severe cases. The air entry may be so poor that the stridor is not loud. It is by no means easy to distinguish it from asthma or acute bronchiolitis. If there is hoarseness the diagnosis of laryngotracheobronchitis is easy, but usually this is absent. One has to listen carefully in order to decide whether there is laryngitis or not. When one needs to know the diagnosis in order to decide the best line of treatment in a severely dyspnoeic child, laryngoscopy may be performed. The stridor of laryngitis could be confused with the noisy ruttle of an infant with *bronchitis* and tracheal exudate. According to Zach and colleagues (1981) recurrent croup is frequently allergic in origin.

Acute epiglottitis may be due to haemophilus influenzae, staphylococcus or pneumococcus. It occurs predominantly in the two to seven year old age group (Addy *et al* 1972). Mild respiratory symptoms change to a severe illness, often with dysphagia and the child rapidly becomes ill, with increasing dyspnoea from obstruction of the airway, There is a low-pitched stertor, with a louder and lower-pitched coarse expiratory rattle, resembling a snore, but the increasing dyspnoea may be more prominent than increasing stridor. There may be large cervical lymph nodes, dysphagia, drooling and an intensely sore throat. The inspiratory stridor decreases as respiratory efforts increase. The voice is muffled rather than hoarse, and is therefore unlike the voice of the child with virus laryngitis. On laryngoscopy, a swollen inflamed epiglottis will be seen, but *the procedure is dangerous and should only be performed by the expert with equipment for tracheostomy at hand, for it may precipitate acute obstruction.* It is vital to distinguish acute epiglottitis from croup, but it can be difficult. In both there is inspiratory stridor. But the rapid deterioration with pallor, high fever, dyspnoea, dysphagia and salivation, favour the diagnosis of epiglottitis, whereas hoarseness and a barking cough suggest croup.

A mild *laryngitis* following a cold does not usually occasion anxiety; but if it occurs in a child already suffering from congenital laryngeal stridor, there are serious grounds for anxiety, because the child may rapidly develop severe dyspnoea.

Laryngeal oedema may follow *trauma* resulting from instrumentation. It may follow a *corrosive substance* or *inhalation of smoke* from a burning house.

Laryngeal spasm may occur in *tetany,* due to hypocalcaemia resulting from rickets, coeliac disease, hypoparathyroidism or renal failure. There is a high-pitched inspiratory stridor, lasting usually for a few minutes or for a single inspiration.

A *retropharyngeal abscess or retropharyngeal lymphadenitis* commonly follow an upper respiratory tract infection. There is dysphagia, head retraction, mouth breathing and fever. The abscess may be seen in the back of the throat or even felt by the finger.

References

Addy MG, Ellis PDM, Turk DC. Haemophilus epiglottitis. *Br Med J* 1972; **1:** 140.

Holinger PH, Johnston KC. The infant with respiratory stridor. *Pediatr Clin North Am* 1955; 403.

Ludman H. Hoarseness and stridor. *Br Med J* 1981; **1:** 715

Phelan PD, Gillam GL, Stocks JG, Williams HE. The clinical and physiological manifestation of the infantile larynx. *Austr Paediatr J* 1971; **7:** 135.

Pracy R. Stridor in children. *Proc Roy Soc Med* 1965; **58:** 267.

Quinn-Bogard AL, Potsic WP. Stridor in the first year of life. *Clin Pediatr* 1977; **16:** 913.

Smith GJ, Cooper DM. Laryngomalacia and inspiratory obstruction in later childhood. *Arch Dis Child* 1981; **56:** 345.

Williams HE, Phelan P, *et al.* Haemangiomas of larynx in infants. *Austr Paediatr J* 1969; **5:** 149.

Zach M, Erben A, Olinsky A. Croup, recurrent croup, allergy and airways hyper-reactivity. *Arch Dis Child* 1981; **56:** 336.

Hoarseness

Hoarseness in a newborn baby is likely to be due to trauma or to a congenital defect.

Hoarseness may result from prolonged crying and in the case of an older child from prolonged shouting, as in games.

The causes may be enumerated as follows:

> Newborn
>> Trauma to the larynx by forceps or intubation
>> Damage to the recurrent laryngeal nerve or vagus by traction
>
> Newborn or later
>> Laryngeal web, cyst, tumour, stenosis
>> Weakness of laryngeal muscles
>>> Myasthenia gravis, Werdnig-Hoffmann syndrome
>> Cretinism
>> Infection: laryngitis, especially viral, but also diphtheria, tuberculosis, syphilis
>> Foreign body
>> Mediastinal pressure by lymph nodes or tumour
>> Rickets (laryngismus stridulus)
>> Cerebral tumour
>> Farbers disease (chronic granulomatous disease)

The history is essential in order to determine the duration of the hoarseness.

Generalized muscular weakness is most likely to be due to the Werdnig-Hoffmann syndrome; but in the newborn baby it could be due to myasthenia gravis if the mother has it.

Rickets used to be a cause of attacks of hoarseness under the name laryngismus stridulus. Vincristine may cause a recurrent laryngeal nerve palsy.

Other causes of hoarseness, except that due to acute laryngitis, are diagnosed on laryngoscopy.

Chest pain

The most frequent cause of chest pain is stitch; this is a cramplike pain on one side of the lower part of the chest or upper part of the abdomen, occurring on exertion after a meal. It is probably due to strain on the peritoneal ligaments attached to the diaphragm. Chest pain is otherwise unusual in children. It is often psychogenic, and may be a featue of overventilation (p. 137).

Pleural friction or pleural pain causes a knife-like stabbing pain, worse on respiration or coughing. The usual causes are pneumonia or epidemic pleurodynia (Bornholm disease).

An unrecognized *injury*, such as a fractured rib, should be considered as a possible cause.

Pericarditis may result from rheumatic fever, tuberculosis, pyogenic organisms or a virus infection (e.g. coxsackie virus).

True *angina* is a rare symptom, occurring in association with rheumatic disease of the aortic valves.

Acute shoulder-tip pain should suggest pleural friction or referred pain from a *ruptured spleen*.

Chest pain may be found on accurate examination to be a rib pain. This could be due to osteitis or a tumour. Tietze's syndrome (chondro-osteopathia costalis tuberosa) consists of pain in a rib due to a walnut-sized firm painful swelling in the anterior cartilaginous area of the ribs.

References

Abrahams A. Stitch. *Practitioner* 1959; **182:** 771.
Driscoll DJ, Glicklich LB, Gallen WJ. Chest pains in children. *Pediatrics* 1976; **57:** 648.
Weidemann H-R. Tietze's syndrome. *Helvet Pediat Acta* 1972; **27:** 25.

Haemoptysis

Haemoptysis is an unusual symptom in childhood. It is most unlikely to be due to tuberculosis. It hardly ever occurs in primary tuberculosis, but could occur in the adult type in the older child. It is unusual in lobar pneumonia.

It is frequently not easy to decide whether blood has been brought up from the chest or from the stomach (e.g. after a nose bleed).

Haemoptysis should be distinguished from red colouration of the sputum by *rifampicin*.

Causes of haemoptysis include:

Blood diseases
Whooping cough
Trauma (e.g. a broken rib)
Foreign body in the lung
Bronchiectasis (probably the commonest cause)
Fibrocystic disease of the pancreas
Heart failure
Uraemia
Bronchial polyp
Pulmonary abscess
Malignant disease
Pulmonary haemosiderosis (rare)
Enterogenous cyst (rare)
In the tropics—paragonimiasis

The importance of blood diseases when there is unexplained haemoptysis must be emphasized. The possibility of a foreign body must never be forgotten in many obscure pulmonary conditions in children.

An enterogenous cyst is a rare cause of haemoptysis. There may be a cough and dysphagia.

Symptoms related to the nose

EPISTAXIS

Epistaxis is rare in infancy but common in later childhood. Causes:
> Nose picking, trauma
> Foreign body (usually causing a unilateral sanguino-purulent
>> discharge)
> Veins in nasal septum: telangiectasia
> Acute coryza: measles and other virus infections
> Whooping cough
> Diphtheria, syphilis (both serosanguineous discharge)
> Tuberculosis
> Blood diseases
> Tumours and polyp
> Terminal renal or hepatic disease
> Atrophic rhinitis

HALITOSIS

It is difficult to find a discussion of the causation of halitosis. Most of the textbooks seen by me, whether general or devoted to otorhinolaryngology, make no mention of the symptom. One book devoted a page to the condition, but listed such unlikely causes as mercury, iodide, bismuth or lead poisoning, cirrhosis of the liver, nasal allergy, 'chronic gastrointestinal disorders', spicy foods, and a low fat diet. Carious teeth are mentioned as a cause, but I doubt whether this is common. The symptom may arise from food debris between teeth which are too close together for proper cleaning to be possible.

Halitosis in an ill child may be due to acute tonsillitis, diphtheria or Vincent's infection, bronchiectasis or lung abscess.

Severe halitosis of recent origin, especially if there is a nasal discharge, would suggest a *foreign body in the nose*. The symptom may be due to the child eating onions or garlic.

Atrophic rhinitis occurs predominantly at puberty or later, but may begin in early infancy. It is almost confined to girls. It often starts after

156

some illness. In adolescence it is worse at the time of menstruation. The nasal cavity becomes greatly widened and the halitosis is extreme. It is often a familial feature.

I consider that it is true to say that if atrophic rhinitis and a foreign body in the nose have been eliminated, it is unlikely that one will find the cause of halitosis in an otherwise well child.

References

Drug and Therapeutics Bulletin. Halitosis. 1969; **7:** 79.

Taylor M, Young A. Histopathological and histochemical studies on atrophic rhinitis. *J Laryngol and Otol* 1961; **75:** 574.

NASAL OBSTRUCTION AND MOUTH BREATHING

Not all mouth breathing is due to nasal obstruction. It may be due to habit: it is a common feature of mental subnormality.

Nasal obstruction (really postnasal obstruction) in the newborn may be due to choanal atresia unilateral or bilateral, or to reserpine taken by the mother. In older children it may be due to allergy, nasal polypi, deflection of the septum or a foreign body.

Nasal congestion may be caused by phenothiazines.

COLDS AND NASAL DISCHARGE

The term *snuffles* refers to a clear mucoid nasal discharge sometimes seen in babies in their first few weeks. The reason for the discharge is uncertain. On microscopy there is no excess of polymorphonuclear white cells, such as would suggest infection, and no excess of eosinophils, such as would suggest allergy. The baby blows bubbles as he breathes and may have some difficulty in feeding because of blockage of the nose. It cures itself in a few weeks.

Even the youngest babies may develop a *cold,* and the common complication of otitis media may result. Other complications include laryngitis and bronchopneumonia. The baby may have difficulty in breathing because he does not open his mouth when the nose is obstructed. He may fail to gain weight or actually lose weight. Some babies develop diarrhoea when they have a cold. An ordinary respiratory infection in an infant or young child may lead to alarming dehydration requiring hospital treatment. Two of the most troublesome complications of colds in the young child are a postnasal discharge and asthmatic bronchitis (p. 144). Culture of the nasal discharge in a baby suffering from a cold may yield haemolytic streptococci.

Allergic rhinitis is commonly mistaken for colds in older infants and children. The persistence of the nasal discharge, the fact that it is clear and mucoid, together with the continual sneezing, should alert one to the true diagnosis. If the child is never free from a nasal discharge, if the child's nose is running when there has been no history of exposure to infection, or if there is a strong family history of allergy, one would suspect allergic rhinitis rather than coryza. The presence of a wheeze would suggest allergy, though the difficulty of a cold precipitating an attack of asthmatic bronchitis is discussed on p. 144. When in doubt, a nasal smear should be examined under the microscope: if the proportion of eosinophils exceeds three per cent, one would think that allergic rhinitis is likely.

When a child has a purulent nasal discharge between colds, he must be presumed to have an *antrum infection*. This can occur even in infancy. In making this diagnosis, which is confirmed by direct inspection of the nares and by X-ray of the antrum, one must distinguish the usual muco-purulent discharge at the end of a cold. An antrum infection is a fairly common complication of fibrocystic disease of the pancreas.

A unilateral purulent nasal discharge suggests a *foreign body* in the nose. When diphtheria was prevalent, a serosanguineous unilateral discharge suggested *nasal diphtheria*. A unilateral nasal discharge, with obstruction of the airway on the same side of the nose, may be due to *unilateral choanal atresia*.

A persistent nasal discharge is an early feature of Riley's syndrome (p. 41). Certain *drugs* may be responsible for nasal congestion or discharge. They include reserpine given to the mother during pregnancy, causing nasal congestion in the neonate, and in later childhood iodides, propranolol or trimeprazine.

SNEEZING

Sneezing is a normal frequent event in young babies in the first two or three months. A mother is likely to think that her baby has a cold.

Older children and adults commonly sneeze at the beginning of a *cold*.

Hay fever or other *allergic rhinitis* is by far the most likely cause of frequent sneezing.

A *foreign body* in the nose may possibly cause persistent sneezing.

Intractable sneezing is rare. The subject has been reviewed by Co (1979). Possible causes include in particular temporal lobe epilepsy or a sequel of ecephalitis.

References

Co S. Intractable sneezing. Case report and literature review. *Arch Neurol* 1979; **36:** 111.

Symptoms related to the mouth and throat

STOMATITIS AND GINGIVITIS

Stomatitis may be due to the following causes:
>   Infection
>   Allergy
>   Avitaminosis
>   The effect of drugs
>   The Stevens-Johnson syndrome

Infections causing stomatitis include herpes, Vincent's infection, the coxsackie virus and monilia. It is probable that other viruses may cause it. Herpes causes vesicles on the tongue without necrosis, while

Vincent's organisms cause necrotic ulcers on the tips of papillae and involve the gums and tonsils. Vincent's infection is confirmed by the smell and by a smear for spirochaetes. Coxsackie stomatitis closely resembles herpes, with small vesicles on the tongue and mucous membranes, but with more tendency to lymph node involvement. Hand, foot and mouth disease is usually due to coxsackie virus: there are vesicles on the tongue, hands and feet—and occasionally on the knees. It clears spontaneously. Thrush infection resembles curds of milk on the tongue and buccal mucosa, but the white patches cannot be removed by a swab. *Allergic aphthae* are indistinguishable from those of herpes.

Stomatitis may be caused by *avitaminosis,* especially ariboflavinosis and other deficiencies of the vitamin B complex, particularly in children on synthetic diets without adequate vitamin supplements. Scurvy may cause it.

Drugs which cause stomatitis include actinomycin D, cotrimoxazole, ethosuximide, gold, griseofulvin, lincomycin, meprobamate, 6-mercaptopurine, methotrexate, niclosamide, phenothiazines, tetracycline, troxidone and vincristine.

The Stevens-Johnson syndrome is more common in boys than girls. There is a severe stomatitis, with erythematous papular lesions, vesicles or bullae beginning on the extensor surfaces of the extremities, and spreading to the trunk, neck and scalp. There may be lesions on the conjunctivae, nares, anorectal junction, vulva and urethral meatus. The child is poorly and feverish, and may have kidney, joint or pulmonary involvement. The cause is not always known, but it may be due to anticonvulsants (barbiturates, carbamazepine, troxidone), aspirin, clindamycin, penicillin, quinine, rifampicin, or sulphonamides. Another cause is a mycoplasma infection.

Gingivitis may be due to the following causes:

    Infection
    Drugs
    Avitaminoses
    Dental caries
    Overcrowding of teeth
    Malocclusion
    Mouth breathing
    Familial type

The gums in gingivitis are red, boggy and bleed easily.

Infections which cause it include herpes, Vincent's infection, thrush, streptococcal and staphylococcal organisms. Herpes zoster or herpes simplex may cause vesicles on the gums with underlying inflammation. Vincent's infection and thrush have already been described. Staphylococcal gingivitis is usually found in children severely ill from another cause. The gums in streptococcal gingivitis are characteristically bright red and the child is ill.

The principal *drug* which causes gingivitis is phenytoin. The gingivitis subsides within three to six months of discontinuing the drug. The severity of the gingivitis is related to the blood level of the drug. (Kapur *et al* 1973).

Avitaminoses, especially scurvy, cause the gums to be inflamed and liable to bleed.

Dental decay and stagnating food between teeth, often associated with overcrowding of teeth, are causes. *Malocclusion* is often related.

Mouth breathing causes gingivitis, but the gum trouble is more often due to a short upper lip providing an inadequate lip seal and so drying the gingivae.

There is a rare familial type of *fibromatous gingivitis,* resembling the gingivitis caused by phenytoin.

Cacogeusia (unpleasant taste in the mouth).

This may be due to acetazolamide, ergotamine, heavy metals or tricyclic antidepressants.

ENLARGEMENT OF THE TONGUE

Enlargement of the tongue is found in:
>   Hypothyroidism
>   Angioma, lymphangioma
>   Rare diseases—Beckwith's syndrome, mucopolysaccharidoses, glycogenoses, amyloidosis, gangliosidosis, mannosidosis, Sandhoff's disease.

Beckwith's syndrome includes a large tongue, umbilical hernia, hypoglycaemia, congenital asymmetry, microcephaly, visceromegaly, facial naevus, renal dysplasia and a risk of Wilms' tumour.

References

Cohen MM, Gorlin RJ, *et al*. The Beckwith-Wiedemann syndrome. *Am J Dis Child* 1971; **122**: 515.

Kapur RN, Girgis S, *et al*. Diphenylhydantoin induced gingival hyperplasia: its relationship to dose and serum level. *Dev Med Child Neurol* 1973; **15**: 483.

DRYNESS IN THE MOUTH

This may be due to *dehydration*, or a variety of *drugs*, including amitriptyline, amphetamine, anticholinergic drugs, antihistamines, atropine, carbamazepine, clonidine, codeine, cyclopentolate, diazepam, fenfluramine, haloperidol, hyoscine, imipramine, isoniazid, methylphenidate, niclosamide, the phenothiazine group and vitamin A overdosage. Cyclopentolate drops may cause an acute toxic psychosis, a dry mouth, ataxia and delirium. It is a feature of amphetamine addicts. Dryness of the mouth may occasionally be due to mouth breathing, or to overventilation (p. 000).

Reference

Adcock EW. Cyclopentolate toxicity in pediatric patients. *J Pediatr* 1971; **79**: 127.

SALIVATION AND DROOLING

Conditions to consider include the following:
>   Normal variation
>   Eruption of a tooth
>   Mental subnormality
>   Abnormality of nervous control—cerebral palsy, motor neurone disease, facial palsy, polyneuritis, myasthenia, myotonia dystrophica
>   Stomatitis
>   Drugs and poisons
>   Oesophageal atresia
>   Perforation of the pharynx
>   Familial dysautonomia (rare)

Most normal babies lack control of the flow of saliva until 12 months or so of age. Some seem to have more saliva than others, and their clothes are constantly wet. Salivation is a common sign of teething. Drooling sometimes continues for years without apparent reason. It is sometimes associated with mouth breathing. Mentally defective children, being late in all aspects of development, except occasionally sitting and walking, are late in controlling the saliva, and this may be one of the troublesome features of mental deficiency from the mother's point of view. Children with cerebral palsy, especially of the athetoid type, are particularly liable to 'drool' for several years, partly, perhaps, because of incoordination of the tongue and lips.

It seems likely that drooling is more often due to failure to swallow or retain saliva than to excessive salivation (Smith & Goode, 1970). This difficulty may be due to a variety of conditions such as cerebral palsy, facial palsy, myasthenia, myotonia dystrophica, or stricture of the oesophagus.

Drooling may be associated with excessive salivation caused by stomatitis, iodides or mercury poisoning. Salivation is a feature of poisoning by organophosphorus insecticides, thallium, fungi, or the anticholinesterase eye drops phospholine iodide. Nitrazepam and clonazepam used in the treatment of epilepsy may cause excessive salivation and lachrymation. Other drugs causing salivation include chlordiazepoxide, dicylomine, ethionamide, and haloperidol. Salivation may be a feature in the newborn baby whose mother is a heroin addict.

Salviation is feature of oesophageal atresia or perforation of the pharynx (p. 65).

Reference

Smith RA, Goode RL. Sialorrhoea. *N Engl J Med* 1970; **283**: 917.

TRISMUS

Trismus is an unusual symptom in children. Probably the commonest causes are mumps, antiemetic drugs or trauma. It must be distinguished from a bony abnormality consisting of partial ankylosis or more commonly hypoplasia of the temporomandibular joint. A rare bony abnormality is myositis ossificans progressiva.

The following conditions may cause trismus:

Mumps

Dental abscess: pericoronitis—around an incompletely erupted tooth

Peritonsillar abscess

Otitis media

Osteitis

Tetanus

Serum sickness (effusion into the joint)

Rheumatoid arthritis

Costen's syndrome (see p. 187)

Epilepsy

Hysteria

Trauma, including dislocation

Drugs

Rare

myotonia atrophica

tumours

rabies

These are mostly self-explanatory. Perhaps the most important cause to eliminate is a dental abscess or inflammation around an unerupted tooth. *Drugs* which may cause trismus include particularly metoclopramide and the tranquillizing group, strychnine in an overdose, and antihistamines.

THE TEETH

Delayed dentition is common in normal children. There are wide variations in the age at which the first tooth appears. Some babies are born with a tooth or teeth, while others may not cut the first tooth until after the first birthday.

The following are causes of abnormal delay in dentition and of teeth being missing:

Supernumerary teeth, particularly upper central and lateral incisors, impeding the eruption of the permanent ones.

Overlong retention of deciduous teeth, for unknown reasons.

Crowding of the jaw—as a result of the teeth being unduly large or the jaw being unduly small. These are often familial features.

Cretinism.

Premature loss of deciduous teeth. This may be due to decay or rarely to hypophosphatasia (in which there may be rickets, with a low plasma phosphatase).

Missing teeth, apart from the usual loss of teeth, may be due to *ectodermal dysplasia.* There may be missing upper lateral incisors, lower third molars or premolars. The condition affects predominantly the permanent teeth and is familial. There are likely to be other signs of the disease—a dry skin, sparse hair and abnormal nails.

There is a rare form of *familial anodontia.*

Yellow staining of the teeth is usually due to tetracycline (taken by the mother in pregnancy, or by the child): it may also be due to neonatal hyperbilirubinaemia.

TOOTH GRINDING

Tooth grinding in sleep may occur in a normal child, but tooth grinding in a child who is awake is usually an indication of mental subnormality.

It is said to be an occasional side effect of fenfluramine.

SNORING

The usual cause of loud snoring is adenoids.

The mechanism was discussed by Birch (1969): when the child is supine, and especially when mouth-breathing, the tongue falls back so that the soft tissue of the mouth and throat approximate, and vibrations in the posterior pillars of the fauces, and to a lesser extent in the soft palate, with inspiration, cause the characteristic noise.

Reference

Birch CA. Snoring. *Practitioner* 1969; **203:** 383.

SORE THROAT

Infectious mononucleosis may cause pharyngitis or tonsillitis with exudate or membrane. Petechiae on the palate are said to be a common feature. It is not possible on inspection to distinguish a streptococcal tonsillitis due to viruses. Vincent's infection may be suspected by the expert on account of the characteristic smell.

Diphtheria may be strongly suspected because of the membrane (which must be distinguished from the closely resembling membrane following tonsillectomy), but the diagnosis has to be confirmed in the laboratory. The possibility of agranulocytosis and other blood diseases has to be remembered.

Soreness of the throat often precedes by minutes other features of hay fever.

DIFFICULTY IN SUCKING AND SWALLOWING

The diagnosis of the cause of sucking and swallowing problems in infancy is liable to be a matter of great difficulty. I have reviewed the subject fully elsewhere (1969). I suggested the following classification:

1   Gross congenital anatomical defects
        Palate—cleft
        Tongue—macroglossia, cysts, tumours
        Retronasal space—choanal atresia
        Mandible—micrognathia
        Temporomandibular joint—ankylosis, hypoplasia
        Pharynx—cyst, diverticulum
        Oesophagus—atresia, fistula, stenosis, web
        Thorax—vascular ring
        Laryngeal cleft
2   Neuromuscular defects
        Rumination, tongue thrusting
        Delayed maturation—normal variation, prematurity, mental
            subnormality
        Cerebral palsy
        Cranial nerve nuclei or tracts
        Bulbar or suprabulbar palsy
        Congenital laryngeal stridor

Muscular dystrophy
Hypotonias
Rare
  Myotonia dystrophica
  Myasthenia gravis
  Möbius syndrome (congenital facial diplegia)
  Cornelia de Lange syndrome
  Riley's syndrome
  Prader-Willi syndrome
3 Acute infections
  Stomatitis
  Oesophagitis
  Poliomyelitis
  Diphtheria
  Tetanus
  Botulism, rabies
4 Effect of drugs.

Space will not permit a full discussion of all these numerous conditions, and I propose to mention a few only. Even an expert is liable to find the establishment of the diagnosis a matter of considerable complexity.

For the most part the group consisting of gross congenital anatomical defects is not difficult to diagnose.

A submucous cleft may be missed. Pointers to it include a bifid uvula, or a palpable V-shaped notch at the midline posterior border of the hard palate, replacing the normally palpable posterior nasal spine. Sometimes there is a transluscent membrane replacing the median raphe, with a short palate. There is likely to be nasal speech and nasal regurgitation of fluid.

Swallowing difficulties are common in *micrognathia,* whether or not it is associated with a cleft palate (Pierre Robin syndrome). The receding chin fails to support the tongue in its normal forward position, impinges against the posterior wall of the pharynx, obstructing respiration and causing feeding difficulties and cyanotic attacks.

Obstructive lesions in the *oesophagus* may be suggested by the story that the child can swallow liquids but not solids.

The *vascular ring* is discussed on pp. 134, 150. An abnormally placed subclavian artery ('dysphagia lusoria', the game of nature), frequently causes no symptoms, but in some it causes difficulty in swallowing.

Choanal atresia is discussed on pp. 129, 158.

A congenital laryngeal cleft causes feeding difficulties with stridor and choking, and closely simulates a tracheo-oesophageal fistula.

The differential diagnosis of the large group of neuromuscular defects is much more difficult. In many, delayed maturation of the swallowing mechanism is the principal difficulty. This occurs in mentally subnormal children, with or without cerebral palsy, and may occur for no apparent reason—and is thus usually termed 'birth injury'—but with no firm evidence of it. It is normal for the very small preterm infant to have difficulty in sucking and swallowing, and therefore the mentally subnormal child, being late in all aspects of development, may have the same difficulties as that of the preterm baby. There is incoordination of the relevant muscles—that of the palate and pharynx in particular. The normal infant displays the tongue-thrusting reflex if solid material is placed on his tongue in the early weeks, but loses this response as he matures, and so is able to take solids by six or seven months: but the mentally subnormal child is later in losing this response, and in addition is late in learning to chew.

It is not known why some infants have delayed development of the bulbar centres necessary for the swallowing mechanism. In some there is transient palatal pharyngeal or cricothyroid incoordination or defective tongue movements. Some apply the term suprabulbar paresis for this condition. These difficulties may last only a few weeks or months, followed by full recovery. They are almost always found in children with Riley's syndrome of familial dysautonomia (p. 41) and in the Prader–Willi syndrome (p. 20): they occur in the Cornelia de Lange syndrome, in children with severe hypotonia, and in the Möbius syndrome (congenital facial diplegia) and the similar condition of myotonia dystrophica. The child with cerebral palsy, in addition to the commonly associated mental subnormality, has stiffness and incoordination of the muscles concerned with swallowing. In some of these children there are other cranial nerve palsies.

It is not clear why many children with *congenital laryngeal stridor* have swallowing difficulties.

Infections which may cause swallowing difficulties include stomatitis and oesophagitis—viral or monilial, diphtheria (causing polyneuritis) and poliomyelitis (bulbar palsy). Swallowing difficulties are commonly seen in *tetanus, botulism* and *rabies.* Johnson *et al.* (1979), studying 10 cases of *infant botulism,* found that early symptoms were constipation and weakness, followed by difficulty in sucking and swallowing, lethargy, ptosis and weakness of facial and extraocular muscles.

Drugs which may cause dysphagia include haloperidol, metoclopramide and clonazepam. Maternal heroin addiction or phenothiazines taken in late pregnancy may be a cause.

The exact diagnosis can be difficult. The first stage is to observe the facial and limb movements and to examine the cranial nerves for signs of spasticity or weakness. One watches the child take a drink of water, and offers the baby a finger to suck in order that one can determine whether he is able to suck. The tongue is examined for wasting and fasciculation, as in anterior horn cell lesions. The movements of the palate are observed for signs of bulbar palsy, and the configuration of the palate for signs of a submucous cleft. Other signs of cerebral palsy and mental subnormality are looked for.

Special investigations necessary include laryngoscopy, oesophagoscopy, cinéradiography and a lateral X-ray of the neck for delineation of the airway and soft tissue masses.

References

Illingworth RS. Sucking and swallowing difficulties in infancy. Diagnostic problems of dysphagia. *Arch Dis Child* 1969; **44:** 655.

Johnson RO, Clay SA, Arnon SS. Infant botulism, diagnosis and management. *Am J Dis Child* 1979; **133:** 586.

Symptoms related to the eye

BLURRING OF VISION: AMBLYOPIA

When a child who has previously had normal vision complains of blurring of vision, careful examination and investigation are essential.

Unless it is recent, blurring of vision may be due to an *error of refraction*.

Blurring of vision may be a premonitory symptom of *migraine*, or an emotional disturbance, including *overventilation* or *malingering*. These diagnoses are dangerous and should only be made after exclusion of organic disease. No symptoms should be said to be merely psychological without positive evidence of psychological disturbance after organic disease has been excluded.

The symptoms may be due to exudate on the surface of the cornea.

Drugs which cause amblyopia include acetazolamide, antiepileptic drugs, antihistamines, barbiturates, chloramphenicol, chloroquine, ergotamine, ethambutol, gentamicin, haloperidol, ibuprofen, indomethacin, isoniazid, kanamycin, meprobamate, nalidixic acid, PAS, phenothiazines, piperazine, sulphonamides, tetracycline and tricyclic antidepressants. *Solvent sniffing* may be a cause.

DETERIORATION AND
LOSS OF VISION

Significant deterioration and gradual loss of vision in childhood is rare. It may be due to papilloedema, optic neuritis, optic atrophy, iridocyclotis, glaucoma, cataract, retinitis pigmentosa, demyelinating disease of the nervous system or drugs.

Papilloedema may be due to an intracranial space-occupying lesion, hypertension, meningoencephalitis, hydrocephalus, degenerative diseases of the nervous system or drugs (notably corticosteroids, imipramine, nalidixic acid, tetracycline or vitamin A excess).

BLINDNESS

It is easy to make the mistake of thinking that a baby is blind, because he shows no interest in his surroundings, when his lack of interest is due to mental subnormality: as he matures it becomes clear that he can see. The optic disc of normal babies is pale, and one can readily and wrongly diagnose optic atrophy. The most important indication of a visual defect in a baby is a roving nystagmus.

The following conditions carry a risk that a child will have a visual defect:

> Rubella, cytomegalovirus, toxoplasmosis, very rarely chicken-pox, in early pregnancy
>
> Prematurity and retinopathy of prematurity
>
> Mental subnormality, cerebral palsy, hydrocephalus, craniostenosis
>
> Fixed strabismus
>
> Delayed treatment of a squint (suppression of squinting eye)
>
> Rare metabolic diseases—cystinosis, Lowe's syndrome (eye and kidney abnormality)
>
> Marfan's disease (arachnodactyly and dislocated lens)
>
> Rheumatoid arthritis (causing iridocyclitis or cataracts)
>
> Drugs taken in pregnancy (e.g. antimitotic drugs, chloroquine, phenothiazine, quinine, radioactive iodine, thalidomide and warfarin)

The preterm baby, especially if a very low birth weight, is at risk of the retinopathy of prematurity: this causes blindness if fully developed, or in less severe cases myopia and strabismus (Phelps 1981).

Optic neuritis may be due to neuromyelitis optica or multiple sclerosis, or drugs (barbiturates, chloramphenicol, clioquinol, ethambutol, ibuprofen, indomethacin, isoniazid, PAS, streptomycin or sulphonamides). Optic atrophy may be caused by chloramphenicol, diodoquin, isoniazid of PAS, but the more usual cause is long-lasting papilloedema.

Sudden loss of vision was discussed by Duffner & Cohen (1978) and by Barnet and colleagues (1970). Very short-lasting loss ov vision may be the beginning of an attack of migraine. The following are other causes of loss of vision:

> Retrobulbar neuritis and papilloedema: intracranial space-occupying lesions, Schilder's disease
>
> Hypertension or uraemia
>
> Retinal artery occlusion
>
> Trauma
>
> Acute anoxia—shock, cardiac arrest, carbon monoxide, cardiac surgery, vertebral angiography

Drugs—arsenic, chloramphenicol, isoniazid, methanol, penicillamine, quinine, streptomycin, thallium, solent sniffing

Infections— ophthalmia neonatorum, toxoplasmosis, toxocara:

Tropics—trachoma, keratomalacia, onchocerciasis, toxoplasmosis.

The mentally subnormal infant is more likely than others to have an associated visual defect, including optic atrophy.

For suppression of vision in one eye with a squint, see p. 175.

CATARACT

The following are causes of cataracts in childhood:

Congenital
Rubella syndrome
Mongolism
Trauma
Drugs, especially corticosteroids
Rheumatoid arthritis
Diabetes mellitus
Rare
  Head-banging
  Myotonia congenita
  Galactokinase deficiency
  Hypoparathyroidism and tetany
  Mucopolysaccharidoses
  Niemann-Pick syndrome
  Rothmund-Thomson syndrome
  Abetalipoproteinaemia
  Congenital ichthyosis
  Craniofacial dysostosis
  Incontinentia pigmenti
  Ectodermal dysplasia
  Hypophosphatasia
  Fabry's disease
  Homocystinuria
  Fanconi's syndrome

Lowe's syndrome
Punctate epiphyseal dysplasia
Alport's syndrome (deafness)
Marfan's syndrome

An opacity due to toxocara can resemble that due to retinoblastoma in infancy.

Apart from the *genetic forms* of cataract, the common congenital form is that due to the *rubella syndrome:* but in the rubella syndrome the cataract may develop after birth, during the first year. The virus has been isolated from a surgically removed cataract as late as 2 years after birth.

About 10 per cent of *mongols* develop cataracts, usually after the first ten years or so, but sometimes earlier.

About 10 per cent of children on continuous *corticosteroid* therapy for a year or more develop a cataract. Such prolonged therapy is sometimes (unwisely) used for *rheumatoid arthritis*, which may itself cause iridocyclitis and a lens opacity. *Diabetes mellitus* only rarely causes a cataract in childhood.

It is said that prolonged *head-banging* may cause a cataract to develop after a few years (Spalter *et al.* 1970).

Galactokinase deficiency is a recently described condition. The incidence is said to be 1 in 50,000 births. There is galactose in the urine, indicated by the clinitest, and a cataract; there is no hepatomegaly or jaundice, and no mental subnormality. There is a high blood galactose (Sidbury 1974).

Various *drugs*, other than corticosteroids, may cause lens opacities: they include antimitotic drugs, carbamazepine, chlorambucil, chloroquine, indomethacin and the phenothiazines. Isoniazid may cause *keratitis* (Macfane 1973).

References

Barnet AB, Manson J, Wilner E. Acute cerebral blindness in children. *Neurology* 1970; **20:** 1147.

Duffner PK, Cohen ME. Sudden bilateral blindness in children. *Clin Pediatr* 1978; **17:** 705.

MacFane PA. The adverse effect of some drugs on the eye. *Prescriber's journal* 1973; **13:** 68.

Phelps DL. Vision loss due to retinopathy of prematurity. *Lancet* 1981; **1:** 606.

Sidbury JB. Some inferences from galactokinase deficiency. *Pediatrics* 1974; **53**: 309.

Spalter HF, Bemporad JR, Sours JA. Cataracts following head-banging in children. *Arch Ophthalmol* 1970; **83**: 182.

NYSTAGMUS

By far the commonest cause of nystagmus in an infant is a defect of vision such as optic atrophy. This should be considered to be the diagnosis until proved otherwise. The nystagmus in such children is often but not always of the roving type, unlike the finer nystagmus due to other conditions.

The following are the main causes of nystagmus:
> Sitting in a moving vehicle
> Defect of vision and astigmatism
> Congenital nystagmus
> Antiepileptic and other drugs
> Albinism
> Spasmus nutans
> Friedreich's ataxia, ataxia telangiectasia (p. 193)
> Cerebellar ataxia, tumour, abscess
>> Infratentorial tumours
> Hypothyroidism

Various *drugs* can cause nystagmus. They include in particular anticonvulsants, colistin, diphenoxylate and salicylates.

Nystagmus is almost invariable in *albinism,* and it is usual in *spasmus nutans* (p. 207) in which there are jerky head movements, ceasing when the child concentrates on an object.

Nystagmus may be caused by various diseases of the cerebellum or cerebellar tracts—such as Friedreich's ataxia, congenital ataxia, tumour or abscess. *Friedreich's ataxia* is a progressive hereditary disease, whose features include ataxia, absence of the knee jerks, plantar extensor responses and pes cavus with rombergism. Schulman & Crawford (1969) described four cases of congenital nystagmus associated with hypothyroidism.

Reference

Schulman JD, Crawford JD. Congenital nystagmus and hypothyroidism. *N Engl J Med* 1969; **280**: 708.

DIPLOPIA

Diplopia is caused usually by muscle imbalance, especially convergent paralysis. It may be caused by neurological disease, encephalitis, iridocyclitis, cataract or dislocation of the lens. It occurs in botulism.

A blow-out fracture of the orbit, with a 'black eye', may be followed in up to 4 or 5 days by diplopia.

A variety of *drugs* may cause diplopia: they include antihistamines, barbiturates, carbamazepine, chloroquine, chlorpropamide, diazepam, fenfluramine, imipramine, indomethacin, nalidixic acid, phenytoin, primidone, quinine, sulphonamides, vincristine and vitamin A excess.

Unilateral diplopia may be caused by a meibomian cyst on the eyelid; mucus or exudate alters the refraction of the eye and leads to blurring. Unilateral diplopia could also be caused by dislocation of the lens or by corneal lesions.

STRABISMUS

It is essential that a squint should be diagnosed shortly after the age of six months, because if left untreated the child will develop amblyopia as a result of suppressing the squinting eye. In the same way if a congenital cataract is not removed sufficiently early, the eye will remain blind: and a child with marked asymmetry of refraction or visual acuity may suppress vision in one eye.

It is normal for some degree of strabismus to occur before the age of six months, but a fixed squint at any age is always abnormal, so that the child should be referred to an ophthalmologist as soon as possible. A fixed squint is commonly found in cerebral palsy, microcephaly and hydrocephalus. The sudden development of a squint could be due to *ophthalmoplegic migraine* (Raymond and colleagues 1977): manifestations include third nerve palsy, headache and vomiting. Other causes include *trauma, cerebral tumour* or *haemorrhage, encephalitis, tuberculous meningitis, botulism, myasthenia, cavernous sinus thrombosis, cerebral vascular abnormalities, Guillain-Barré syndrome.* An important and treatable condition which causes a fixed squint in the first few weeks is the retinoblastoma.

Squints are due to imbalance of muscle, as a result of weakness or maldevelopment of the muscle or faulty innervation; to differences in the refraction of the two eyes; to hypermetropia or to a visual defect in one eye—such as that due to a corneal opacity or the retinopathy of prematurity (Phelps 1981). A squint is an unusual side effect of *nalidixic acid* and of *tricyclic antidepressants*.

When the squint is of the paralytic type (non-comitant), due to paralysis of muscle, the eyes are straight except when moved in the direction of the paralysed muscle, when diplopia occurs.

When the squint is concomitant (non-paralytic), as it usually is, all muscles move the eyes normally, but they do not work in conjunction. The two eyes are in the same relative position to each other whatever the direction of the gaze. There is no diplopia.

In young infants one can determine whether there is a squint by noting the position of the light reflex on each cornea when a torch is held in front of the child (Stanworth 1974). The reflex should be in the centre of the pupil or at a corresponding point on the two corneas.

In testing an older child, one covers one eye while with the other he looks at an auriscope light 13 to 15 inches in front of him. When the card is slowly moving away, the eyes should not move if the eyes are straight. When the fixating eye is covered the other eye should not move unless a squint is present. If there is a convergent squint, there will be a lateral movement: if there is a divergent squint, there will be a medial movement. The examiner watches the eye which is being uncovered. A false appearance of a convergent squint is caused by epicanthic folds: the examiner should pinch the nose in such a way that the folds disappear—when it will be easier to see whether there is or is not a squint.

References

Phelps DL. Vision loss due to retinopathy of prematurity. *Lancet* 1981; **1:** 606.
Raymond LA, Tew J, Fogelson MH. Ophthalmoplegic migraine of early onset.
    J Pediatr 1977; **90:** 1035.
Stanworth A. Squint in the first two years. *Medicine* (U.K.) 1974; **27:** 1614.

MYOPIA

The following are the known causes of myopia (Gardiner & James 1960):

> *Congenital and familial.* Myopia is commonly a familial feature. There may be other congenital conditions, such as colobomata or albinism
>
> *Maternal toxaemia or hypertension.* A history of these conditions is frequent when myopia is severe
>
> *Malnutrition* in utero. Prematurity and particularly dysmaturity are common precursors. *Retrolental fibroplasia* may result in myopia
>
> *Social.* Myopia is more common in the poor than in the well to do
>
> *Degenerative conditions* usually commence after the age of four. They may lead to retinal degeneration or detachment of the retina.
>
> *The effect of drugs (rare).* These include corticosteroids, tetracycline, sulphonamides and acetazolamide

Reference

Gardiner P, James G. Myopia. *Brit J Ophthalmol* 1960; **44**:172.

PHOTOPHOBIA

Photophobia may be due to hysteria. It is experienced by some children with migraine. Other causes include:

> Meningitis
> Foreign body in the eye
> Iridocyclitis, phlyctenular conjunctivitis
> Corneal ulcer
> Measles
> Albinism
> Drugs—atropine eye drops, ethosuximide, mercury, PAS, troxidone.
> Vitamin A deficiency
> Rare—congenital glaucoma
> > Acrodermatitis enteropathica

Cystinosis
Botulism
Retinitis pigmentosa

It is a troublesome symptom in phlyctenular conjunctivitis, which is usually due to tuberculosis; there are white or grey papules 1–2 mm in diameter on the cornea or bulbar conjunctiva, with injection of the surrounding sclera and profuse lachrymation.

It is sometimes an early symptom in *congenital glaucoma.*

LACHRYMATION AND EPIPHORA

The newborn baby does not usually shed tears when he cries, and often does not do so until he is 4 to 6 weeks old, unless there is injury to the eye. When he begins to shed tears, the eyes may water (epiphora) if the nasolachrymal duct has not completely opened: this opens spontaneously in almost all cases in a few weeks or months (Muller *et al* 1978). Other causes of lachrymation are as follows:

Maternal heroin addiction
Malposition of the punctum as a result of facial palsy, chronic
    blepharitis or trauma
Trauma: eyelash in the canaliculus
    Other foreign bodies
Pain in the eye (mainly injury or iridocyclitis)
Infection—conjunctivitis, including phlyctenular conjuncti-
    vitis due to tuberculosis
Measles
Bad smells
Eyestrain
Hay fever
Thyrotoxicosis
Drugs—arsenic, bromides, mercury, nitrazepam.

Conjunctivitis does not usually cause pain: if there is pain one should suspect that there is iritis.

Reference

Muller K, Burse H, Osmers F. Anatomy of the nasolacrymal duct in newborn:
    therapeutic considerations. *Eur J Pediatr* 1978; **129:** 83.

COLOUR VISION

Colour vision may be affected by ethambutol. White vision may result from troxidone: yellow vision from barbiturates, digoxin, streptomycin, sulphonamides or thiazide diuretics: blue or purple vision may be caused by nalidixic acid. Loss of colour vision may be a symptom in retinitis pigmentosa—as may night blindness.

PTOSIS

In *congenital ptosis* there is a defective development or absence of the levator palpebrae superioris or a defect in the superior rectus. It occurs in the *fetal alcohol syndrome.*
Rare causes include:

> *Horner's syndrome*—a disturbance of the cervical sympathetic chain, with unilateral miosis, apparent enophthalmos, ptosis, absence of facial sweating and heterochromia of the iris. It may occur in association with Klumpke's paralysis.
>
> *Myotonic dystrophy* (p. 189) and congenital facial diplegia (Möbius syndrome). In both there is an immobile face and open mouth
>
> *Myotubular myopathy*
>
> *Myasthenia gravis*
>
> *Dystrophic ophthalmoplegia.* This may start at any time from infancy to adult life, usually with ptosis as the first symptom. It is slowly progressive, and is confined to the levators of the eyelid and external ocular muscles. Later there is weakness of the lateral and vertical eye movements.
>
> *Marcus Gunn* phenomenon—ptosis until the mouth is opened, when the eyelid is simultaneously raised
>
> *Smith–Lemli–Opitz* syndrome
>
> *Tumours*—rhabdomyosarcoma, neuroblastoma
>
> *Abetalipoproteinaemia*
>
> *Encephalitis.* Wernicke's encephalopathy
>
> *Botulism*
>
> *Drugs*—sulthiame or vincristine

PROPTOSIS

Proptosis is an uncommon symptom (Vanselm 1980).

Rare causes are:

Thyrotoxicosis

Craniostenosis, craniofacial dyostosis

Tumours—neuroblastoma, angioma, rhabdomyosarcoma, retinoblastoma, teratoma, glioma, neurofibroma, osteoma, histiocytosis x.

Cysts or cystic swellings—dermoid, orbital encephalocele, anterior meningocele, mucocele of the paranasal sinus.

Orbital cellulitis, ethmoiditis.

Cavernous sinus thrombosis, arteriovenous aneurysm.

Haemorrhage—blood diseases, pertussis

Trauma—fractured base of skull

Fibrocystic disease of the pancreas (rare) (Strauss *et al* 1969)

In *orbital cellulitis* there is proptosis, limitation of eye globe movement, oedema of the conjunctiva and eyelids. It can readily be confused with *cavernous sinus thrombosis,* which is usually secondary to infection around the orbit, sinus or face. There are rigors and fever, and the child is ill. The signs tend to be more localized in orbital cellulitis. In cavernous sinus thrombosis the CSF may show raised protein and white cells: cranial nerves 3, 4, 5 and 6 may be involved.

References

Haynes RE, Cramblett HG. Acute ethmoiditis: its relationship to orbital cellulitis. *Am J Dis Child* 1967; **114:** 261.

Strauss RG, West PJ, Silverman FN. Unilateral proptosis in cystic fibrosis. *Pediatrics.* 1969; **43:** 297.

Vanselm JL. Proptosis in paediatrics. *S African Med J* 1980; **57:** 662.

Symptoms related to the ear

EAR PAIN AND EAR DISCHARGE

Pain

The usual cause of ear pain is *acute otitis media*. Other causes are as follows (Smyth 1978)

> The pinna—injury, boil, herpes
>
> External auditory meatus—boil, foreign body, herpes, otitis externa, injury
>
> Referred pain—from lower molar tooth, temporomandibular joint, throat, possibly cervical spine

Discharge

When a mother complains that her child's ear discharges she usually refers to wax. A purulent discharge is usually due to otitis media but it could be due to a foreign body or boil in the external auditory meatus, or to otitis externa. A clear watery discharge after a head injury suggests cerebrospinal fluid in association with a fracture of the skull.

Reference

Smyth GDL. *Diagnostic Ear, Nose and Throat.* London: Oxford University Press, 1978.

DEFECTIVE HEARING

A child may appear to be deaf because he does not listen—perhaps because he is engrossed in an interesting occupation, or because of indiscipline or bad manners. A mentally defective infant is likely to be slow to respond to sound and to be wrongly suspected of deafness.

A child with infantile autism may appear to be deaf because of lack of social responsiveness.

If a parent suspects deafness it is likely that her fears are well founded, and a full testing should be carried out by an expert.

It must be a standard practice to check the hearing of all children with delayed or defective speech.

Conditions liable to be associated with deafness include the following

Important congenital conditions
Genetic (familial) deafness
Prenatal—rubella, cytomegalovirus, syphilis, drugs—(quinine, streptomycin, kanamycin, gentamicin, neomycin, vancomycin, thalidomide)
Mental subnormality
Cerebral palsy
Cleft palate
Mongolism
Cretinism
Acquired conditions
Neonatal hyperbilirubinaemia
Extreme prematurity. Severe anoxia or acidosis at birth
Prolonged naso-tracheal intubation
Recurrent otitis media, glue ear, adenoids
Meningitis, measles, mumps, congenital syphilis
Trauma
Drugs
Rare congenital syndromes
Congenital nephritis. Alport's syndrome
Waardenburg's syndrome
Treacher–Collins syndrome
Klippel–Feil syndrome
Surcardiac syndrome (p. 221)
Leopard syndrome
Pendred's syndrome (deafness with goitre)
Hurler's syndrome
Albinism
Retinitis pigmentosa
Osteogenesis imperfecta, osteopetrosis
Acoustic neuroma

Before other factors are considered one should examine the ears with an auriscope in order to eliminate blockage of the meatus by wax.

About 30 per cent of children born by mothers who had *rubella* in the first three months of pregnancy will have some defect of hearing. It should be noted that this may be only partial or it may be confined to one ear, or it may develop in the early years after infancy. In making a diagnosis (which is essential for genetic counselling) one must not be misled by the absence of a history of rubella in pregnancy. In a survey of 354 cases Sheppard *et al.* (1977) found that 45 per cent of mothers of affected children gave a history of rubella: 13 per cent had an undiagnosed rash in pregnancy: 16 per cent gave a history of contact only: and 25 per cent were unaware of any contact and had been well throughout.

Cerebral palsy and mental subnormality are strongly associated with deafness. Some 20 to 25 per cent of all children with cerebral palsy have some degree of deafness. Children with athetosis are more likely to have a hearing defect than those with the spastic form of cerebral palsy.

Hyperbilirubinaemia in the newborn period, whether due to prematurity, haemolytic disease or other causes, predisposes to deafness. In the fully-developed case there are other signs of kernicterus such as athetosis. A history of severe jaundice in the newborn period should alert one to the possibility of deafness in later months and years.

There is some association between deafness and premature delivery or severe anoxia at birth. Galambos and Despland (1980) listed the main perinatal risk factors for deafness as follows: acidosis (in particular), but also anoxia, low Apgar score, number of days on assisted ventilation.

Most children with a *cleft palate* develop deafness.

Some infants with *hypothyroidism* have a hearing defect. Balkany *et al* 1979 found a significant hearing loss in two thirds of 103 *mongols*—a factor which would add to their mental handicap.

Meningitis and recurrent otitis are important causes of deafness. The danger that recurrent attacks of otitis may cause deafness, particularly if perforation of the drum is allowed to occur, is an important reason for the prompt treatment of otitis media. The development of deafness in association with a mass of adenoids is a strong indication for adenoidectomy. The so-called 'glue-ear' or serous otitis media may be a sequel of repeated and usually inadequately treated otitis media. Grommets themselves after a time may damage the ear drum and cause deafness (Fox 1980).

Congenital syphilis, now rare in Britain, is an important cause of deafness in some countries.

A variety of *drugs* cause deafness. Some of these may affect the child when given to the pregnant woman. The main ones are actinomycin, ampicillin, capreomycin, chloroquine, colistin, cotrimoxazole, dihydrostreptomycin, erythromycin lactobionate, ethacrynic acid, framycetin, frusemide, gentamicin, ibuprofen, indomethacin, kanamycin, medroxyprogesterone, neomycin, nortriptyline, propranolol, quinine, rifampicin, salicylates, streptomycin, tobramycin, vancomycin and vincristine

Of the many rare congenital syndromes (Arthur 1965) associated with deafness, Waardenburg's syndrome is probably the most common. It consists of a white forelock, heterochromia of iris and congenital deafness.

Conclusion

There are many possible causes of deafness and many factors which increase the likelihood of deafness. These 'risk' factors should alert one to the possibility of deafness. It must be remembered that the child born with defective hearing cannot know that he does not hear well. It is our responsibility to make the diagnosis. Every child with delayed or defective speech must have his hearing tested by an expert.

The method of clinical diagnosis has been described in detail in my book (Illingworth, 1980). Suitable test sounds are the crinkling of paper, a small hand bell, the sound PS or PHTH (for high tones) and OO (for low tones), on a level with the ear and 30–45 cm away, out of sight of the baby. In the first three months the baby may respond by a startle reflex, by blinking the eyes, by momentarily stopping sucking his dummy, by crying, or by quieting if he is already crying. Between three and four months he begins to respond by turning his head to sound.

References

Arthur LJH. Some hereditary syndromes that include deafness. *Dev Med Child Neurol* 1965; **7**: 3395.

Balkany TJ, Downs MP, *et al.* Hearing loss in Down's syndrome *Clin Pediatr* 1979; **18**: 116.

Fox AM. Grommets don't work. *Pediatrics* 1980; **65**: 1198.

Galambos R, Despland P. The auditory brain stem response evaluates risk factors for hearing loss in the newborn *Pediatr Res* 1980; **14**: 159

Illingworth RS. *Development of the infant and yound child, normal and abnormal.* 7th Edn. Edinburgh: Churchill Livingstone, 1980.
Sheppard S, Smithells RW, *et al.* National congenital rubella surveillance 1971–75. *Health Trends* 1977; **9**: 38.

TINNITUS

The complaint of buzzing in the ears (tinnitus) may be psychological.

Tinnitis may be caused by antihistamines, carbamazepine, quinine and salicylates.

The symptom may originate from an acoustic nerve tumour.

A rare cause is an intracranial arteriovenous communication. It is worth while looking for distended veins on the face and scalp, and auscultating the skull for a continuous bruit.

VERTIGO

Vertigo is such a subjective symptom that it is not easy to assess it in children (Eviatar & Eviatar 1977). The young child cannot describe what he feels; and the fact that he is experiencing vertigo may not be recognised. Vertigo commonly precedes a faint or fit, or occurs with a change of posture when he has been ill or is anaemic. It could be a *psychological symptom*, and may be due to *overventilation* (p. 137).

The causes of vertigo include:
    Benign paroxysmal vertigo
    Epidemic vertigo and vestibular neuronitis
    Epilepsy
    Hypoglycaemia
    Migraine (premonitory symptom)
    Drugs
    Rare
      Cerebellar lesions
      Cerebral tumours
      Labyrinthitis after mumps
      Sequela of meningitis or head injury
      Chronic otitis media

Ramsay Hunt syndrome—facial palsy with herpes of the
      external auditory canal
Occlusive disease of the vertebrobasilar vessels
Multiple sclerosis

Benign paroxysmal vertigo (Rabe 1974, Dunn & Snyder 1976) is a
mysterious but distressing condition, occurring mainly at about 1 to 3
years of age, in which there is a sudden attack of severe vertigo lasting
for seconds or minutes, sometimes with nystagmus or vomiting. The
child is terrified, becomes pale and sweats and may cling to the
parents, fall, stagger or cry for help. The attacks may recur after an
interval of days or months, ceasing after a period varying from four
months to four years. Vestibular caloric tests always show absence or
usually short duration of the normally induced nystagmus. The
C.S.F. and E.E.G. are normal. It was suggested by Koehler (1980) that it
can be a migraine equivalent. It is most important to distinguish these
attacks from epilepsy; the most important distinguishing feature is the
absence of loss of consciousness in benign paroxysmal vertigo.

Vertigo may be a manifestation of *epilepsy* especially when there is a
focus in the temporal lobe, and it may be a premonitory symptom of
migraine or a symptom of *hypoglycaemia.*

Epidemic vertigo and vestibular neuronitis (which may or may not be
the same thing) occurs usually a few days after an upper respiratory
tract infection, with recurring attacks of vertigo without neurological
signs, but with abnormal labyrinthine responses to hot and cold. They
are thought to be of virus origin and are infectious. The child recovers
in days or weeks.

Rare causes of vertigo include *cerebellar tumour and abscess,* and the
acoustic neuroma, labyrinthitis complicating mumps, a *posterior fossa
tumour, chronic otitis media* and the *Ramsay Hunt syndrome* (facial
palsy with herpes of the external auditory canal), *multiple sclerosis*
(Molteni 1977) and *occlusive disease of the vertebrobasilar vessels.* In the
later condition there are attacks of vertigo, followed later by the
development of ataxia. Diagnosis is by vertebral angiography.

Vertigo may be due to certain *drugs,* especially acetazolamide,
amitriptyline, antihistamines, carbamazepine, clonazepam, clonidine, colistin, diazepam, dicyclomine, ethosuximide, fenfluramine,
gentamicin, griseofulvin, imipramine, indomethacin, isoniazid,
kanamycin, meprobamate, minocycline, nalidixic acid, pethidine,
phenytoin, phenothiazines, phensuximide, piperazine, polymyxin,

primidone, salicylates, sulphonamides, thiazides, thiabendazole and trimethoprim. It may be due to solvent sniffing.

References

Dunn DW, Snyder H. Benign paroxysmal vertigo in childhood. *Am J Dis Child* 1976; **130:** 1099.
Eviatar L, Eviatar A. Vertigo in children: differential diagnosis and treatment. *Pediatrics* 1977; **59:** 833.
Koehler B. Benign paroxysmal vertigo in childhood, a migraine equivalent. *Eur J Pediatr* 1980; **134:** 149.
Molteni RA. Vertigo as presenting symptom of multiple sclerosis in childhood. *Am J Dis Child* 1977; **131:** 553.
Rabe EF. Recurrent paroxysmal non-epileptic disorders. *Curr Probl Pediatr* 1974; **4:** 3.

Face Pain

Pain in the face may arise from a molar tooth, an acute antrum infection, a boil in the ear, or osteitis. Pain from herpes is rare in childhood.

Pain may be due to Costen's temporomandibular syndrome. There is muscle spasm over the joint with a tender point in the temporalis muscle. The pain may be due to asymmetry of the bite, tooth grinding or gum chewing: it is rare before adolescence.

References

Schwartz L, Chayes CM. *Facial pain and mandibular dysfunction.* Philadelphia: Saunders, 1969.
Sutcher HD, Lerman MD. Temporomandibular syndrome. *JAMA* 1973; **225:** 1248.

Facial Palsy

The following are the usual causes of facial palsy:
Newborn Babies
  Pressure in *utero* against the facial nerve
  Injury by forceps
  Nuclear agenesis (rare)
  Möbius syndrome (rare) or myotonia dystrophica (rare)
Older Children
  Bell's palsy
  Post-ictal
  Mastoiditis
  Poliomyelitis or encephalitis
  Infectious mononucleosis
  Cerebral tumour
  Herpes of the external auditory meatus
Rare
  Facioscapulohumeral type of muscular dystrophy
  Hypertension
  Melkersson's syndrome
  Cardiofacial syndrome
  Guillain-Barré syndrome
  Increased intracranial pressure
  Anaphylactoid purpura

The facial palsy of the newborn infant usually clears up in a few weeks. Though facial palsy is usually ascribed to pressure by forceps, it is known that almost all are of antenatal origin and are caused by pressure *in utero* against the facial nerve (Hepner 1951). When the facial palsy does not improve, one suspects the more serious agenesis of the facial nucleus.

The *Möbius syndrome* is also termed congenital facial diplegia. There is striking immobility of the face with hardly any movement, so that the child does not smile and shows little expression when crying. Though the level of intelligence is usually below the average, these children are liable to be considered severely defective when in fact they are only slightly subnormal or even within normal limits. The cause is probably a failure of development of the facial and extraocular muscles. *Myotonia dystrophica* (sometimes called dystrophia myotonica) gives a similar facial appearance. It is characterised by hypotonia, mental retardation, myotonia, progressive muscle wasting, baldness, cataracts and gonadal atrophy. Early weakness in the facial muscles is followed by weakness in the neck, forearm extensors, hand, vasti, quadriceps and ankle dorsiflexors. The mouth tends to hang open and there is a droopy immobile face. There is myotonia, and wasting of the sternomastoid muscle. The mother is affected, but not the father. There may be a history of reduced fetal movement and hydramnios. The E.M.G. is characteristic.

Facial palsy developing in the older child is usually *Bell's palsy*: or it can result from mastoid infection or from herpes of the external auditory meatus (Ramsay Hunt syndrome). The possibility of poliomyelitis should be considered, even though there is no other evidence of paralysis. There may be facial weakness for a few hours after a fit (Todd's paralysis). It has complicated infectious mononucleosis.

Facial palsy of supranuclear type may be due to a *cerebral tumour*, especially a glioma of the pons.

Weakness of the facial muscles may develop in infancy or early childhood in the *facioscapulohumeral type of muscular dystrophy*.

Lloyd, Jewitt, and Still (1966) noted the frequency with which facial paralysis occurs in children with *hypertension*. The facial palsy is of lower motor neurone type. It was found in 20 per cent of 35 severely hypertensive children, possibly as a result of haemorrhage into the facial canal.

Melkersson's syndrome consists of facial palsy, chronic or recurrent oedema of the face and a furrowed tongue.

Cayler (1969) described the association of transient facial palsy with *congenital heart disease* and other defects.

Bilateral facial palsy occurs in the *Guillain–Barré syndrome*.

It may occur in anaphylactoid purpura (Meadow 1979) and in increased intracranial pressure.

References

Cayler GG. Cardiofacial syndrome. *Arch Dis Child* 1969; **44:** 69.

Hepner WR. Some observations on facial paresis in the newborn infant. *Pediatrics* 1951; **8:** 494.

Lloyd AVC, Jewitt DE, Still JDL. Facial paralysis in children with hypertension. *Arch Dis Child* 1966; **41:** 292.

Meadow R. Schönlein–Henoch syndrome. *Arch Dis Child* 1979; **54:** 822.

Clumsiness and Ataxia

It seems to me to be irrational to write separate sections on the clumsy child and ataxia, because there are all gradations between the slight clumsiness of innumerable 'normal' children and severe disabling ataxia, with overlapping of the causes (Gubbay 1975). Consequently I have tried to separate clumsiness and chronic ataxia on the one hand from acute ataxia.

The causes of clumsiness and chronic ataxia are mainly as follows:

Normal variations
Delayed motor maturation: often familial
Emotional factors
Mental subnormality
Minimal cerebral palsy of the spastic, ataxia or athetoid types
Visuospatial defects
Chorea
Muscular dystrophy
The effect of drugs: lead or mercury poisoning
Post traumatic, postencephalitic
Cerebral tumour
Mirror movements
Hypothyroidism
Rare
  Klippel-Feil syndrome
  Degenerative diseases of the CNS. Multiple sclerosis, leucodystrophies
  Lipoidoses
  Congenital oculomotor apraxia (Cogan's syndrome)
  Syndrome with chronic liver disease
  Ataxia telangiectasia
  Basilar artery migraine
  Abetalipoproteinaemia
  Wilson's disease
  Hartnup disease
  Argininosuccinicaciduria
  Phenylketonuria
  Maple syrup urine disease

Riley's syndrome (p. 41)

Von Hippel-Lindau syndrome—retinal changes, cerebellar ataxia

Pelizaeus-Merzbacher disease

Refsum's syndrome

Sjögren's syndrome—cataract, ataxia, mental subnormality (p. 46)

The child who was late in learning to walk is usually late in learning to walk steadily, and falls more than others of the same age who learnt to walk sooner. I have frequently seen ataxia diagnosed in such cases.

Mothers commonly complain that one of their children falls a great deal, always has bruises on his legs, or seems awkward with his hands. The teacher complains that the child writes badly, holds his pencil in an odd way and is poor at physical training. Such children may have difficulty in tying shoelaces or buttoning coats. They may swing the arms in an odd way, bump into furniture, misjudge distance (as in going through a doorway) and frequently break objects. They find needle threading a hopeless task: they are awkward in dressing, drawing, writing or feeding themselves. They tend to write with the whole body, with the tongue protruding and the paper at an unusual angle, while the free hand roams. They sometimes have difficulty in distinguishing right from left. They cannot throw a ball properly. These children often concentrate badly and are overactive and impulsive. They find reading difficult and may indulge in mirror writing. They may have difficulties in spatial appreciation. All the symptoms are made worse by scolding. Affected children commonly present as behaviour problems. They get into constant trouble at school, for teachers are apt to think that they are just naughty, dull, lazy or awkward. They may present as truancy. They often hate games because they are so bad at them and may be unpopular and ridiculed by their fellows. They may develop manifestations of insecurity, such as stuttering, excessive shyness, silly behaviour or bed-wetting.

On superficial examination these children look normal and intelligent. They may have an IQ well above the average, though some are merely average or below average. On neurological examination abnormal signs may be found. Whereas a normal child of three can stand for a few seconds and at four quite steadily on one foot, many of the clumsy children at the age of five, six or seven are unsteady when standing on one foot. They cannot jump like a three-year-old or hop like a five-year-old. When building a tower of ten cubes they have some tremor of the hand and may knock the tower down accidentally before it is completed. In timed tests of fine manipulation, such as the placing of small pegs into a peg board, they are far below the average in performance. They are poor at placing shaped objects through holes or at making designs with blocks or at copying letters. In the various tests performed by the psychologist, the performance is much inferior to the verbal tests.

There are wide normal variations in children, and these variations are often familial. Sometimes they are of emotional origin and are related to insecurity, yet many 'clumsy' children, though regarded as 'normal' but 'naughty' by their teachers, are not really normal—they show evidence of organic disease.

Mentally subnormal children tend to be more clumsy with the hands and other movements than normal children; it is said that small-for-dates children are more likely to be clumsy than children who were of average birth weight.

The term 'minimal brain dysfunction' or 'minimal brain damage' is applied by some to this condition. (See also 'overactivity' p. 196). In some of these children there are minimal signs of cerebral palsy of the spastic or athetoid types.

Clumsiness may be related to myopia or to visuospatial difficulties. In some there is merely ataxia; they are examples of 'congenital ataxia'. Some have a slight tremor which interferes with fine hand movements.

Awkwardness and clumsiness with poor writing and emotional disturbance are common features of early *chorea,* and should alert one to this if the child had been normal previously. *Muscular dystrophy* may be the cause of the clumsiness. In the common Duchenne variety there is commonly a history of late walking, indications of slight mental subnormality, clumsiness, awkward running, frequent falls and a particular difficulty in climbing stairs. The diagnosis is confirmed by the serum creatine phosphokinase and muscle biopsy. There is a rare form of congenital myopathy which is manifested by persistent clumsiness.

Numerous *drugs* cause mild to severe clumsiness or ataxia; probably the commonest is phenytoin and other antiepileptic drugs. A variety of other drugs may be responsible, in particular, antihistamines, chlordiazepoxide, colistin, cyclopentolate, diphenoxylate, indomethacin, niclosamide, piperazine, polymyxin, sedatives and tranquillisers, streptomycin, sulthiame and vincristine.

Some children are clumsy because of *mirror movements*. When one hand tries to get a button through a button hole, the opposite free hand makes the same movements. As a result of these mirror movements the child finds it difficult to tie shoelaces and to carry out innumerable daily tasks.

Some children with the *Klippel-Feil* syndrome have a similar difficulty. They cannot let go of something with one hand while grasping with the other. This makes it difficult to climb a ladder.

Ataxia may occur in *hypothyroidism* (Hagberg & Westphal 1970). Macfaul *et al* 1978 described neurological abnormalities in 30 patients where treatment started before the age of two. Ten were clumsy, 16 had a squint, 3 had nystagmus, 6 had speech defects and 15 had minor motor abnormalities.

Rendle–Short *et al* (1973) described the features of *Cogan's syndrome* of congenital oculomotor apraxia: the children are unable to turn the eyes in a horizontal position when asked to do so, and may be thought to be blind in early weeks. There may be jerky movements of the head, difficulty in changing direction suddenly when running, lateness in walking and mild mental subnormality.

Rosenblum *et al* (1981) described six children with ataxia, chronic liver disease, areflexia, sensory loss and paresis of gaze, possibly due to vitamin E deficiency.

A wide variety of *degenerative diseases of the nervous system* and *metabolic diseases* cause clumsiness.

Ataxia telangiectasia is a hereditary condition. The telangiectases appear at about 4 to 6 years of age, first on the bulbar conjunctiva, and then on the ear, on the face in a butterfly distribution, and later on the palate and sternum. There are frequent sinus and respiratory infections due to defective humoral and cellular immunity. Mental deterioration ensues, with dysarthria, drooling and athetosis. There may be ovarian hypoplasia, and a risk of the development of lymphoma.

Golden & French (1975) described eight children with *basilar artery migraine*, who had ataxia, vertigo and headache in attacks.

In *Hartnup disease* there are episodes of ataxia with pellagra-like skin lesions. In *maple syrup urine* disease there are episodes of ataxia and convulsions, and the urine smells of maple syrup. The *Pelizaeus-Merzbacher* syndrome is a sex-linked slowly degenerative disease with nystagmus, ataxia, tremors and spasticity. *Refsum's* syndrome is characterised by ichthyosis, the development of nerve deafness, retinitis pigmentosa, ataxia and mental deterioration.

Acute ataxia. Acute ataxia could be due to hysteria. It may be caused by *acute labyrinthitis* (p. 185),|*encephalitis, cerebral tumour* or *trauma.*

Solvent sniffing and *alcohol* may cause severe ataxia. Solvent sniffing amongst school children and adolescents is a serious problem in Canada and the United States. It behoves all of us to remember its possibility in Great Britain. Fumes from glues and plastic cements used in ready-made building kits, aeroplane glues, lacquer enamels, nail polish remover and paint thinner, contain such substances as benzene, carbon tetrachloride, toluene, xylene, alcohol, acetone and amyl acetate; and petrol contains naphtha. All these substances are CNS depressants. They may arouse a feeling of exhilaration, but later ataxia, diplopia or confusion may arise. It is said to be common in New York slums.

Because of the possibility of a *cerebral tumour or abscess,* the fundi must be examined for papilloedema.

References

Golden GS, French JH. Basilar artery migraine in young children. *Pediatrics* 1975; **56:** 722.

Gubbay SS. *The clumsy child.* Philadelphia: Saunders, 1975.

Hagberg B. Westphal O. Ataxic syndrome in congenital hypothyroidism. *Acta Paediatr Scand* 1970; **59:** 323.

Macfaul R, Dorner S, *et al.* Neurological abnormalities in patients treated for hypothyroidism from early life. *Arch Dis Child* 1978; **53:** 611.

Rendle–Short J. Appleton B, Pearn J. Congenital ocular motor apraxia; paediatric aspects. *Austr Paediatr J* 1973; **9:** 263.

Rosenblum JL, Keating JP, *et al.* A progressive neurologic syndrome in children with chronic liver disease. *N Engl J Med* 1981; **304:** 503.

Abnormal Gait

Abnormality of gait may be due to any of the causes of ataxia (p. 190). Other causes include:

Hysteria (older children, after about 7 years of age).

Hip conditions such as subluxation commonly cause a waddling gait. The same gait is seen in cases of muscular dystrophy involving the muscle around the hip. Other diseases of the hip, such as Perthes' disease, cause a limp.

Cerebral palsy of the spastic type causes a characteristic gait: its nature depends partly on the distribution of the cerebral palsy—hemiplegia or diplegia. The hemiplegic child walks with a limp, partly because of the shortening of the affected leg, and he characteristically carries the affected arm adducted, partly across the abdomen.

Hypotonia causes a characteristic gait. The causes include benign congenital hypotonia, poliomyelitis and rarely peripheral neuritis (pp. 229, 232).

Paraesthesiae

Paraesthesiae are difficult to assess in children. The obvious cause of paraesthesiae in the legs is sitting with the legs crossed, or pressure of the edge of a chair against the back of the thigh.

Paraesthesiae may be one of the premonitory symptoms of *migraine* or a feature of *temporal lobe epilepsy*.

Tetany may result from hysterical overventilation, sulthiame, or hypoparathyroidism, and lead to paraesthesiae.

The symptom may be due to *drugs*—acetazolamide, amitriptyline, chlorothiazide, ergotamine, imipramine, kanamycin, nalidixic acid, nitrofurantoin, niclosamide, piperazine, polymyxin, streptomycin, sulthiame, trimethoprim, thiabendazole, or vincristine. Ergotamine may cause tingling, numbness and chilling of the extremities.

Overactivity

It is difficult to define the term overactivity with precision (Safer & Allen 1976). Many mothers think that their children are 'overactive', and complain that they are always on the go and never sit still, when in fact they are normal. This sort of behaviour is usual in the child from five to ten or so. The healthy six-year-old is always on the go: he does not walk, he runs; when his mother holds one hand he skips and hops. What is normal at one age, however, is not normal at another. As children mature they lose much of this excessive activity. In this section I will discuss what one may term 'unusual overactivity'. This is commonly accompanied by lack of concentration, ready distractability and short attention span. The children tend to be impulsive, clumsy, excessively talkative and even destructive. Their movements are more purposeless than just increased in amount. These children wear their mothers out and exhaust their teachers. The condition is more common in boys. The term *'minimal brain dysfunction'* or *'minimal brain damage'* is applied by some to this condition—and to clumsiness and some hundred other symptoms—though there is no laboratory or psychological test which indicates that there was brain damage (Varga 1979, Rie & Rie 1980, Carey & McDevitt 1980). It is now becoming recognised that the condition of 'minimal brain damage' is a myth, and that the term should be abandoned. (Wender & Wender 1976, Carey & McDevitt 1980). There may be a biochemical basis for the problem, involving biogenic amines (Shaywitz *et al* 1978, Rapoport & Ferguson 1981). There may be an underlying variant in monoamine metabolism.

The main causes of 'unusual overactivity' may be summarized as follows:

Normal variation
Delayed maturation
Heredity
Prenatal anoxia, alcohol, toxaemia, maternal smoking
Neonatal hyperbilirubinaemia
Personality
Excessive restraint
Boredom
Poor teaching or motivation. Overcrowded classes

Emotional problems: insecurity
Mental subnormality
Autism
Temporal lobe epilepsy
Lead poisoning
Drugs

Unusual overactivity may be a *familial* trait. It may be partly a matter of an inherited personality characteristic. It must not be assumed that an overactive child has suffered 'brain injury' without first enquiring about the behaviour of the mother or father at that age.

Mental subnormality is a common cause of unusual overactivity in the young child, partly because mentally subnormal children mature more slowly than normal ones. As a result they are late in growing out of overactivity. Overactivity is often a feature of *autism, temporal lobe epilepsy,* or the result of excessive restraint.

Certain *drugs* may be responsible for overactivity. They include chlordiazepoxide, clonazepam, phenobarbitone, phenytoin, primidone and the tricyclic antidepressants. It has been suggested that food additives, such as tartrazine, may be a factor but if they are, they probably play a role in only a few children (Stare *et al* 1980).

References

Carey WB, McDevitt SC. Minimal brain dysfunction and hyperkinesis *Am J Dis Child* 1980; **134:** 926.

Rapoport JL, Ferguson HP. Biological validation of the hyperkinetic syndrome. *Dev Med Child Neurol* 1981; **23:** 667.

Rie HL, Rie ED. *Handbook of brain dysfunctions.* New York: John Wiley, 1980.

Safer D, Allen RP. *Hyperactive children: diagnosis and management.* Baltimore: University Park Press, 1976.

Shaywitz SE, Cohen DJ, Shaywitz BA. The biochemical basis of minimal brain dysfunction. *J Pediatr* 1978; **92:** 179.

Stare FJ, Whelan EM, Sheridan M. Diet and hyperactivity. Is there a relationship? *Pediatrics* 1980; **66:** 521.

Varga J. The hyperactive child. *Am J Dis Child* 1979; **133:** 413.

Wender PH, Wender EH. Minimal brain dysfunction myth. *Am J Dis Child* 1976; **130:** 900.

Undue Excitement

This may be due to *hypoglycaemia*. It may also be caused by a variety of *drugs*, notably acetazolamide, antihistamines, chlordiazepoxide, diazepam, imipramine, mepacrine, nitrazepam, nitrofurantoin, nortriptyline, phenobarbitone, alcohol or poisons. The symptoms could be due to a drug of addiction, or solvent sniffing.

Aggressiveness and Temper Tantrums

Undue aggressiveness and temper tantrums are usually behaviour problems, and like most behaviour problems result largely from a conflict between the child's personality and developing mind with that of the personality and attitudes of his parents and other environmental factors. But the symptoms may also be due to disease, biochemical changes, epilepsy and drugs. *Any debilitating disease such as anaemia* may have a bad effect on a child's temper.

A developing cerebral tumour may cause personality changes.

Hypoglycaemia may be accompanied by aggressive behaviour. When a child suddenly, and for no apparent reason, without injury or thwarting, has a sudden outburst of temper and aggressiveness, *temporal lobe epilepsy* is a possibility. Some *drugs* and in particular barbiturates but also tricyclic antidepressants, may cause aggressive and difficult behaviour.

Undue Irritability

Undue irritability in the newborn baby may be due to *cerebral oedema, cerebral damage* or the *effects of anoxia*. It may be the result of *drugs* taken by the mother in pregnancy, such as the tricyclic antidepressants, barbiturates or phenothiazines, or to smoking in pregnancy (Zelson 1973). It may be a withdrawal symptom from drugs of addiction taken by the mother: the onset of symptoms may be delayed for a few days after birth.

The most likely cause of persistent undue irritability in a well child is *insecurity*, due probably to mismanagement—lack of real love, or excessive strictness and punishment. To some extent the irritability may be due to familial personality traits.

It may be due to lassitude, boredom, anaemia or any illness, such as a urinary tract infection.

A young baby's excessive irritability may be due to *phenylketonuria*. The infant with *coeliac disease* may vomit and become irritable when given cereals.

Pink disease, due to mercury in teething powders or other substances should no longer be seen. It is characterised by pinkness of the hands and feet, excessive sweating, constant crying and photophobia.

When a school child habitually arrives home in a bad temper, the most likely cause is *hypoglycaemia,* responding rapidly to a meal. Otherwise he may have been bullied at school by a teacher or child.

Drugs are an important cause of excessive irritability, and the worst offender is phenobarbitone. This may have a paradoxical effect of causing insomnia and irritability, particularly in mentally subnormal children. Primidone, which breaks down into a barbiturate, may have a similar action. Other drugs which may cause the symptoms include acetazolamide, aminophylline, amphetamine, antihistamines, clonazepam, ephedrine, fenfluramine (on withdrawal), imipramine, methimazole, sulthiame, thyroxine and troxidone.

Cyclopentolate, cycloserine, ethionamide, hyoscine and fenfluramine may give rise to a psychotic reaction and irritability.

Reference

Zelson C. Infant of the addicted mother. *N Engl J Med* 1973; **288:** 1393.

Confusion, Delirium and Hallucinations

A short-lasting confusional state may be a premonitory symptom of *migraine*. The child may have partial aphasia for a few minutes, and sometimes other neurological symptoms. The development of the headache helps to establish the diagnosis. Confusion may be the result of a fit or head injury. It may result from overventilation (p. 137). It is a common feature of hypoglycaemia.

Temporal lobe epilepsy may be manifested by a confusional state or by abnormal behaviour of various kinds.

Heat stroke or *dehydration* may be a cause.

Lobar pneumonia and other acute infections may be accompanied by delirium or confusion, especially when there is severe malnutrition.

Reye's syndrome (encephalopathy with fatty degeneration of the viscera) should be considered.

Various *drugs* may be responsible, in particular alcohol, amitriptyline, amphetamine, antihistamines, bromides, carbamazepine, chlordiazepoxide, cephalexin, cotrimoxazole, cylopentolate, diazepam, digoxin, ethionamide, ethosuximide, fenfluramine, griseofulvin, hyoscine, indomethacin, mepacrine, methylphenidate, monoamine oxidase inhibitors, nitrofurantoin, phenytoin, piperazine, primidone and sulthiame.

Hallucinations may be a feature of *temporal lobe epilepsy*. They may be due to solvent sniffing, cannabis, LSD and various poisons.

The causes of *delirium* are similar to those of coma, though infections such as pneumonia, or drugs and intracranial causes, are the most important.

Coma

Coma may be defined as prolonged profound unconsciousness, and delirium as a state of confusion, disorientation, irrational conversation or excitability. The most important causes to consider first are diabetes or hypoglycaemia, head injury, drugs or cerebral haemorrhage.

Causes of coma include the following:

Metabolic conditions
> Diabetes mellitus: hyperglycaemia, hypoglycaemia
> Hyponatraemia, hypernatraemia
>> Dehydration—Heat stroke
> Addison's disease
> Liver or kidney failure
> Hyperammonaemia
> Infections—encephalitis, meningitis, meningococcal septicaemia
> Reye's syndrome
> Malaria
> Typhoid fever

Cerebral trauma—head injury, child abuse
> Haemorrhage, abscess, tumour
> Thrombosis—e.g. sickle cell
> Burn encephalopathy (p. 222)

Epilepsy—post convulsion
Stokes-Adams syndrome of atrioventricular block, causing attacks of unconsciousness
Drugs and poisons
Hysteria

The first cause to consider is *diabetic acidosis* or *hypoglycaemia* due to insulin overdose. The smell of acetone in the breath, the presence of sugar in the urine and a blood sugar test should promptly establish the diagnosis of diabetes. A rare but important form of diabetic coma is the *nonketotic hyperosmolar form* with hyperglycaemia, dehydration, fits, mild or moderate diabetes, but without significant acidosis or ketosis.

Hyponatraemia and *dehydration* or *heat stroke* are important causes of coma, especially in mentally subnormal children when they have a respiratory or alimentary tract infection. Overventilation should support the likelihood of the hypernatraemic type of dehydration. Hypernatraemia may also be caused by errors in the constitution of feeds— either by making them too concentrated, or by carelessly adding salt instead of sugar to feeds (Stern *et al* 1972).

Infective hepatitis can be acute and lead to coma in a few hours. The Kussmaul breathing of uraemia should point to renal failure.

Hyperammonaemia may be caused by any of five inborn errors of metabolism involving the urea cycle. It is manifested in infancy or early childhood by vomiting, irritability, lethargy, fits, and often hypertonia and hepatic enlargement. Acute episodes may be precipitated by infection, anaesthetics or surgical procedures (Sinclair 1979).

Severe infections may lead to a coma. In the tropics malaria is an obvious cause, but other infections may cause coma in a severely malnourished child. Encephalitis or meningoencephalitis may be causes.

For Reye's syndrome see p. 73.

Head injury, including child abuse, is an important cause, as are the other intracranial conditions listed.

Coma may follow a severe *epileptic convulsion:* but when a known epileptic presents in coma, one should remember that he might have taken an overdose of antiepileptic drugs.

Numerous drugs and *poisons* may cause coma, and clinical examination may provide vital clues (Maragos 1978). A hot dry skin may suggest belladonna poisoning. Perspiration may suggest salicylates, LSD or organophosphates. Nystagmus may suggest poisoning by ɔhenytoin or barbiturates. Overventilation suggests salicylates, paraldehyde, methyl or ethylene glycol. Needle marks point to narcotics. Small pupils suggest narcotics, barbiturates or phenothiazines. Dilated pupils suggest belladonna, amphetamine or antihistamines.

Drugs and poisons which may cause coma include alcohol, amphetamine, aminophylline, antihistamines, barbiturates, carbon monoxide, cyclopentolate (mydriatic), diphenoxylate, fenfluramine, haloperidol, iron, isoniazid, kerosene, lead, mushroom poisoning, organophosphates, meprobamate, phenothiazines, piperazine, phenytoin and thallium.

Solvent sniffing is a cause which is apt to be forgotten.

The parents' statement that the child could not have had access to drugs must never be taken to eliminate poisoning (p. 138).

Sometimes one strongly suspects narcotic poisoning but evidence is lacking; a therapeutic test of naloxone may provide that evidence.

Recurrent attacks of coma may be due to deliberate administration of drugs by the mother as a form of *non-accidental injury* or the *'reverse Munchausen syndrome'* (Verity *et al* 1979). One has known such a child being investigated in hospital for recurrent coma who relapsed into coma each time the mother visited him.

A diagnosis which is always a dangerous one is *hysteria*. As always, the diagnosis can only be made on the basis of absence of evidence of organic disease on full investigation and follow-up, together with positive evidence of hysteria.

References

Arieff AI, Carroll HJ. Nonketotic hyperosmolar coma with hyperglycaemia. *Medicine* 1972; **51**: 73.

Maragos GD. The unconscious child. *Paediatrician* 1978; **7**: 142.

Sinclair L. *Metabolic disease in childhood.* Oxford: Blackwell Scientific Publications, 1979.

Stern GM, Jones RB, Fraser ACL. Hyperosmolar dehydration in infancy due to faulty feeding. *Arch Dis Child* 1972; **47**: 468.

Verity CM, Winckworth C, *et al.* Polle syndrome: children of Munchausen. *Br Med J* 1979; **2**: 422.

Drowsiness

Undue drowsiness may be due merely to *fatigue* or *lack of sleep* if the child is otherwise well.

It may be due to any *serious illness,* including febrile conditions, meningitis, diabetic acidosis and uraemia.

A variety of *drugs* cause drowsiness. They include the antiepileptic drugs, antihistamines, diphenoxylate, fenfluramine, indomethacin, meprobamate, methimazole, nalidixic acid, P.A.S., the phenothiazines and tranquillizing drugs. *Poisons* should be considered. As in the case of coma, drugs may be administered by the mother as child abuse or the Polle syndrome.

Drowsiness may be due to dehydration including heatstroke. It may be due to hypernatraemia caused by the baby's feeds being made up too concentrated. It is sometimes an early symptom of hypoglycaemia.

In newborn babies cold injury causes drowsiness.

Drowsiness and apathy are a feature of severe malnutrition and kwashiorkor.

Involuntary Movements

A wide variety of involuntary movements of differing types and severity may occur at any age in childhood (Marsden 1974). Below is a summary of the causes.

The newborn and young infant

All normal infants exhibit the *Moro and startle reflexes* in the first three months. These reflexes may be exaggerated when there is cerebral irritability. The Moro reflex consists of a sudden abduction of the arms at the shoulder, with extension of the elbows and opening of the hands, followed by adduction as if in an embrace. It is probably due to vestibular reflexes set up by movement of the neck. The startle reflex results from a loud noise; it differs from the Moro reflex in that there is flexion of the elbows and the hands remain closed.

Normal children when asleep in the first few weeks have *sudden jerky movements* resembling the startle reflex.

All normal infants in the early weeks show frequent *jaw trembling*.

Many newborn infants show a rapid *jittery movement* of the limbs. It occurs particularly in the presence of hypocalcaemia: for distinction from convulsions see (p. 208).

Hiccoughs are normal in young infants after a feed.

Tics are extremely common in children. They usually consist of blinking the eyes, twitching the face, inappropriate mouth opening ('gaping'), shrugging the shoulders, sniffing or clucking the tongue. They are usually single (i.e. one of the above), but may be multiple and complex, and therefore readily confused with chorea. They are more common in boys than in girls. The onset is more often at about the age of seven years than at other ages, about 90 per cent beginning before the age of ten. They frequently disappear at puberty, but some persist throughout life. One tic usually lasts several months. Tics may be brought on by home conflicts and other causes of insecurity, but the cause cannot always be found. *Tics* may be a side effect of *amphetamine* or *methylphenidate*.

The rare *Gilles de la Tourette syndrome* usually begins before the age of ten; there are tics, head jerkings and later complex movements with involuntary noises—barking, grunting, hissing or uttering of obscenities.

Tics are commonly confused with *chorea*. The essential distinguishing feature is the fact that in a tic the same movement is constantly repeated; in chorea one never knows which movement is going to occur next. It is not by any means easy, however, to distinguish a complex tic from chorea of mild degree. In chorea one sees the characteristic hand posture when the child is asked to hold the hands out pronated. Severe chorea cannot be confused with tics because of the many other obvious features; but mild chorea may closely resemble tics.

I have often had children referred to me with the diagnosis of chorea, when the true diagnosis was mere *overactivity*. They did not show the varied uncoordinated movements of chorea. One has also seen chorea confused with bizarre movements of *hysteria* or with sudden jerky movements of a nervous 'highly strung' child.

Athetosis constitutes 10 to 15 per cent of all cases of cerebral palsy. It is probably most often related to anoxia in utero or during delivery, but may be familial; it may be due to kernicterus which is now rarely seen; often the cause cannot be determined. The slow writhing movements of athetosis disappear in sleep.

Athetoid movements—often termed choreoathetosis—occur in many rare degenerative diseases of the nervous system; they include *Huntington's chorea*, in which fits are a common early feature, followed by slowness of movement, dysarthria, rigidity, ataxia, tremors and mental deterioration (Folstein *et al* 1981).The first manifestation is sometimes isolated chorea. *Wilson's disease* (hepatolenticular degeneration) often begins with an attack indistinguishable from acute infective hepatitis, and later there may be hepatic cirrhosis, dysarthria, dysphagia, a fixed rigid face, inappropriate laughter, tremors, haemolytic crises, pericorneal pigmentation (Slovis *et al*

1971): the *Hallervorden–Spatz* and *Creutzfeld–Jakob syndromes*, both with progressive dementia: the *Lesch–Nyhan syndrome*, of hyperuricaemia, self-mutilation, dystonic or athetoid movements, mental subnormality, attacks of opisthotonos, mainly in boys: the *Pelizaeus–Merzbacher syndrome, ataxia telangiectasia: Lowe's syndrome* of mental subnormality, cataract, abnormal aminoaciduria, renal tubular defect, rickets, and the development of hypotonia, *disseminated lupus, encephalitis, cerebral thrombosis or tumour* (Paradise 1960); *benign familial non-progressive chorea: paroxysmal choreoathetosis* (Kinast *et al* 1980, Sleigh & Lindenbaum 1981)—a non-progressive condition in which choreiform movements are precipitated by startling or anxiety, responding to phenytoin.

Dystonia musculorum deformans (torsion spasm) begins between the age of five and ten, with hypertonus of the calf muscles, leading to inversion and adduction of the foot, and later a fixed flexion and adduction of the hip with lordosis, torticollis and involuntary twisting movements.

For Sandifer's syndrome see p. 259.

Many *drugs* cause dystonic or choreiform movements and sometimes attacks of opisthotonos. They include especially metoclopramide (Castels-Van Daele *et al* 1970), prochlorperazine and other phenothiazines; symptoms include a stiff neck, torticollis, facial grimacing, oculogyric crises, dysarthria, dysphagia and trismus. Other drugs with similar effect include amitriptyline, amphetamine, antihistamines, carbamazepine, cephalosporins, chloroquine, diazoxide, ethosuximide, fenfluramine, haloperidol, imipramine, phenytoin and carbon monoxide or methaqualone (mandrax) poisoning.

Tremors

Tremors are normal in children, but are more often seen in *clumsy or mentally subnormal ones*. The tremor is seen particularly on fine manipulation, as when building a tower of cubes.

For jitteriness in the newborn, see p. 208.

Tremors in the young baby may be related to *maternal drug addiction*, including particularly alcohol; tremors may persist for several weeks in the *fetal alcohol syndrome*. Other drugs taken in pregnancy and which may cause tremors in the baby, include diazepam, diphenhydramine, heroin, pentazocine and phenothiazines.

Drugs taken by the child and sometimes causing tremors, include aminophylline, phenothiazines and terbutaline. Tremors are a feature of *thallium poisoning* and may result from *solvent sniffing*—often with associated ataxia and exaggerated reflexes (Seshia *et al* 1978).

Other causes of tremors include *Wilson's disease* (p. 205), *brain stem and cerebellar lesions* (intention tremor), *encephalitis, hypoglycaemia* and *thyrotoxicosis*. *Spasmus nutans* (rare) (Hoefnagel & Biery 1968) is a peculiar condition seen in infants aged usually three to about 24 months, in which there are rhythmical jerking movements of the neck, usually in the lateral or horizontal direction, ceasing when they concentrate on something. The child often has a characteristic way of looking at objects out of his eye corners and may tilt his head to one side. The movements disappear in sleep. There is usually nystagmus, often more marked on one side than the other. The movements are increased by holding the head; they disappear spontaneously by the age of three or four.

Hiccoughs

Apart from the occasional normal hiccoughs of child (or adult), hiccoughs after infancy may be caused by a *subphrenic abscess* or by *ethosuximide*. *Epidemic hiccough* may be due to encephalitis, but more often hiccough, lasting one to seven days followed by recovery, follows a *respiratory infection*.

For spasmodic torticollis see p. 258.

For convulsions see p. 208.

References

Castels-Van Daele M, Jaeken P. *et al*. Dystonic reactions in children caused by metoclopramide. *Arch Dis Child* 1970; **45**: 130.

Folstein S, Abbott M, Moser R, *et al*. Hereditary disorders of dystonic movement. *The Johns Hopkins Hosp Med J* 1981; **148**: 104.

Hoefnagel D, Biery B. Spasmus nutans. *Dev Med Child Neurol* 1968; **10**: 32.

Kinast M, Erenberg G, Rotner AD. Paroxysmal choreoathetosis: report of 5 cases and review of the literature. *Pediatrics* 1980; **65**: 74.

Marsden CD. Involuntary movements. *Medicine (UK)* 1974; **32**: 1904.

Paradise JL. Sydenham's chorea without evidence of rheumatic fever. *N Engl J Med* 1960; **263**: 625.

Seshia SS, Rajani KR, *et al*. The neurological manifestations of chronic inhalation of leaded gasoline. *Dev Med Child Neurol* 1978; **20**: 323.

Sleigh G. Lindenbaum RH. Benign (non-paroxysmal) familial chorea. *Arch Dis Child* 1981; **56**: 616.

Slovis TL, Dubois RS, Rodgerson DO, Silverman A. The variable mani-
    festations of Wilson's disease. *J Pediatr* 1971; **78**: 578.
Torup E. A follow-up study of children with tics. *Acta Paediatr Uppsala* 1962;
    51: 261.

Convulsions

Convulsions occur in about seven per cent of all children and about one per cent of all newborn babies. They occur in about 20 per cent of mentally subnormal children, except mongols, in whom convulsions are rare; they occur in about 35 per cent of all children with cerebral palsy—50 per cent of those with spastic hemiplegia, 40 per cent of those with spastic quadriplegia but in fewer of those with diplegia. They occur in about 10 per cent of athetoids, but rarely in those with congenital ataxia.

It is often difficult to decide whether an infant or child has had a convulsion or not. Unless one is able to witness the episode oneself, accurate history-taking is essential. It may be impossible to diagnose without witnessing the episode, and even then it may be difficult. A convulsion in a newborn baby rarely presents as an obvious major fit (Rose & Lombroso 1970). It commonly presents as mere twitching of a limb or limbs and fluttering of the eyelids. The twitchings may migrate from one limb or part of the body to another. Conjugate deviation of the eyes would be a vital indication of a fit, as would hypertonus in a twitching limb. Convulsive movements have to be distinguished from the normal sudden jerks in sleep or awakening, and from the agitation and tremulousness of a baby when hungry. Classic movements of a limb, indicating a convulsion, cannot be stopped by flexing the limb, whilst jittery tremulous movements can (Brown *et al* 1972). Jittery tremors may be provoked by external stimuli.

Apnoeic or cyanotic attacks (p. 128) may be a form of convulsion, or the result of one. One has seen a convulsion wrongly diagnosed because of the attacks of pallor and shock in *intussusception*. The rigidity, flushing and staring eyes of a *masturbating* older infant or child may wrongly suggest an epileptic fit, as may sudden attacks of *paroxysmal vertigo* (p. 186). A child with *spastic hemiplegia* may have twitching of the affected limbs without loss of consciousness so that the diagnosis of a convulsion may be missed. The distinction from *faints* can be difficult (p. 220), as may be the distinction from *hysterical convulsions* or *tetany* (p. 210). The diagnosis of *temporal lobe epilepsy* may be missed because of the bizarre symptoms, such as sudden outbursts of rage without apparent reason.

When obtaining the history about episodes in an older child which might be convulsions, probably the most important question to ask is whether the mother has noticed anything unusual in the eyes during an episode: conjugate deviation of the eyes—lateral or vertical— would be conclusive evidence of a convulsion. It is also useful to ask a mother to imitate the child's movements or 'twitching' in the episode. Special investigations, such as the EEG, may or may not help, for in grand mal epilepsy the EEG is frequently normal between attacks.

Convulsions are the end result of a wide variety of pathological processes. From the nature of the convulsions one can rarely make a diagnosis of the cause, for most convulsions, with the principal exception of petit mal and infantile spasms, look alike. Every effort must be made to establish the correct diagnosis, because only then can the appropriate treatment be prescribed; hence hospital investigation is always necessary.

The common causes vary with age. The commonest causes in a newborn baby are *hypoxia, hypoglycaemia, hypocalcaemia,* and *infection,* but there are numerous rare *metabolic diseases* which may cause convulsions in the newborn period (Eriksson & Zetterstrom 1979, Lockman 1980). In some developing countries *tetanus* is the commonest cause. *Febrile convulsions* are rare in the first six months. From six months to five years the commonest diagnosis will be a *febrile convulsion,* though *breath-holding fits* are common. After the age of two or three, epileptic fits become common and after the age of five the usual diagnosis will be *epilepsy.* Petit mal is very rare below the age of three.

Fits in the newborn period

Brain defect or damage by hypoxia (prenatal or perinatal), including cerebral oedema, haemorrhage, cysts or structural defects, are a significant cause of neonatal convulsions. Convulsions on the first day are more likely to be due to anoxia; on the second or third day they are more likely to be due to cerebral haemorrhage.

If there is a serious brain defect, the cranial circumference may be unusually small, but it is not always so. If there is cerebral oedema or a subdural effusion, the fontanelle is likely to be bulging and the sutures may be widely separated. There may be retinal haemorrhages, but such haemorrhages are often found in normal babies. In most full-term infants the symptoms of cerebral haemorrhage commonly develop on about the third day, the infant having been previously well. The child suddenly has cyanotic attacks or convulsions, may vomit and go off his food. There may be bulging of the fontanelle. He may develop atelectasis and so develop respiratory symptoms which mask the real cause, a cerebral haemorrhage.

Neonatal hypoglycaemia. Neonatal hypoglycaemia occurs particularly in babies who are small in relation to the duration of gestation, in babies of toxaemic mothers, in boys rather than in girls, in the smaller of twins and in babies of diabetic mothers. It follows birth injury or cold injury, and may be associated with the respiratory distress syndrome, kernicterus, Beckwith's syndrome (umbilical hernia with macroglossia and hypoglycaemia), adrenocortical hyperplasia, infections and glycogenoses. The symptoms begin a few hours after birth in most babies, but a few develop them up to five or six days later. They consist of twitches, cyanotic attacks and convulsions. It is important to establish the diagnosis promptly in order that appropriate treatment can be given.

Neonatal tetany. Neonatal hypocalcaemia is most often seen about the fifth to the seventh day, and is due mainly to the inability of the newborn baby to handle the high phosphorus content of the cow's milk. It is also related to physiological hypocalcaemia, which occurs particularly between the third and the fifth or sixth days. It may occur when the mother has suffered from hyperparathyroidism or diabetes in pregnancy. There may be associated *hypomagnesaemia.* The symptoms are convulsions which are indistinguishable from other convulsions. The typical carpopedal spasm of tetany in older children is rarely seen. A positive Chvostek's sign does not establish the diagnosis because it occurs in normal babies. It is important that the correct diagnosis should be made in order that treatment can be given. The prognosis is better for this condition than it is for other causes of convulsions in the newborn period.

Less frequently hypocalcaemia occurs on the first day or two in low-birth-weight babies and placental insufficiency. Causes include mainly cerebral malformations, anoxia, birth injury and maternal diabetes or infection. The prognosis is then not so good.

Important *infections* which may cause convulsions in the newborn period include particularly septicaemia due to the Group B streptococcus, the staphylococcus and gram negative bacteria, and pyogenic meningitis. In neonatal meningitis there is usually no neck stiffness or other sign of meningitis, and there may be no bulging of the fontanelle. The baby is just ill and no good reason is found for it until a lumbar puncture reveals the diagnosis. Other infections include otitis media and pneumonia. Neonatal tetanus is common in certain countries abroad in which goat or cow dung, mud or other undesirable materials are applied to the umbilicus at birth (Marshall 1968). The first symptom is usually difficulty in sucking at the age of five or six days, followed by stiffness of the laws and generalized spasticity. Twitchings develop and spasms occur spontaneously or in response to stimulation. The child lies stiffly with flexed extremities or opisthotonos, with a risus sardonicus, stiff jaws, or a stiff upper lip on feeding, and short spasms accompanied by little snorts or grunts.

Rare infections which may cause convulsions include toxoplasmosis, generalized herpes, cytomegalovirus and malaria in tropical countries.

Convulsions may be due to *hyponatraemia* or *hypernatraemia*.

All other causes of convulsions in the newborn period are rare. They include pyridoxine dependency, faulty carbohydrate metabolism (galactosaemia, fructosaemia, lactic acidosis, lactose intolerance, glycogenoses, and a wide variety of inborn errors of metabolism, mostly with abnormal aminoaciduria. (Lockman 1980): they include isovaleric acidosis, argininosuccinicaciduria, citrullinaemia, propionic, acidaemia, methyl malonic acidaemia, hyperglycaemia, hyperammonaemia; oast house syndrome, carnosinaemia, hyperprolinaemia, beta-alaninaemia, Leigh's disease and maple syrup urine disease.

Kernicterus commonly presents at the age of five to nine days in infants with hyperbilirubinaemia, as a result of haemolytic disease or prematurity. Fits may be a feature.

The narcotic withdrawal syndrome may be a cause. When the mother is a morphine or heroin addict the baby at birth will suffer the symptoms of withdrawal—extreme irritability, convulsions and excess salivation.

Drugs given for the treatment of neonatal asphyxia, such as nikethamide or ethamivan, may cause convulsions is only a small overdose is given.

Convulsions after the newborn period

    The following conditions should be considered:
        Febrile convulsions
        Breath-holding attacks
        Brain defects
          Subdural effusion
          Head injury
        Epilepsy including infantile spasms
        Sequelae of immunization
        Hypoglycaemia, hypocalcaemia
        Dehydration and its repair
        Infection, including malaria
        Poisons
        Rare
          Acute infantile hemiplegia, sickle-cell crises, haemolytic uraemic syndrome, acute nephritis:
          Metabolic diseases—including phenylketonuria and the rare inborn errors of metabolism.

After the first weeks of life and up to the age of four to five years the commonest cause of fits is the so-called *febrile convulsion*. This condition is the source of much confusion. It is important to distinguish it from epilepsy because the treatment and the prognosis are different. The following are the criteria necessary for making the diagnosis (Livingston & Pauli 1976):

1 Febrile convulsions are definitely unusual before the age of six months, and they should not be diagnosed after the age of five years. The peak age incidence is eighteen months.

2 They only occur with a rapid rise of temperature, and there must be a history of the child having been off colour and probably off his food for a few hours before the fit occurred.

3 Fits occurring more than 12 hours after the onset of an illness are almost certainly not febrile convulsions, unless there is a complication such as otitis media developing after a sore throat, and causing a new rise in temperature.

4   The fits should not last more than ten minutes.

5   They should be general and not focal.

6   There must be no history of fits without a precipitating infection.

7   There is normally only one fit with the rapid rise of temperature: rarely there may be another fit, but it should not be more than 12 to 18 hours after the first (Livingston *et al.* 1973).

8   There must not be residual weakness of a limb (Todd's paralysis) after a fit.

9   The EEG between fits is normal.

I should be particularly cautious about diagnosing a benign febrile convulsion if the child were mentally subnormal or had cerebral palsy, because epileptic fits are so common in these conditions. Accurate diagnosis is important: fewer than 3 per cent satisfying these criteria will have fits later, while 97 per cent of children with other fever-precipitated fits will later have epilepsy.

There are some important difficulties with regard to the diagnosis. Firstly, fever may precipitate fits in epileptics. Hence the criteria above must be satisfied. In particular there must be no history of fits between the 'febrile convulsions'. Secondly, any severe convulsion may cause a rise of temperature. Hence the finding of an elevated temperature following a fit does not prove that an infection caused the fit.

If a child has an infection which caused both an elevation of temperature and a fit, the temperature may have dropped in transit to the hospital. Hence the finding of definite infection together with the appropriate history may be more important for the diagnosis than the finding of an elevated temperature.

A family history of febrile convulsions is commonly obtained, but a family history of definite epilepsy would arouse doubts about the diagnosis of febrile fits. An extremely important source of error is pyogenic meningitis in the infant or young child, for in about 15 per cent the onset is with fever and a convulsion, and in half of these presenting in that way there is no meningism—no neck stiffness, no Kernig sign or other indication of meningitis: hence the recommendation (Ouelette 1974, Rutter & Smales 1977) that all young children presenting with fever and a fit should have a lumbar puncture performed.

Breath-holding convulsions may occur at any age between about six months and five years, and very rarely after that age. The usual age of onset is six to eighteen months. The child when thwarted or hurt may cry, hold his breath in expiration, or cry, 'till all the air has gone out of his lungs', as a parent said. The child rapidly becomes blue, and if he holds the breath for a further ten or fifteen seconds, he becomes limp. If he holds the breath for a further ten or fifteen seconds, he will have a major convulsion indistinguishable from epilepsy. There is often opisthotonos, and occasionally vomiting or wetting. The basic cause of the attack is reduced cardiac output resulting from reduced cardiac return as a result of the increased intrathoracic pressure from breath-holding. It is said that there is often a hyper-sensitive oculocardiac reflex—slowing of the heart on compression of the eyeball. It is important to note the exact sequence of events, for this sequence helps one to distinguish the attacks from epileptic fits. In a typical epileptic fit the child has a sudden convulsion, becoming stiff first, then twitches and becomes blue. There is no aura and no preceding stimulus (pain or thwarting). If there is a cry it is synchronous with the tonic phase; this is followed by the clonic phase. Cyanosis occurs late in the epileptic fit, not at the beginning, as it does in a breath-holding attack. A fit following anger or a fright is unlikely to be epilepsy.

Toronto neurologists (Lombroso & Lerman 1967) have described a pallid type of breath-holding attack usually following pain or a fright; in it there is rapid loss of consciousness with pallor but without preceding cyanosis. This is a form of syncope. In both types there is commonly a family history of similar fits.

Many make the mistake of thinking that breath-holding attacks are merely a behaviour problem, occurring only when the child cannot get his own way. In fact they commonly occur when the child has a fall or other injury. It has been suggested that there is some association with hypochromic anaemia. Antiepileptic drugs do not affect the frequency of the attacks—a useful therapeutic test when one is in doubt. The EEG is normal and no other investigation is necessary.

Brain defects. Congenital brain defects, such as cerebral agenesis or porencephalic cysts, are an important cause of fits in the older baby. In a high proportion of these there will be associated mental subnormality or neurological signs suggesting cerebral palsy. Fits are an unusual complication of congenital hydrocephalus. In the first year of life and perhaps in the first two years brain defects are a more common cause of fits than epilepsy.

Subdural effusion and head injury. Convulsions occur as a result of a serious head injury, but they also occur as a result of subdural effusion which often presents without evidence of injury. In child abuse all possibility of it being anything but accidental is stoutly denied. All small children receive some bumps on the head in falls, and it seems that a subdural effusion may result from an apparently minor injury or from violent shaking. The presenting symptom is a convulsion or a too rapidly enlarging head. The diagnosis is made by ophthalmoscopic finding of retinal haemorrhages, by transillumination of the skull and by subdural tap.

Epilepsy may occur in infancy, but it should be regarded as being probably secondary to some cause such as brain defect or metabolic condition.

Infantile spasms. The so-called infantile spasms have also been termed 'salaam spasms', 'myoclonic seizures' and 'hypsarrhythmic attacks'. They consist of sudden rapid flexion of the trunk, lasting a fraction of a second. The subject was fully reviewed by Jeavons and Bower (1964). In 70 per cent of cases the attacks begin during the first six months, particularly at about four to six months of age. They usually cease by the age of eighteen months, but are commonly replaced by major convulsions. They are not examples of *petit mal* epilepsy, with which they are commonly confused. The attacks may result from a wide variety of causes (Matsumoto *et al*, 1981), including gross *brain malformations or damage, anoxia, subdural effusion, phenyl-ketonuria, syphilis, meningitis* and *intracranial infections, hypo-glycaemia, neurodermatoses* (e.g. tuberous sclerosis, neurofibro-matosis, the Sturge–Weber syndrome of facial port wine stain with mental subnormality), *cerebral palsy and fits, Tay-Sachs' disease* and other causes. In a third no cause can be found. One of the known causes is *Aicardi's syndrome* (Willis & Rosman 1980) of agenesis of the corpus callosum, mental subnormality and chorioretinopathy.

A suggested cause is *pertussis immunisation:* but as there are some 30 known causes of infantile spasms, and as they characteristically occur at just the age at which pertussis immunisation is being carried out, and in view of the fact that there is no laboratory or other investigation which can prove that the infantile spasms are the result of the immunisation, the connection is, to say the least, exceedingly doubtful. One has seen two children who developed infantile spasms within 48 hours of diptheria and tetanus immunisation alone.

There are several ways in which immunisation could cause a convulsion. The injection itself could immediately cause a breath-holding attack: in an older child it could cause a faint, and sometimes a faint may be accompanied by convulsive movements: the fever which commonly follows within a few hours of the pertussis immunisation could cause a benign febrile convulsion, or could precipitate a fit in an epileptic: but in none of those cases is there 'brain damage': Lastly every immunisation carries some risk, and very rarely pertussis immunisation can cause brain damage (as can pertussis itself). But if a child has a convulsion within a few hours of a pertussis immunisation, one must on no account give another dose of it: one would give the diphtheria and tetanus injections alone.

In 97 per cent of cases of infantile spasms the EEG is characteristic, showing the so-called hypsarrhythmia—sudden high peaks of electrical activity.

Infantile spasms have to be distinguished from petit mal, which occurs in an older age group (p. 215). One has seen a diagnosis of 'colic' when the correct diagnosis was infantile spasms.

Hypoglycaemia. Convulsions may be due to hypoglycaemia, other than that due to insulin overdosage. It is of vital importance that the diagnosis should be established, because recurrent hypoglycaemic attacks with convulsions cause irreparable brain damage. The fit is commonly preceded by weakness, pallor and sweating. Proper history-taking is important: a history of fits occurring only in the early hours of the morning, or a long time after a meal should suggest the need to perform a fasting blood sugar estimation to eliminate hypoglycaemia.

Hypoglycaemia may be due to hyperplasia or tumour of the islets of Langerhans, hypopituitarism, adrenocortical insufficiency, glycogenoses, hepatic disease or carbohydrate intolerance. With regard to the latter, an example is fructose intolerance, in which the child has hypoglycaemic symptoms such as vomiting, malaise and tremors on eating sweets (p. 12). Investigation for these conditions is laborious and should be carried out in hospital.

Hypocalcaemia after the newborn period is due to a variety of causes, including rickets, steatorrhoea, alkalosis, hypoparathyroidism or damage to the parathyroid glands following thyroidectomy for thyrotoxicosis. In older children hysterical overventilation may cause tetany. Tetany due to rickets occurs especially between the age of four months and three years. The clinical diagnosis of rickets is made by the thickened epiphysis of the wrist and the enlarged costochondral junctions. There is commonly some anaemia and hypotonia. The diagnosis can only be suspected on clinical grounds, but it must be confirmed by X-ray of the wrist or costochondral junctions and the serum alkaline phosphatase. Owing to the relative frequency of resistant rickets in Britain, one must not be misled by the history that adequate doses of Vitamin D have been given, though tetany in resistant rickets is rare.

Fits due to tetany are commonly indistinguishable from other major convulsions. Occasionally, however, one may see the typical limb posture of tetany—the thumb drawn into the palm of the hand, the hands abducted with the wrists flexed, the fingers flexed at the metacarpo-phalangeal joints and extended at the distal joints.

Dehydration following gastroenteritis and sometimes respiratory tract infections may be accompanied by convulsions. The causes are varied, and include electrolyte disturbances such as hyponatraemia, hypernatraemia and hypocalcaemia; over-rapid hydration; hydraemia as a result of overhydration; hyperthermia; and cerebral thrombosis. It may result from giving too much fluid without sufficient sodium or from hydrating too rapidly.

Infections—such as post-infectious encephalomyelitis associated with the common infectious diseases, whooping cough and toxoplasmosis are causes of fits. Post-infectious encephalomyelitis commonly follows an acute infectious disease, but may occasionally precede the rash in the case of the exanthems or the parotid swelling in the case of mumps. Occasionally the encephalitic symptoms occur without the appearance of the rash or the mumps, the diagnosis being made by virological means.

Subacute sclerosing panencephalitis ('SSPE') is a rare condition beginning with ordinary fits, but followed later by sudden rhythmical convulsive movements, dementia and death. It is due to a slow virus infection, usually measles. The EEG is characteristic.

Tetanus causes spasms which may be confused with epileptic fits. The excessive muscle tone and stiffness between convulsive movements and their occurrence with the slightest stimulus, with a history of trauma, should point to this diagnosis.

A convulsion may be a symptom of the acute onset of *poliomyelitis*.

Drugs and Poisons. The possibility of poisoning should be borne in mind when a child has an obscure illness. Numerous poisons and drugs may cause convulsions; they include amitriptyline, anti-histamines, camphor, chlorpromazine, corticosteroids, dicophane, insecticides, insulin overdosage, lead, phenothiazine, plants and strychnine.

The so-called *acute infantile hemiplegia* is the result of a variety of conditions, such as infections, injury, congenital heart disease, disseminated lupus erythematosus, periarteritis, sickle-cell anaemia, polycythaemia, thrombocytopenic purpura and dehydration (Carter & Gold 1967). The child has a major and often protracted convulsion followed by coma, and is then found to have a hemiplegia with mental subnormality.

Convulsions after infancy

> Febrile convulsions (until the age of five)
> Epilepsy
> Breath-holding attacks (until the age of five)
> Faint, syncopal attacks. Rare—surcardiac syndrome
> Hysteria, overventilation tetany
> Brain disease or injury
> Infections—encephalitis, meningitis, poliomyelitis, pertussis, malaria
> Metabolic conditions—hypoglycaemia, hypoparathyroidism (rare)
> Nephritis, hypertension, haemolytic uraemic syndrome (p. 52)
> Burn encephalopathy
> Drugs and poisons

Febrile convulsions and breath-holding attacks have virtually ceased by the age of five, but are common before then, especially between the age of one and three or four years.

Many of the conditions already mentioned must be considered in the older child. The most common cause of fits after the fifth year is *epilepsy*. Many children are thought to have *petit mal* when in fact they have *grand mal*. The distinction is important for the treatment of the two conditions is different.

Petit mal consists of brief lapses of consciousness, lasting up to 20 seconds, without a preceding aura, without convulsive movements and not followed by sleep. The attacks are commonly called 'dizzy spells' or 'fainting turns'. The child may stop, stand and stare. There may be flickering of the eyelids and a momentary upward deviation of the eyes, but there is no twitching of the limbs. Not more than five per cent of affected children fall in an attack. There is no change of colour. The child may drop an object held in the hand and may wet himself. The attacks can almost always be precipitated by forced over-ventilation.

Petit mal is distinguished from infantile spasms by the following features:

1   The age incidence. Infantile spasms occur mainly at four to six months and cease by three. *Petit mal* is rare before three, occurs predominantly between the age of four and eight years, usually ceasing by puberty (when it may be replaced by *grand mal*).

2   The duration of the attacks. The duration of *petit mal* is longer than that of infantile spasms, which consist of a sudden jack-knife flexion lasting a fraction of a second.

3   Infantile spasms are almost always associated with mental deficiency, while in 95 per cent of children with *petit mal* the IQ is normal.

4   The EEG is different. The EEG in infantile spasms shows sudden peaks of electrical discharge: that of *petit mal* shows three per second spike and wave activity.

Petit mal is distinguished from *grand mal* by the following points:

1   The rarity of *petit mal*. *Petit mal* is a relatively rare form of fits in children. It occurred in two to three per cent of 15,102 epileptics seen at the Johns Hopkins Hospital at Baltimore.

2   The nature of the fit. Convulsive twitching in limbs suggests *grand mal*. A fall usually signifies *grand mal*, for a change in posture is very rare in *petit mal*. Stiffness in an attack signifies *grand mal*. A change of colour is against the diagnosis of *petit mal*.

3   The duration of the fit. *Grand mal* can be momentary, but it usually lasts longer. A *petit mal* attack lasts not more than 20 seconds, but there may be a rapid succession of *petit mal* attacks.

4   *Petit mal* attacks can usually be precipitated by overventilation. The child is instructed to blow 100 times a piece of paper 12 inches away.

5   *Grand mal* attacks are commonly followed by sleep and sometimes by vomiting. This does not apply to *petit mal*.

6   The EEG is different. The EEG is abnormal in children with *petit*

mal, showing the three per second spike and wave activity. It is often normal in children with *grand mal*.

There are many different kinds of epileptic fit. In *temporal lobe epilepsy* there may be aurae consisting of hallucinations of smell, taste, sight or hearing. There may also be feelings of fear or abdominal pain. Chewing and odd movements may occur. There may be sudden tachycardia, blanching followed by blushing, paroxysmal confusion, meaningless words, senseless laughter, delusions or hallucinations, and catastrophic rage, with violent unexplained outbursts of temper. It may follow anoxia, pyogenic meningitis, encephalitis, head injury, a long fit of any cause, Schilder's disease, tuberous sclerosis or phenylketonuria (Ounsted *et al* 1966).

Psychomotor epilepsy may show itself by sudden unexplained temper tantrums. These should be considered when an epileptic child has unexplained outbursts of temper and screaming. Epileptic auto- matism occurs in children—leading to sudden irrational acts, such as walking fully clothed into a lake.

By no means all epileptic children have tonic and clonic phases in a fit. Some have unexplained falls and are limp when picked up, with- out twitching.

A sudden instantaneous onset of headache or of abdominal pain, lasting a few minutes only and followed by sleep may be a mani- festation of epilepsy.

It can be difficult to distinguish *faints* from fits. Faints are definitely rare in a young child, but from early puberty to adolescence they are common. A faint usually occurs on change of posture or on prolonged standing (as in school prayers), while a fit may occur at any time (particularly on awakening or on going to sleep). If a mother tells me that her child 'faints' when sitting in a chair I would certainly say that her diagnosis was incorrect, an epileptic fit being far more likely. Likewise if a child suddenly 'faints' when playing it is far more likely to be an epileptic fit. Loss of colour or limpness can occur with either faint or fit. Convulsive movements can occur during a faint: they do not definitely point to the diagnosis of epilepsy. In a study of 362 blood donors who became faint when blood was withdrawn, 47 lost consciousness: 25 of these (53 per cent) had a convulsion during the period of unconsciousness. An EEG is normal in many cases of *grand mal* epilepsy, and a fit resembling a faint would be *grand mal*, not *petit mal*.

Rabe (1974) described the *surcardiac syndrome,* an autosomal recessive condition consisting of congenital deafness, prolonged Q.T. interval and fainting attacks, starting in late infancy or early childhood. Sandifer's syndrome of dystonic movements in association with oesophageal reflux could be confused with convulsions.

Syncopal attacks may occur in children with a prolonged Q.T. interval without deafness: they may also occur when there is a posterior fossa tumour. Cough syncope occurs with asthma. Syncopal attacks occur in cases of untreated Fallot's tetralogy in association with periodic supraventricular tachycardia. Scott and her colleagues (1976) described syncopal attacks with bradycardia and vertigo in the 'sick sinus' syndrome. Extension of the neck may cause unconsciousness if there are fused cervical vertebrae (Illingworth, 1956).

Hysteria and hysterical overventilation tetany are unusual in children (p. 137). They are confined to older children—after the age of six or seven years. The hysterical fit is not difficult to distinguish from epilepsy, but when a mother describes an attack of hysterical overventilation tetany it is easy to make a wrong diagnosis. The history of overventilation followed by tingling in the extremities and stiffness of the hands and feet (perhaps with a description of carpopedal spasm), should make one think of tetany.

With regard to brain diseases, the various neurodermatoses may cause convulsions. As for tuberous sclerosis, the mother may have the typical lesions, but children do not usually have the facial lesions in the first five years: over 90% of affected babies, however, with tuberous sclerosis when examined by the Wood's lamp, show the typical patches of hypopigmentation even in the newborn period.

The frequency of convulsions in children with mental subnormality or cerebral palsy was noted on p. 208. Fits are common in various *degenerative diseases of the nervous system.*

A severe head injury, a cerebral abscess or a subdural effusion may be followed in months or years by convulsions. In some ten per cent or more of children in whom convulsions follow these conditions, the first fit may not occur until ten years or more after the damage to the brain.

Intracranial infections, including meningitis and encephalitis, continue to be important causes of fits. Post-infectious encephalomyelitis following the common infectious diseases is also important.

Metabolic conditions are important causes of fits. They include in particular hypoglycaemia, whether spontaneous or the result of insulin overdosage, and the effects of dehydration and repair. The symptoms of ketotic hypoglycaemia commonly begin after the first birthday, especially in low-birth-weight babies who have remained small and thin. The symptoms may be drowsiness in the morning before eating or at other times of food deprivation. The diagnosis is established in hospital.

Fits may be due to *hypoparathyroidism*. There may be a history of late teething, muscular pains, a dry skin, and mental deterioration. There may be moniliasis of nails and the oral mucosa, loss of hair and cataracts.

Convulsions are an important complication of *acute nephritis*, when there is associated hypertension. A child with acute nephritis should be referred to hospital in order that appropriate treatment should be given to prevent fits if the blood pressure is dangerously high.

In the first 48 hours after a burn, not necessarily a severe one (Warlow & Hinton 1969), a child may begin to vomit and then develop fluctuating levels of consciousness, twitching, hypertension or respiratory arrest. It is probably due to cerebral oedema.

Poisons, especially lead, are important causes of fits. Other poisons include carbon tetrachloride, dicophane, lead, mercury, monoamine oxidase inhibitors, pyrethrum, rotenone and strychnine.

More than 70 *drugs* are suspected of causing fits (Chadwick 1981, Davies 1981). They include acetazolamide, aminophylline, amitriptyline, amphetamine, antihistamines, carbamazepine, chloroquine, corticosteroids, cycloserine, diphenoxylate, imipramine, isoniazid, metoclopramide, nalidixic acid, the phenothiazines and pyrimethamine.

References

Brown JK, Cockburn F, Forfar JO. Clinical and chemical correlations in convulsions in the newborn. *Lancet* 1972; **1:** 135.

Carter S, Gold A. Acute infantile hemiplegia. *Pediatr Clin North Am* 1967; **14:** 851.

Chadwick DW. Convulsions associated with drug therapy. *Adverse Drug Reaction Bulletin* 1981; **No. 87:** 316.

Davies DM. *Textbook of adverse drug reactions.* Oxford: Oxford University Press, 1981.

Eriksson M, Zetterstrom R. Neonatal convulsions. *Acta Paediatr Scand* 1979; **68:** 807.

Illingworth RS. Attacks of unconsciousness in association with fused cervical vertebrae. *Arch Dis Child* 1956; **31**: 8.

Jeavons PM, Bower BD. Infantile spasms. *Clinics, No. 15* London: Heineman, 1964.

Livingston S, Bergman W, Pauli LL. Febrile convulsions. *Lancet* 1973; **2**: 1441.

Livingston S, Pauli LL. Febrile fits. *Br Med J* 1976; **2**: 1530.

Lockman A. Neonatal seizures, diagnosis and treatment. In *Pediatrics Update.* Oxford: Blackwell Scientific Publications, 1980.

Lombroso CT, Lerman P. Breath-holding spells (cyanotic and pallid infantile syncope). *Pediatrics* 1967; **39**: 563.

Marshall F. Tetanus of the newborn. *Adv in Pediatrics* Vol 15. Year Book Publishing Co, 1968.

Matsumoto A *et al.* Infantile spasms. Etiological factors, clinical aspects and long term prognosis in 200 cases. *Eur J Pediatr* 1981; **135**: 239.

Ouelette EM. Febrile convulsions. *Pediatr Clin North Am* 1974; **21**: 467.

Ounsted C, Lindsay J, Norman R. Biological factors in temporal lobe epilepsy. *Clinics in Dev Med No. 22.* London: Heinemann, 1966.

Rabe EF. Recurrent paroxysmal non-epileptic disorders. *Curr Probl Pediatr* 1974; **4**: 3.

Rose AL, Lombroso CT. Neonatal seizure states. *Pediatrics* 1970; **45**: 404.

Rutter N, Smales ORC. Role of routine investigation in children presenting with their first febrile convulsion. *Arch Dis Child* 1977; **52**: 188.

Samson JH, Apthorp J, Finley A. Febrile seizures and purulent meningitis. *JAMA* 1969; **210**: 1918.

Scott O, Macartney FJ, Deverall PB. Sick sinus syndrome. *Arch Dis Child* 1976; **51**: 100.

Warlow CP, Hinton P. Early neurological disturbance following relatively minor burns in children. *Lancet* 1969; **2**: 978.

Willis J, Rosman NP. The Aicardi syndrome versus congenital infection: diagnostic considerations. *J Pediatr* 1980; **96**: 235.

Neck Stiffness

Neck stiffness may be a symptom or sign of the utmost importance in childhood, in that it may point to meningitis. On the other hand it may be a trivial matter of no importance. Stiffness in lateral movement of the neck in a newborn baby may be related to a sternomastoid tumour. After the newborn period the commonest causes are the 'rheumatic' stiff neck, cervical adenitis and drugs. The principal causes of neck stiffness are as follows:

> Meningism, meningoencephalitis, poliomyelitis
> Tetanus
> Intracranial haemorrhage, abscess, tumour
> Vertebral anomalies, injury, infection (osteitis)
> > Discitis
> Effects of lumbar puncture
> 'Rheumatic' stiff neck
> Rheumatoid arthritis
> Retropharyngeal abscess
> Cervical lymphadenitis
> Meningeal leukaemia
> Myositis ossificans progressiva
> Cerebral palsy of the spastic or rigid type
> Drugs

The neck stiffness of *meningism* and meningitis consists of stiffness in flexing the neck, but not in lateral movement. Ideally the child should be in the sitting position when the test is carried out. The neck is fully extended and then flexed. Resistance may be felt throughout the movement of flexion or only in the terminal part of the movement, when the chin is almost touching the sternum. It is important to watch the child's face when testing for meningism, for if there is meningism there is almost always pain on flexing the neck. A wince of pain in the last part of the movement may be the only convincing sign of meningism. The pain is usually felt in the lumbar region, but is sometimes felt in the muscle at the back of the neck. The child with meningism may be unable to kiss his knees. When he sits up in bed he exhibits the tripod sign, placing both arms behind him so that he does not fall back owing to spasm of the glutei, erector spinae and hamstrings.

Meningism occurs in a variety of infections in childhood, such as pneumonia, pyelonephritis, otitis media, tonsillitis, infective hepatitis, mumps, malaria and typhoid fever. It occurs in many virus infections of the nervous system, such as poliomyelitis, encephalitis, the post-infectious encephalomyelitides and pyogenic meningitis. It also occurs after an intracranial haemorrhage or in the presence of a cerebral abscess or a tumour.

Limitation of movement without pain occurs as a feature of *congenital anomalies of the vertebrae*, including fusion of vertebrae.

The so-called *'rheumatic stiff neck'* is a mysterious entity, at one time ascribed to sitting in a draught. The so-called 'rheumatic' stiff neck has nothing to do with rheumatic fever. Tenderness of the muscles distinguishes it from meningism; the pain in the rheumatic stiff neck is mainly on lateral or rotatory movement rather than on flexion. It may be due to a virus infection.

Stiffness of the neck, usually but not always without pain, occurs commonly in *rheumatoid arthritis*.

Pain on movement of the neck with stiffness may result from *inflamed cervical lymph nodes or from a retropharyngeal abscess.*

Myositis ossificans progressiva commonly begins in the neck muscles; there is a deposition of bone between muscle bundles, gradually spreading through the trunk muscles over a period of years. The bone can readily be felt by the examiner's hand.

Neck stiffness and opisthotonos may be a side effect of the phenothiazines or metoclopramide.

Reference

Illingworth RS. Myositis ossificans progressiva. *Arch Dis Child* 1971; **46**: 264.

Scoliosis

The causes of scoliosis can be classified as follows:

       Postural—the scoliosis disappearing when the child bends
           over
       Compensatory—due to unequal length of the legs
       Structural—persisting when the child bends over
         Unknown causes
         Muscular dystrophy, late stage
         Poliomyelitis
         Rare—hemivertebra
           Congenital asymmetry
           Fragilitas ossium
           Neurofibromatosis

Marfan's syndrome
Friedreich's ataxia
Prader–Willi syndrome

The clinical diagnosis of most of these conditions is straightforward, though radiological examination is needed for the diagnosis of hemivertebra and perhaps fragilitas ossium. Marfan's syndrome is diagnosed on the arachnodactyly, tall slender build, subluxation of the lens of the eye and an aortic valve lesion, often with other abnormalities. Scoliosis is a common finding in the *Prader–Willi* syndrome (p. 20). It may result from defective leg growth in rheumatoid arthritis involving one knee.

References

Holm VA, Laurnen EL. Prader Willi syndrome and scoliosis. *Dev Med Child Neurol* 1981; **23**: 192.
Zorab PA. *Scoliosis*. London: Heinemann, 1969.

Hypotonia and/or generalized Weakness

The assessment of muscle tone is part of the routine examination of infants in a welfare clinic or elsewhere. The assessment is made as follows:

1 Feeling the muscle. The hypotonic muscle, as in a mongol, feels flabby.

2 Assessing the resistance to passive movement. One tests in particular the elbow, wrist, hip, knee and ankle. In hypertonic children there is increased resistance, and in hypotonic children the resistance is reduced. One has to distinguish voluntary resistance by the child.

3 Assessing the range of movement. This is increased in the hypotonic child and decreased in the hypertonic child. For instance, in the case of the mongol, who is always hypotonic, having flexed the hip to a right-angle, abduction is so full that both legs will lie flat extended on the couch. Abduction of the hip is reduced in hypertonia. Dorsiflexion of the ankle is reduced in hypertonia and increased in hypotonia.

4   One shakes the limb—holding the arm below the elbow and the leg below the knee. The amount of movement of the hand or wrist gives a good idea of the muscle tone.

A severely hypotonic infant lies in the characteristic frog-like posture with the hips abducted and externally rotated, the limbs being in contact with the couch. In ventral suspension the baby cannot hold the head up, and the four limbs hang down lifelessly, with no flexion at hip, knee or elbow. There is complete head lag when he is pulled to the sitting position.

Hypotonia at birth is usually due to severe anoxia. It can be caused by drugs taken by the mother in pregnancy, notably alcohol, barbiturates, chlorpropamide, diazepam, librium, magnesium sulphate (in labour), propranolol.

Apart from the hypotonia due to anoxia, by far the commonest cause of severe hypotonia with weakness is the Werdnig–Hoffmann syndrome.

Numerous papers have been written about hypotonic or 'floppy' infants, and various classifications have been suggested. The classification below is modified from that of Dubowitz (1980).

Hypotonia with weakness
> Werdnig–Hoffmann infantile spinal muscular atrophy.
>> Motor neurone disease (rare)
> Duchenne   muscular   dystrophy.   Kugelberg–Wehlander muscular dystrophy
> Congenital muscular dystrophy (rare) Myotonic dystrophy (rare p. 189)
> Peroneal muscular atrophy (rare)
> Injury to cervical spinal cord at birth
> Rare metabolic diseases—glycogenoses, lipoidoses, mucopolysaccharidoses, McArdle's syndrome, Lowe's syndrome, myoglobinuria, hypoparathyroidism, familial periodic paralysis, Leigh's syndrome, Krabbe's syndrome, Refsum's syndrome (p. 194) neuromyelitis optica (Devic's syndrome), porphyria.
> Dermatomyositis (p. 40), Myasthenia gravis (p. 40)
>> Disseminated lupus (p. 34)

Acute illness
  Guillain–Barré syndrome
  Polyneuropathies
  Poliomyelitis. Pseudopoliomyelitis
  Diphtheria
  Botulism, rabies
 Hysteria
 Drugs
Hypotonia without significant weakness
  Mongolism and other severe mental subnormality
  Benign congenital hypotonia
  Hypotonic form of cerebral palsy
  Rare syndromes—Prader–Willi, Marfan, Ehlers–Danlos and
    congenital laxity of ligaments, Riley's syndrome
  Other metabolic conditions—rickets, coeliac disease, hypo-
    thyroidism, hypercalcaemia, renal tubular acidosis

In the *Werdnig–Hoffmann syndrome* hypotonia is present at birth or develops in the first few weeks. The tendon jerks are usually absent and there may be fasciculation of the tongue. There is indrawing of the chest with inspiration. Contractures develop early. Few survive the first birthday.

Motor neurone disease is rare in childhood. There is progressive weakness, wasting and fasciculation of the tongue with loss of reflexes.

The commonest form of *muscular dystrophy* is that of *Duchenne,* affecting boys. Half the affected boys are late in walking (after the age of 18 months), and some mental subnormality is common, so that they are often somewhat late in other aspects of development. Weakness develops, especially noticeable on climbing stairs. The weakness involves the proximal muscles before the distal ones and the lower limbs before the upper. Toe walking may occur. There is a waddling gait, especially when the boy is tired or running. He cannot perform a standing jump; he cannot rise directly from the supine position—displaying the Gower manoeuvre of rolling over and climbing up the thighs. The prominence of the calf muscles may be obvious.

A benign variant is the Kugelberg–Wehlander syndrome, developing mainly in adolescence, with proximal weakness in the first place.

There may be severe hypotonia in the rare congenital muscular dystrophy; the weakness is mainly proximal and it is not progressive.

For *myotonic dystrophy* as a cause of weakness see p. 189.

In *peroneal muscular atrophy,* which is also rare, weakness develops in the evertors and dorsiflexors of the ankle: reflexes are lost, toe walking may occur, and hammer toes may develop.

Injury to the cervical spinal cord may occur, mainly in a breech delivery. There may be considerable hypotonia, with absent tendon jerks. The intercostal muscles may be paralysed and there is in-drawing of the lower part of the chest on inspiration. The whole picture resembles that of the Werdnig–Hoffmann syndrome, but in that condition the child will cry feebly if the foot is pricked, whereas in the child with cervical cord injury there is usually no cry.

There are many metabolic diseases associated with hypotonia and/or weakness. In *Pompe's type of glycogen storage disease* there is hypotonia from infancy, a large tongue, weakness, mental subnormality and cardiac enlargement. In the *sulphatide lipoidosis* (metachromatic leucodystrophy) weakness and hypotonia begin in the first year, with mental deterioration, optic atrophy and nystagmus: the motor nerve conduction time is prolonged. In *McArdle's syndrome* of phosphorylase deficiency there may be weakness and cramps on exertion. In *paroxysmal myoglobinuria* there are muscle cramps and weakness with myoglobin in the urine. In *familial periodic paralysis* there are attacks of severe weakness in association with potassium deficiency. In *Leigh's subacute necrotizing encephalomyelopathy* there are hypotonia, ocular palsies, weakness, mental deterioration, dysphagia and failure to thrive. For *Refsum's* syndrome see p. 194. *Neuromyelitis optica* (Devic) may occur at any age: there may be flaccid paralysis, loss of tendon jerks, sensory loss and optic neuritis. *Porphyria* (p. 108) may be manifested by flaccid paralysis, abdominal pain and fits. Hypotonia with sucking and swallowing difficulties may be a feature of *myasthenia gravis,* of the transitory type in the newborn, or of the persistent type.

Amongst the acute conditions is the *Guillain–Barré syndrome,* a condition of varied aetiology, of which virus infections and an im-munisation sequela is an example. There is the rapid onset of flaccid paralysis, often including the facial muscles, with loss of tendon jerks. The CSF finding of high protein with normal cell count is characteristic.

There are several causes of *polyneuritis* (Evans 1979). They include *serum sickness,* the *Guillain–Barré syndrome, degenerative polyneuro-pathies,* and cases due to *metabolic, toxic* or *systemic disease,.* It sometimes follows *rubella immunisation* or *tetanus toxoid*. Tasker & Chutorian (1969) described 17 children between infancy and adolescence with distal weakness and sensory changes. The polyneuritis lasted for varying periods from 16 months to several years. There was decreased nerve conduction time and a raised CSF protein. Polyneuritis is a common sequel of *diphtheria*, and may result from *typhoid fever, typhus, mumps, leprosy* and *poisons*. It may be caused by lead poisoning, chloramphenicol, isoniazid, nalidixic acid or nitrofurantoin.

Botulism is an unusual cause of polyneuropathy (Berg 1977, *Medical*) *Journal of Australia* 1978). An affected child develops constipation, followed in a week or two by the rapid development of bulbar and limb weakness, ptosis, hypotonia and loss of reflexes. The condition may resemble poliomyelitis, the Guillain–Barré syndrome or myasthenia. There is a rare *hypertrophic interstitial polyneuropathy* (Anderson *et al* 1973) with delayed motor development, hypotonia, weakness, absent reflexes, a high CSF protein and delayed motor nerve conduction.

Drugs may cause muscle weakness, mainly by causing peripheral neuritis. They include azathioprine, chloroquine, colistin, cyclophosphamide, cycloserine, diazepam, ethionamide, gentamicin, gold, isoniazid, kanamycin, lead, meprobamate, 6-mercaptopurine, metronidazole, neomycin, nitrofurantoin, tricyclic antidepressants, triamcinolone and vincristine.

Hysteria is an unusual cause of flaccid paralysis with sensory changes.

Hypotonia without significant weakness occurs in mongolism and many other conditions. All mongols are hypotonic.

Benign congenital hypotonia is a non-specific condition, which is non-progressive and tends to improve. The usual age at which affected children are able to walk is five or six years.

There is a rare *hypotonic form of cerebral palsy*, in which there is generalised hypotonia; the exaggerated tendon jerks, the positive stretch reflex, ankle clonus and extensor plantar response establishes the diagnosis. These children become spastic as they get older. Many wrongly diagnose hypotonia in the common spastic form of cerebral palsy on account of the excessive head lag when the child is pulled up into the sitting position.

Several rare syndromes are associated with hypotonia without weakness. Hypotonia is an early feature of the *Prader–Willi syndrome*

(p. 20). It occurs in *Marfan's syndrome* of arachnodactyly, hyper-extensible joints, iridodonesis and congenital heart disease. There may be hypotonia in the *Ehlers–Danlos syndrome* of cutis hyperelastica and in *Riley's syndrome* of familial dysautonomia (p. 41).

There is a minor degree of hypotonia in many cases of rickets.

References

See p. 232.

Localized Weakness

Weakness of an arm or of the legs without generalized weakness may be due to the following conditions:

> Erb's palsy, Klumpke's palsy
> Pseudoparalysis of scurvy
> Todd's paralysis after an epileptic fit
> Trauma—pulled elbow, nerve damage by injection
> Spinal tumour, abscess, lipoma
> Diastematomyelia, syringomyelia
> Poliomyelitis: transverse myelitis
> Hysteria

The commonest cause of weakness of an arm from birth is Erb's palsy. There is weakness of flexion of the elbow, wrist drop, and the 'chauffeur's tip position' of the hand. The limb is hypotonic—a point of importance, for I have seen it confused with spastic hemiplegia. The hypertonia of the muscles in mild spastic hemiplegia may be so slight that it cannot be detected until the child is older; but in the ipsilateral leg there is likely to be an exaggerated knee jerk and there may be reduced dorsiflexion of the ankle. In cold weather the affected hemiplegic arm and leg are cold as compared with the normal side. In Erb's palsy the biceps jerk is reduced, while in spastic hemiplegia it is increased. After infancy there is no problem, for Erb's palsy almost always disappears within a few days or weeks of birth. Klumpke's paralysis is due to damage to the seventh and eighth cervical nerve roots and the first dorsal. There is weakness of the hand and often ipsilateral ptosis and a small pupil if the sympathetic fibres are also involved.

232   *Localized weakness*

Pseudoparalysis of a limb may be due to scurvy, the child not using the limb because it hurts owing to the subperiosteal haemorrhage.

After a major epileptic fit there may be weakness of a limb or of arm and leg, lasting usually for a few hours and occasionally for a few days *(Todd's paralysis)*.

The radial nerve is commonly damaged by unwisely giving an intramuscular injection into the arm: the sciatic nerve may be damaged by incorrect choice of site for injections in the lower limb. The triple vaccine may cause brachial neuritis, though given correctly.

Trauma may cause apparent weakness of a limb as does scurvy. Trauma includes fractures, an important cause of which in the early years is child abuse.

A *lipoma* in the region of the cauda equina is an important cause of progressive weakness of the lower limbs, usually with loss of sphincter control (Dubowitz *et al* 1965). The lipoma can be seen and palpated in the region of the sacrum or buttock.

Diastematomyelia is a condition in which the spinal cord is split and tethered by a spicule of bone. It leads to progressive weakness of the legs. It is sometimes revealed by a patch of pigmentation or hair over the spine.

Local paralysis may be caused by poliomyelitis and other viruses, including the coxsackie and viruses of the acute infectious diseases. A few cases of muscle weakness, resembling poliomyelitis, have occurred 4 to 11 days after an asthmatic attack (Lancet 1980). There may be severe flaccid paralysis of a limb or occasionally of several limbs, preceded by muscle pain, as in poliomyelitis. There is no sensory loss. It may be due to a neurotropic virus.

Goodyer (1981) has reviewed the various manifestations of hysteria in children, especially paralysis, aphasia, aphonia, disturbances of vision and gait, and torticollis.

References

Anderson RM, Dennett X, Hopkin I, Shield LK. Hypertrophic interstitial polyneuropathy in infancy. *J Pediatr* 1973; **82:** 619.
Berg BO. Syndrome of infant botulism. *Pediatrics* 1977; **59:** 321.
Dubowitz V. Muscular dystrophy and related disorders. *Postgrad Med J* 1965; **41:** 332.
Dubowitz V. The floppy infant. *Clinics in Developmental Medicine No. 76* London: Heinemann, 1980.

Dubowitz V, Lorber J, Zachary RB. Lipoma of the cauda equina. *Arch Dis Child* 1965; **40:** 207.

Evans OB. Polyneuropathy in childhood. *Pediatrics* 1979; **64:** 96.

Goodyer I. Hysterical conversion reactions in children. *J Child Psychol Psychiat* 1981; **22:** 179.

Illingworth CM. Pulled elbow, a study of 100 patients. *Br Med J* 1975; **2:** 672.

Lancet (Leading article). Post-asthmatic pseudopoliomyelitis in children. 1980; **1:** 860.

Medical Journal of Australia (Leading article). Infant botulism. 1978; **2:** 228.

Sinclair L. *Metabolic disease in childhood.* Oxford: Blackwell Scientific Publications, 1979.

Tasker W, Chutorian AM. Chronic polyneuritis of childhood. *J Pediatr* 1969; **74:** 667.

Stiffness or Spasticity of Limbs

Many infants in the first days and weeks have greater than usual muscle tone with exaggerated tendon jerks and often with ankle clonus. Unless there are other abnormal signs, such as smallness of the head circumference in relation to the baby's weight or delayed motor development, one pays little attention to it. The signs usually disappear as the child grows older.

Weakness due to spasticity or hypertonia is nearly always a manifestation of *cerebral palsy*. The differential diagnosis depends on the distribution of the spasticity. If a child with spastic quadriplegia has been spastic from birth, the cause would almost certainly be cerebral palsy—but if he was normal at first and then became spastic, other causes must be considered. If the disease was of acute onset, it could be due to encephalitis (such as a post-infectious encephalomyelitis), or to an intracranial vascular accident, such as thrombosis due to dehydration. If the spasticity is of gradual onset, it may be due to one of the numerous degenerative diseases of the nervous system, such as Schilder's disease—which is manifested by the gradual development of blindness, deafness and spasticity beginning in early childhood. There are so many degenerative diseases of the nervous system that it would be impossible to review them all here. The reader should refer to any of the textbooks of paediatric neurology, such as that of Menkes or Drillien & Drummond. Other causes of progressive spasticity involving all four limbs include craniovertebral abnormalities, such as basilar impression and the Klippel–Feil syndrome of fused cervical vertebrae with other anomalies. Neuromyelitis optica and its near relative disseminated sclerosis are other causes of spasticity of rapid onset. It should be noted that the spasticity of cerebral palsy may increase as the child grows older, and the development of deformities, such as dislocation of the hip and joint fixation due to muscle contracture may give a false impression that the child has a progressive neurological disorder.

When the spasticity of cerebral palsy is almost entirely confined to the lower limbs, it is easy to diagnose spastic paraplegia, while more careful examination of the upper limbs when the child is building a tower of bricks or performing a timed bead-threading test, will show that there is minimal involvement of the upper limbs, so that the true diagnosis is cerebral diplegia. True spastic paraplegia is rare, and should alert one to the possibility that the lesion is spinal and not cerebral. The spinal lesion may be a tumour, cyst or other anomaly, and it should be looked for, because it may be treatable.

Excessive muscle tone, restricting the range of movement in a joint, may be confused with *deformities of joints,* such as *arthrogryposis* or other congenital abnormalities. Reduced range of movement in a joint such as the hip could be ascribed to increased muscle tone when it is due to *contracture of the muscles,* as a result of the child (usually severely mentally defective or hypotonic) always lying in one position.

The *development of excessive muscle tone in a previously normal child* suggests the following possibilities:

Encephalitis or meningitis if acute, and other infections of the
central nervous system, including tetanus
Demyelinating or degenerative disease of the nervous system
Cerebral or spinal abscess or tumour
Brain damage—perhaps decerebrate rigidity—due to
anoxia (e.g. cardiac arrest)
meningo-encephalitis
cerebral tumour or haemorrhage
Drugs

Spasticity of extrapyramidal type can be caused by diazoxide, phenothiazines, haloperidol, tricyclic antidepressants and metoclopramide.

The number of conditions involved is so considerable, covering a large section of the whole of paediatric neurology, that it would not be profitable to discuss them here. An affected child should be investigated by a paediatrician.

References

Drillien CM, Drummond MB. *Development problems in early childhood.* Oxford: Blackwell Scientific Publications, 1977.
Menkes JH. *Textbook of child neurology.* Philadelphia: Lea and Febiger, 1974.

Inequality of Limb Length

It is said that prenatal maldevelopment of a limb may be caused by the mother taking abortifacients, ergot, cannabis, a contraceptive pill, haloperidol, imipramine, methotrexate, phenytoin, or warfarin, or by uterine abnormalities—fibroids, a bicornuate uterus, oligohydramnios or by hyperthermia in early pregnancy. Irradiation in pregnancy may be a factor. Other drugs are suspected of occasionally causing limb deformities.

Sharrard (1979) listed the causes of abnormality of limb length as follows:

1 Congenital bone abnormalities
   Short femur or tibia
   Coxa vara
   Dislocation of hip
2 Soft tissue abnormalities
   Arterio-venous fistula
   Haemangioma (Klippel–Trenaunay syndrome)
   Neurofibromatosis
   Arthrogryposis
3 Abnormality of bone growth
   Achondroplasia
   Fibrous dysplasia
   Pseudoarthrosis of tibia

4 Trauma to the epiphysis
5 Infection—overgrowth due to chronic osteitis
   tuberculosis
   osteitis involving the epiphysis
6 Neurological—poliomyelitis
   cerebral palsy
7 Total growth abnormalities
   Congenital asymmetry

Limb shortening may be a sequel of irradiation damaging the growing end of the bone: and it may follow injection of contrast material into the femoral artery.

The haemangioma involving a lower limb may not be obvious: the limb is enlarged: the slight naevoid markings may be difficult to detect.

A neurofibroma can cause limb enlargement without necessarily other signs, such as café-au-lait pigmentation.

Cerebral palsy causes shortening of arm or leg, obvious if there is hemiplegia: poliomyelitis causes more shortening.

Congenital asymmetry is a strange condition in which one side of the body is bigger than the other: hence the old term 'hemi-hypertrophy': the difficulty lies in deciding which of the two sides is 'normal'. Many features are commonly combined with the asymmetry: they include features of the Russell and Silver syndromes (Reister & Scherz 1964)— shortness of stature, increased gonadotrophin output, early sexual development with retarded bone age, café-au-lait pigmentation, incurved little finger, turning down of the angles of the mouth and a small triangular face; there is an increased incidence of malignant disease, especially Wilms' tumour, and neurofibromatosis. There may be syndactyly and retinal changes.

References

Reister HC, Scherz MG. Silver syndrome. *Am J Dis Child* 1964; **107**: 410.
Ringrose RE, Jabbour JT, Kelle DK. Hemihypertrophy. *Pediatrics* 1965; **36**: 434.
Sharrard WJW. *Paediatric orthopaedics and fractures.* Oxford: Blackwell Scientific Publications, 1979.

Limitation of Joint Movement

Limitation of joint movement from birth may occur in the *fetal alcohol syndrome* (Hanson 1977) *arthrogryposis, punctate epiphyseal dysplasia* (achondroplasia-like appearance with cataract, related to warfarin administration in pregnancy), and the *nail-patella syndrome*—hypoplasia of patella, dystrophic nails and elbow dysplasia. It also occurs in *diastrophic dwarfism* and *Pfaunler's syndrome*.

Joint contractures, often involving only the fifth finger, may occur in diabetes mellitus.

References

Grgic A, Rosenbloom AL, *et al.* Joint contracture—common manifestation of childhood diabetes mellitus. *J Pediatr* 1976; **88:**584.

Hanson JW. Alcohol and the fetus. *Br J Hosp Med* 1977; **18:** 126.

Simila S, Vesa L, Wasz–Hockert O. Hereditary onycho-osteodysplasia (nail patella syndrome). *Pediatrics* 1970; **46:** 61.

Bow Legs and Knock Knees

Some degree of *bow legs* is normal in late infancy. If the bowing is more marked than usual, so that when the child is lying down there is a gap of over 5 cms between the medial femoral condyles, when the internal maleoli are in contact with the legs extended, one should take an X-ray to exclude rickets or *Blount's disease*. Blount's disease is a likely diagnosis if the bowing is unilateral; it is more common in Negroes and in Finland. The X-ray shows irregular ossification on the medial side of the upper tibial epiphysis, leading to beaking on the posteromedial aspect of the metaphysis.

Knock knee is normal in toddlers, especially at around the age of three, except when extreme—there being a gap of over 10 cms between the internal malleoli when the child is lying down with the legs extended; in that case an X-ray should be taken.

Reference

Sharrard WJW. Knock knees and bow legs. *Br Med J* 1976; **1:** 826.

Toe Walking and Toeing in

Some *normal toddlers* walk on their toes by habit. There are no signs of spasticity or other disease: the tendon jerks are normal, the plantar responses are flexor, there is a normal range of abduction at the hip and of dorsiflexion of the ankle. Special investigation is unnecessary. A child may walk on his toes because of a painful heel.

A *prematurely born baby* on reaching what would have been term, is liable to bear his weight on his toes rather than on the sole of his foot.

By far the commonest cause of toe walking is *cerebral palsy of the spastic type.* If the toe walking is unilateral, there will be the usual signs of spastic hemiplegia—the characteristic gait, shortening of the affected leg and arm, some wasting of the affected limbs, limited dorsiflexion of the affected ankle, relative coldness of the affected limbs as compared with the normal ones, limited abduction of the hip, exaggerated knee jerk and plantar extensor response on the affected side, and possibly ankle clonus. If both lower limbs are involved, there will almost certainly be signs of at least slight involvement of the arms, if the child is old enough to perform fine repetitive movements.

An unusual cause is *congenital shortening of the Achilles tendon.* The absence of the other signs of cerebral palsy and especially of an exaggerated knee jerk, limited abduction of the hip or of an extensor plantar response, should make a mistaken diagnosis unnecessary. If the limitation of dorsiflexion of the ankle is due to spasticity, dorsiflexion will be normal when the knee is flexed. If the limitation is due to shortening of the Achilles tendon, the dorsiflexion will remain limited on flexion of the knee.

An early sign of *dystonia musculorum deformans* is often toe walking ('The ballet-dancer's foot). (See p. 206).

Other causes of toe walking are *infantile autism, muscular dystrophy, peroneal muscular atrophy* (p. 229) and *a spinal cord tumour.* Toe walking in Duchenne muscular dystrophy is said to be a postural adjustment to keep the weight-line behind the hip and in front of the knees at the same time in the face of ileo-tibial band tightness and quadriceps weakness.

Toeing in is almost always a self-curing condition in the young child; in the commonest form the whole limb is rotated medially, the child

238

walking with the knees partly turned in to face each other. A less common form is the metatarsus varus in which there is adduction and varus deformity of the foot, the child walking with the knees forward or turned slightly outwards.

Bilateral talipes in a girl is commonly (in about 40 per cent) associated with congenital hip dislocation. Whenever in boy or girl there is *significant* talipes, one should satisfy oneself that the hip is normal.

Reference

Sharrard WJW. Intoeing and flat feet. *Br Med J* 1976; **1**: 888.

Limp, Limb and Joint Pains

When a young child begins to limp, or an older child complains of limb pains, it may be impossible to distinguish bone pain from muscle or joint pain. The young child cannot even say where the pain is; he may be old enough to say that the pain is somewhere in the thigh, but he cannot localize it further; and the younger child just refuses to bear weight and cannot complain of pain. When a young child begins to limp, there is often a history of minor trauma, but so there is in many other small children, who fall when running, fall off trees or have other knocks and bumps. When there is no history of definite injury, and no signs of injury, inflammation or arthritis, one often obtains a history of preceding upper respiratory tract infection. That, too, is difficult to assess, because such infections are so common in this age group. *The accurate diagnosis of the cause of a limp (or refusal to bear weight) can be very difficult and often impossible* (Illingworth 1978). When older children complain of vague limb or back pains, and no abnormal signs can be found, the pain may be due to the normal vigorous pursuits of youth, such as dances, violent games or skateboards. *Traumatic periostitis* may result from a twist or sprain. Recovery occurs in 7 to 10 days. The X-ray may show a periosteal reaction about a week after the injury.

When a previously well child begins to limp, one examines the shoe for a protruding nail, crinkling of the sole or excessive tightness; one then examines the child's lower limbs for a sore place, local heat or bone tenderness (due to fracture), not forgetting to look for enlarged tender inguinal lymph nodes. One then examines the ankle and knee joints for pain on movement and heat on palpation, and the hip joint in order to determine whether the range of movement, particularly in abduction and rotation, is full and painless. One remembers the frequency with which pain in the knee is pain referred from a diseased hip.

Finally one examines the spine for the range of movement, and the abdomen in case the limp is related to psoas spasm due to intra-abdominal inflammation.

I have tried to arrange the causes of limp and limb pains on an anatomical basis, despite overlap. Pain in the lower limbs may be referred from the abdomen (e.g. psoas spasm in appendicitis) or from the spinal cord or vertebrae. Pain in the knee is commonly pain referred from the hip. When a tibia is fractured (as in a road traffic accident), the pain may be confined to the tibia, when in addition there is injury to the hip.

For limp due to shortening of a limb see p. 235.

The following are other causes to consider:

> *Soft tissue*—Trauma: nail in shoe etc: ingrowing toe nail:
>> Inguinal adenitis
>> Sickle-cell disease
>> Collagen diseases
>
> *Muscle*—growing pains
>> Trauma. Effects of intramuscular injection. Strain
>> Duchenne muscular dystrophy
>> Early poliomyelitis
>> Weakness of a limb
>> Cramp—McArdle's syndrome: dehydration
>> Trichiniasis, myositis, other infection
>> Porphyria
>
> *Tendons and ligaments*
>> Sprain, stress
>> Pes cavus, flat foot
>> Achilles tendonitis. Tight Achilles tendon
>
> *Bursitis*—calcaneal

Periosteum—trauma: non-accidental injury
  Scurvy
  Rubella syndrome
  Caffey's disease (p. 35)
  Vitamin A excess
Bone—Trauma: fracture: non-accidental injury
  Stress fracture of the heel
  Slipped femoral epiphysis
  Osteitis: sickle-cell disease
  Tumour—leukaemia, Hodgkin's disease, cyst, osteoid
       osteoma, Gaucher's disease
  Rickets

Osteochondritis
  Perthes' disease of the hip
  Scheuermann's disease of the spine
  Osteochondritis dissecans
  Chondromalacia patellae
  Osgood-Schlatter's disease of the tibial tuberosity
  Freiberg's disease of the metatarsal head
  Köhler's disease of the heel
  Kienböck's disease of the carpal lunate

Drugs
Psychological
Joints—Trauma: pulled elbow; strain—hypermobility
  Transient synovitis: osteitis
  Infections e.g. dysentery, salmonella, yersinia, brucellosis,
  Pyogenic cocci, including meningococci
  Tuberculosis, syphilis
  Viruses—mumps, rubella, rubella vaccine, influenza,
       chickenpox, hepatitis B, glandular fever, arbovirus,
       adenovirus, cytomegalovirus.
  Mycoplasma
Rheumatic fever
Rheumatoid arthritis. Psoriasis
Connective tissue disorders—disseminated lupus, dermato-
       myositis, periarteritis, scleroderma, Sjögren's disease.
Spondylo-arthropathy. Ankylosing, spondylitis. Spondylo-
       listhesis

Blood diseases—anaphylactoid purpura, haemophilia, Christmas disease, leukaemia, sickle-cell disease, haemoglobinopathies.

Tumours—haemangioma, histiocytosis X etc.

Immunological diseases—agammaglobulinaemia, serum sickness

Miscellaneous—sarcoid
  Ulcerative colitis, Crohn's disease, Whipple's disease
  Fibrocystic disease of the pancreas
  Subacute bacterial endocarditis
  Reiter's disease, Behçet's disease
  Mucocutaneous lymph node disease (p. 35)
  Gout

Trauma—foreign body in joint

Drugs

Psychological conditions

I shall pick out only a few of these for discussion, either because they are common or important or because attention has recently been drawn to them. Before discussing any one of these, one must emphasize the importance of considering *non-accidental injury* as a cause of limp, limb pains or joint pains. The only objective evidence of a fracture of a bone may be the slight heat on palpation over the break.

One may fail to elicit the history of the particular childhood activity which has caused the limb pain by sprain or strain.

Inguinal lymphadenitis as a cause of a limp may be missed if not specifically looked for.

Many children are thought to have rheumatic fever when they have growing pains—a misnomer, because the pains occur predominantly before the period of maximum growth. Apley found that one in every 25 Bristol school children had such pains. The pains are nonarticular, involving mainly the thigh and calf muscles, mainly at night in bed. The cause is unknown. The ESR is normal, an important fact which eliminates rheumatic fever. Øster and Nielsen (1972) in a study of 2718 school children aged 6 to 19 years, found that the peak age of growing pains was 11, and at that age approximately 20 per cent of boys and 30 per cent of girls complained of them. The overall incidence in boys was 12·5 per cent and in girls 18·4 per cent. Twenty eight per cent of those with growing pains also had headaches and 27 per cent had abdominal pain, either simultaneously or at different times. The children were otherwise normal.

Some boys with *Duchenne muscular dystrophy* have pain in the legs. *Poliomyelitis* may cause severe limb pain in the preparalytic stage, due to spasm in the muscles about to be paralysed. *Transient myositis* may cause severe pain with fever (Tepperberg 1977). Myalgia may be due to *trichiniasis* due to eating uncooked meat: there may be fever, orbital oedema and eosinophilia.

Arthritis may follow *rubella immunisation* and last for a week or weeks, often beginning about six weeks after the injection with arm or leg pain due to brachial or lumbosacral radiculitis. In older children and adolescents, rubella may cause arthritis.

Scurvy causes acute leg pains because of subperiosteal haemorrhage: in Britain scurvy is extremely rare, but it is liable to occur in severely defective children.

A *slipped femoral epiphysis* occurs especially between 10 and 15 years, especially in overweight boys. It is bilateral in 20 per cent. The symptom is a limp with little pain. On examination there is limited abduction of the hip.

Tumours of bone are of great importance and the diagnosis can readily be missed unless specifically looked for. Leukaemia and Hodgkin's disease must be considered when a child complains of persistent limb pain.

Osteoid osteoma occurs at any age, but mainly in children, and more often in boys (Orlowski & Mercer 1977). It involves especially the tibia and femur, but may affect other bones, including the vertebrae. It causes chronic pain, often severe, especially at night and on exertion. The pains may be of a boring or aching nature, relieved by aspirin. It may be referred from the upper end of the femur to the knee. There is local tenderness and wasting may occur in older children. Below the age of 8 years the affected limb may be longer than the other. The X-rays show no abnormality at first, but later show thickening of the cortex with a lucent area in the bone.

Transient synovitis of the hip is common (Jacobs 1971). The age of onset is usually between 18 months and seven years, and it is rather more common in boys. There may be a history of a preceding cold or minor injury, of doubtful significance. The symptom is refusal to bear weight, or limp, or vague pain in the knee or hip, with limitation of movement. The symptoms usually last a few days, and may be relieved by avoidance of weight bearing. Special investigations are of little help, except that an X-ray is necessary to eliminate Perthes' disease and other conditions: in transient synovitis there may be slight widening of the joint space of the hip, but the X-rays are difficult to interpret. The E.S.R. is raised in about half of all cases. The white cell count is usually normal, but there may be leucopenia or eosinophilia. The condition may be difficult or impossible to distinguish from early Perthes' disease—and some children, thought at first to have transient synovitis of the hip, prove on follow-up examination to have Perthes' disease.

The age of onset of *Perthes' disease* is usually 2 to 10 years. It presents with a limp and limitation of hip movement, with pain in the region of the hip or knee, but often no pain at all. It is sometimes found incidentally when an X-ray is taken for another purpose, and the child has had no symptoms to suggest Perthes' disease. It may be bilateral. On examination there is limitation of abduction, external rotation and extension of the hip, but especially of abduction.

Osteochondritis dissecans is associated with pain in the knee, especially over the lateral aspect of the medial condyle of the femur. It is due to a fragment of bone underlying the articular cartilage of the knee becoming avascular. *Chondromalacia patellae* occurs in the older child, with pain mainly in the front of the knee, and sometimes with a story of the knee 'giving way' or 'locking'—a similar story to that of the child with a 'clicking knee'—commonly due to a discoid meniscus (Snellmann & Stenström 1960). In the case of chondromalacia, there is tenderness behind the patella and discomfort on rubbing the patella against the end of the femur.

Leg pain may be due to *Achilles tendonitis* (Shapiro *et al,* 1974): there is warmth and tenderness of the Achilles tendon.

A *pulled elbow* is a common mishap in small children under the age of about five (Illingworth 1975). The child suddenly shows sign of pain in the upper limb or will not move the arm. The pain is usually in the region of the elbow, but in about a quarter of all cases it is localized to the wrist; in others the pain is referred to the forearm or shoulder. The diagnosis is frequently missed, but correct diagnosis is important because it can be cured instantly by appropriate manipulation. It is due to the head of the radius being pulled partially through the annular ligament.

Pyogenic arthritis, or osteitis near a joint, can readily be confused with rheumatic fever. The diagnosis is made more difficult when two or three joints are involved in osteitis. When there is any doubt (as there often is) a blood culture should be taken before penicillin is given. Arthritis is common in the mucocutaneous lymph node syndrome (p. 35).

Rheumatic fever is now rare in Britain. Its main features are arthritis, lassitude, fever and often carditis, following (in about a third of all cases) a known previous throat infection. In the remaining two thirds the streptococcal infection may be proved by estimation of the anti-streptolysin O titre and culture of haemolytic streptococci from the throat swab. The arthritis is typically a 'flitting polyarthritis', involving mainly (and almost entirely) the knee, ankle, wrist and elbow, only occasionally the hip, and rarely other joints. Hip involvement in rheumatic fever is unusual. The arthritis starts in one joint and clears after two or three days, moving to other joints in rotation, but the arthritis may involve one joint only or at least treatment is given so promptly that other joints are not involved. Occasionally there may be a mere complaint of pain in joints without detectable arthritis. In my experience all children with arthritis due to rheumatic fever are unwell. If a child complains of pains in the joints and yet feels well and full of energy, rheumatic fever can be almost excluded. Fever may be short-lasting and subside before the child is referred to a doctor. The ESR is invariably high (unless there is heart failure due to carditis, in which case the ESR is normal in about a quarter of all cases). If the ESR was not very high (e.g. if it were merely 15 to 20 mm in an hour, micro-Westergren method), I would almost exclude the diagnosis of rheumatic fever as a cause of the arthritis. Other useful investigations are the antistreptolysin O titre (which should be over 200 units) and the presence of C reactive protein (CRP). Both these tests are positive in almost a hundred per cent of cases in the acute stage.

There is almost always a raised sleeping pulse rate in the early stage (e.g. over 100 per minute), but there is often a sinus bradycardia (e.g. pulse rate of 60 per minute) in the early convalescent stage. If the pulse rate is fast, the sleeping pulse rate alone is of value, because tachycardia due to emotional factors must be excluded. The murmur of an obvious carditis may clinch the diagnosis; but in the early stage of such a murmur it is essential to distinguish a functional murmur. Almost one in two of all children have an innocent murmur. In many, the diagnosis is obvious: in others considerable clinical experience is needed to satisfy oneself that the murmur is not organic in origin. A child with fever, hyperthyroidism, severe anaemia or marked tachycardia may have an innocent murmur. It is not easy to describe in words the difference between a functional and an organic murmur. The functional murmur is either soft or musical and high pitched. It is commonly of short duration, tends to be late in systole, to be louder when the child lies down than when he is upright, and is often increased by exertion. Some describe the murmur as being on occasion 'vibratory' or 'twanging' in character. Functional murmurs are not confined to any one part of the heart. They may be mainly apical, along the sternal border or at the base.

Duckett Jones in the United States devised criteria for the establishment of the diagnosis of rheumatic fever. These were subsequently modified by the American Heart Association and the Medical Research Council, as follows:

Major criteria
1 Carditis, revealed by:
   (a) Development of an organic apical systolic murmur or an aortic diastolic murmur under observation
   (b) Change in heart size of more than 15 per cent on a standard X-ray film
   (c) Pericarditis, shown by rub or effusion
   (d) Congestive failure under the age of 25 years, without other cause
2 Polyarthritis
3 Chorea
4 Rheumatic nodules
5 Erythema marginatum

Minor criteria
1 Fever—37·4°C or more (by mouth)
2 Raised ESR
3 Evidence of haemolytic streptococcal infection, as shown by the history, ASO titre or throat swab
4 Increased PR interval in the ECG
5 Past history of rheumatic fever

The diagnosis of rheumatic fever was to be based on the presence of two major criteria, or one major and two minor criteria. In practice this method of diagnosis has worked well, but an occasional child with rheumatic fever does not satisfy the criteria, and an occasional child with some other condition does satisfy them.

I have seen many children who were thought to have rheumatic fever when in fact they had *febrile aches and pains in the limbs*.These occur in any infection associated with fever and are nonarticular.

Rheumatoid arthritis

The peak age of onset of rheumatoid arthritis is two to four years, though it may begin long before two—even in the first year (Laaksonen 1966). It is more common in girls than in boys. The presenting symptom is usually pain in a joint. A troublesome presenting symptom or sign, which may last for some months before a joint becomes involved, is unexplained fever. This occurs in some ten per cent of cases. A single joint may be involved or several joints may be painful at one time. When a single joint is involved, it is most likely to be a knee or ankle. The joint becomes enlarged, movement is painful and becomes restricted, and the joint is hot on palpation. There are signs of effusion into the joint. About half of all cases present with involvement of a single joint, and over a period of months no other joint may be involved. Involvement of the small joints of the fingers (especially the proximal interphalangeal joints) is a common and characteristic feature of other cases. There is commonly wasting of the muscles surrounding an affected joint. Muscle weakness is a common complaint. In about a quarter of all cases there is a characteristic salmon pink maculopapular slightly raised rash, consisting of lesions one to two cm in diameter, sometimes oval in shape with a pale centre. The lesions appear mainly in the latter part of the day, especially on the extremities. Pericarditis is a relatively common complication: rare complications include myocarditis and amyloidosis. Secondary scoliosis with gross difference in limb development may occur when a single joint, such as the knee, is affected. The incidence of splenic and lymph node enlargement in rheumatoid arthritis is often exaggerated. It occurs in not more than one in ten of all affected children.

It may be difficult to distinguish rheumatoid arthritis from rheumatic fever (Sills 1973). Rheumatic nodules may occur in both. The following are the main differentiating points in doubtful cases:
1 Stiffness in the mornings strongly favours the diagnosis of rheumatoid arthritis.
2 Duration of joint involvement. Arthritis in one joint does not last

more than a few days in rheumatic fever, even if no treatment is given.

3 Involvement of the neck and proximal interphalangeal joints suggests rheumatoid arthritis.

4 A normal ESR, a negative ASO titre, or the absence of CRP, excludes the diagnosis of rheumatic fever. The ESR is normal in 30 to 40 per cent of children with active rheumatoid arthritis. A high ESR (over 40 mm in an hour, using the micro-Westergren method) is unusual in rheumatoid arthritis; an ESR between 10 and 20 mm would almost exclude the diagnosis of rheumatic fever with arthritis unless there were heart failure. The ASO titre is negative in 80 per cent of children with rheumatoid arthritis, and CRP is absent in 70 per cent. These tests are positive in 99 per cent of children with rheumatic fever and arthritis.

5 Iridocyclitis. This occurs in about 15 per cent of children with rheumatoid arthritis.

6 If the child is under five, he would almost certainly be ill if he had rheumatic fever and would have obvious carditis. I would almost exclude rheumatic fever if a four-year-old had arthritis without carditis. Under three, rheumatic fever is exceedingly rare. Unfortunately tests for the rheumatoid factor do not often help in children. The tests are rarely positive in the absence of rheumatic nodules.

Polyarthritis, lasting 1 to 4 months, may follow about 3 weeks after a mild gastrointestinal illness, consisting of abdominal pain, fever and diarrhoea, due to *yersinia* infections.

Psoriasis usually precedes arthritis by several years. Psoriatic arthritis is indistinguishable from rheumatoid arthritis except that psoriasis characteristically involves the terminal interphalangeal joints, while rheumatoid arthritis involves the proximal joints. The condition commonly begins before the age of sixteen, but the average age of onset is nine years. The rash of psoriasis may precede or follow the development of arthritis. The polyarthritis is commonly asymmetrical: it frequently affects only a single digit at first. In rare cases there is fever, pericarditis and lymph node enlargement.

The connective tissue disorders may closely resemble rheumatoid arthritis: they include *disseminated lupus* (p. 34), *periarteritis* (p. 34), *scleroderma* and *dermatomyositis* (p. 40). About 20 per cent of cases of dermatomyositis present as polyarthritis.

Spondylo-arthropathy usually presents as arthritis of the hip or knee, and less commonly the ankle: later, commonly about six years after the onset, there is sacro-ileitis and/or ankylosing spondylitis (Ansell 1980, 1981). It is much more common in boys, most of them nine or older. A quarter give a history of pain in the heel, due to plantar fasciitis, bursitis or Achilles tendonitis. There may be arthritis in the interphalangeal joints of the toes or the metatarsophalangeal joints. There is sometimes a history of recurrent attacks of transient synovitis of the hip. Six per cent later develop psoriasis, and eight per cent develop ulcerative colitis or Crohn's disease: other complications include iridocyclitis or aortic incompetence.

The so called *gut arthropathy* includes arthritis in association with ulcerative colitis, Crohn's disease, Reiter's disease and other bowel infections, such as salmonella, yersinia, campylobacter and dysentery. Reiter's disease may follow 10 to 20 days after one of these infections—along with conjunctivitis and urethritis. The possibility of one of the above, such as Crohn's disease, should be suspected when in addition to arthritis involving one or two joints, there is loss of weight. Newman & Ansell (1979) described attacks of arthritis in *fibrocystic disease of the pancreas.* North *et al* (1970) described 11 cases of *sarcoid arthritis,* characterised by large painless boggy synovial and tendon sheath effusions involving the wrists, ankles, knees and elbows, running a chronic course with uveitis but no hilar lymphadenopathy, and with no abnormal laboratory findings apart from a raised E.S.R. There was a slowly progressive joint involvement over a two to three year period. All started before the age of four years.

Juvenile gout may be secondary to leukaemia or haemolytic anaemia, but may be primary (familial) (British Medical Journal 1972).

Rarely a mono-arthritis may be due to a *foreign body,* introduced from outside into the joint (e.g. 'Rose thorn arthritis').

Many *drugs* may cause arthralgia or joint effusion (Adverse Drug Reaction Bulletin 1971). Serum sickness may result from diphtheria or tetanus antitoxin. When coiticosteroids are discontinued after prolonged administration there may be joint pains, stiffness, paraesthesiae and malaise (Hargreave *et al* 1969). Mild arthralgia may accompany almost any drug-induced rash. Barbiturates, methimazole, penicillin and sulphasalazine may cause a joint effusion. Carbamazepine, chlordiazepoxide, cimetidine, ethambutol, isoniazid and rifampicin may cause joint pains.

Hypervitaminosis A causes angular stomatitis, hepatomegaly and bone pain with periostitis. Cramps may be caused by ergotamine, lincomycin, nalidixic acid, phenothiazines or thiazide diuretics.

Finally a limp or complaint of joint pain may be an attention-seeking device, and a limp may be due to hysteria.

Pain in the Heel

The diagnosis of the cause of pain in the heel is commonly difficult, and although the causes have largely been covered above, I felt that they should be summarised here in spite of the repetition (Gross 1977).

The main causes are trauma to the soft tissues (e.g. by shoes), infection in the soft tissues, stress fracture, calcaneal bursitis, ankylosing spondylitis, and osteochondritis (Sever, Köhler, Freiberg).

References

Adverse Drug Reaction Bulletin Drug induced aches and pains. 1971; **No. 30:** 88.

Ansell BM. *Rheumatic disorders in childhood.* London: Butterworth, 1980.

Ansell BM. Spondyloarthropathy in childhood: a review. *J Roy Soc Med* 1981; **74:** 205.

Apley J. *The child with abdominal pains,* 2nd ed. Oxford: Blackwell Scientific Publications, 1975.

British Medical Journal. Juvenile gout. Leading article. 1972; **1:** 129.

British Medical Journal. Polyarthritis and yersinia enterocolitica. Leading article. 1975; **2:** 404.

Gross RH. Foot pain. *Pediatr Clin North Am* 1977; **24:** 813.

Hargreave FE *et al.* Steroid pseudorheumatism in asthma. *Br Med J* 1969; **1:** 443.

Illingworth CM. Pulled elbow. *Br Med J* 1975; **2:** 672.

Illingworth CM. 128 limping children with no fracture, sprain or obvious cause. *Clin Pediatr (Phila)* 1978; **17:** 139.

Jacobs BW. Synovitis of the hip in children and its significance. *Pediatrics* 1971; **47:** 558.

Jones TD. The diagnosis of rheumatic fever. *JAMA* 1944; **126:** 481.

Laaksonen A. A prognostic study of juvenile rheumatoid arthritis. Analysis of 544 cases. *Acta Paediatr Scand Suppl* 1966; 166.

Newman AJ, Ansell BM. Episodic arthritis in children with cystic fibrosis. *J Pediatr* 1979; **94:** 594.

North AF, Fink CW, *et al.* Sarcoid arthritis in children. *Am J Med* 1970; **48:** 449.

Øster J, Nielsen A. Growing pains. *Acta Paediatr Scand* 1972; **61:** 329.

Orlowski JP, Mercer RD. Osteoid osteoma in children and young adults. *Pediatrics* 1977; **59:** 526.

Shapiro JR, Fallat RW, *et al*. Achilles tendinitis and tenosynovitis. *Am J Dis Child* 1974; **128:** 486.

Sills EM. Errors in diagnosis of juvenile rheumatoid arthritis. *Johns Hopkins Med J* 1973; **133:** 88.

Snellman O, Stenström RH. Congenital lateral discoid meniscus of the knee joint and its arthrography in children. *Ann Paediatr Fenniae* 1960; **6:** 124.

Tepperberg J. Transient acute myositis in children. *JAMA* 1977; **238:** 27.

Back Pains

The commonest cause of back pain in children is ligamentous strain or intervertebral disc lesions in the lumbosacral spine or neck. They are usually due to athletic and gymnastic exercises to which the child is not accustomed or perhaps suited (Grantham 1977). According to my colleague J. Sharrard F.R.C.S., who has helped me with this section, intervertebral disc lesions are not uncommon in children, but are rarely recognised. The so-called fibrositis is probably non-existent; the symptoms are probably due to ligamentous strain or pain referred from the disc region.

Back pain and related symptoms due to *discitis* were described by Menelaus (1964) and Fischer *et al* (1978). Menelaus described 35 cases seen at Melbourne. The youngest was 10 months old. Symptoms included abdominal pain, vomiting, malaise, back pain, stiff neck, vague pain in the buttocks, knee or thigh, or a limp. On examination there was lordosis, stiffness and sometimes local tenderness in the back, or fever. The X-ray showed narrowing of the disc space.

Ankylosing spondylitis is an important cause of back pain (p. 249).

Scheuermann's disease of the spine, mainly thoracic, causes back pain and sometimes adolescent kyphosis.

Spondylolisthesis (Bleck 1974) is rare before the age of five. It consists of a forward slip of one vertebra over the other. The symptoms are low back pain, sometimes sciatic pain, or a crouched posture due to contracted hamstrings.

Back pain may be of *psychological origin.* As always, this is a dangerous diagnosis, and I repeat that the diagnosis should only be made on the basis of positive evidence of psychological disturbance after elimination of organic disease on full investigation and follow-up.

References

Bleck EE. Spondilolisthesis. *Dev Med Child Neurol* 1974; **16:** 680.

Fischer GW *et al.* Diskitis. *Pediatrics* 1978; **62:** 543.

Grantham VA. Backache in boys. *Practitioner* 1977; **218:** 226.

Menelaus MB. Discitis. *J Bone and Joint Surg* 1964; **46B:** 16.

Schaller J, Bitnum S, Wedgewood RJ. Ankylosing spondylitis with childhood onset. *J Pediatr* 1969; **74:** 505.

Local Muscle Wasting

Local muscle wasting must be distinguished from *lipodystrophy, congenital absence of muscle* and *congenital asymmetry. Lipodystrophy* commonly affects the face at first, but may be confined to the lower limbs. As the term implies, there is loss of fat but not of muscle.

Congenital absence of muscle, such as that of the pectoralis major, can be confused with muscle wasting: it is related to the mother's ingestion of abortifacients in pregnancy. *Congenital asymmetry* (p. 236) can be confused with muscle wasting.

The usual causes of local muscle wasting are the following:

Nerve injury—by injection, pressure, surgery

Polyneuritis

Muscular dystrophy: peroneal muscular atrophy

Poliomyelitis, spastic hemiplegia

Spina bifida, diastematomyelia, spinal tumour, syringomyelia or cervical spondylosis

The limbs involved in *spastic hemiplegia* are wasted, but not markedly so, and not nearly as much as a limb affected by poliomyelitis.

Local muscle wasting may result from *infections,* either by damage to a nerve or by direct effect on a muscle. Those involved are usually the radial or sciatic nerves. Because of the risk of damage to nerves, no intramuscular injection should ever be made into the arm. The outer aspect of the thigh is a safer place for an injection than the buttocks, though rarely some local wasting follows. If triamcinolone is injected for the management of hay fever, it should be given deeply into muscle (and never into the arm): failure to inject deeply leads to wasting of subcutaneous and muscle tissue.

For polyneuritis, see p. 229.

Asymmetry of the Head

It is extremely common to find that a young baby's head is flat on one side, because he has consistently laid on that side, while it bulges out at the other side. The skull becomes more symmetrical as he grows older, and no treatment is necessary.

Many babies are born with some degree of cranial asymmetry, and it is of no importance.

Extreme asymmetry may be due to craniostenosis—premature closure of the cranial stutures. As surgical treatment may be possible and necessary, it is important to establish the diagnosis—by palpation of the ridge of fused sutures and X-ray.

Other causes, both rare, are a *partial Treacher–Collins syndrome* or other anomaly of the first arch, or *congenital asymmetry.*

A Small Head

The size of the head is closely related to the size of the cranial contents. If the brain does not grow normally, the head is likely to be unusually small. Hence the measurement of the head circumference is an important part of the developmental assessment of an infant, in that it may add confirmatory evidence of defective mental development or of early hydrocephalus. The measurement of the head circumference should be just as much part of the routine examination of a baby in a baby clinic, doctor's surgery or hospital, as is the examination of the hips for congenital subluxation or the back for a congenital dermal sinus, and—after three or four months—a rough test of hearing.

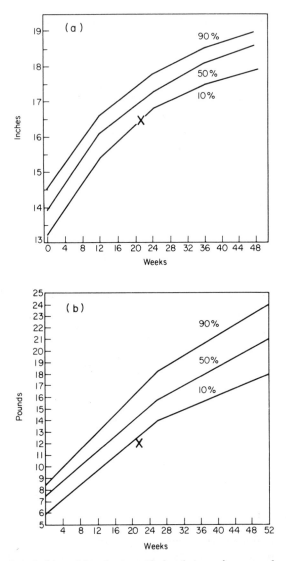

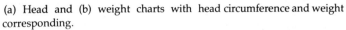

(a) Head and (b) weight charts with head circumference and weight corresponding.

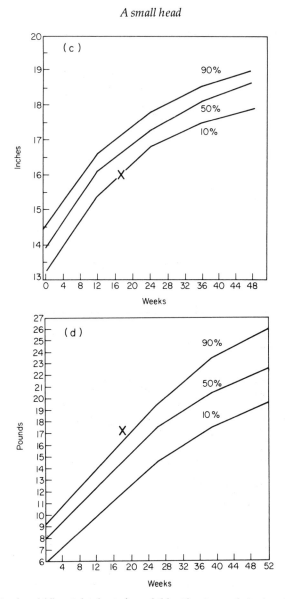

(c) Head and (d) weight charts for a child with microcephaly showing a small head in relation to weight.

It is easy to make an erroneous diagnosis of microcephaly and therefore of mental deficiency when in fact the child is normal. It is necessary to be aware of the other causes of smallness of the head circumference.

When a child has an unusually small head, one should consider the following conditions:

Normal variation
Small baby
Familial feature
Microcephaly
Craniostenosis

A small baby is likely to have a smaller head than a big baby, and a big baby is likely to have a bigger head than a small baby. *Hence the maximum head circumference must be related to the size of the baby.* This can be done by plotting the head circumference and the weight on the relevant centile charts. The two normally coincide, though a small or large head may be a familial feature which affects the position on the chart. Hence when the head is unusual, one must see both parents.

The fact that the head circumference corresponds exactly with the fiftieth centile by no means proves that the head is normal. The child might have microcephaly if he is a particularly big baby, or hydrocephalus if he is a particularly small baby.

When there is true microcephaly, the head is not only unusually small, but it is badly shaped, tapering off towards the vertex.

Craniostenosis or premature closure of the cranial sutures is a rare cause of undue smallness of the head. The fused sutures may be palpated by the experienced finger, but the diagnosis is established by X-ray. The anterior fontanelle would be closed.

A Large Head

Erroneous diagnosis or unnecessary suspicion of the presence of hydrocephalus is common. The usual error is to fail to relate the size of the head to the size of the baby. The best (and the easiest) measurement to which to relate the head size is the weight (Illingworth & Lutz 1965, Illingworth & Eid 1971). A big baby is likely to have a bigger head than a small baby. Serial measurements are more important than single ones: serial measurements enable one to determine whether a child's measurement is deviating from his position on the centile chart. It is commonly forgotten that if there is an unusually fast rate of increase of head size, as shown on the head chart, the most common cause is a correspondingly rapid increase in the size of the baby: hence the position of the centile head chart must be compared with the position on the centile weight chart.

Another common source of error is the genetic or familial one. There may be a familial tendency to have an unusually large (or small) head.

Two other sources of error are common. The *preterm baby* has a relatively large head: and an older infant (e.g. nine to twelve months of age) with 'failure to thrive' has a relatively large head because the brain suffers less from malnutrition than the rest of the body.

Significant causes of head enlargement are as follows:

Hydrocephalus
Subdural effusion
Cerebral tumour or cyst
Megalencephaly (rare)
Hydranencephaly (rare)
Cerebral gigantism (rare) and other rare conditions

The diagnosis of *hydrocephalus* would be confirmed by the finding of a bulging fontanelle, widely separated sutures, and serial measurements plotted on the centile chart which indicate that the head size in relation to the weight of the child is enlarging excessively.

The child with *achondroplasia* has a large head, partly because of a slight ventricular enlargement and partly because of *megalencephaly*, a large brain, usually of poor quality. (For discussion of 109 cases of megalencephaly, see Lorber & Priestley 1981.)

Hydranencephaly is a rare condition in which the head seems to be full of cerebrospinal fluid with compression of brain tissue. The diagnosis is made in part by transillumination in a darkened room.

In *cerebral gigantism* (Sotos and Cutler, 1977), there is a prominent forehead, acromegalic features, excessive growth in height, large hands and feet, clumsiness and mental subnormality. There is excessive growth in the first three or four years.

The head is liable to be unduly large in sulphatide lipoidosis and gangliosidosis.

References

Illingworth RS, Lutz W. The measurement of the infant's head circumference and its significance. *Arch Dis Child* 1965; **40:** 672.

Illingworth RS, Eid E. Head circumference in relation to weight, chest circumference, supine length and crown rump length in the first six months of life. *Acta Paediatr Scand* 1971; **60:** 333.

Lorber J, Priestley BL. Children with large heads. *Dev Med Child Neurol* 1981; **23:** 494.

Sotos JF, Cutler EA. Cerebral gigantism. *Am J Dis Child* 1977; **131:** 625.

Torticollis

Apart from the sternomastoid tumour, the 'rheumatic' stiff neck, habit and the effect of drugs, all the causes of torticollis are rare, though several are important for treatment. The causes may be classified as follows:

Muscle—Sternomastoid tumour (congenital torticollis)

Myositis ossificans progressiva (rare)

'Rheumatic' stiff neck

Poliomyelitis (weakness of muscle)

Cervical vertebrae and joints

Rheumatoid arthritis

Klippel–Feil syndrome, Sprengel's deformity, odontoid anomaly

Scoliosis (p. 225)

Osteitis, tumour

Trauma: subluxation of atlanto-axial joint: strain

Soft tissues—tonsillar abscess, cervical adenitis

Eye—ocular torticollis

Ear—vestibular disturbance

Intracranial—posterior fossa tumour. AV malformation

Oesophagus—Sandifer's syndrome

Unclassified—Paroxysmal torticollis, spasmodic torticollis. Spasmus nutans

Drugs

Psychological—Habit, hysteria, tic.

'*Congenital torticollis*' is due to a sternomastoid tumour, itself the result of pressure in utero against the sternomastoid muscle—or perhaps rarely the result of damage during delivery. The tumour is felt a few days after birth and torticollis with rotation of the neck develops shortly after. There may be associated cranial and mandibular asymmetry and other indications of the effect of oligohydramnios. A particular risk is a dislocated hip.

Myositis ossificans is a rare disease commonly beginning with a stiff neck and torticollis (Illingworth 1971, p. 225).

The so-called 'rheumatic' stiff neck may be myositis of virus origin. There is local tenderness.

Neck stiffness, occasionally with torticollis, is often a feature of rheumatoid arthritis.

The *Klippel–Feil syndrome* is diagnosed by the short neck, limitation of neck movement and X-ray, and the *Sprengel deformity* by the high position of the scapula.

Ocular torticollis is a posture adopted by the child to maintain binocular vision and avoid a squint when there is paresis of an ocular muscle, usually the superior oblique. The head is tilted and rotated. The symptoms often appear at about two or three years of age.

A *cerebellar tumour* may cause the child to rotate or tilt the occiput towards the shoulders on the affected side.

Sandifer's syndrome (Werlin *et al* 1980) consists of oesophagitis (with or without hiatus hernia) with dystonic movements or episodes of body stiffening, resembling fits, sometimes preceded by food intake, coughing or sneezing.

Snyder (1969) described 12 cases of *paroxysmal torticollis* in infants aged two to eighteen months. They experienced two to three attacks a month, consisting of torticollis, crying, pallor and vomiting on rotating the head. The attacks lasted 10 minutes to 14 days, and there was spontaneous recovery by the age of five. It was suggested that the cause was a labyrinthitis or vestibular neuronitis. Sanner & Bergström (1979) described a similar condition.

Spasmodic torticollis may be a *tic*. There are sudden single lateral movements of the neck. For spasmus nutans see p. 207.

Torticollis and dystonic movements are a frequent side effect of metoclopramide, phenothiazines and haloperidol (p. 206).

Some infants, children and adults keep the head tilted to one side for no apparent reason. Bizarre postures may occur in *hysteria*.

References

Illingworth RS. Myositis ossificans progressiva. *Arch Dis Child* 1971; **46:** 264.

Sanner G, Bergström B. Benign paroxysmal torticollis in infancy. *Acta Paediatr Scand* 1979; **68:** 219.

Snyder CH. Paroxysmal torticollis in infancy. *Am J Dis Child* 1969; **117:** 458.

Werlin SL, D'Souza BJ, *et al.* Sandifer syndrome: an unappreciated clinical entity. *Dev Med Child Neurol* 1980; **22:** 374.

Opisthotonos

Opisthotonos in the newborn must be distinguished from the posture assumed by a baby delivered by *face presentation*. Such babies are not hypertonic, unless they have cerebral palsy.

Causes of true opisthotonos include the following:

> Severe kernicterus
>
> Airway obstruction—retropharyngeal abscess, tracheal obstruction, vascular ring
>
> Oesophagitis
>
> Sequela of meningitis, encephalitis, cerebral haemorrhage, cardiac arrest
>
> Tetanus, rabies
>
> Gaucher's disease, Tay-Sach's disease, Lesch-Nyhan syndrome
>
> Cerebral tumour
>
> Neck injury
>
> Drugs—especially metoclopramide and phenothiazines, but also chloroquine

Attacks of arching of the back are sometimes an early sign of athetosis.

Asymmetry of the Chest

When the chest is notably asymmetrical the following conditions should be considered:

    Congenital deformity
    Congenital absence of the pectoralis major
    Scoliosis
    Intrathoracic disease—atelectasis, pleural effusion, air-containing cyst, etc.
    Congenital asymmetry (hemihypertrophy, hemiatrophy)

Congenital absence of the pectoralis major is not rare. Simple inspection together with awareness of the possibility will establish the diagnosis. The condition may cause confusion in the X-ray of the chest, by making one side of the chest appear to be more translucent than the other. It may be combined with syndactyly (Poland's syndrome) and may then be due to the use of an abortifacient.

Crying

All babies cry long before they laugh, and the causes of crying (or laughing) are not always clear.

Many of the causes of crying are obvious. The usual ones are hunger, wind or other discomfort. Some babies cry when the light is put out; others cry when the light is put on; all are likely to cry if the limbs or head are tightly held by one's hand.

One may summarize the causes of crying as follows:

A. Infants

   1   *Crying without disease*

        Hunger due to fear of overfeeding
        Thirst
        Discomfort—wind, cold, heat, itching, evening colic, wet napkin, loud noises
        Cow's milk allergy

261

Teething
Irritability on the breast
Personality
Crying on passing urine
Habit
Loneliness: desire to see surroundings, or to be picked up
Fatigue
Food forcing
Child abuse
Drug withdrawal (newborn). Use of drugs
Unexplained

2 *Crying with disease*
Infection
Headache, earache
Strangulated hernia. Torsion of testis.
Intestinal obstruction and intussusception
Pink disease
Phenylketonuria
Coeliac disease
Autism

B. Older children (excessive crying only)
Personality
Insecurity
Habit
Hunger
Fatigue
Puberty
Early chorea
Illness
Child abuse
Autism

The obvious cause of crying by an infant is hunger. A sensible mother feeds her young baby when he wants it, whether in the day or night. Rigid ideas about the feeding schedule, due to fears of causing 'bad habits', lead to a great deal of crying. Another rigid idea which leads to much crying from hunger is the fear of overfeeding. Many babies cry from hunger because someone is so obsessed by the fear of overfeeding them that they are half-starved. A baby's cry may be due to thirst caused by hypernatraemia as a result of making the feeds with dried milk too strong (for instance, a heaped measure of milk powder in an ounce of water).

Discomfort from any cause may lead to crying. Causes include excessive cold or excessive heat, pruritus (as from eczema), a wet napkin or a sudden loud noise. For 'evening colic' see p. 101.

Allergy to cow's milk (p. 13) is a possible cause of excessive crying. It is a difficult diagnosis to establish with certainty, and apart from laboratory investigation, trials with and without cow's milk are likely to be needed.

Teething is a convenient condition to blame when a baby, six months or more of age, cries excessively, especially in the evening. It is reasonable to suggest that the eruption of a tooth through the periosteum may cause pain; but *much of the crying which is ascribed to teething is in fact related to habit formation in connection with sleep, due to parental mismanagement.* The usual age at which this sleep problem arises is nine to twelve months. The baby discovers that if he cries when put to bed he will be picked out of his cot and taken downstairs—and so he cries every time when put to bed. He may also discover that if he cries as soon as he awakens he will be picked up and taken either downstairs or into his parents' bed—and so he cries out every night. This crying is commonly ascribed by parents to 'indigestion' or 'awful wind', when in fact it is purely a habit which they have themselves caused.

Irritability and screaming in the newborn period when the baby is put to the breast is an annoying symptom, which leads to some babies being put to the bottle. Mavis Gunther ascribed it to the baby's nose becoming obstructed by his upper lip when feeding, or being blocked by the mother's breast tissue. It may be partly due to the mother trying to force the baby to suck, or fearing that the baby will bite her, so that she withdraws as soon as he begins to suck. The problem settles down within about ten days if patience is shown.

However wise the management, some babies cry excessively, and one can only ascribe it to the *personality*—which is largely inherited. Some babies seem to sense their mother's anxiety and tenseness and cry as a result.

Babies commonly cry, often with a shriek, when *passing urine*. It is a normal feature, especially around the age of six months.

Many babies cry when left alone and are quiet when picked up. Many intelligent babies, from the age of six weeks or so, are not content to be left lying down with nothing to see. They are quiet when propped up so that they can see the fascinating activities of the kitchen.

In the weaning stage much crying is due to *efforts to force the child to take food,* especially food which he does not like, or not allowing him to feed himself when he wants to. Rarely such crying may be due to food allergy.

It must be admitted that much crying by infants occurs without discoverable cause. If the crying continues when the child is picked up and fed, it must be assumed that it is due to some discomfort—perhaps *abdominal pain or headache.* Crying is usual when the baby feels tired.

Crying when the baby is unwell may be due to *infection,* such as otitis media or pyelonephritis, or to intestinal obstruction (if there is also vomiting). One must examine the *hernial orifices* for a strangulated hernia and look for torsion of the testis. The acute onset of screaming attacks should suggest the possibility of *intussusception.*

Pink disease should no longer occur, because mercury is no longer a constituent of teething powders, but one must remember the possibility of the mother having obtained a teething powder from an old stock, or having applied an ointment containing mercury.

Crying is a feature of *phenylketonuria* until by proper treatment the serum phenylalanine level is reduced to normal. Crying is a common feature of coeliac disease, until gluten is excluded.

In older children excessive crying may be a feature of the *personality.* It may be due to insecurity, and one must investigate the home and school background.

Crying at night is usually due to *habit formation,* the habit having continued from infancy. The child repeatedly cries out at night because he knows that his mother will come to him, perhaps read to him, play with him, give him a warm drink or take him into her own bed.

A child may cry because he is *hungry or tired.* Children at *puberty* commonly burst into tears with little or no provocation.

When an older child is excessively lachrymose one must eliminate organic disease, such as *anaemia* or *pyelonephritis* or a persistent *streptococcal throat infection.*

When a child who previously behaved normally becomes unusually tearful, one must consider early *chorea.* Emotional behaviour is a common early symptom. *Autism* is an occasional cause.

Despite the most careful history-taking and investigation, it may be impossible to determine the exact cause of excessive crying: but the more carefully the history is taken, the fewer are these cases. Some of them may be related to the mother's fatigue, or to domestic friction. Some complaints of a baby's constant crying represent a mother's urgent call for help, in a 'pre-battering' situation.

Drugs may cause weepiness; they include amphetamines, bromides, methylphenidate and phenobarbitone.

Reference

Illingworth RS. *The normal child.* London: Churchill Livingstone, 8th Edn. 1982.

Types of Cry

There is an increasing interest in the nature of the cry of infants. Analysis of the cry by spectrographic methods has yielded interesting and useful information (Michelsson & Wasz-Hockert 1980): the cries of the asphyxiated, hypothyroid, mongoloid and other abnormal babies all have their special characteristics when studied by these methods. Fisichelli and Karelitz (1963) showed that normal infants cry more rapidly after a stimulus than do children with brain abnormalities. Babies with cerebral irritability, meningitis, hydrocephalus and kernicterus have a shrill, high pitched cry.

A hoarse gruff cry is characteristic of *hypothyroidism*.

The hoarseness of *laryngitis* is characteristic. More important is the presence of hoarseness in a child with stridor dating from birth.

The cat-like cry of the *'cri-du-chat' syndrome* is characteristic. This occurs in defective microcephalic infants. There is often some degree of hypertelorism, an antimongoloid slant of the eyes and low-set ears. It is associated with deletion of the distal portion of the short arm of one of the 4 to 5 chromosomes (Kajii *et al* 1966). The crying of the child with the *Cornelia de Lange syndrome* is said to sound like a bleating lamb (McArthur & Edwards 1967).

Other characteristic cries are the weak cry of the child with *amyotonia congenita* (or similar muscle weakness) or the child with myasthenia gravis, and the whimper of the *seriously ill* child.

The child with pneumonia may have a grunting type of cry.

References

Fisichelli VR, Karelitz S. The cry latencies of normal infants and those with brain damage. *J Pediatr* 1963; **62:** 724.

Kajii T, Homma T, *et al.* Cri du chat syndrome. *Arch Dis Child* 1966; **41:** 97.

McArthur RG, Edwards JH. De Lange syndrome. Report of 20 cases. *Can Med Ass J* 1967; **96:** 1185.

Michelsson K, Wasz-Hockert O. The value of cry analysis in neonatology and early infancy. In Murry T, Murry J. (Eds) *Infant communication: cry and early speech.* Houston: College–Hill Press: 1980, p. 124.

Insomnia and Sleep Disturbance

Refusal or failure to sleep is almost always a behaviour problem due to mismanagement, but because organic factors may be contributory, the subject will be briefly mentioned here.

The following are the main causes of defective sleep:

> Mismanagement, including hunger
> Evening colic (p. 101)
> Mental subnormality
> Vomiting, diarrhoea, polyuria, frequency of micturition
> Pruritus
> In the older child—insecurity, fears, anxieties
> Drugs

Mismanagement may consist of leaving the infant crying from hunger because of the fear that night feeds cause bad habit formation. Usually, however, sleep disturbance arising from mismanagement begins later in infancy, especially at about nine to fifteen months, when the child is allowed to discover that as soon as he cries (e.g. when put to bed, or on awakening), his mother will pick him up, take him downstairs, play with him, give him a warm drink or take him into her own bed.

Some *mentally subnormal children* have an inverted sleep rhythm, sleeping by day and being wakeful at night.

Anything causing *vomiting, diarrhoea, polyuria* or *frequency of micturition* will cause sleep disturbance.

Pruritus, as from infantile eczema or scabies, may cause troublesome insomnia.

In the older child, *bad habit formation* beginning in infancy is the main cause of insomnia.

Other causes of sleep disturbance in the older child are *worries and anxieties about home or school, fear of the dark or of shadows on the wall.*

Certain *drugs* may cause insomnia. They include amphetamine, diazepam, diphenoxylate, ephedrine, griseofulvin, imipramine, methylphenidate, niclosamide, and vincristine. Fenfluramine may cause nightmares. Barbiturates or antihistamines may have a paradoxical effect and cause sleeplessness.

Sleep walking is a common problem of normal children, mainly after the age of four or five years, occurring mainly in deep stage 4 sleep early in the night. It is often a familial feature. Sometimes it seems to be more common when the child has had a large meal shortly before going to bed: but usually there is no discoverable cause.

Nightmares occur equally with or more commonly than sleep walking: most children have occasional episodes. They tend to occur particularly at the onset of an infection, or when there is a sudden loud noise. If they are excessively frequent, they may be due to insecurity at home or school.

Reference

Illingworth RS. *The normal child.* London: Churchill Livingstone, 8th Edn, 1982.

Mental Subnormality

When one considers the obvious fact that approximately half the population has an I.Q. of less than 100, it is clear that backwardness is a common problem. Not all backwardness is due to a low level of intelligence, and many other conditions have to be kept in mind when one is considering the problem of a backward child.

The most common cause of backwardness in childhood is mental subnormality, and that condition will be considered first. I have discussed developmental diagnosis and the diagnosis of mental subnormality in detail elsewhere (Illingworth, 1980). Below is a summary of the main points in the diagnosis.

The first essential to the diagnosis of mental subnormality is a thorough knowledge of the normal and variations from the normal which do not amount to disease. One needs this knowledge in order to determine how far an infant has developed as compared with an average baby. One must also know the factors which may have affected his development, and know whether these factors will have a permanent effect or a reversible one. It is also useful to know about conditions which somewhat increase the likelihood that a child will be retarded—the factors which place him 'at risk' of mental subnormality.

One may summarize the factors which place him 'at risk' of mental subnormality as follows:

> Family history of mental subnormality
> Maternal rubella and other virus infections in the first three months of pregnancy
> Low birth weight, especially in relation to the duration of gestation
> Maternal toxaemia, antepartum haemorrhage
> Multiple pregnancy
> Cerebral palsy
> Congenital deformities
> Convulsions in the newborn period, other than those due to hypocalcaemia
> Hyperbilirubinaemia in the newborn period
> Severe anoxia at birth, or cerebral haemorrhage

One must not exaggerate the importance of any of these factors. For instance, a mentally subnormal mother may give birth to a normal child. Even a mongol woman may give birth to a normal infant. Maternal rubella in the first three months is hazardous to the fetus. Innumerable low-birth-weight infants are mentally normal or superior. Maternal toxaemia only slightly increases the risk of abnormality in the fetus. Any major congenital deformity, such as a cleft palate or congenital heart disease, slightly increases the risk of mental handicap. Many children who suffered severe anoxia at birth are mentally and physically normal. Cerebral palsy, neonatal convulsions other than those due to hypocalcaemia, and hyperbilirubinaemia (e.g. serum bilirubin over 20 mg per cent), significantly increase the risk of a mental handicap.

It follows that one must take the history of any of the factors above, but that one must not pay too much attention to them. One bears them in mind and is alerted to the increased risk, but does not exaggerate their importance. The next step (after the newborn period) is to obtain a history of milestones of development, so that one can assess the rate of development from birth until the present time.

The physical examination must include neurological examination for signs of cerebral palsy and other conditions. The diagnosis of mongolism and cretinism should be obvious. The examination must include in particular a measurement of the maximum circumference of the head, because the size of the head is governed largely by the growth of the cranial contents. If the brain does not grow normally, the head is usually small. The head circumference of mentally subnormal infants is nearly always small in relation to their weight, unless they have hydrocephalus, megalencephaly or hydranencephaly.

With regard to the developmental examination, it is essential to remember the all important principle that the mentally subnormal child is backward in all aspects of development, except occasionally in the motor field (sitting and walking). Hence the full term mentally subnormal baby at birth resembles a premature baby, in that he tends to sleep a large part of the day and night, he may have difficulty in sucking and swallowing, regurgitate and fail to demand feeds. He is then late in passing the milestones of development. He is late in beginning to smile at his mother (average in normal full term infants—four to six weeks); he is late in following with his eyes and turning his head to sound (average three or four months), he is late in reaching out and grasping objects without their being placed in his hand (average five months), in chewing (average six or seven months), in helping his mother to dress him by holding his arm out for a sleeve, in imitating byebye and playing patacake (all average 10 months), and later in speech. (The average child begins to combine words spontaneously at 21 to 24 months.) He is likely to be late in feeding himself with a cup without help (average 15 months) and in acquiring sphincter control (average 18 months for the first signs). Above all he shows less interest in his surroundings and concentrates badly, being easily distracted. He is late in ceasing to take objects to the mouth, and in ceasing to cast objects to the ground, one after the other. (Average in both about 15 months).

The diagnosis of mental subnormality is a most serious one to make, and it can only be made after careful consideration of the history, the child's development to date, the findings on examination, and an interpretation of the significance of each. It is wrong even to breathe a suspicion that the child is mentally defective until one is certain of one's ground, for it will cause the gravest distress and anxiety to the parents. I would strongly advise the family doctor to seek the opinion of an expert before imparting his diagnosis to the parents.

Reference

Illingworth RS. *Development of the infant and young child, normal and abnormal.* Edinburgh: Churchill Livingstone, 7th Edn, 1980.

Other causes of General Backwardness

All these factors are relevant to the subject of underachievement at school—performance at school below the level which should correspond to the child's tested intelligence.

I have described the factors in detail elsewhere (Illingworth 1974). The factors are outlined in this and subsequent sections.

Many conditions other than mental subnormality may cause generalized backwardness in infancy and especially in later childhood.

For convenience I have listed them in three groups—factors in the child, in the home, in the teaching—though realizing that there is some overlapping between these groups. They may be summarized as follow:

a Factors in the child
>   Delayed maturation: 'Slow starter'
>   Physical problems, such as cerebral palsy
>   Sensory problems—defective eyesight or hearing
>   Learning disorders
>   Personality—laziness, daydreaming, emotional block
>   Insecurity
>   The effect of failure
>   Poor concentration
>   Autism
>   Schizophrenia
>   Drug addiction

b Factors in the home or environment
>   Emotional deprivation
>   Malnutrition
>   Poor home—low expectation, poor example, etc.

c Factors in the teaching
>   Poor teaching
>   Lack of motivation
>   Absence from school
>   Changes from school to school
>   Special school instead of ordinary school

Factors in the child

Delayed maturation

Though delayed maturation is not as common as some parents imagine, it is a real entity. An infant may be retarded in all aspects of development and yet prove to be normal later. This could not be expected if there were microcephaly—and this fact alone indicates the importance of including a measurement of the maximum head circumference in the examination of a baby. The diagnosis of mental subnormality in infancy, unless it is severe, is difficult: the diagnosis of mental subnormality in an infant with a head of normal size in relation to weight is more than difficult—it is dangerous.

Delayed maturation causes trouble at school—the child doing badly in the subjects of the curriculum, and yet doing well later.

Physical problems

Cerebral palsy or muscular dystrophy may cause serious retardation apart from the commonly associated mental subnormality. Amongst other things these conditions reduce the child's opportunity for learning.

Defective vision and hearing

When a child has poor eyesight or hearing from birth, he cannot know that he does not see or hear properly. It is the responsibility of others to make the diagnosis.

Delayed reading

This is a major cause of backwardness at school.

The most common cause of delay in learning to read is mental subnormality, and this diagnosis must be eliminated with the help of a psychologist before other causes, such as specific learning disorders, are considered (Ingram & Mason 1965, Schechter 1971).

A child may be delayed in learning to read as a result of bad environmental conditions, emotional deprivation or insecurity. He may be delayed by poor teaching, repeated or prolonged absence from school or by a visual or auditory defect, or poor concentration with overactivity. There is some relationship between delayed talking and reading with delay in the establishment of handedness.

Having eliminated the above factors, one should then consider the so-called 'learning disorders'.

Learning disorders

Learning disorders include dyslexia (difficulty in reading), dysphasia (difficulty in learning to speak), dysgraphia (difficulty in writing), and difficulties in spelling or spatial appreciation. They are more common in boys. Affected children are often clumsy in their movements. The difficulties commonly occur in combination. These children tend to leave too small or too large a space between written letters; they often write at an acute angle; they frequently reverse letters, such as *h* and *y*, *d* and *b*. They commonly read from right to left, and interpret, for instance, BUT as TUB, MEAT as MATE, SAW as WAS, transposing letters or syllables, and getting the order of the letters wrong. I saw a page of a boy's arithmetic book, with all the sums calculated like this:

$$16 + 1 = 71$$
$$13 + 1 = 41$$

Some of the children indulge in mirror writing. They may have inadequate auditory discrimination of speech sounds, interpreting, for instance, BUD as BUT, even though their actual hearing is normal. They may show an inability to synthesize into correct words letters which have individually been sounded correctly—interpreting, for instance CLOCK as COCK. They fail to recognize or remember the shape of letters, however often they are told them, and confuse letters of similar shape. They may be able to spell out the word correctly but be unable to write it; they cannot correlate sound with the written word. Most of the children have difficulty in the establishment of handedness and in learning right-left differentiation. They are commonly ambidextrous or left-handed. They tend to read slowly and hesitantly, wriggling and distorting the face as they read. As they mature the concomitant signs and symptoms may disappear, leaving nothing but the reading difficulty. These difficulties often cause serious problems and embarrassment at school, and may lead to behaviour problems such as truancy.

A proper I.Q. test must be carried out before the diagnosis can be established—and it is important that the diagnosis should be made, in order that the teacher can understand that the child's poor performance is not just due to carelessness, and in order that the appropriate treatment can be arranged. This consists of combining the visual, auditory and kinaesthetic senses—the child being shown letters and words, hearing them and feeling them at the same time.

An important cause of dyslexia seems to be delay in maturation, some children being late in reading, just as others are late in walking or acquiring sphincter control. It is probably that in many cases there is a combination of factors.

The personality

The personality of the child has an important effect on his progress at school. Laziness is partly a personality problem, partly the effect of bad influence of others, and partly lack of interest in the work—which may be a matter of the child's lack of aptitude for a particular subject or the way in which the subject is taught. Daydreaming may interfere with school work. Sensitive children may develop emotional blocks to learning when they are afraid of the teacher or are being unduly hurried.

Insecurity

Insecurity is a most important cause of backwardness in intelligent children. The insecurity may be due to difficulties at home, to bullying at school or fear of a teacher. It has a powerful effect in lowering the standard of a child's work. *Failure* in work has a bad effect on a child's progress. Success leads to success, and failure to a further lowering in the standard achieved.

Poor concentration

The most common cause of defective concentration is low intelligence—or an intelligence quotient below that of other members of the class. But it may also be due to the child being gifted, finding the work too easy, or to his having interests and aptitudes outside the school curriculum.

Poor concentration may be due to daydreaming, to insecurity, or to finding the work too easy. It may be due to boredom, dislike of the work, lack of motivation in the teaching, or dislike of the teacher. It may be due to a defect of the eyesight or of hearing. *Drugs* are an important cause of defective concentration. They include antiepileptic drugs, antihistamines, fenfluramine and tricyclic antidepressants. Barbiturates are particularly important offenders—either by causing drowsiness or irritability, or by a direct action on the brain, interfering with learning and memory. Antiepileptic drugs may also interfere with folate metabolism, which can affect performance.

Frequent petit mal attacks may result in defective concentration. The so-called 'petit mal status' consists of a rapid succession of attacks: these attacks may interfere with school work.

Infantile autism

This is a serious condition in which the child from the earliest infancy shows no affection, preferring toys to persons. He has no desire to be picked up and cuddled when he is a baby. He may be poor at sucking, late in smiling, surprisingly undemanding if left alone and annoyed on being disturbed. He may cry unusually rarely—or cry excessively. He may fail to respond to the human voice while he responds to other sounds. His speech is seriously retarded. He may use words and intonate them well, but they bear no relation to the person listening to them and no relation to the existing situation. His head is of normal size and shape and he looks intelligent; yet he functions as a mentally defective child. He disregards his parents and tends to avert his gaze when spoken to. He is really an extreme introvert and isolates himself from the world. He may play with one toy in an obsessional way for hours, and is often especially fond of spinning toys: and he hates to change his occupation, having an intense desire for 'sameness'. He likes one particular routine, one particular toy or furniture arrangement and may develop a panic reaction if change occurs. He may adopt bizarre attitudes and postures, flicking his fingers in front of his eyes and walking on his toes. The cause is unknown (Ornitz & Ritvo, 1976), but unfavourable intrauterine or genetic factors may be relevant. (Folstein & Rutter 1977, Finegan & Quarrington 1979).

When the diagnosis of autism is suspected, an expert should see the child.

Schizophrenia

The symptoms of schizophrenia (Wolff & Barlow 1979) are severe impairment of emotional relationships, solitariness, remoteness, lack of feeling for people, abnormal postures, striking immobility (katatonia) or aimless overactivity, ritualistic mannerisms (e.g. rocking and spinning), pathological preoccupation with particular objects, resistance to change, excessive or abnormal response to sensory stimuli—for example insensitivity to pain or other discomfort—illogical anxieties, hallucinations (rare in autism), and irrelevance of speech. The parents cannot understand the child; a book by professional parents (Wilson 1968), gives a vivid description of their own schizophrenic son. Schizophrenia is very rare before school age while autism manifests itself in early infancy: there is a much stronger genetic factor in schizophrenia than in autism.

Sometimes psychoses are superimposed on mental deficiency and this increases the difficulty of assessment.

Factors in the home

Factors in the home have a profound effect on the child's progress from infancy onwards (Illingworth 1968, 1974). They include the home interests and example, the opportunities for the child to learn outside the home and school, praise for good work, expectation of success, and the right attitude to homework (implying that it is an understood thing that the homework will be done after the meal on returning from school). Other important factors include love and security, the amount of conversation between child and parent and its quality, the provision of suitable play material, the chance to develop independence, loving discipline, a good example, good nutrition and the prevention of disease, the encouragement of special interest, the encouragement of questions and argument, ambition but not over-ambition, regular school attendance and the expectation of success. A poor home causes a considerable degree of retardation. Some parents actively discourage the child from doing his homework—or provide no place in which he can work away from the family and the television set.

Poor teaching

Backwardness may be due to poor teaching. Unless the teacher likes the child and the child the teacher, there are likely to be learning difficulties. Some teachers use the methods of threats, punishment, ridicule and sarcasm, instead of encouragement and praise, and then blame the child for not doing well. Lack of motivation is an important cause of backwardness: when a subject is badly taught and made uninteresting, the children are not likely to do well in it.

Prolonged absences from school are usually due to faulty management at home, but may be due to illness. Children are kept off school far too readily—and miss a great deal of education as a result. They are kept away from school for the most trivial cough or wheeze—and yet are taken shopping and attend the child welfare clinic with the baby brother. Frequent moves from school to school cause an emotional upheaval, and the child may find that work is being taught differently, or that he has missed much that has been taught. It has been shown that frequent short spells of absence from school cause more deterioration in performance than one long period of absence.

Some children are retarded by being sent to a special school instead of an ordinary school. The standard of education cannot be as high in a special school, where there is a wider scatter of age groups and intellectual levels in a class than in an ordinary school, and where less time is devoted to lessons.

References

Finegan J, Quarrington B. Pre- peri and neonatal factors and infantile autism. *J Child Psychol Psychiat* 1979; **20:** 119.

Folstein S, Rutter M. Genetic influences and infantile autism. *Nature* 1977; **265:** 726.

Illingworth RS. How to help a child to achieve his best. *J Pediatr* 1968; **73:** 61.

Illingworth RS. *The child at school: a paediatrician's manual for teachers.* Oxford: Blackwell Scientific Publications, 1974.

Ingram TTS, Mason AW. Reading and writing difficulties in childhood. *Br Med J* 1965; **2:** 463.

Ornitz EM, Ritvo ER. The syndrome of autism: a critical review. *Am J Psychiat* 1976; **133:** 609.

Schechter MD Dyslexia *Austr Paediatr J* 1971; **7:** 123.

Wilson L. *This stranger my son.* London: John Murray, 1968.

Wolff S, Barlow A. Schizoid personality in childhood: a comparative study of schizoid, autistic and normal children. *J Child Psychol Psychiat* 1979; **20:** 29.

Backwardness in Individual Fields of Development

In considering individual fields of development one must make due allowance for prematurity; e.g. if a baby were born two months prematurely, the average age for beginning to smile would be four to six weeks plus two months.

Smiling

All mentally subnormal and most autistic children are late in beginning to smile at the mother. A blind child will probably be late in beginning to smile.

Sitting and walking

The common causes of lateness in sitting and walking are:
>Mental subnormality
>Delayed motor maturation, usually familial
>Hypertonia—cerebral palsy
>Hypotonia
>Muscular dystrophy
>Emotional deprivation: institutional care
>Lack of opportunity to sit and walk: illness
>Excessive caution and timidity: dislike of bumps

By no means all mentally subnormal children are late in learning to sit and walk, but most are. A few mongols learn to sit at the usual age, but almost all are late in learning to walk.

When a child is late in sitting or walking, and no other abnormality can be found, it is common to find that the mother, father or sibling behaved in the same way. We presume that this is a matter of delayed maturation.

Cerebral palsy, particularly of the spastic and athetoid types, delays walking and in severe cases may make it impossible. The hypotonias delay sitting and walking. A child with the Werdnig–Hoffmann syndrome may never walk. Children with the more benign hypotonia may walk at five or six years of age. Children with *muscular dystrophy* of the Duchenne type are late in learning to walk. About half of boys with Duchenne muscular dystrophy have not started to walk alone by 18 months; but a confusing feature of these boys is the frequently associated mild mental retardation, which in itself delays walking.

Children brought up in an institution are late in sitting and walking, partly because of emotional deprivation and partly because of lack of practice. If a child is kept on his back for prolonged periods, the age of sitting and walking is delayed.

Obesity almost certainly does not delay walking.

Many children refuse to walk without a hand held, long after they have become sufficiently mature to walk unaided,

Congenital subluxation of the hip does *not* delay walking. Many children are referred to orthopaedic surgeons on account of lateness in walking. This is irrational, and such children should be referred to the paediatrician.

Delayed sphincter control and enuresis

The following are the main causes of delayed control of the bladder:

> Delayed maturation, usually a familial feature (primary enuresis)
> Mental subnormality
> Mismangement of toilet training
> Severe constipation
> Emotional deprivation
> Organic causes
>> Bladder-neck or urethral obstruction
>> Ectopic ureter entering the vagina. Ureterocele
>> Diverticulum of the anterior urethra
>> Meningomyelocele
>> Sacral agenesis
>> Diastematomyelia
>> Lipoma of the cauda equina
>> Epispadias
>> Ectopia vesicae
>> Absent abdominal muscles with gross expansion of the posterior urethra
>> Traumatic: after a circumcision operation
>> Epilepsy

Many psychiatrists maintain that enuresis is entirely a psychological problem, while many paediatricians hold that there are two types of enuresis, primary and secondary, the primary kind being that in which the child has never been dry at night, and the secondary variety in which the child is dry for a period of months or years and then begins to wet the bed. They feel that the primary type usually has an organic basis, there being delay in maturation of the relevant part of the nervous system, some children being late in acquiring control of the bladder, just as others are late in learning to sit, walk or talk. In this variety there is usually a family history of the same complaint. If one of identical twins wets the bed, the other does; but if one of non-identical twins does, the likelihood of the other doing so is much less. No one would deny that psychological difficulties can be added to the problem of the child with primary enuresis. For instance, the mother is likely to smack the child for wetting his bed, may ridicule him or try to shame him for it—and so make him worse. If she shows excessive anxiety about his toilet training, she is likely to cause emotional disturbance and add to his problem. I have discussed the problem in detail elsewhere.

The *mentally subnormal* child, being late in almost all aspects of development, is likely to be late in acquiring sphincter control.

Mismanagement of toilet training may cause delay in control of the bladder or relapse once control has been achieved. It may add psychological factors to the problem of delayed maturation. Mismanagement consists usually of excessively enthusiastic 'potting', compelling the child to sit on the pottie when he wants to get off and smacking him for not using it. Occasionally a parent does not give the child a chance to use the pottie when he wants it, and delays the acquisition of control. It is the usual thing for a mother to smack her child for wetting the bed—until she finds that it does not help, and then she merely scolds him. MacKeith (1972) wrote that the sensitive or critical period is important; when the child has reached that degree of maturation which enables him to learn to control the bladder, mismanagement of toilet training is particularly liable to delay the acquisition of control. Unkindness or strict methods are especially important. Parents can delay the acquisition of control, but they can do little to accelerate it until the nervous system is ready.

A child brought up in an institution, or otherwise exposed to *emotional deprivation*, is likely to be late in acquiring control of the bladder.

The organic causes of urinary incontinence were fully reviewed in the article by Smith (1967). When a child has constant dribbling incontinence, day and night, urethral valves may be the cause in the boy, or an ectopic ureter or ureterocele in a girl. The older boy may dribble only after micturition, because some urine remains in the posterior urethra until the voluntary squeeze of the external urethral musculature relaxes, thus allowing the urine to dribble through. A diverticulum of the anterior urethra acts in the same way. The ectopic ureter in the girl may open into the urethra, or between the urethral and vaginal orifice, or near the hymen. In boy or girl, the diagnosis should immediately be suspected if there is dribbling incontinence. When the mother's story is equivocal, one should see that the child has a dry nappy on (if he still has one), and then observe when it becomes wet, by examining it every ten minutes or so.

The other organic causes, such as meningomyelocele, ectopia vesicae, absent abdominal muscles or lipoma involving the cauda equina, are obvious if looked for. The 'neurogenic bladder' is diagnosed by the dribbling of urine, the patulous anus, perineal anaesthesia, and the fact that urine can be expressed by firm suprapubic pressure. It is easy to miss the diagnosis of epispadias by failing to examine the penis. Diastematomyelia is less easy to diagnose. It may be associated with a meningomyelocele, or there may be a tuft of hair in the middle of the back which draws attention to the possibility of an underlying bone deformity. In addition to the incontinence there may be progressive weakness of the legs. The diagnosis is established by X-ray studies. Sacral agenesis may be impossible to diagnose without X-ray studies. If only one or two segments are missing, a gap may be felt on palpation. When there is complete sacral agenesis, the buttocks are flat, the intergluteal cleft is small, and there may be lower limb deformity. There may be other orthopaedic abnormalities, or an imperforate anus. The symptom is usually urinary incontinence of the dribbling variety, often with recurrent urinary tract infection. One should examine for a patulous anus (Thompson *et al* 1974). The condition is sometimes related to maternal diabetes.

Incontinence following circumcision may be the result of putting a stitch through the urethra.

Bed-wetting in the case of an epileptic child may be the result of a fit.

Secondary enuresis is usually due to psychological stress or insecurity. The cause may lie in worry at home or school, a move from house to house, a move to a new school or a spell in hospital. It is important to realise that when a child has recently acquired control of the bladder, anything causing frequency or polyuria is liable to cause enuresis, especially when this develops at the sensitive or critical period. Hence in all cases one should examine the urine for sugar (i.e. for diabetes mellitus) and for the specific gravity (for renal failure and other causes of polyuria). One must also examine a clean specimen under the microscope for excess of white cells and for organisms and culture it in order to eliminate a urinary tract infection.

Berg *et al* (1977) studying 40 children with day and night incontinence, and 46 with incontinence only at night, found that day and night incontinence in boys is commonly associated with soiling, and that one in two girls with it has bacteriuria. This may be the result of the wetting rather than the cause.

Gross constipation is an occasional cause of wetting.

Delayed speech

The following are the usual causes of delayed speech:
> Mental subnormality
> Delayed maturation, usually a familial trait
> Emotional deprivation
> Deafness
> Multiple pregnancy (twins)
> Psychoses—autism and schizophrenia
> Aphasia
> Unknown causes

The most common cause of delayed speech is *mental subnormality*. Probably all mentally subnormal children are late in learning to speak. Otherwise, the usual cause is delayed maturation: one nearly always finds that the mother, father or sibling was late in learning to speak.

A child brought up in an institution or otherwise subjected to *emotional deprivation* is likely to be late in learning to speak. Delayed speech is an almost universal finding on follow-up examination of children who have suffered child abuse (Lynch 1978).

An important cause of delayed speech is *deafness*, which may be only for high tones. One must not be put off by the story that the child hears footsteps and many other noises. Suitable high tones for testing the child's hearing are the sounds PS, PHTH, and the crumpling of tissue paper, assuming that he cannot see the source of sound and that the source of sound is on a level with the ear and reasonably near (e.g. within one or two feet).

Twins are often late in speech—perhaps because the mother has less time to talk to twins than to singletons. The delay is unlikely to be due to the twins understanding each other without speaking properly.

Children with *infantile autism* or *schizophrenia* are late in speaking. For hysterical aphasia or aphonia, see Arajarvi 1965.

Delayed speech is *not* due to laziness, it is *not* due to 'everything being done for him', it is *not* due to tongue tie, and it is most unlikely to be due to jealousy. There is some association between delayed speech and delay in the establishment of handedness.

Whatever the causes, parents and doctors should realize that a child fails to speak because he cannot speak. Adults tend to talk less to him, so that he hears less and is still further retarded.

Emotional causes include emotional deprivation, such as that due to institutional care, insecurity and worries. Poor teaching may be a cause.

We cannot always determine the cause of delayed speech. We do know that many children who are late in learning to speak are subsequently late in learning to read or write. When a child of three or four years of age is not saying any words and his hearing is known to be normal, and he is not autistic or mentally defective (i.e. has aphasia), the outlook is uncertain. All children with delayed speech development should be referred to an expert for diagnosis.

Indistinct speech

Indistinctness of speech is usually due to substitution of letters, of which the commonest is the substitution of 'th' for 's'—the central lisp, due to protrusion of the tongue between the teeth when pronouncing the 's'. It is readily treated by the speech therapist, though milder ones cure themselves. The speech therapist may treat other substitutions, but it is uncertain how much of the improvement to be expected is due to therapy and how much to maturation, for most of these substitutions are self-limiting.

Nasal speech is due to a cleft palate, a submucous cleft, or adenoids. A submucous cleft may be suspected because of a history of nasal regurgitation in infancy, and the finding of a bifid uvula, decreased palatal movement on phonation and a palpable notch on the posterior edge of the hard palate. It may follow adenoidectomy.

Dysarthria. When a child has previously spoken normally, the sudden onset of dysarthria may be a premonitory symptom of *migraine* (p. 92).

It may be a symptom of a wide variety of *degenerative diseases of the nervous system, cerebral tumour or congenital syphilis.*

It may be due to certain *drugs,* namely diazepam, imipramine, metoclopramide, phenytoin; primidone or sulthiame.

When a child has never spoken normally, dysarthria may be due to cerebral palsy, in which there is spasticity or incoordination of the muscles of speech, or to a cleft palate (or submucous cleft), structural abnormalities of the jaw, including malocclusion and macroglossia. Malpronunciation of the sounds m, n, ng, may be due to nasal obstruction. It has to be distinguished from dyslalia and severe lisp.

References

Arajarvi T. Elective mutism in children *Ann Paediatr Fenniae* 1965; **11**: 46.

Berg I, Fielding D, Meadow R. Psychiatric disturbance, urgency and bacteriuria with day and night wetting. *Arch Dis Child* 1977; **52**: 651.

Lynch MA. The prognosis of child abuse. *J Child Psychol Psychiat* 1978; **19**: 175.

MacKeith RC. Is maturation delay a frequent factor in the origins of primary nocturnal enuresis? *Dev Med Child Neurol* 1972; **14**: 217.

Smith ED. Diagnosis and management of the child with wetting. *Aust Paediatr J* 1967; **3**: 193.

Thompson IM, Kirk RM, Dale M. Sacral agenesis *Pediatrics* 1974; **57**: 236.

Mental Deterioration

The usual causes of mental deterioration are as follows:

       Emotional causes. Insecurity. Emotional deprivation
       Poor teaching
       Absences from school
       Moves from school to school
       Development of visual or auditory defects
       Metabolic diseases
       Degenerative diseases of the nervous system
       Severe hypoglycaemia, including insulin overdosage
       Lead poisoning
       Cerebral tumour or abscess
       Meningitis, encephalitis, cerebral thrombosis
       Head injury
       Effect of epilepsy
       Drugs

Psychoses
Severe malnutrition
Development of thyroid deficiency
Muscular dystrophy

At any age a child's progress may slow down as a result of *insecurity*, anxiety, worries or emotional deprivation. Laziness and loss of interest in the work in hand may also be important factors. Insecurity in its broadest sense is one of the main causes of backwardness in intelligent children.

A child may develop a *defect of hearing or eyesight*, after having been previously normal, with the result that his school work deteriorates.

A variety of *metabolic diseases* leads to deterioration of a child's intelligence. They include particularly abnormalities of aminoacid and carbohydrate metabolism. There are so many of these diseases that it is not useful to attempt to relate particular symptoms to particular diseases. The classification by Lagos (1971) is useful, because it is based on the age of onset of symptoms. Unfortunately there is some overlapping between the groups: but the classification does help one to refer to any of the larger textbooks of paediatrics for further information. All are rare. The classification (modified) is as follows:

1   *Deterioration starting at birth*
    Phenylketonuria
    Pyridoxine dependency
    Maple syrup urine disease (fits, vomiting, hypotonia)
    Homocystinuria (resembling Marfan's syndrome, with dislocation of the lens, long fingers, but with fits and thromboses)

2   *Starting in the first two years*
    Amaurotic family idiocy
    Hyperuricaemia (Lesch–Nyhan disease: p. 206)
    Subacute necrotizing encephalopathy (feeding difficulties, vomiting, hypotonia, weakness, respiratory problems)
    Leucodystrophies
      Sulphatide lipoidosis (starting at 12 to 18 months, with motor weakness, hypotonia, fits)
      Krabbe's disease (normal till 4 to 6 months: fits)
      Pelizaeus–Merzbacher disease (starting in first year: nystagmus, choreoathetosis)

      Hypersarcosinaemia, carnosinaemia, hyperlysin-
        aemia
      Canavan's disease
      Gaucher's disease (hypertonia, splenomegaly)
      Niemann–Pick disease (especially Jews)
      Generalized gangliosidosis
      Mucopolysaccharidoses
      Glycogen storage disease
      Tuberous sclerosis

3 *Starting after two years*
      Amaurotic family idiocy (late forms)
      Myoclonic epilepsy
      Schilder's disease (blindness, deafness, spasticity)
      Subacute sclerosing panencephalitis (commonly
        related to measles virus)
      Heller's infantile dementia (no neurological signs)

Severe hypoglycaemia, which is usually caused by insulin over-dosage, but which may arise spontaneously in association with fits, may lead to severe irreversible mental deficiency.

Lead poisoning causes serious mental deterioration. Mentally subnormal children are more likely to eat dirt or to take objects to the mouth than normal children, and so are more likely than others to develop lead poisoning—and so to deteriorate.

There are scores of *degenerative diseases of the nervous system,* mostly hereditary. They include in particular Friedreich's ataxia and Schilder's disease. Degenerative diseases of the nervous system are difficult to distinguish from an intracranial space-occupying lesion, and it follows that the necessary investigations should be carried out in hospital.

Meningitis, encephalitis or head injury may cause serious mental subnormality in a previous normal child. Intracranial thrombosis as a result of dehydration or other causes may occur in infancy and have the same effect.

Epilepsy does not in itself cause serious mental deterioration, though epileptic fits may themselves be caused by the cerebral lesion which also causes mental deterioration. *Petit mal* is not usually associated with mental deterioration, though frequent attacks may cause a child in class to lose the thread of the discussion. A rapid succession of *petit mal* attacks (*petit mal status*), is particularly liable to cause school difficulties. Subictal epilepsy consists of a series of electrical discharges which causes some of the features of epilepsy, such as confusion, without convulsive movements. Temporal lobe epilepsy is more likely than other forms of epilepsy to be associated with some deterioration. Major fits, if prolonged, may damage the brain by anoxia. Finally psychological problems associated with epilepsy may cause a child's school work to deteriorate.

Drugs given to an epileptic, especially barbiturates, or other drugs in an overdose, may have a retarding effect, leading to drowsiness, defective concentration and deterioration. Drug addiction may cause progressive mental deterioration.

Psychoses such as schizophrenia cause serious deterioration in a child's performance.

References

Lagos JC. *Differential diagnosis in pediatric neurology*. Boston: Little Brown, 1971.

Symptoms related to the genito-urinary tract

URINARY TRACT INFECTION

A urinary tract infection is difficult to diagnose with certainty in general practice (and there are often difficulties in making the diagnosis in hospital). Mistakes are commonly made in two directions: the diagnosis is made when there is in fact no urinary infection, and it is missed when there is an infection. The reasons for the mistakes are varied. Many regard scalding on micturition or frequency as definitely indicating an infection, and regard these symptoms as necessary before making the diagnosis. Both of these beliefs are incorrect. Discomfort on micturition may be due to meatal ulcer or balanitis in the boy, or soreness of the vulval region, as in a nappy rash, in the girl. There are many other causes of frequency (p. 290). These symptoms are the exception rather than the rule in a urinary tract infection. In an acute infection the common symptoms are fever, vomiting, rigors, meningism and febrile convulsions (under the age of five). There may be abdominal discomfort and sometimes diarrhoea. There is unlikely to be tenderness in the loin. Another common misbelief is the idea that there must be albumin in the urine or that the presence of albumin confirms the diagnosis. In fact albumin is present in less than half of all cases. Frank haematuria is definitely unusual. In a chronic urinary tract infection the only symptoms are commonly lack of energy, poor appetite and other vague symptoms which do not point to the urinary tract. Outside hospital the only satisfactory method of obtaining a culture of urine is the dipslide or one of its modifications, in which the child passes urine on to a dipslide or the dipslide is inserted into the clean urine container, put into the sterile bottle provided and sent to the laboratory.

DELAYED MICTURITION IN THE NEWBORN

Delayed micturition in the newborn baby was discussed by Moore & Galvez (1972), and by Johnston (1976). Johnston found that 67 per cent pass urine in the first 12 hours, 25 per cent in the next 12 hours, and 7 per cent only after 24 hours. He suggested that sometimes there is no discoverable cause for transient urinary retention. Absence of micturition with an empty bladder and without ascites (which would suggest rupture of the urinary tract with urethral obstruction), indicates severe bilateral renal agenesis. Other causes to consider include:

> Restriction of fluid
> Tubular or cortical necrosis
> Renal agenesis
> Bilateral renal vein thrombosis (p. 293)
> Congenital nephrotic syndrome
> Nephritis
> Neurogenic bladder
> Urethral diverticulum
> Ureterocele

References

Johnston JH. Abnormalities of micturition in the neonte. *Br J Hosp Med* 1976;
   16: 462.
Moore ES, Galvez MB. Delayed micturition in newborn period. *J Pediatr* 1972;
   80: 867.

SUPPRESSION OR RETENTION OF URINE

For convenience these will be discussed together.

The causes of suppression or retention of urine can be listed as follows:

> Normal—newborn
> Behaviour problem
> Urethral obstruction
>> Valves in posterior urethra
>> Congenital contracture of vesical outlet
>> Hypertrophy of the verumontanum
>> Labial adhesions
>> Hydrocolpos
>> Congenital stricture
> Anterior sacral meningocele, sacral teratoma, retrovesical cyst
> Neuromuscular disease—spina bifida, myelitis, tumour of the
>>> cord, sacral agenesis, poliomyelitis, transverse myelitis,
>>> Guillain–Barré syndrome
> Diverticulum at the base of the bladder
> Faecal impaction
> Meatal ulcer
> Foreign body
> Stone
> Transient–instrumentation
> Trauma
> Acute nephritis
> Drugs—phenothiazine group

Retention of urine is a rare behaviour problem, an unusual attention-seeking device.

Dribbling of urine with a poor stream in the case of a baby suggests urethral obstruction. Sacral agenesis (p. 281) may cause the same symptoms. Labial adhesions or hydrocolpos are readily diagnosed by inspection of the vulva.

Faecal impaction is diagnosed by rectal examination.
Imipramine may cause difficulty in micturition.

Oliguria

Oliguria may be due to:

>   Fever, dehydration, shock
>   Acute nephritis, haemolytic uraemic syndrome
>   Acute tubular necrosis
>   Renal vein thrombosis
>   Incompatible transfusion
>   Drug—carbamazepine

FREQUENCY OR SCALDING ON MICTURITION

It is normal for a baby in the first few months to scream on micturition.
Some scalding on micturition may be due merely to the urine being
concentrated as the result of a raised temperature in an infection.

When an older child complains of discomfort on micturition, a local
examination of the genital area should be carried out. A common
cause is a nappy rash, a meatal ulcer or soreness of the vulva. It
could result from sulphonamide crystalluria. Other drugs which may
cause dysuria include amitriptyline, chlordiazepoxide, imipramine
and isoniazid.

Dysuria may be caused by a urinary tract infection. Acute nephritis
may be accompanied by pain on micturition with some frequency.

It is a serious mistake to treat a child as a urinary tract infection on
the basis of symptoms without establishing the diagnosis in the
laboratory.

Frequency or scalding are not usually prominent symptoms of
urinary tract infection unless there is cystitis.

Frequency may result from pelvic appendicitis, and so an incorrect
diagnosis of urinary tract infection is made, especially when on urine
examination an excess of white cells is found.

A toddler who is learning control of the bladder always has urgency
and cannot wait once he feels the desire to pass urine. Children with
enuresis of primary type often retain this urgency for some years.

A toddler may develop what appears to be frequency of micturition, when it is in reality an attention-seeking device. The child discovers that as soon as he demands to pass urine his mother drops everything and rushes him to his potty: he then demands to pass urine every few minutes, and his mother in her anxiety to train him does not realise the true nature of the frequency.

Drugs which may cause frequency and polyuria include antihistamines, carbamazepine, demeclocycline (ledermycin), fenfluramine and Vitamin D excess.

POLYDIPSIA AND POLYURIA

The causes are mainly the following:

> Habit polydipsia (probably the commonest cause)
> Diabetes mellitus, diabetes insipidus
> Renal failure: chronic nephritis etc
> Renal tubular acidosis, hypercalcaemia
> Rare syndromes—salt-losing type of adrenocortical hyperplasia, Conn's syndrome, Bartter's syndrome, De Toni–Fanconi syndrome
> Catecholamine-secreting tumour (eg phaeochromocytoma (p. 42) rare)
> Carbohydrate malnutrition (p. 12).
> Drugs—clonazepam, Vitamin D excess

Habit polydipsia in child or adult has to be distinguished by complex laboratory procedures from polydipsia of organic origin, such as diabetes mellitus (Dies *et al* 1961, Kohn *et al* 1976).

Conn's syndrome includes polyuria, polydipsia, alkalosis, hypokalaemia, hypertension, albuminuria and a urine of low specific gravity. *Bartter's syndrome* consists of polyuria, hyperaldosteronism, alkalosis, weakness, short stature, vomiting, thirst and a craving for salt, developing any time in infancy or later.

Thirst may or may not be a feature when there is polyuria. Young babies or mentally subnormal children may become dehydrated as a result of not experiencing thirst. Babies with *nephrogenic diabetes insipidus* may have to be almost forced to take more fluid than they demand.

References

Dies F, Rangel S, Rivera A. Differential diagnosis between diabetes insipidus and compulsive polydipsia. *Ann Int Med* 1961; **54:** 710.

Kohn B, Norman ME, Feldman H, Thier SA. Singer I. Hysterical polydipsia in children. *Am J Dis Child* 1976; **130:** 210.

HAEMATURIA

The commonest causes of haematuria are acute nephritis, infection, obstruction and tumours. The causes may be summarized as follows:

Blood diseases, especially anaphylactoid purpura, leukaemia etc. Scurvy. Haemolytic uraemic syndrome.

Connective tissue or collagen diseases

Kidney—nephritis, focal nephritis, pyelonephritis, tuberculosis. Glandular fever (rare cause)

Tumours. Wilms' tumour. Polycystic kidney. Angioma

Hydronephroisis

Calculi. Crystalluria

Renal vein thrombosis, infarction. Varices. Angioma, telangiectasia

Tropical infections—schistosomiasis, malaria

Trauma

Ureter—stone

Bladder—foreign body, tumour, haemorrhage, cystitis

Urethra—foreign body

Effect of exertion or cold

Factitious haematuria

Drugs, poisons

Unexplained

Blood diseases which cause haematuria include haemophilia, haemorrhagic disease of the newborn, sickle-cell anaemia, thrombocytopenic purpura and leukaemia Haematuria commonly follows Henoch-Schönlein purpura, as a result of a complicating nephritis. Scurvy, glandular fever and the collagen diseases are occasionally accompanied by haematuria.

Acute nephritis is now a rare cause of haematuria in Britain, but in tropical countries it is common, especially in association with infections of the skin. The symptoms may be acute, with headache, vomiting, fits or puffiness of the eyes, but there may be no visible oedema.

Recurrent haematuria is commonly due to focal nephritis. Roy *et al* (1973) referred to Berger's disease, sudden haematuria in association with respiratory infection. Naked eye haematuria is an unusual feature of pyelonephritis.

Tuberculosis of the kidney is now rare in Britain. The tuberculin test will be positive. The diagnosis is confirmed by the finding of sterile pyuria, detection of tubercle bacilli in the centrifuged deposit, and isolation of the tubercle bacillus on culture or guinea-pig inoculation.

Tumours and cysts of the kidney include the nephroblastoma (Wilms' tumour), polycystic disease and angioma of the renal pelvis. Wilms' tumour occurs particularly in the first four years. It may be associated with aniridia, Beckwith's syndrome, congenital asymmetry, the von Hippel–Lindau syndrome (p. 329), bilateral retinoblastoma, neurofibromatosis or anomalies of the urinary tract. The symptoms or signs are principally abdominal swelling, haematuria, dysuria, abdominal pain and sometimes fever.

Renal calculi are rare in children except in tropical countries unless they are confined to bed for prolonged periods with orthopaedic conditions.

Renal vein thrombosis occurs mainly in the first few months of life, commonly following an infection elsewhere (McFarland 1965). The diagnosis is suspected when a child suddenly develops haematuria, a renal mass and perhaps oedema. The kidney is palpable in half the cases. There may be thrombocytopenia, uraemia, albuminuria and acidosis. *Infarction of the kidney* may occur in subacute bacterial endocarditis.

Conditions in the bladder include polypi, diverticula and foreign bodies. The latter are important in girls. I have seen a child admitted to hospital on ten occasions on account of haematuria, before a safety pin was found in the bladder. Polypi and diverticula are diagnosed by cystograms and cystoscopy. Haemorrhagic cystitis may result from an adenovirus infection of the bladder, cyclophosphamide, or bacillus proteus cystitis and urethritis (blood appearing especially at the end of micturition) (Mufson *et al* 1973).

Bleeding may arise from a *urethral caruncle* in a girl or a *meatal ulcer* in a boy. The blood in such a case would be seen at the end of micturition. Urethral obstruction may cause haematuria.

In an occasional child haematuria follows *exertion* (Illingworth & Holt, 1957).

Drugs which cause haematuria include anticoagulants, acetazolamide, aminophylline, bacitracin, cephalosporins, cyclophosphamide, kanamycin, methicillin, PAS, phensuximide, phenytoin, salicylates, sulphonamides and troxidone.

Factitious haematuria has to be considered when there are no other obvious causes (Outwater *et al* 1981): it may be a feature of the 'Munchausen by proxy' syndrome, in which the mother adds blood to the child's urine.

After the most complete investigation, including renal biopsy, it may be impossible to determine the cause of the haematuria.

For conditions causing a colour change in the urine suggestive of haematuria, see below.

References

Illingworth RS, Holt KS. Transient rash and haematuria on exercise and emotion. *Arch Dis Child* 1957; **32**: 254.

McFarland JB. Renal vein thrombosis. *Q J Med* 1965; **34**: 269.

Mufson MA, Belshe RB, *et al.* Cause of acute haemorrhagic cystitis in children. *Am J Dis Child* 1973; **126**: 605.

Outwater KM. *et al.* Factitious hematuria. *J Pediatr* 1981; **98**: 95.

Roy L, Fish AJ, *et al.* Recurrent macroscopic hematuria, focal nephritis and mesangial deposition of immunoglobulin and complement. *J Pediatr* 1973; **83**: 767.

West CD. Asymptomatic hematuria and proteinuria in children. *J. Pediatr* 1976; **89**: 173.

CHANGES IN THE COLOUR OF THE URINE

The following conditions are associated with unusual colouration of the urine:

Dark colour
Concentration, as in fever
Dark yellow
Bile
Carotene-containing foods

Red
  Nitrofurantoin
  Haemoglobinuria
  Favism
  Infection of baby's alimentary tract by serratia marcescens
  Rhodamine B in foodstuffs
  Blackcurrant juice, blackberries, rose hip syrup
  Beeturia
  Drugs
Red brown
  Urates
  Porphyria
  Myoglobinuria
Dark brown or black
  Alkaptonuria
  Tyrosinosis
  Melanosis
  Nitrofurantoin
Blue
  Hypercalcaemia
  The result of copper clasp on the nappy holder.
Haemoglobinuria occurs when there is rapid haemolysis.

The red colour of the urine in *beeturia* is due to the pigment betanin in the beet. The red colour changes to yellow when alkali is added, and returns to red on acidification (Tunnessen *et al* 1969).

Urates disappear on boiling.

In porphyria, the urine may be normal in colour when passed, but changes to Burgundy red on exposure to light. There may be haemolytic anaemia, photosensitivity and hypertrichosis.

The urine in myoglobinuria is red brown and gives a positive benzidine or guaiac test (Boroian & Attwood 1965). It follows crush injuries, electric shocks, severe exercise or other causes. There may be muscle pains, chills and vomiting.

In alcaptonuria the urine becomes dark on standing. The nappie may show a black stain. The urine gives a colour change with Benedict's reagent and ferric chloride gives a fleeting blue colour.

Some *drugs*, other than those mentioned in the table, may colour the urine red or red brown. They include rifampicin, sulphonamides, quinine and pamaquin. Dorbanex (laxative) may

Drugs that colour the urine

Urine colour	Associated drug or chemical	Urine colour	Associated drug or chemical
Blue	Methyelne blue	Pink and red to red brown —cont'd	Emodin (alkaline urine) Eosins (red with green fluorescence) Hematuria producers (mercuric salts, irritants, etc.) Hemolysis producers Phenindione (Danilone, Hedulin, Indon) Phenolic metabolites (glucuronides) Phenolphthalein (alkaline urine) Phensuximide (Milontin) Porphyrins Prochlorperazine (Compazine) Santonin (alkaline urine) Thiazolsulfone (Promizole) Urates (especially newborn infants and during tumour lysis)
Brown to black	Aniline dyes Cascara Chlorinated hydrocarbons Hydroxyquinoline Melanin Methocarbamol (Robaxin) Naphthalene Naphthol Nitrites Phenol Phenyl salicylate (salol) Pyrogallol Quinine Resorcinol (resorcin) Rhubarb Santonin Senna Thymol		
Green (blue plus yellow)	Anthraquinone Arbutin Bile pigments Eosins Methocarbamol (Robaxin) Methylene blue Resorcinol (resorcin) Tetrahydronaphthalene Thymol	Rust	Chlorzoxazone (Paraflex)
		Yellow or brownish	Danthron (Dorbane) (acid urine) Heavy metals (bismuth, mercury) Liver poisons (jaundice) Alcohol Arsenicals Carbon tetrachloride Chloral hydrate Chlorinated hydrocarbon Chlorobutanol (chlorbutol, Chloretone) Chloroform Cinchophen Naphthalene Neocinchophen Nitrofurantoins Pamaquine (Aminoquin, Beprochine, Gamefar, Plasmoquine, Praequine, Quipenyl) Sulfonamides Tribromoethanol with amylene hydrate (Avertin)
Magenta to purple	Fuchsin Phenolphthalein		
Orange orange red	Phenylazopyridine (Pyridium)		
Orange red brown	Combinations of phenylazopyridine (Pyridium) and other drugs used as urinary antiseptics; many of the trade names begin with *azo* Santonin		
Pink and red to red brown	Aminopyrine Anthraquinone and its dyes Antipyrine (Pyrazoline) Chrysarobin (alkaline urine) Cinchophen Danthron (Dorbane) (pink to violet—alkaline urine) Diphenylhydantoin (Dilantin)	Yellow or green	Carotene-containing foods Methylene blue Riboflavin Vitamin B complex Yeast concentrate

make the urine pink. A blue colour in the nappie may be due to a pseudomonas or serratia marcescens infection (Thearle *et al* 1973).

The table on p. 296, reproduced with permission from Shirkey's book *Pediatric Therapy* (1972), summarizes the colour changes which may result from drugs.

References

Boroian TV, Attwood CR. Myoglobinuria. *J Pediatr* 1965; **67:** 69.
Shirkey HC. *Pediatric therapy*. St Louis: Mosby, 1972.
Thearle MJ, Wise R, Allen JT. Blue nappies. *Lancet* 1973; **2:** 499.
Tunnessen WW, Smith C, Oski FA. Beeturia. *Am J Dis Child* 1969; **17:** 424.

PAIN IN THE PENIS

This is an unusual symptom, apart from pain on passing urine. Pain in the penis may be due to irritation at the bladder neck, as by a stone.

PAIN OR SWELLING IN THE SCROTUM

The obvious causes are:

      Hernia or hydrocele (They may be both present)
      Torsion of the testis
      Epididymo-orchitis or orchitis alone
      Tumour of testis (especially embryonal carcinoma)
        Cysts, Angioma
      Trauma
      Oedema
      Filariasis in Tropics

Unless there has been definite injury, pain in the scrotum should be regarded as being due to torsion of the testis until proved otherwise. The torsion may be that of the spermatic cord or the testicular appendages: in the latter case there may be a localized spot of tenderness at the upper pole of the testis.

Torsion can occur at any time in childhood, from the first day onwards. It is more common in the first year. The pain often starts in sleep or during exercise; it commonly begins in the inguinal region of the abdomen just above the internal inguinal ring and may be referred to the abdomen. The testis may untwist and retwist, with recurrence of pain. There is often vomiting and shock. The correct diagnosis is urgent, so that surgical treatment can be given immediately.

Torsion of the testis can be confused with epididymitis but that is exceedingly rare in the absence of a urinary tract infection or other gross urological abnormality. It has to be distinguished also from the orchitis of mumps and tuberculosis, testicular neoplasm or injury, or haemorrhage in purpura. Orchitis apart from mumps is very rare; and orchitis in mumps hardly ever occurs prior to puberty. Orchitis could be confused with a strangulated hernia.

References

Kelalis PP, Stickler GB. The painful scrotum: torsion vs epididymo-orchitis. *Clin Pediatr* 1976; **15:** 220.
Perera WSN. The red-hot scrotum: a 10 year review. *Records of the Adelaide Children's Hospital.* 1979; **2:** 185.
Williamson RCN. Death in the scrotum. Testicular torsion. *N Engl J Med* 1977; **296:** 338.

Oedema

Generalized oedema

Newborn infants, especially those prematurely born, may have general oedema and scleroderma (Lancet 1979). Other causes in the newborn include

    Congestive heart failure
    Immaturity of the kidney
    Haemolytic disease. Haemoglobinopathies
    Maternal diabetes
    Hypoxia
    Vitamin E deficiency
    Severe infection
    Cold injury
    Dystrophia myotonica

After the newborn period, the causes are mainly the following:
Hypoproteinaemia
  Defective protein intake, kwashiorkor, beriberi
  Nephritis and the nephrotic syndrome
  Steatorrhoea: fibrocystic disease of the pancreas
  Protein loss with burns, eczema, suppuration; protein-
    losing enteropathy, diarrhoea
  Syphilis
  Liver disease, galactosaemia
  Unexplained
Heart failure. Constrictive pericarditis
Increased capillary permeability
  Anaemia. Anaphylactoid purpura. Positive pressure ven-
    tilation
  Allergy: aspirin sensitivity: angioneurotic oedema
Excess intake of sodium or fluid, excessive infusion
  Feeding errors
  Sodium retention (heart, liver, kidney disease: steroids)
Diabetes mellitus, on starting treatment
Miscellaneous
  Yellow nail syndrome
  Intestinal lymphangiectasia (diarrhoea, failure to thrive,
    oedema)
  Collagen diseases

This classification is not entirely accurate, partly because of the overlapping of the basic causes. Despite all investigations, the cause may remain obscure (Fisher 1966).

Dystrophia myotonica is a rare cause of general oedema in the newborn (Pearse & Höweler 1979).

Oedema without albuminuria may be the presenting symptom in *fibrocystic disease of the pancreas*. It may occur in other examples of the sprue syndrome (Gordon 1961).

The *nephrotic syndrome* is the end result of wide variety of conditions, including *disseminated lupus, renal vein thrombosis, syphilis, amyloid disease, diabetes and quartan malaria*. It may be *congenital*. It may be caused by heavy metals, ampicillin, daunorubicin, penicillamine, phenindione, potassium perchlorate, rifampicin, sulphonamides, thioridazine or troxidone. It may result from the use of outdated tetracycline.

The oedema of nephritis may be asymmetrical in distribution: this may be particularly noticeable on the face, owing to the child lying on one side in sleep.

Generalized oedema due to *heart failure* is rare in children. The diagnosis will not necessarily be obvious. There may be a murmur or cyanosis pointing to congenital heart disease, but heart failure may occur without a murmur in paroxysmal tachycardia, coarctation of the aorta, Fallot's tetralogy (in early infancy), transposition of the vessels or anomalous venous drainage, and when heart failure develops the murmur of a patent ductus or of a ventricular septal defect may disappear. Heart failure may also occur without a murmur in myocarditis, fibroelastosis or severe anaemia.

Aspirin sensitivity may manifest itself by generalized oedema.

A variety of allergic causes may be responsible for angioneurotic oedema, but it is not normally easy to detect the allergen.

Excessive sodium or fluid intake is usually due to an excessive intravenous infusion. Faulty feeding may result in oedema in premature infants; too concentrated a formula may lead to oedema by causing hypernatraemia.

Slight oedema lasting for a few days occurs in some ten per cent of children when treatment of *diabetes mellitus* is commenced (Klein *et al.*, 1962).

Oedema of the upper part of the body alone is likely to be due to *obstruction of the superior vena cava,* and oedema of the lower part of the body alone may be due to *obstruction of the inferior vena cava* (or to ascites and its causes).

For the yellow nail syndrome see p. 331.

Oedema of the hands and feet, and sometimes elsewhere, may be an early sign of *dermatomyositis* or *periarteritis*. It occurs in the *Kawasaki syndrome* (p. 35).

Face, eyelids and conjunctiva

Oedema of the face may be caused by the following conditions:

      Part of general oedema

      Rubbing the eyes excessively (especially hay fever), crying,
          conjunctivitis

Angioneurotic oedema. Sensitivity to eye drops
Drugs
Infections around the face: acute sinusitis, orbital cellulitis
Cavernous sinus thrombosis
Dermatomyositis
Infectious mononucleosis, measles; trichiniasis
Melkersson's syndrome (rare)

The commonest cause of oedema of the conjunctiva (with sometimes oedema of the eyelid) is crying or severe rubbing of the eyes because of itching caused by *hay fever.* Some swelling of the eyelids may result from eye infections or allergy to eye drops.

Angioneurotic oedema may be due to a variety of allergens, hereditary deficiency of C₁ esterase inhibitor (Lancet 1973), or drugs—clonidine, disodium cromoglycate, demeclocycline and tartrazine used as colouring matter in drugs and foods. It may also be due to allergy to cow's milk protein (p. 13).

Other drugs may cause oedema of the face; by far the commonest is aspirin. Others include amitriptyline, cephaloridine, clonazepam, chlordiazeposide, cotrimoxazole, demeclocycline, ethosuximide, imipramine, indomethacin, iodides, methimazole, nitrofurantoin, penicillin, primidone, troxidone and Vitamin A excess.

Oedema of the face may be caused by infection in the vicinity, including *acute sinusitis, boils, dental abscess, orbital cellulitis, cavernous sinus thrombosis* or *osteitis of the frontal bone.* As for *acute sinusitis,* acute ethmoiditis is the most important, certainly in the young child (Healy 1981). The ethmoid sinus is always present at birth: the maxillary sinus is not usually important until after the age of 18 months, and the frontal sinus is not usually liable to infection till 7 or 8 years. Acute ethmoiditis presents as periorbital oedema or cellulitis: there is occasionally local pain or tenderness. It may be complicated by orbital cellulitis or cavernous sinus thrombosis (p. 180).

Melkersson's syndrome (Kunstadter 1965) consists of chronic swelling of the face, peripheral type of facial palsy (unilateral, bilateral or relapsing), and furrowed tongue. The facial palsy may precede the other symptoms by several years.

Arm

Oedema of the arm of a newborn baby may be due to an arm presentation.

A mother may be greatly alarmed when she picks up a baby from his bed in the morning and finds that one arm is swollen, cold and blue. There is pitting oedema. This is due not to the child lying on the affected arm, but to the arm having become uncovered when the temperature of the room is low. In a few hours the oedema disappears and the arm becomes normal in colour and appearance.

Abdominal wall

Shaul (1981) noted oedema of the abdominal wall in neonatal appendicitis (p. 104), and in necrotizing enterocolitis in the newborn. It may occur in peritonitis.

Legs

Congenital asymmetry may be confused at first with oedema. In this condition one half of the body is larger than the other, but there is no oedema. Oedema of the limbs is often a feature of *cold injury* in the newborn period.

Unilateral limb enlargement from birth may be due to a *lymphangioma* or *arteriovenous abnormality* (Klippel–Trenaunay syndrome) but there is not usually oedema. If the oedema is unilateral, and dates from birth, *Milroy's oedema* should be considered. This is largely lymphatic and there is little pitting. Enlargement of a limb or digit may be a manifestation of *neurofibromatosis* or of *congenital asymmetry*.

Oedema of both legs in a girl, or in boy in whom the testes cannot be palpated, suggests *Turner's syndrome*.

Oedema of both legs may result from *ascites*.

Sickle-cell anaemia may cause oedema of the limbs.

Oedema may be due to *compression stenosis of the left common iliac vein* by an overriding right common iliac artery ('iliac compression syndrome'). (Cockett *et al* 1967).

Genitalia

Oedema of the genitalia is common in normal newborn infants.

Oedema of the scrotum may be caused by an insect bite or sensitivity to detergents used for washing the nappies or pants (Cochran 1970). The cause of oedema of the scrotum is not always clear (Nicholas *et al*, 1970, Kaplan 1977). The onset is often rapid, with little pain, sometimes slight fever, clearing up in 12 to 48 hours. It might be allergic in origin, or due to bites or superficial cellulitis in association with an abrasion or pustule.

Oedema of the scrotum has to be distinguished from epididymitis, in which there would be marked tenderness, and from torsion of the testis, which may present as oedema with local tenderness. It could also be confused with rupture of the urethra with extravasation of urine.

Oedema of the scrotum can be an early manifestation of anaphylactoid purpura.

Lower part of body

This may be due to an adherent pericardium or obstruction of the inferior vena cava.

Sternum

This occurs at the onset of mumps (Gellis & Feingold 1976). Oedema over the sternum occurs in almost 6 per cent of cases of mumps, usually developing 5 to 8 days after the commencement of the glandular swelling, and lasting about 5 days.

References

Cockett FB, Thomas ML, Negus D. Iliac vein compression—its relation to ileofemoral thrombosis and the post-thrombotic syndrome. *Br Med J* 1967; **2**: 14.
Cochran W. Severe dermatitis and biological detergents. *Br Med J* 1970; **2**: 362.
Fisher DA. Obscure and unusual edema. *Pediatrics* 1966; **37**: 506.
Gellis SS, Feingold M. Mumps and presternal oedema. *Am J Dis Child* 1976: **130**: 417.
Gordon RS. Protein losing enteropathy in the sprue syndrome. *Lancet* 1961; **1**: 55.

Healy G. Acute sinusitis in childhood. *N Engl J Med* 1981; **304**: 779.

Kaplan GW. Acute idiopathic scrotal oedema. *J Pediatr Surg* 1977; **12**: 647.

Klein R, Marks JF, *et al*. The occurrence of peripheral edema and subcutaneous glycogen deposition following the initial treatment of diabetes mellitus in children. *J Pediatr* 1962; **60**: 87.

Kunstadter RH. Melkersson's syndrome. *Am J Dis Child* 1965; **110**: 559.

Lancet Leading article. Hereditary angioneurotic oedema. 1973; **1**: 1044.

Lancet Leading aritcle. Anasarca in the newborn. 1979; **2**: 729.

Nicholas JL, Morgan A, Zachary RB. Idiopathic edema of the scrotum in young boys. *Surgery* 1970; **67**: 847.

Pearse RG, Höweler CJ. Neonatal form of dystrophia myotonica. *Arch Dis Child* 1979; **54**: 331.

Pittman FE, Harris RC, Barker HG. Transient edema and hypoproteinemia. *Am J Dis Child* 1964; **108**: 189.

Shaul WL. Clues to the early diagnosis of neonatal appendicitis. *J Pediatr* 1981; **98**: 473.

Delayed Puberty in the Girl and Amenorrhoea

By the term delayed puberty I mean absence of menstruation by the age of sixteen. By primary amenorrhoea I mean the absence of menstruation; by secondary amenorrhoea I mean amenorrhoea after one or more menstrual perdiods.

Much the commonest finding in delayed puberty is merely that it is a normal variation, frequently familial. Puberty is delayed by severe malnutrition or severe general disease. Girls of small build are likely to reach puberty later than those of big build; so, for obscure reasons, are those in large families. Delayed puberty could rarely be related to hypothyroidism. Rare cases include the following:

> Turner's syndrome and other forms of gonadal dysgenesis
> Pituitary disease, especially craniopharyngioma: gonadotrophin deficiency
> Testicular feminisation syndrome:
> > ovarian insufficiency

For *Turner's syndrome,* see p. 19. Most children with this syndrome are small in height. *Pituitary dwarfism* may be unexplained, or due to a tumour: the child is dwarfed but with normal proportions, and usually with no secondary sexual characteristics. Pituitary disease is unlikely if physical growth is normal. *Gonadotrophin deficiency* may be congenital. Affected children may be tall, and there will be no secondary sexual characteristics.

The *testicular feminisation syndrome* is characterised by a normal female appearance with normal or increased height and normal breast development with pale areolae. There is little or no body hair, pubic or axillary. There is often a family history of amenorrhoea.

If there is no sign of puberty by the age of 16, and there is no relevant family history, full investigation is required.

When there are normal secondary sex changes, but no menstruation, disease is unlikely to be found. About 10 per cent of girls do not menstruate until there is full breast development or a bone age of thirteen or fourteen. Much the commonest cause of delayed menarche in the presence of normal secondary sexual characteristics is malnutrition, deliberate or otherwise. Frisch *et al* (1980) noted the high incidence of primary or secondary amenorrhoea in 89 young ballet dancers; there was a strong correlation between the occurrence of amenorrhoea and excessive thinness. Menstruation does not occur, or ceases to occur, when the weight drops below a critical level.

It is usual for menstruation to be irregular or scanty for several months after the first period has occurred. It is normal for a year or more to elapse between the first and second period and for six months to elapse between periods in the second year. Approximately 40 periods occur before the regular adult pattern is established.

Amenorrhoea commonly occurs during the summer, or when there is emotional stress, as on starting school, especially when weight reduction occurs.

Amenorrhoea may result from anatomical causes, including in particular *hydrocolpos* or *haematocolpos,* readily found on physical examination. Another rare cause, readily found on physical examination, is the *adrenogenital syndrome,* in which there is enlargement of the clitoris with small stature. *Hyperthyroidism* or *hypothyroidism* are rare causes of amenorrhoea.

Drugs which may cause amenorrhoea include those causing hyperprolactinaemia. It may follow the use of the contraceptive pill.

Relevant drugs are haloperidol, methyldopa, metoclopramide, phenothiazines or tricyclic antidepressants.

Pregnancy may be the cause of the amenorrhoea.

Reference

Frisch R E, Wyshak G, Vincent L. Delayed menarche and amenorrhoea in ballet dancers. *N Engl J Med* 1980; **303:** 17.

Some Other Gynaecological Problems

Vaginal bleeding

A small amount of vaginal bleeding in the girl between the age of five and ten days is normal. It is due to maternal oestrogens and is not related to haemorrhagic disease of the newborn.

Vaginal bleeding at any subsequent age, without associated signs of puberty, should raise the possibility of trauma, foreign body or possibly a tumour. It may also occur as a result of blood disease. The blood may arise from the vulva, vagina or uterus. The blood may have come from the urethra.

Vaginal bleeding is rarely the first indication of sexual precocity.

It is said that ethosuximide can cause vaginal bleeding.

It is essential that vaginal bleeding before the age of puberty should be investigated because of the importance of possible causes.

Vaginal discharge

It is normal for the newborn girl in the first few days to have a thin vaginal discharge, and between the fifth and the tenth day some bleeding may occur.

After infancy a clear mucoid discharge is common and of no significance. Unless it is offensive or purulent it should be ignored. It may be due to lack of cleanliness, to eczema, nappy rash or to mild itching leading to rubbing. A small girl playing in a sandpit may readily introduce some sand into the vagina by direct contact with the sand or by the hands. Soreness may be associated with masturbation. At puberty some leucorrhoea is physiological, resulting from oestrogen stimultion.

Vaginitis may be due to threadworms, candida infection, *E. coli*, staphylococci, treptococci, gonococci or virus infections such as herpes (Singleton 1980). A blood-stained discharge may be due to Shigella or group A streptococci. Trichomonas infection is rare before puberty. Infection is liable to occur because of the proximity of the vagina to the anus, the lack of labial fat pads, the lack of pubic hair, the wrong wiping direction and dirty fingers.

The possibility of sexual abuse has to be remembered.

Whenever a child has a purulent vaginal discharge or blood in the discharge, the possibility of a *foreign body* must be remembered. This may be demonstrated by X-ray. If necessary the vagina may be inspected by a Kelly cystoscope. Henderson & Scott (1966) found soiled toilet paper in the vagina of a child with vaginal discharge. In their review they noted that others had found the following foreign bodies in girls with a vaginal discharge: safety pins, hairpins, folded paper, crayons, twigs, splinters of wood, cherries, paper-clips, beads, bits of toys, pencil erasers, sand, stones, marbles, cotton, shells, nuts, corks and insects.

A rare cause of vaginal discharge is a tumour.

Dysmenorrhoea

This is rare for two or three years after the onset of menstruation, because the menstrual cycles are usually anovular. It can be suggested by the mother or older girls, and the commonest cause of dysmenorrhoea in the young adolescent is psychological.

Menorrhagia

The commonest cause of abnormal uterine bleeding in an adolescent is hyperplasia of the endometrium—a self-limiting condition which does not require treatment.

Other important causes of excessive blood loss are anaemia, blood disease and an incomplete abortion.

References

Henderson PA, Scott RB. Vaginitis caused by toilet tissue. *Am J Dis Child* 1966;
    111: 529.
Singleton AF. Vaginal discharge in children and adolescents. *Clin Pediatr* 1980;
    19: 799.
For general references see
Beynon CL. Menstrual problems in adolescence. *Practitioner* 1975; **214**: 192.
Dewhurst CJ. *Gynaecological disorders of infants and children*. London: Cassell,
    1974.
Root AW. Endocrinology of puberty. *J Pediatr* 1973; **83**: 187.

Delayed Puberty in the Boy

By delayed puberty I mean the absence of signs of puberty by the age
of seventeen.
    The following causes of delayed puberty must be considered:
        Normal variation
        Familial factors
        Malnutrition and severe chronic illness
        Pituitary disease
        Isolated deficiency of gonadotrophins
        Gonadal defects
            Cryptorchidism
            Effect of operation
            Mumps
            Torsion of testis (delayed treatment)
            Myotonic dystrophy (rare)
            Klinefelter's syndrome (rare)
            Male pseudohermaphroditism (rare)
            Male Turner's syndrome (rare)
    There are considerable *normal variations* in the age of onset of
puberty, often familial. It tends to be later in large families. Boys of
small build are likely to reach puberty later than those of big build. As
in the case of the girl, malnutrition or severe illness may delay the
onset of puberty, but obesity does not.

Pituitary disease includes in particular the craniopharyngioma and the chromophobe adenoma. There is severe growth failure. Optic atrophy, particularly unilateral, may point to the diagnosis. Fröhlich's syndrome is so rare that it can be virtually ignored; in order to make the diagnosis there must be evidence of disease of the hypothalamus, with polyuria, polydipsia and glycosuria, obesity and dwarfism.

Isolated deficiency of gonadotrophins may be associated with anosmia (Kallman's syndrome). It is also found in the Laurence–Moon-Biedl syndrome of polydactyly, retinitis pigmentosa and dwarfism, and occurs in association with neurofibromatosis.

Gonadal defects include the undescended testis, testicular atrophy following postpubertal mumps or an operation, and Klinefelter's syndrome. In Klinefelter's syndrome the penis is of normal size, but the testes are small and there is gynaecomastia.

The male Turner's syndrome is characterized by genital under-development, shortness of stature, webbing of the neck, a low posterior hair line, low-set ears, mental subnormality, coarctation of the aorta and cubitus valgus.

The causes of delayed puberty should be sought if there are no signs of puberty by the age of seventeen.

Reference

Root AW. Endocrinology of puberty. *J Pediatr* 1973; **83**: 187.

Sexual Precocity

The Girl

Sexual precocity in a girl may be either isosexual or heterosexual (Harris 1981). The former implies the early appearance of pubertal features appropriate to the sex of the patient, while the latter implies the development of male secondary sexual characteristics such as enlargement of the clitoris.

The causes of precocity are as follows:

Constitutional sexual precocity

Rare

Intracranial tumours

Hydrocephalus

Hypothyroidism

Polyostotic fibrous dysplasia

Adrenocortical tumour. Hepatoma

Heterosexual

Congenital adrenal hyperplasia

Ovarian tumour

Exogenous androgens

Sexual precocity before the age of nine years is the so-called 'constitutional' type, i.e., without any disease, in 90 per cent of cases. It can occur at a few months of age. The sequence of changes may be the same as that of an older child; but the first sign of sexual precocity may be vaginal bleeding alone, pubic hair alone or breast changes, or any combination of these. The child is usually tall for her age at first, but owing to premature closure of the epiphyses, smallness of stature is the end result. It is important that endocrinological investigations should be carried out in order to eliminate the other causes (Sigurjonsdottir & Hayles 1968). The 17-oxosteroid output is higher than in ordinary children of the age but normal for puberty. At puberty a vaginal smear shows oestrogenization.

It should be noted that breast enlargement may occur without other signs of puberty in normal children, and pubic hair can occur without breast enlargement or other signs of puberty (Altchek 1972). In these cases the stature is average, and the urinary 17-oxosteroids are normal for the age. Gonadotrophins are either not found in the urine or at a low level normal for the age. The vulva has a normal atrophic appearance and vaginal and urethral cells are not oestrogenized. The skeletal maturation, the urine and plasma oestrogens are normal for the age. When there is breast enlargement without any other sign of puberty (premature thelarche) the areola is usually pale and unpigmented.

Sometimes vaginal bleeding without pubic hair may occur in a young child, and not recur for some years until normal adolescence occurs. The stature would be average for the age, and there would be no oestrogenization in the vaginal smear.

Intracranial conditions should be revealed in the ordinary physical examination of the child, including ophthalmoscopy for papill-oedema.

Polyostotic fibrous dysplasia (Albright's syndrome) consists of sexual precocity, pigmentation of one side of the body (perhaps only a patch on the buttocks or thigh), with X-ray evidence of fibrous dysplasia in the femur or other bones on the same side as the pigmentation. The exact mechanism of the sexual precocity is uncertain. Vaginal bleeding commonly precedes other signs of precocity.

Adrenocortical tumours usually make themselves obvious by the rapid onset of puberty, often with the full appearance of Cushing's syndrome, obesity of the buffalo type, with little fat in the extremities, a plethoric facies, hypertension, commonly stunting of growth and hypertrichosis. There is an excess of 17-oxogenic steroids in the urine. The common cause is a carcinoma.

Sexual precocity also occurs in association with *adrenocortical hy-perplasia*, which is normally associated with pseudohermaphro-ditism. There is enlargement of the clitoris from birth, usually with advanced skeletal maturation and increased 17-oxosteroids in the urine.

When the cause of sexual precocity is an *ovarian tumour*, the vaginal bleeding tends to be marked, with minimal breast changes and pubic hair. The diagnosis should be suspected if vaginal bleeding precedes the development of pubic hair or of breast changes. The tumour is usually felt on bimanual examination. If there is a granulosa cell tumour, there is a great excess of oestrogens in the urine, and in the case of a teratoma there is an excessive output of gonadotrophins from the tumour.

Exogenous androgens, as used in the treatment or prevention of excessive height, may cause heterosexual precocity.

The Boy

Whereas in 90 per cent of cases of sexual precocity in girls the cause is 'constitutional' and not related to disease, the majority of cases in boys are due to serious disease.

As a rule, if the penis is fully developed as at puberty, and the testes are normal in size for puberty, the cause is likely to be intracranial. If the penis is large but the testes are small and undeveloped the cause is likely to be in the adrenal.

The causes of sexual precocity are as follows:

Isosexual
  Constitutional
  Hypothalamic tumour, hydrocephalus, postencephalitis
  Hypothyroidism (Hemady *et al* 1978)
  Congenital adrenal hyperplasia
  Hepatoma
  Tumour of testis
  Exogenous androgens
Heterosexual
  Feminising tumour of adrenal cortex
  Exogenous oestrogens

As in the girl, breast enlargement may be due to the child ingesting oestrogen tablets.

Gynaecomastia

When a boy has enlargement of the breast, the following conditions have to be considered:

Normal newborn breast enlargement
Normal gynaecomastia of adolescence
Disease involving the skin, pituitary, thyroid, lung, adrenal, liver, kidney, testis. Malnutrition. Paraplegia
Klinefelter's syndrome
Effect of drugs

Enlargement of the breast is normal in newborn full-term male babies, but rare in prematurely born ones. An obese boy may appear to have breast enlargement, but the appearance is due to nothing more than fatty tissue.

Gynaecomastia is common in *adolescence*. In a study of 1855 non-obese adolescent boys, it was found in 38·7 per cent. The figure for the 14–14½ year old group was 64·6 per cent. In 23·3 per cent the enlargement was unilateral. It persisted for up to 2 years in 27·1 per cent and up to 3 years in 7·7 per cent. It may be unilateral (Nydick *et al* 1961). The serum oestradiol is high in relation to testosterone (Carlson 1980).

Sexual precocity 313

Gynaecomastia is occasionally seen in various diseases in adults, including generalized skin conditions, severe malnutrition, acromegaly, thyrotoxicosis, carcinoma of the lung, feminising adrenocortical tumour, cirrhosis of the liver, renal failure, or tumour of the testis. It may occur in paraplegic patients. It is not clear how many of these conditions cause gynaecomastia in children.

Gynaecomastia may be a feature of *Klinefelter's syndrome*. Some 25 per cent of such children are mentally subnormal. The testes are small for the age. The diagnosis is established by the buccal smear and chromosome analysis.

The following *drugs* may cause gynaecomastia: amphetamine, anabolic steroids, cannabis, cimetidine, cytotoxic drugs, digitalis, gonadotrophins, griseofulvin, imipramine, isoniazid, oestrogens, P.A.S., phenothiazines, progesterone, reserpine, spironolactone, testosterone, tricylic antidepressants and vincristine. It has resulted from digoxin poisoning.

References

Altchek A. Premature thelarche. *Pediatr Clin North Am* 1972; **19:** 543.
Annotation. Gynaecomastia. *Br Med J* 1964; **2:** 1548.
Carlson HE. Gynecomastia. *N Engl J Med* 1980; **303:** 795.
Harris F. Isosexual precocious puberty in a 9 year old boy. *J Roy Soc Med* 1981; **74:** 318.
Hemady ZS, Siler–Khodr TM, Najjar S. Precocious puberty in juvenile hypothyroidism. *J Pediatr* 1978; **92:** 55.
Lee PA. The relation of concentration of serum hormones to pubertal gynecomastia. *J Pediatr* 1975; **86:** 212.
Nydick M, Bustos J, Dale JH, Rawson RW. Gynecomastia in adolescent boys. *JAMA* 1961; **178:** 449.
Sigurjonsdottir TJ, Hayles AB. Precocious puberty. *Am J Dis Child* 1968; **115:** 309.

Recurrent Infections

Most children suffer recurrent infections, and in most cases the cause is unknown. Malnutrition is a factor, but the mechanism is not fully understood: concomitant and interrelated factors include poverty, poor housing and dirt. Infants in developing countries, when not fully breast fed, suffer greatly from recurrent gastroenteritis. Common respiratory infections, colds and tonsillitis, reach their peak when the child starts school, or in the case of the preschool child, when he attends a nursery, or when an older sibling starts school and brings the infection home. After two or three years at school the incidence of these infections falls off steeply. The infections are largely viral, but some are streptococcal infections of the throat. Repeated virus infections do not usually denote a recognized immunological deficiency.

Knowledge of relevant immunological factors is rapidly increasing: the subject is a highly complex one (Janeway 1967). A whole volume of *Pediatric Clinics of North America* (May 1977, p. 275 to 425) was devoted to this subject. There are more than 40 immunological deficiency syndromes.

A simple (and oversimplified) grouping of causes is as follows:

Unknown

Malnutrition

Defective leucocyte activity and function

Thymic dependent lesions

Other immunological deficiencies—complement, opsonins, gammaglobulin

Splenectomy

Obstruction of secretions: foreign bodies.

Abnormal communications with the cerebrospinal fluid pathways

Domestic or other reservoir of infection

Defective leucocyte function occurs in a variety of conditions.

Granulopenia occurs mainly because of infections, drugs and serious blood diseases such as leukaemia (Kauder & Mauer 1966). It may be caused by innumerable drugs, such s chloramphenicol: these are discussed in the section on anaemia (p. 46) and purpura (p. 55).

Cyclic neutropenia is a rare condition in which approximately every

314

three weeks there are mouth ulcers and other infections, with fever and arthralgia. In *exocrine pancreatic insufficiency* there are neutropenia, dwarfism and infections. (p. 11).

Several rare diseases are related to defective leucocyte function.

Chronic granulomatous disease (Farber's disease) is an x-linked recessive condition with a specific metabolic abnormality of granulocytes which render them unable to kill ingested bacteria. The condition usually manifests itself in the early months with repeated staphylococcal infections, granulomatous lesions of the skin, synovia (arthritis) and viscera, hoarseness, failure to thrive, lymphadenopathy, hepatosplenomegaly and hypergammaglobulinaemia. The *Chediak-Higashi syndrome* is an autosomal recessive, with undue susceptibility to infection, pyoderma, oral ulcers, decreased pigment in the skin and hair, and later neutropenia.

In *thymic dependent lesions* there is a special tendency to virus and candida infections. There is normal primary immune function, phagocytosis and inflammatory response, but there are deficiencies in tests of cell-mediated functions. They include *Di George's syndrome* of congenital aplasia of the thymus, hypoparathyroidism, tetany, abnormal susceptibility to viral and fungal infections, failure to thrive and anomalies of the great vessels. The increased susceptibility to infection in *ataxia telangiectasia* (see p. 193) and the *Wiskott-Aldrich syndrome* and purpura and eczema (p. 58) are largely thymic dependent.

Impaired inflammatory response results from a lack of inhibition of certain complement components: there is a special susceptibility to staphylococcal infections. A familial deficiency has been described.

The *gamma globulin deficiencies* include agammaglobulinaemia, hypogammaglobulinaemia and dysgammaglobulinaemia. *Burton's disease* is an example of hypogammaglobulinaemia: it usually develops in the second year, with recurrent staphylococcal or haemophilus influenzae infections, and often with arthritis (especially boys). Buckley *et al* (1972) described undue susceptibility to infection in association with hyperimmunoglobulinaemia E.

Splenectomy, especially in the first five years, and especially in the first two post-operative years, carries with it a risk of overwhelming infection, often pneumococcal (Bisno 1971). It is probable that the underlying cause of the splenectomy is irrelevant, though this is not accepted by all. There is an increased susceptibility to infection in hereditary splenic hypoplasia and in asplenia with or without congenital heart disease (Hjelt & Hakosalo, 1959). Increased susceptibility to infections after splenectomy has also been described in adults (Desser & Ultmann, 1972).

Obstruction of secretions commonly causes infection. Examples are incompletely opened naso-lachrymal duct in infancy, the preauricular sinus, congenital dermal sinus, otitis media with adenoidal hypertrophy and fibrocystic disease of the pancreas (obstruction by unduly thick secretions). The recurrent pulmonary infections in Riley's syndrome (familial dysautonomia) are probably due to bronchial hypersecretion and obstruction.

Foreign bodies in the ear, nose, bronchus and vagina commonly cause persistent and recurrent infections. Infection resulting from a urethral catheter is continuous rather than recurrent until the catheter is removed and the infection is treated.

Recurrent meningitis is usually due to a communication between the subarachnoid space and the air sinuses, mastoid, ear or skin (by a congenital dermal sinus). Cerebrospinal fluid rhinorrhoea may be due to a congenital defect in the cribriform plate or elsewhere, or result from injury (see symposium *Proc. Roy. Soc. Med.*, 1974).

Recurrent antrum or skin infections may result from frequent reinfection from a reservoir or infection in the home (or school). When a child has a chronic or recurrent antrum infection, it is important to ensure that neither of the parents or other person in the home has a similar infection. Domestic animals may be a reservoir of infection, streptococcal or otherwise. Threadworm and roundworm infections are difficult to eradicate because of the presence of infection in other members of the family, school mates and dust. Recurrent herpes infections may arise from a reservoir in the family.

Recurrent urinary tract infection may be related to an underlying congenital structural defect; radiological investigation is necessary for every case of urinary tract infection.

References

Bisno AL. Hyposplenism and overwhelming pneumococcal infection: a reappraisal. *Am J Med Sci* 1971; **262**: 101.
Buckley RH, Wray BB, Belmaker EZ. Extreme hyperimmunoglobulinemia E and undue susceptibility to infection. *Pediatrics* 1972; **49**: 59.

Desser RK, Ultmann JE. Risk of severe infection in particular with Hodgkin's disease or lymphoma after diagnostic laparotomy and splenectomy. *Ann Int Med* 1972; **77**: 143.

Hjelt L, Hakosalo J. Congenital asplenia. *Annales Paediatr Fenniae* 1959; **5**: Suppl 12.

Janeway CA. Recurrent infections. In: Green M, Haggerty RJ (Eds) *Ambulatory Pediatrics*. Philadelphia: Saunders, 1977.

Kauder E, Mauer AM. Neutropenias in childhood. *J Pediatr* 1966; **69**: 147.

Symposium. Recurrent meningitis. *Proc Roy Soc Med* 1974; **67**: 1141–1154.

Symptoms related to the Skin

PRURITUS

Pruritus, or the itch, is a common symptom in childhood. Perhaps the commonest causes are infantile eczema or urticaria, irritation by contact with wool or a sweat rash. The following are the main causes to consider:

Irritation by wool next to skin
Sweat rash
Urticaria
Insect bites
Pediculosis
Ringworm infection
Chilblains
Threadworms (pruritus ani)
Scabies
Pyogenic skin infections, prickly heat (tropics)
Chickenpox
Eczema
Psoriasis
Lichen planus
Pityriasis rosea
Dermatitis herpetiformis
Serum sickness
Mycosis fungoides
Jaundice

Uraemia
Leukaemia
Reticuloses
Diabetes mellitus
Psychological factors
Drugs

There are other conditions which cause pruritus, but the above are the principal ones. The list is such a long one that it would not be profitable to discuss the differential diagnosis. Urticaria, scabies and the effect of drugs will alone be mentioned further.

The most common cause of *urticaria* is sensitivity to insect bites, such as fleas from a dog or cat or other household pet. It may also be due to foods, inhalants, bites, stings, infection by fungi or parasites, candida, reticuloses, infectious mononucleosis and virus infections. It may be due to *allergy to cow's milk* (p. 13). It is often aggravated by aspirin. Severe psychological stress may cause urticaria. It may have an immunological basis.

Scabies is diagnosed by the burrows, found especially on the sides of the fingers, wrists, anterior axillary folds, buttocks and in infants scalp and soles of feet, together with the intense itching and frequently the history of itching in members of the family. The diagnosis may be confused by the secondary wheals, vesicles, bullae, eczema or pustules, and by unwise topical applications.

Innumerable *drugs* may cause urticaria or pruritus. They include amitriptyline, aminophylline, antibiotics, antihistamines, antisera, aspirin, barbiturates, carbamazepine, chloral, chloramphenicol, clindamycin, cloniine, chloroquine, codeine, colistin, dichloralphenazone, dphenoxylate, erythromycin, gold, griseofulvin, imipramine, indomethacin, isoniazid, lincomycin, meprobamate, methimazole, nalidixic acid, opiates, penicillin, phenothiazines, phenytoin, piperazine, quinine, rifampicin, salicylates, streptomycin, sulphonamides, tetanus toxoid, tetracycline, vitamin A and corticosteroid ointment.

Urticaria may be due to sensitivity to topical applications (to the antibiotic or to the base or vehicle used). Urticaria may also be caused by tartrazine and other azo dyes, and by sodium benzoate and 4-hydroxybenzoic acid used as preservatives in pickles, sauces, instant coffee and other foods.

References

British Medical Journal. Chronic urticaria. Leading article. 1976; **3**: 68.

Delayney JC. Response of patients with asthma and aspirin sensitivity to tartrazine. *Practitioner* 1976; **217**: 285.

HAIR LOSS AND HYPERTRICHOSIS

Hair Loss

Loss of hair may be due to the following conditions:

Head rolling
Trichotillomania
Alopecia areata. Mongolism
Ringworm and other infections
Pituitary, thyroid, parathyroid or adrenal insufficiency
Abnormalities of hair structure—trichorrhexis, pili torti, monilethrix
Any severe chronic illness or acute weight loss
Vitiligo
Rare syndromes
  Ectodermal dysplasia
  Progeria
  Dystrophia myotonica
  Argininosuccinicaciduria
  Acrodermatitis enteropathica
  Disseminated lupus
Drugs

Infants often denude their heads in a patch or patches by *head rolling*. Toddlers and other children sometimes acquire the habit of pulling their hair out; it is usually a manifestation of insecurity.

Alopecia areata may be due to several causes. The hair tends to break off 2 or 3 mm from the root. The broken hair is the shape of an exclamation mark, being thicker at the top than the base. It may be associated with agammaglobulinaemia. There is an association between *mongolism* and alopecia areata, probably dependent on an autoimmune mechanism (Du Vivier & Munro 1974). Alopecia in the case of older children sometimes follows psychological stress, as in adults.

Ringworm is diagnosed by fluorescence under Wood's light or by detection of the fungi in potassium hydroxide on a slide.

Trichorrhexis nodosa is a condition in which there are nodular swellings on the hair with fractures of the hair shaft. *Pili torti* consist of twisted hairs. The condition is hereditary and is sometimes associated with deafness. Affected infants are commonly born without hair. After some growth of hair, the eyelashes, hair of scalp and hair of eyebrows fall out. *Monilethrix* is a developmental anomaly of the hair shaft. The diagnosis is made by microscopy.

Hair loss may be the sequel of any *chronic illness* or acute weight loss.

Numerous *rare syndromes* are associated with hair loss. They are listed in the books by Rook, Wilkinson & Ebling (1979), Bruinsma (1977) and Verbov (1979). For acrodermatitis enteropathica see p. 326.

Drugs which cause hair loss include amphetamine, anticoagulants, antimetabolites, bismuth, carbamazepine, carbimazole, chloroquine, ethambutol, ethionamide, fenfluramine, gentamicin, gold, heparin, indomethacin, mepacrine, nitrofurantoin, P.A.S., phenytoin, primidone, propylthiouracil, sodium valproate, thallium, trimethoprim, troxidone, vitamin A excess. Hair loss may follow several weeks after anticoagulant therapy.

Hypertrichosis

Generalised hypertrichosis is often racial. Other causes, except those related to drugs, are rare. They include the following:

Endocrine—Cushing's syndrome (p. 27), adrenocortical hyperplasia, adrenal insufficiency

Other metabolic—porphyria (p. 108), mucopolysaccharidoses.

Severe weight loss or malnutrition. Degenerative diseases of the nervous system. Lipodystrophy

Chromosomal—Turner's syndrome, trisomy E

Cornelia de Lange syndrome

Leprechaunism

Congenital asymmetry

Epidermolysis bullosa

Dermatomyositis

Drugs

Syndrome of hereditary gingival hyperplasia with hypertrichosis (Winter and Simpkiss 1974)

Hirsutism may result in the female from administration of *androgens*.

It may occur in ovarian and adrenal diseases and in Turner's syndrome. A hairy face may occur in the *fetal alcohol syndrome*.

Local hypertrichosis or patches of excessive hair occur in the *hairy naevus, linear naevus sebaceous syndrome*, (Gellis & Feingold 1970) and on the back in relation to *diastematomyelia* or *congenital dermal sinus*.

Of the several mucopolysaccharidoses, *Hurler's syndrome* is the most likely to be associated with hirsutism: there is progressive hepatosplenomegaly, cataract and mental deterioration.

The *Cornelia de Lange syndrome* presents with a characteristic facies in which the eyebrows are continuous with each other. There is hirsutism, malformation of the hands with a proximally-placed thumb, and mental subnormality.

Various *drugs* cause hypertrichosis. They include anabolic steroids, corticosteroids, diazoxide, minoxidil, penicillamine, phenytoin and streptomycin.

References

Bruinsma W. *A guide to drug eruptions*. Oosthuizen, Holland: De Zwaluw, 1977.
Du Vivier A, Munro DD. Mongolism and alopecia areata. *Proc Roy Soc Med* 1974; **67**: 596.
Forbes A. Hypertrichosis. *N Engl J Med* 1965; **273**: 602.
Gellis SS, Feingold M. Linear nevus sebaceous syndrome. *Am J Dis Child* 1970; **120**: 138.
Rook A, Wilkinson DS, Ebling FJG. *Textbook of dermatology* 4th edn. Oxford: Blackwell Scientific Publications, 1979.
Verbov J. *Modern topics in paediatric dermatology* London: Heinemann, 1979.
Winter GB, Simpkiss MJ. Hypertrichosis and hereditary gingival hyperplasia. *Arch Dis Child* 1974; **49**: 394.

ICHTHYOSIS

Ichthyosis simplex (xeroderma) is a dominant inherited condition.
Rare causes include
    Ichthyosiform erythroderma (lamellar ichthyosis of the newborn), ichthyosis following the collodion skin syndrome (harlequin fetus).

Refsum's syndrome—heredopathia atactica polyneuritiformis, an error of lipoid metabolism. Ichthyosis develops in childhood and is followed soon by polyneuritis, deafness, retinitis pigmentosa, night blindness.

Sjögren–Larsson syndrome—ichthyosis, spasticity, mental subnormality.

Rud's syndrome—dwarfism, fits, mental subnormality, hypogonadism.

Netherton's syndrome—girls. Abnormal hair shafts, allergic manifestations, renal disease, deafness and dwarfism.

Ichthyosis nigricans—sex-linked recessive, males: early infancy—large scattered brown-black scales: often mental subnormality.

Various chromosome abnormalities

References

Frost P, Van Scott EJ. Ichthyosiform dermatoses: classification based on anatomic and biometric observations. *Arch Dermatol* 1966; **94**: 113.

Lancet leading article Scaly skin. 1978; **2**: 615.

Rayner A, Lampert RP, Rennert OM. Familial ichthyosis, dwarfism, mental retardation, renal disease and deafness. *J Pediatr* 1978; **92**: 766.

PIGMENTATION

Hyperpigmentation

Normal pigmentation includes racial factors: sunburn: freckles (ephelides): mongolian pigmentation: some café-au-lait spots.

Mongolian pigmentation (Naevus of ITO or OTA) is universal in coloured races, and is said to be universal in Eskimos: it may occur in white races. It is found in babies on the lumbosacral area and often in front of the ankle and occasionally on the arms. In white children it has a blueish grey colour, like a bruise: in coloured children the affected area is darker than the surrounding skin. Jacobs and Walton (1976) found mongolian pigmentation in 95·5 per cent of coloured children and in 9·6 per cent of white children.

Café-au-lait lesions are normal unless multiple and large. Single lesions—one to three cm long occur in 20 per cent of normal children. If they are more than six in number, and are more than four to six cm long, they should be regarded as neurofibromatosis until proved otherwise. Crawford (1978) suggested that the diagnosis of neurofibromatosis in a child should be made on the basis of two or more of the following—five or more café-au-lait spots, biopsy, family history and a characteristic bone lesion.

Causes:

   (i) Neurofibromatosis (Von Recklinghausen's disease)

  (ii) Tuberous sclerosis (Epiloia). A quarter of all cases of epiloia have café-au-lait spots with mountain ash leaf-shaped white macules and hypopigmented areas.

 (iii) Silver's syndrome

 (iv) Association with pulmonary stenosis and mental subnormality (Watson 1967)

  (v) Gaucher's syndrome

 (vi) De Toni–Fanconi syndrome (p. 15)

(vii) Phaeochromocytoma

Patchy pigmentation

Neurofibromatosis

Albright's syndrome (Polyostotic fibrous dysplasia) (p. 311). This consists of a patch of brownish pigmentation, sometimes small, on one buttock or thigh, in association with an area of osteoporosis in the femur on the same side (and sometimes in other bones) with sexual precocity in girls.

Fanconi's syndrome—skeletal defects, especially in the arm, with blood changes: sometimes rain-drop macules.

Multiple lentiginoses—a dominant condition with multiple pigmented skin lesions, mental subnormality, dwarfism, deafness, hypertelorism, nystagmus and heart lesions.

Peutz–Jeghers syndrome—pigmentation around the nose, mouth, nails, hands; pigmentation in the oral mucosa: intestinal polyposis.

Incontinentia pigmenti—linear and patchy pigmentation on the trunk or limbs, following a vesicular eruption in infancy, with mental subnormality: it is more common in girls.

Diffuse pigmentation

Yellow—jaundice: mepacrine skin staining
  carotinaemia: excessive intake of carrots (p. 117)
Blue or blue black—chlorpromazine, chloroquine, acanthosis nigricans
Brown or grey brown—heavy metals, phenothiazines, repeated transfusions
  Addison's disease, Gaucher's disease
  Niemann–Pick disease, xeroderma pigmentosum
Bronze—phototherapy (neonate)
  Other rare conditions causing diffuse or extensive patchy pigmentation include:
    Xeroderma pigmentosum—pigmented areas related to photo-sensitivity, telangiectasia, large freckles, keratoses
    Cushing's syndrome
    Thyrotoxicosis
    Pellagra and sprue
    Hartnup disease (error of tryptophane metabolism, ataxia, pellagra-like lesions)
    Porphyria. Violaceous skin
    Effect of drugs—antimalarial drugs, arsenic, bismuth, busulphan, clonazepam, corticosteroids, cytotoxic drugs, gold, griseofulvin, mercury, nitrofurantoin, phenothiazines, phenytoin, silver, vitamin A excess

Hypopigmentation

Patchy hypopigmentation and hyperpigmentation occurs in vitiligo, epiloia (tuberous sclerosis), and the Rothmund–Thomson syndrome (p. 329).

A white forelock is a feature of the Waardenburg syndrome (p. 184).

Hypopigmented areas follow lesions of eczema and many skin rashes, such as nappy rashes, in coloured children. Depigmented areas occur in pityriasis alba, naevus depigmentosus and lichen sclerosus.

Generalised hypopigmentation may occur in albinism, phenyl-ketonuria, hypopituitarism and the Chediak–Higashi syndrome, a recessive, consisting of hypopigmentation of the skin, hair and eyes, with a predisposition to infection and later to lymphoma.

References

Bleehan S. Disorders of melanin pigmentation. *Br J Hosp Med* 1975; **13**: 590.

Crawford AH. Neurofibromatosis in the pediatric patient. *Orthop Clin North Am* 1978; **9**: 11.

Jacobs A, Walton R. Mongolian pigmentation. *Pediatrics* 1976; **58**: 218.

Wall LM. Disorders of pigmentation. *Medicine (UK)* 1980; p. 1582.

Watson GH. Café-au-lait spots, pulmonary stenosis and dull intelligence. *Arch Dis Child* 1967; **42**: 303.

PHOTOSENSITIVITY

Photosensitivity may be caused by the following conditions:

Drugs—amitriptyline, antidepressants, antiemetics, anti-histamines, barbiturates, carbamazepine, chloroquine, cotrimoxazole, cytotoxic drugs, demeclocycline (leder-mycin), diphenoxylate, frusemide, gold, griseofulvin, imipramine, nalidixic acid, phenothiazines, sulphon-amides, tetracyclines, thiazide diuretics, viprynium

Topical—cosmetics

Pellagra

Rare

   Porphyria

   Cockayne's syndrome (p. 328)

   Hartnup disease

   Bloom's syndrome (p. 328)

   Xeroderma pigmentosum

   Ultraviolet light causes a rash in pellagra and disseminated lupus

BULLOUS OR VESICULAR SKIN LESIONS

Bullous skin lesions occur in a wide variety of conditions, including the following:
Scalds
Impetigo
Urticaria
Urticaria pigmentosa (mast-cell disease), blisters, pigmented maculopapular eruption, transient urticaria
Pemphigus neonatorum
Rare
Erythema multiforme
Epidermolysis bullosa. Lesions usually present at birth: blisters on pressure areas
Bullous disease of childhood—a persistent or recurrent disease, involving especially the pubis, scalp and trunk (Ramsdell *et al* 1979). It usually starts in the first 10 years, with remission in a few months to three years
Incontinentia pigmenti—erythema in the young female infant, followed by vesicles or bullae by the age of about four months, and later by linear pigmentation
Toxic epidermal necrolysis: Resembles scalded skin. Usually staphylococcal: also caused by barbiturates, phenytoin, penicillin, sulphonamides
Acrodermatitis enteropathica—a chronic probably recessive disease, usually starting in the first 18 months—vesicular or bullous warts on extremities or around mouth and anus; loss of hair; diarrhoea. May be due to zinc deficiency (Moynahan 1974)
Porphyria; vesicles or bullae on exposure to sun
Syphilis
Cockayne's syndrome
Drugs—acetazolamide, antimitotics, barbiturates, bromides, chloral, chlordiazepoxide, clonidine, frusemide, meprobamate, nalidixic acid, nitrazepam, penicillamine, phenytoin, rifampicin, salicylates, sulphonamides, thiazide diuretics, tricyclic antidepressants (e.g. imipramine)

Vesicular eruptions may be due to any of the causes of photosensitivity.

Vesicular eruptions in the newborn have resulted from infection by haemophilus influenzae (Halal *et al* 1978), staphylococcus aureus, the cytomegalovirus and herpes. After the newborn period the commonest cause is chickenpox; it can also be caused by herpes simplex or zoster, or the coxsackie virus (hand, foot and mouth disease—causing vesicles on the tongue, hands and feet, and sometimes on the knees). Dermatitis herpetiformis is a relapsing condition, bullous or vesicular, affecting the limbs and trunk.

For the Stevens–Johnson syndrome see p. 160.

References

British Medical Journal. Leading article. Drug induced bullous eruptions. 1981; **1**: 421.

Halal *et al.* Congenital vesicular eruption caused by haemophilus influenzae Type B. *Pediatrics* 1978; **62**: 494.

Moynahan E J. Acrodermatitis enteropathica: a lethal inherited zinc deficiency syndrome. *Lancet* 1974; **2**: 399.

Ramsdell W, Jarratt M, *et al.* Bullous disease of childhood. *Am J Dis Child* 1979; **133**: 791.

ERYTHEMA NODOSUM

Erythema nodosum is a non-specific response to:

1 Bacteria—streptococci, tuberculosis, BCG, leptospira, pasteurella, yersinia.
2 Viruses e.g. cat scratch fever.
3 Fungal infections.
4 Drugs—barbiturates, bromides, iodides, penicillin, salicylates, sulphonamides, thiouracil; and may follow the discontinuation of corticosteroids.
5 Sarcoid, ulcerative colitis, Crohn's disease.

ECZEMATOUS SKIN LESIONS

Eczematous skin lesions occur in a variety of diseases other than infantile eczema. They include:

Contact dermatitis
Nappy rash

Rare
　Mycoses
　Histiocytosis X
　The Wiskott–Aldrich syndrome of purpura and eczema
　Agammaglobulinaemia
　Phenylketonuria
　Ataxia telangiectasia
　Ahistidinaemia
　Acrodermatitis enteropathica
　Coeliac disease
　Hartnup disease
　Mucopolysaccharidoses
Drugs which may cause it include amitriptyline, antihistamines, iodides, kanamycin, meprobamate, neomycin, penicillin, phenothiazines, quinine, salicylates and sulphonamides, streptomycin, thiazide diuretics.

TELANGIECTASIA

Some degree of telangiectasia on the back of the neck in infancy, and on the interscapular area in older children, is normal. Much the commonest cause of telangiectasia otherwise is prolonged use of topical corticosteroids. Other causes are rare; they include:

Osler–Rendu–Weber syndrome. This is a dominant genetic condition, the most common manifestations of which are telangiectasia on the face and in the nasal mucous membrane (causing epistaxis, not often before puberty). There may be similar lesions in the retina, larynx, bone and gastrointestinal tract. There may be a large head, due to megalencephaly, multiple angiomata and cirrhosis of the liver.

Louis–Bar syndrome of ataxia telangiectasia.

Bloom's syndrome—facial telangiectasia with a butterfly distribution, with dwarfism and photosensitivity.

Cockayne's syndrome—facial telangiectasia with a butterfly distribution, loss of facial subcutaneous fat, characteristic facies, retinitis pigmentosa, cataract, deafness and kyphosis, photosensitivity, dwarfism and mental subnormality.

Rothmund–Thomson syndrome—telangiectasia, cataract, sparse
hair and dwarfism.

Blue bleb syndrome—blue nodular naevi on the skin with intestinal
telangiectasia.

Turner's syndrome—with intestinal telangiectasia.

Wyburn–Mason syndrome—facial telangiectasia with cerebral
arteriovenous aneury sm.

Bonnet–Dechaume–Blanc syndrome of facial telangiectasia with involvement of the retina and brain.

NAEVI

The common naevi are:

> The 'stork-bite' naevi on the inner end of the upper eyelid of
> the newborn baby, disappearing after a few months.
>
> The wedge-shaped naevus on the forehead of the newborn
> baby. There is always a coexistent naevus on the back
> of the neck. These naevi disappear in a few months.
>
> The strawberry naevus, which is capillary or cavernous,
> appearing a few days after birth, growing for up to 6
> months and disappearing within 5 to 10 years.
>
> The cavernous haemangioma—a markedly elevated naevoid
> mass.
>
> Facial port wine stain.
>
> The Sturge–Weber syndrome—facial port wine stain which
> includes the forehead, with a naevus in the pia,
> calcifying after a few months, with cerebral palsy,
> mental subnormality and fits.
>
> Pigmented naevi and melanomata.

Rare:

> Fabry's syndrome (angiokeratoma corporis diffusum), with
> purplish black naevi, and naevi in the skin, cardio-
> vascular, pulmonary and renal systems.
>
> Kasabach–Merrit syndrome—cavernous haemangioma with
> thrombocytopenia.
>
> von Hippel–Lindau syndrome—naevi involving the retina,
> skin and cerebellum, sometimes with polycystic
> kidney, haemangioma of liver and Wilms' tumour.

Klippel–Trenaunay syndrome—enlarged leg, slight neavoid staining of skin.

Maffucci's syndrome—multiple haemangiomata with dyschondroplasia and abnormal growth of long bones.

Osler–Rendu–Weber syndrome (p. 328).

Blue bleb syndrome (p. 87).

Disseminated haemangiomatosis—very numerous skin naevi.

Linear naevus sebaceous. Naevi present on face at birth, linear naevi on body, skull abnormalities, hirsutism, fits, mental subnormality.

Xeroderma pigmentosum.

See also telangiectasia (p. 328).

References

Esterly NB, Solomon LM. Pigmentary lesions and hemangiomas. *J Pediatr* 1972; **81**: 1003.

Øster J, Nielsen A. Nuchal naevi and interscapular telangiectases. *Acta Paediatr Scand* 1970; **59**: 416.

NAIL LESIONS

Numerous conditions affect the nails.

Absence of nails—may be genetic

Hypoplasia of nails—

Drugs in pregnancy—phenytoin or anticoagulants

Prone sleeping (Culley 1981): most infants sleeping in the prone position have one foot drawn up and one extended and rotated. The toes of the foot drawn up are flexed and the toe nails abnormal, hypoplastic or curved.

Familial genetic factors are the commonest cause other than the above. Bass (1968) described a rare familial condition in which there was absence of the middle phalanges with hypoplasia of nails.

Nail-patella syndrome (see p. 237)

Hypoparathyroidism—deformed or atrophic nails

Friable nails—chondroectodermal dysplasia
Fungus infection, rheumatoid arthritis, hypoparathyroidism
Pitted nails—psoriasis, candidiasis
Hollow nails—(koilonychia)
Familial, iron deficiency, hypothyroidism, hyperthyroidism
Yellow—Congenital lymphoedema (Kleinman 1973). This syndrome consists of yellow or greenish nails, with accentuated convexity and sometimes cross ridging, with congenital generalised lymphoedema: the yellow colour of the nails may precede the development of lymphoedema by several years.
Tetracycline in pregnancy
Psoriasis
Red half-moon—heart failure
Red purple—porphyria
Brown—tetracycline in pregnancy
Fungal infection
Chronic renal disease
Adriamycin, arsenic, bleomycin, chloroquine, cyclosphosphamide, doxorubicin, phenolphthalein, silver
Black—pseudomonas infection
Blue—mepacrine, argyria
Blue half-moon—Wilson's disease.
White—anaemia, cirrhosis
White hands—hypoalbuminaemia
For other conditions, see Samman and Zaias.

Reference

Bass HN. Familial absence of middle phalanges and nail dysplasia. *Pediatrics* 1968; **42**: 318.
Culley P. Unilateral outward-turning leg in infancy. *Br Med J* 1981; **1**: 1236.
Giocobetti R, Esterly NB, Morgan ER. Nail hyperpigmentation secondary to therapy with Doxorubicin. *Am J Dis Child* 1981; **135**: 317.
Kleinman PK. Congenital lymphedema and yellow nails. *J Pediatr* 1973; **83**: 454.
Samman PD. In: Rook A, Wilkinson DS, Ebling FJG. *Textbook of dermatology.* Oxford: Blackwell Scientific Publications, 1979.
Zaias N. *The nail in health and disease.* Lancaster MTP Press, 1980.

Side Effects of Drugs (general)

Nearly all drugs have unpleasant side effects, and it was felt that a book concerning the common symptoms of disease would not be complete without a brief account of the side actions of drugs used to treat disease—side effects which are commonly confused with the result of the disease. There are several reasons why it is easy to miss the fact that a child's symptoms are the side effect of the drug, and not due to the disease for which the drug is being given, (Vere, 1976): the reaction may be bizarre, the reaction may closely mimic a common disease, the reaction to the drug may be delayed, and the clinical picture may be so complex that the side effects of the drug are not recognised. For further reference concerning side effects of drugs, see the books by Davies (1981) and Dukes (1979).

At the risk of some oversimplification, one may group the side effects of drugs as follows, according to the tissue predominantly involved:

1 Action on the skin—rashes, erythematous, urticarial, scarlatiniform, morbilliform, erythema multiforme, erythema nodosum, exfoliative dermatitis, purpura, acne, striae, photosensitivity, pigmentation, hair loss or hypertrichosis, Stevens–Johnson syndrome, disseminated lupus, fixed drug eruptions.

2 Action on the brain, psychological or otherwise. Advantageous—the patient thinking that he is better, although the drug had no relevant pharmacological action. Disadvantageous—the patient imagining that the drug is causing untoward symptoms. Direct action on the brain—causing confusion or other symptoms.

3 Action on the eye—causing cataract, optic atrophy, papilloedema, retinal changes, conjunctivitis.

4 Action on the ear—causing deafness or ataxia.

5 Action on the heart.

6 Action on the liver—hepatitis.

7 Action on the kidney—albuminuria, haematuria, nephrotic syndrome.

8 Action on the blood.

Predominantly red cells—haemolysis, megaloblastic anaemia, hypoplastic anaemia.

Predominantly white cells—granulopenia, agranulocytosis.
Predominantly platelets—thrombocytopenic purpura.
Action on several of the blood elements.
Action on clotting mechanisms.
Action on the haemoglobin—methaemoglobinaemia.
9 Action on the alimentary tract—abdominal pain, ulceration, bleeding, vomiting, diarrhoea, constipation.
10 Allergic and anaphylactoid reactions. Asthma.
11 Drug fever.
12 Collagen disease—disseminated lupus, periarteritis.
13 Superinfection—especially moniliasis.
14 Drug resistance and antagonism.
15 Drug dependence and addiction.
16 Action on the fetus when drug taken in pregnancy.

Drug reactions are usually due to overdosage, intolerance, side effects including secondary effects, idiosyncrasy, hypersensitivity and allergy.

In the section to follow, I have made no attempt to list side effects in order of frequency. This would be impossible. Some of the side effects mentioned are probably rare, but it was felt that a fairly comprehensive list would be useful for the family doctor.

Some rashes caused by drugs

Acne—actinomycin D, barbiturates, bromides, chloral, corticosteroids, ethambutol, ethionamide, iodides, isoniazid, phenytoin, tetracycline, thiouracil and troxidone.
Bullous eruptions.
Disseminated lupus erythematosus.
Erythema multiforme—barbiturates, chloral, codeine, penicillin, phenolphthalein, phenytoin, salicylates, sulphonamides, tetracycline and thiazide diuretics.
Erythema nodosum (p. 327).
Exfoliative dermatitis—anticonvulsants, chloroquine, gold, griseofulvin, isoniazid, nitrofurantoin, penicillin, phenothiazines, phenytoin, salicylates, streptomycin, sulphonamides, thiouracil and troxidone.
Eczema.

Fixed drug eruptions—anticonvulsants, antihistamines, barbiturates, chlordiazepoxide, iodides, mepacrine, meprobamate, penicillin, phenolphthalein, quinine, salicylates, sulphonamides and tetracycline.

Lichen planus—antimalarials, arsenic, gold and P.A.S.

Photosensitivity rashes.

Pigmentation. Purpura.

Stevens–Johnson syndrome—antiepileptic drugs, clindamycin, penicillin, rifampicin, long acting sulphonamides.

Toxic epidermal necrolysis—barbiturates, nitrofurantoin, penicillin, phenytoin, sulphonamides.

Urticaria.

References

Davies DM. *Textbook of adverse drug reactions*. Oxford: Oxford University Press, 1981.

Dukes MNG (Ed). *Meyler's side effects of drugs*. Amsterdam: Excerpts Medica, 1979.

Forfar J. Drugs and the fetus. *Update* 1981; **22**: 1469.

Vere DW. Drug adverse reactions as masqueraders. *Adverse drug reaction bulletin* 1976; **No. 60.**

Side effects of Individual Drugs

Some of the side effects listed are rare. Selected important side effects are in italics.

Acetazolamide (Diamox)—action on blood, kidney, liver; confusion, depression, diarrhoea, drowsiness, excitement, fever, fits, glycosuria, haematuria, headaches, irritability, melaena, paraesthesiae, polydipsia, rash, renal calculus, taste disturbance, vertigo, vision blurring, vomiting.

Actinomycin D—action on blood, alopecia, deafness, diarrhoea, intestinal ulceration, oral ulcers, rash.

Adrenaline—*fainting, nervousness, pallor, sweating,* tremor.

Aminophylline—*agitation,* anxiety, coma, *death,* dehydration, delirium, fever, fits, haematemesis, haematuria, headache, overventilation, rashes, respiratory paralysis, restlessness, shock, thirst, tremor, vertigo, vomiting.

Amitriptyline (Tryptizol)—abdominal pain, action on blood and liver; ataxia, blurring of vision, constipation, *drowsiness,* dry mouth, dysuria, excitement, fatigue, fever, fits, hallucinations, headache, ileus, mouth ulcers, nausea, numbness, oedema of face, oliguria, paraesthesiae, photosensitivity, pruritus, rash, sweating, tremors, vertigo, vomiting, weakness.

Amphetamine—aggressiveness, *anorexia, defective physical growth,* drowsiness, *drug dependence,* dry mouth, hallucinations, hyperthermia, *insomnia,* irritability, jaundice, paranoia, pupils dilated, rash, schizoid reactions, sweating, tearfulness, tics, tremor, weight loss. Withdrawal depression.

Anabolic steroids, e.g. Methandienone (Dianabol), Norethandrolone (Nilevar)—*jaundice,* liver cancer, lower P.B.I., *premature closure of epiphyses,* raised serum lipoids, virilisation.

Antihistamines—action on blood, amblyopia, ataxia, concentration poor, confusion, delirium, dental decay, *drowsiness, dry mouth,* dystonia, dysuria, facial spasms, fainting fits, frequency of micturition, gastric disturbance, hallucinations, headache, insomnia, irritability, lassitude, mouth dry, rash, tachycardia, tinnitus, trismus, urinary retention, vertigo.

Aspirin—see Salicylates.

Azathioprine—*action on blood,* diarrhoea, muscular wasting, pancreatitis, tumour formation.

Bacitracin—action on kidney, anorexia, nausea, pain at site of injection, rash.

Bactrim—see Cotrimoxazole.

Barbiturates—amblyopia, *bad behaviour* (especially in mentally subnormal child), *concentration impaired,* depression, diplopia, *drowsiness, drug dependence,* hepatosplenomegaly, *insomnia, irritability,* megaloblastic anaemia, nystagmus, optic neuritis, purpura, *rash,* Stevens–Johnson syndrome, tearfulness, yellow vision; withdrawal symptoms—delirium, fits, tremors.

Becotide—oral thrush.

Bephenium—diarrhoea, nausea, vomiting.

Betamethasone—see Corticosteroids.

Boric acid—death, diarrhoea and vomiting, haemorrhages, peripheral circulatory failure, red beefy rash.

Bromides—acne, hallucinations, slow thought, *tearfulness.*

Calcium chloride—*gastric irritation.*

Capreomycin—action on kidney, deafness, defective colour vision, hypocalcaemia, hypokalaemia, optic neuritis.

Carbamazepine (Tegretol)—abdominal pain, action on blood, amblyopia, alopecia, adenopathy, anorexia, ataxia, blood pressure rise or fall, cataract, conjunctivitis, confusion, diarrhoea, diplopia, disseminated lupus, dizziness, drowsiness, dry mouth, dystonia, fever, fits, frequency, headache, hyperacousia, jaundice, limb pains, nausea, nystagmus, oliguria, peripheral neuritis, photosensitivity, pruritus, purpura, rash, Stevens–Johnson syndrome, syncope, tinnitus, vomiting.

Carbenicillin—action on blood, hypokalaemia, purpura. See also penicillin.

Cephalosporins—abdominal discomfort, action on blood, kidney and liver; allergy, anorexia, confusion, diarrhoea, fever, nausea, oedema, Parkinsonism, rash, serum-sickness like symptoms, superinfection, thrombophlebitis at injection site, vomiting, wheezing.

Chloral—rash.

Chlorambucil—cataract.

Chloramphenicol—newborn baby—abdominal distension, cyanosis, death, flaccidity, *grey syndrome;* failure to thrive, hypothermia, irregular respirations, loose stools, optic neuritis, pruritus, rash, vomiting.

Older children—*action on the blood,* especially granulopenia; action on liver; optic neuritis, peripheral neuritis, enterocolitis.

Chlordiazepoxide (Librium)—abdominal discomfort, action on blood and liver; anorexia, arthralgia, ataxia, confusion, constipation, depression, drowsiness, excitement, paradoxical, *extrapyramidal symptoms,* hostility, hypotension, mania, memory impaired, mouth dry, muscle cramps, nausea, oedema, overactivity, rashes, salivation, urinary difficulty, vertigo, vomiting. Withdrawal—irritability, tremors.

Chloroquine—accommodation impaired, action on blood and liver; *blurred vision,* burning in epigastrium, burning in mouth, *cataract,* colour vision impaired, deafness, diplopia, hair loss and loss of colour, involuntary movements, myopathy, nausea, photosensitivity, pigmentation, pruritus, rashes, *retinal changes* (may be delayed for 4–5 years), torticollis, vomiting.

Chlorothiazide group—action on blood, allergy, cramps, hyperglycaemia, lassitude, melaena, nausea, pancreatitis, paraesthesiae, *potassium loss,* rashes, vertigo.

Chlorpromazine (Largactil)—see Phenothiazines.

Cimetidine—arthralgia, confusion, constipation, diarrhoea, granulopenia, gynaecomastia, headache, muscle pain, rash, vertigo.

Clindamycin—entercolitis, *ulcerative colitis,* Stevens–Johnson syndrome, urticaria.

Clonazepam (Rivotril)—aggressiveness, ataxia, concentration defective, diarrhoea, drooling, drowsiness, dysphagia, fatigue, hypotonia, irritability, oedema of face, overactivity, overeating, parotid swelling, pigmentation, salivary or bronchial hypersecretion, thirst, vertigo.

Clonidine—angioneurotic oedema, dry mouth, insomnia, jaundice, nausea, pruritus, rash, sedation, thirst, vertigo.

Codeine—collapse of lung if cough productive, drying of secretions.

Colistin—*action on kidney,* deafness, muscle weakness, nystagmus, paraesthesiae, vertigo.

Corticosteroids—*acne,* abdominal pain, agranulocytosis, *cataract, Cushing's syndrome, death sudden,* delayed healing, *dermal atrophy, diabetes,* fits, glaucoma, *growth inhibition, hypertension, increased severity of chickenpox, muscle pains, muscle weakness, obesity, operative shock, osteoporosis,* pancreatitis, panniculitis, *peptic ulcer,* pigmentation, *purpura, sodium retention, striae, suppression of pain in infection,* thrombocytopenia, thromboembolic phenomena.

On discontinuing—increased intracranial pressure.

Skin applications—*acne,* burning sensation, *dermal atrophy,* folliculitis, hypertrichosis, miliaria, pruritus, *striae, telangiectasia.*

Corticotrophin (ACTH)—same as corticosteroids; more tendency to acne, allergy, hirsutism, hypertension, pigmentation: less bruising, less dyspepsia, osteoporosis, striae.

Cotrimoxazole—see trimethoprim. Action on blood, skin, kidney, and liver; alopecia, angioneurotic oedema, deafness, diarrhoea, glossitis, hallucinations, headache, nausea, paraesthesiae, photosensitivity, vertigo, vomiting.

Cromoglycate—allergic granulomatosis, anaphylaxis, angioneurotic oedema, pulmonary eosinophilia, urticaria, wheezing.

Cyclopentolate—*acute psychosis*, ataxia, delirium, dry mouth, diarrhoea, visual hallucinations, ileus, vomiting.

Cyclophosphamide—*action on blood* and *liver; alopecia*, amenorrhoea, anorexia, *cystitis, diarrhoea*, glycosuria, headache, intestinal ulceration, lymphoma, malignant disease, myelitis, myocarditis, nail pigmentation, nausea, oral ulcers, pneumonitis, protein-losing enteropathy, pulmonary fibrosis, reduced resistance to virus infections, *sterility*, vomiting.

Cycloserine—action on blood, fits, neurotoxic, psychoses.

Demeclocycline (Ledermycin)—diarrhoea, facial oedema, *photosensitivity*, polydipsia, polyuria, *staining of teeth*, staining of nails, vomiting.

Diazepam (Valium)—action on blood and liver; acute excitement, ataxia, blurred vision, cardiac arrhythmia, constipation, depression, diplopia, drowsiness, dry mouth, dysarthria, hallucinations, headache, hostility, impaired memory, irritability, nausea, rash, *respiratory depression*, sleep disturbed, temperature fall, tremors, vertigo, weakness. Prenatal—hypotonia.

Diazoxide—cardiac arrhythmia, *hypertrichosis*, involuntary movements.

Dichloralphenazone—pruritus.

Dichlorophen—abdominal discomfort, diarrhoea, rash, urticaria, vomiting.

Dicyclomine—rash, salivation, vertigo.

Digoxin—anorexia, *bradycardia, coupling of the beats*, gynaecomastia, nausea, *oliguria*, scotoma, *vomiting*, xanthopsia.

Dioctyl sulphosuccinate—jaundice.

Diodoquin—optic atrophy.

Diphenoxylate (Lomotil)—abdominal distension, areflexia, ataxia, depression, dizziness, drowsiness, fits, hypotonia, insomnia, nausea, nystagmus, pruritus, pupils small, rash, vomiting.

Ephedrine—headache, *insomnia*, nausea, *nervousness*, pallor, palpitation, sweating, tremor.

Ergotamine—abdominal pain, blurred vision, chilling of extremities, cramps, diarrhoea, *gangrene,* headache, nausea, *numbness,* papilloedema, taste disturbance, *tingling,* vomiting.

Erythromycin—abdominal pain, allergy, deafness, diarrhoea, fever, *jaundice* (mainly the estolate), nausea, rash, vomiting, wheezing.

Ethacrynic acid—electrolyte disturbance, deafness, pancreatitis, ventricular fibrillation.

Ethambutol—arthralgia, fever, gastrointestinal symptoms, hair loss, headache, jaundice, loss of colour vision, rash, *reduced visual acuity,* retrobulbar neuritis.

Ethamivan (Vandid)—*convulsions.*

Ethionamide—abdominal pain, acne, alopecia, anorexia, diarrhoea, jaundice, mental changes, peripheral neuritis, photosensitivity, rash, salivation, vomiting.

Ethosuximide (Zarontin)—abdominal pain, action on blood, kidney and liver; anorexia, confusion, depression, disseminated lupus, drowsiness, fatigue, headache, hiccough, nausea, Parkinsonism, photophobia, psychosis, rash, facial swelling, stammer, stomatitis, vaginal bleeding, vertigo, vomiting.

Fenfluramine—alopecia, confusion, depression, diarrhoea, diplopia, drowsiness, dry mouth, dyskinesia, headache, insomnia, lethargy, nightmares, opisthotonos, poor concentration, rash, tooth grinding, urinary frequency, vertigo, vomiting, withdrawal—*agitation.*

Flufenamic acid—diarrhoea.

Framycetin—deafness.

Frusemide—bullous skin, deafness, hypokalaemia, pancreatitis, photosensitivity.

Gentamicin—*action on ears, kidney,* alopecia, blurred vision, muscle weakness, permanent vestibular damage, psychological disturbance.

Gold—*action on blood, kidney, liver,* photosensitivity, pruritus, *rashes,* stomatitis.

Griseofulvin—action on blood, kidney, liver, stomach, altered taste and smell, disseminated lupus, gynaecomastia, headache, insomnia, peripheral neuritis, photosensitivity, pigmented genitalia, poor concentration, superinfection, urticaria, vertigo.

Haloperidol (Serenace)—aphonia, depression, drowsiness, dry mouth, dysphagia, fever, involuntary movement, action on liver and skin, salivation, sweating, vision blurred, vomiting.

Hyoscine—*atropine like action,* coma, dryness of mouth, excitement, hallucination.

Ibuprofen—amblyopia, deafness, dyspepsia, jaundice, optic neuritis.

Imipramine (Tofranil)—abdominal pain, accommodation impaired, action on blood and liver, aggressiveness, angioneurotic oedema, anxiety, ataxia, cold extremities, concentration impaired, constipation, delirium, dental decay, difficulty in micturition, diplopia, drowsiness, dryness of mucous membranes, dysarthria, dysphagia, dysuria, excitability, fits, giddiness, glossitis, gynaecomastia, headache, hypothermia, ileus, insomnia, irritability, lactorrhoea, lethargy, nausea, nystagmus, ocular palsy, oliguria, overactivity, palpitation, paraesthesiae, Parkinsonism, peripheral neuritis, photosensitivity, postural hypotension, pruritus, pulmonary infiltration, rashes, renal damage, retrobulbar neuritis, stomatitis, sudden falls, sweating, tachycardia, taste disturbance, tearfulness, tremors, vertigo, vision blurred.

Indomethacin (Indocid)—abdominal distension, action on blood and liver, anorexia, asthma, ataxia, blurred vision, buccal ulcer, confusion, corneal and retinal changes, deafness, death, depression, diplopia, drowsiness, diarrhoea, fever, hair loss, headache, melaena, nausea, necrotizing enterocolitis, neuropathy, oedema, optic neuritis, pancreatitis, peptic ulcer, pruritus, psychological changes, rash, vertigo, vomiting.

Iodides—*acne, coryza,* gastric disturbances, goitre, fever, oedema of eyelids, swelling of salivary glands, urticaria.

Iron—abdominal discomfort, blackening of teeth and stools, constipation, diarrhoea.

Isoniazid—action on blood, kidney, liver; albuminuria, arthralgia, cramp, disseminated lupus, drowsiness, dysuria, excitability, fever, fits, gynaecomastia, headache, mouth dry, optic atrophy, optic neuritis, pancreatitis, *peripheral neuritis,* psychological changes, pulmonary eosinophilia, rash, vertigo, vision blurred, vomiting.

Kanamycin—action on blood, ear, kidney, liver; amblyopia, diarrhoea, muscle weakness, paraesthesiae, rash, superinfection, tinnitus, vertigo.

Lincomycin—abdominal pain, action on blood and liver; altered taste or smell; diarrhoea, muscle pain, overgrowth of yeasts, pruritus, rashes, superinfection, urticaria, vomiting.

Mefenamic acid—diarrhoea, dyspepsia, haemolysis, leucopenia, rash.

Mepacrine (Atabrine)—action on blood, psychosis, rash, *yellow staining of skin.*

Meprobamate (Miltown, Equanil)—action on blood, agitation, anaphylactoid reaction, anorexia, ataxia, blurred vision, bronchospasm, depression, drowsiness, drug dependence, fever, frequency, gastroenteritis, lymphadenopathy, Parkinsonism, proctitis, rash, stomatitis, thirst, vertigo, vomiting, weakness. Withdrawal—insomnia, tremors, twitching.

6-Mercaptopurine—action on *blood, liver;* anorexia, diarrhoea, intestinal ulceration, lupus disseminated, muscular wasting, oral ulcers, vomiting.

Methicillin—kidney damage, rigors.

Methimazole—action on blood and liver; arthralgia, C.N.S. depression or stimulation, fever, hypothyroidism, oedema, pruritus, rash.

Methotrexate—abdominal pain, action on *blood* and *liver;* alopecia, anorexia, diarrhoea, lung infiltration, melaena, nausea, oral ulceration, pulmonary eosinophilia, rash, renal tubular damage, vomiting.

Methylphenidate (Ritalin)—*anorexia,* anxiety, dyspepsia, *growth retardation,* headache, insomnia, irritability, mouth dry, palpitation, psychological disturbance, rash, sweating, tearfulness, tics, tremors.

Metoclopramide (Maxolon)—*dysarthria, dysphagia, dystonia, facial grimacing,* lactorrhoea, *oculogyric crises, opisthotonos,* stiff neck, *torticollis, trismus.*

Morphia—nausea, vomiting.

Nalidixic acid (Negram)—anaemia, action on blood, depression, diarrhoea, drowsiness, false positive for urinary reducing substances, fits, glycosuria, haemolysis, headache, hyperglycaemia, hypertension, increased intracranial pressure, jaundice, muscle weakness, myalgia, nausea, paraesthesiae, photosensitivity, polyarthritis, pruritus, rash, sixth nerve weakness and squint, vertigo, visual disturbance, vomiting.

Neomycin—action on ear, kidney, and liver; muscle weakness, rash, steatorrhoea, wheezing.

Niclosamide—abdominal pain, ataxia, dry mouth, headache, loose stools, nausea, paraesthesiae, rash, sleep disturbed, stomatitis, vomiting.

Nitrazepam (Mogadon)—ataxia, *bronchial hypersecretion*, depression, drowsiness, excitement, increased appetite, lachrymation, memory impaired, *salivation*, taste disturbed.

Nitrofurantoin—action on blood, kidney and liver; alopecia, anaphylaxis, angioneurotic oedema, chills, cyanosis, eosinophilia, fever, fits, haemolysis in presence of glucose-6-phosphate dehydrogenase deficiency, hallucinations, headache, muscle pains, nausea, paraesthesiae, peripheral neuritis, pigmentation, pleural effusion, pulmonary infiltration, rash, teeth discoloured, urine brown, vomiting.

Novobiocin—action on blood and liver; rash, yellow staining of skin.

Nystatin—abdominal pain, diarrhoea.

Oleandomycin—jaundice.

Oestrogens—gynaecomastia.

Oxyphenisatin (Dulcolax)—lupoid hepatitis.

P.A.S. (Para-amino salicylic acid)—abdominal pain, action on blood, kidney and liver; diarrhoea, disseminated lupus, drowsiness, fever, gynaecomastia, haemorrhages, hair loss, lymphadenopathy, optic atrophy, optic neuritis, photophobia, pulmonary eosinophilia, pulmonary infiltration, rash, steatorrhoea, thyroid enlargement, vitamin B deficiency, vomiting.

Paracetamol—granulopenia, haemolysis, hepatitis, pancreatitis.

Paromomycin—abdominal pain, action on kidney, deafness, diarrhoea, headache, nausea, rash, steatorrhoea, superinfection, vertigo, vomiting.

Penicillamine—action on blood, diarrhoea, fever, loss of taste, purpura, rash, vomiting.

Penicillin—*anaphylaxis*, angioneurotic oedema, arthralgia, asthma, conjunctivitis, dermatomyositis, *diarrhoea* when taken by mouth, effusion into joints, *haemolysis*, hypertrichosis, increased intracranial pressure, lachrymation, limb pain, lupus disseminated, periarteritis, polyneuritis, pruritus, pulmonary eosinophilia, rashes, superinfection, visual defect, wheezing.

Pethidine—nausea, vertigo.

Phenacetin—jaundice, action on kidney.

Pheneturide—action on blood, kidney and liver; ataxia, dyspepsia, rash.

Phenothiazine group of tranquillizers (Chlorpromazine (Largactil), Perphenazine (Fentazin), Prochlorperazine (Stemetil), Promazine (Sparine), Thioridazine (Melleril), Trifluoperazine (Stelazine))—abdominal pain, action on blood and liver; catatonia, concentration impaired, constipation, *corneal opacities*, constriction of chest, depression, dental decay, diarrhoea, drowsiness, dry mouth, *extrapyramidal symptoms*, facial oedema, fever, fits, gynaecomastia, headache, hypothermia, inability to sit still, involuntary movements, lactorrhoea, limb pains, muscle rigidity, nasal congestion, neck stiffness, oculogyric crises, oedema, opisthotonos, postural hypotension, paralysis of accommodation, photosensitivity, pigmentation of retina and skin, pruritus, rash, rigidity, stomatitis, sweating, tremors, urinary retention, vertigo, visual blurring.

Phensuximide (Milontin)—action on blood, ataxia, disseminated lupus, drowsiness, haematuria, hepatosplenomegaly, lymphadenopathy, nausea, rash, vertigo.

Phenazopyridine (Pyridium)—action on blood, yellow urine.

Phenylbutazone—action on blood, lymphadenopathy.

Phenytoin (Epanutin)—abdominal discomfort, action on blood, kidney and liver; acne, alopecia, amblyopia, anorexia, arthropathy, *ataxia*, choreoathetosis, concentration defective, conjunctivitis, constipation, decalcification, diplopia, disseminated lupus, drowsiness, dysarthria, fever, *gingivitis*, haematuria, headache, hepatosplenomegaly, *hirsutism*, hyperglycaemia, immunosuppression, interaction with phenobarbitone, phenothiazines, P.A.S., sulthiame; joint effusion, lymphadenopathy, lymphoma, megaloblastic anaemia, mental slowing, mental deterioration, nausea, *nystagmus*, overactivity, periarteritis, pigmentation, pruritus, psychological disturbance, rash, rickets, skull thickening, Stevens–Johnson syndrome, striae, tremors, vomiting.

Piperazine—abdominal pain, accommodation impaired, allergic purpura, ataxia, blurring of vision, coma, confusion, diarrhoea, hallucinations, hypotonia, incoordination, muscle weakness, paraesthesiae, precipitation of fits in epileptics, rashes, tremors, urticaria, vertigo, vomiting.

Polymyxin—action on kidney, ataxia, circumoral numbness, fever, neurotoxic, paraesthesiae, pruritus, rash, slurred speech, vertigo.

Primidone (Mysoline)—abdominal pain, action on blood, alopecia, amblyopia, angioneurotic oedema, ataxia, decalcification, diplopia, disseminated lupus, *drowsiness,* dysarthria, hair loss, *irritability,* lymphadenopathy, megaloblastic anaemia, nausea, *nystagmus,* oedema of eyelids, overactivity, psychoses, rash, vertigo, vomiting.

Propranolol—bronchospasm, hypotension, lassitude.

Pyrazinamide—action on liver, limb pains.

Pyrimethamine—action on blood, convulsions.

Quinine—action on blood and skin, deafness, jaundice, tinnitus, visual defect.

Rifampicin—abdominal pain, action on blood, liver and kidney; bone pain, conjunctivitis, deafness, diarrhoea, drowsiness, dyspepsia, dyspnoea, fever, headache, muscle pain, nausea, pancreatitis, pruritus, rash, red urine, red sputum, red tears; Stevens–Johnson syndrome, vomiting, wheezing.

Ristocetin—action on blood and kidney, albuminuria, thromboses.

Salbutamol—tremors.

Salicylates—*anaemia, angioneurotic oedema, asthma, bleeding* by causing hypoprothrombinaemia or thrombocytopenia, deafness, haematemesis, increase of chronic urticaria, jaundice, nystagmus, *overventilation,* pulmonary eosinophilia, *tinnitus,* vertigo, vomiting. Aspirin particles also cause bleeding by direct action on gastric mucosa.

Sodium fusidate—diarrhoea, vomiting.

Streptomycin—action on blood, *ataxia, deafness,* fever, lupus disseminated, jaundice, muscle weakness, optic neuritis, paraesthesiae, pruritus, rash, wheezing, yellow vision.

Sulphasalazine—action on blood, anorexia, arthralgia, fever, headache, lung changes, muscle pain, nausea, rash, vomiting.

Sulphonamides—*action on blood and liver; crystalluria,* diplopia, disseminated lupus, *drug fever,* headache, lymphadenopathy, myopia, nausea, necrotizing angiitis, optic neuritis, pancreatitis, photosensitivity, polyarteritis, polyneuritis, pulmonary infiltration, rash, vertigo, yellow vision.

Long-acting sulphonamides—*Stevens-Johnson syndrome.*

Sulthiame (Ospolot)—action on blood and kidney; anorexia, ataxia, blurred vision, confusion, depression, drowsiness, dysarthria, headache, loss of weight, nephrotic syndrome, *overventilation*, paraesthesiae, photophobia, psychotic excitement, ptosis, raised blood level of phenytoin, rash, renal calculus, status epilepticus, vertigo, vomiting.

Terbutaline (Bricanyl)—tremors, palpitation.

Testosterone group—acne, jaundice, premature closure of epiphyses, virilization.

Tetanus toxoid—dysarthria, peripheral neuritis, pruritus, sweating, urticaria, wheezing.

Tetracyclines—abdominal pain, action on kidney, anaphylaxis, *bulging fontanelle, diarrhoea,* disseminated lupus, *enamel hypoplasia, enterocolitis,* fever, glossitis, jaundice, myopia, *overgrowth of monilia,* pancreatitis, peptic ulcer, *photosensitivity,* pruritus, rash, thrombocytopenia, *tooth and nail discoloration,* papilloedema, vertigo, *wheezing.*

    Old stocks—abnormal aminoaciduria, Fanconi-like syndrome, nausea, oedema, polydipsia, polyuria, vomiting.

Thiabendazole—dyspepsia, headache, hyperglycaemia, leucopenia, numbness, pruritus, tinnitus, vertigo, xanthopsia.

Thiouracil—acne, action on blood and liver; disseminated lupus, fever, lymphadenopathy, rash.

Thyroxine—*heart failure at onset, loss of weight.*

    Overdose—*advanced skeletal maturation followed by premature closure of epiphyses, diarrhoea, irritability, tachycardia.*

Trimeprazine (Vallergan)—abdominal pain, depression, drowsiness, dry mouth, headache, nasal stuffiness, rash, vertigo.

Trimethoprim—see cotrimoxazole.

Troxidone—abdominal pain, acne, *action on blood and liver;* alopecia, angioneurotic oedema, diplopia, disseminated lupus, drowsiness, effusion into joints, grand mal, haematuria, headache, hiccoughs, irritability, lymphadenopathy, *nephrotic syndrome,* photophobia, rash, Stevens–Johnson syndrome, vomiting, white vision.

Valproate sodium (Epilim)—anorexia, drowsiness, elevation of serum barbiturate, extrapyramidal symptoms, hair loss, headache, **hepatic damage,** nausea, pancreatitis, purpura, vomiting, **weight gain.**

Vancomycin—action on blood, ears, kidney and liver; fever, paraesthesiae, phlebitis, rash, respiratory arrest, rigor, superinfection, thromboses, urticaria.

Vincristine—abdominal pain, *action on blood, alopecia,* ataxia, constipation, diarrhoea, diplopia, headache, hoarseness, insomnia, jaw pain, oral ulcers, pain in fingers, paraesthesiae, peripheral neuritis, pigmentation, pulmonary fibrosis, ptosis, rash, vomiting.

Viomycin—action on ears, kidney and liver; electrolyte disturbances, rashes.

Viprynium—abdominal pain, diarrhoea, nausea, red stools, vomiting.

Vitamin A excess—abdominal pain, anorexia, arthralgia, *bone pain,* brittle nails, diplopia, dry mouth, dry skin, fractures, *hepatosplenomegaly,* hydrocephalus, hypoplastic anaemia, increased intracranial pressure, myalgia, oedema of occiput, papilloedema, *periostitis,* pruritus, sparse hair, *stomatitis,* vomiting.

Vitamin D excess—anorexia, *hypercalcaemia,* nephrocalcinosis, polyuria.

Vitamin K excess—*haemolysis, kernicterus.*

Psychological and Organic

Psychological factors are so commonly associated with organic disease that it is essential to eliminate organic disease before concluding that the cause is entirely psychological. In fact *one should never conclude that a symptom is entirely psychological without positive evidence of a psychological disorder and without eliminating organic disease.* It is then necessary to see the child again in order to make sure that one is right about the absence of organic disease. The difficulty is that organic disease may cause psychological disorders, and psychological disorders may cause somatic symptoms.

Many psychological symptoms are caused by disease. For instance, infections and other diseases which result in a child necessarily or unnecessarily missing school may lead to the child worrying about dropping behind others in his class—and may even make it difficult for him to return to school. A common example of this is asthma: many parents keep their asthmatic child away from school when he has the slightest wheeze (or even a cold which might perhaps lead to a wheeze), and as a result the child drops behind in his work, worries, and wheezes all the more, and so is kept away longer still. It is a difficult vicious circle which must be broken. If a mother is over anxious about the child's health, she makes him neurotic and hypochondriacal.

Many school difficulties which have an organic basis lead to psychological symptoms. Learning disorders commonly present as a behaviour problem such as truancy. Clumsiness of movement commonly leads to unhappiness at school because of the unkindness of the teachers who ascribe the child's bad writing to carelessness and naughtiness. Defects of hearing or seeing lead to troublesome behaviour problems because the child is unable to follow the work of the class. A child who finds the work too much for him, either because of a learning difficulty in a particular subject or because his IQ is lower than that of others in his form or for other reasons, may lose heart, become worried, depressed and insecure.

Epilepsy leads to behaviour difficulties in several ways. The child may be rejected from entry to a school because of the epilepsy, or he may be treated differently from others, being prevented, for example, from swimming. If he suffers from frequent attacks of *petit mal* he may so frequently miss what is being said that he drops behind in his class work. He may have temporal lobe epilepsy, which causes bad behaviour, leading, for instance, to outbursts of temper. It is particularly important to remember that drugs given for epilepsy may make him clumsy, drowsy and irritable and cause poor concentration. Phenobarbitone is particularly liable to cause undue irritability and bad behaviour.

Overactivity, which is sometimes related to prematurity, events during pregnancy or anoxia at birth, leads to difficulties at school, poor concentration and punishment.

On p. 1 it is noted that certain diseases which lead to poor physical growth lead to food refusal because of food forcing. For instance, congenital heart disease is commonly associated with defective physical growth. This leads to the mother worrying about the child's small size, and so she tries to make him eat more—and he refuses.

A baby was referred to me on account of excessive crying. He was found to have phenylketonuria, and when the serum phenylalanine was reduced by an appropriate diet his behaviour promptly improved.

Some bad behaviour is due to hypoglycaemia. It is well known that some children (and adults) become bad tempered when hungry. Others behave badly because they are tired as a result of an infection or anaemia.

Children with an intracranial neoplasm, tuberculous meningitis or chorea may present as a behaviour problem.

Chronic diarrhoea, such as occurs in ulcerative colitis, leads to bad temper and irritability. This may lead some to ascribe the ulcerative colitis to a behaviour problem. Admittedly there are often psychological factors in association with ulcerative colitis.

Several studies have shown that there is a higher incidence of physical handicap in juvenile delinquents than in the normal population. It is possible that the XYY chromosome anomaly may be associated with tallness of stature and deliquency.

Other conditions which may present as behaviour problems include thyrotoxicosis, migraine, anorectal stenosis, bladder neck obstruction, and (rarely) phaeochromocytoma or neuroblastoma.

Children may be embarrassed and unhappy because of their ugliness or other aspects of their physical appearance, such as obesity, sexual precocity, delayed puberty, short stature or lipodystrophy.

In the next few years we may well learn that more aspects of behaviour have a biochemical or chromosomal basis.

More than half of all the symptoms discussed in this book, all of which may be due to organic disease, may also be psychological in origin. For instance, one of the three components of asthma is psychological disturbance (the other two being allergy and infection). There may be a psychological component in allergic rhinitis. A cough may be merely a habit or an attention-seeking device.

Numerous somatic symptoms may arise from psychological problems. They include diarrhoea, abdominal pain, vomiting, frequency of micturition, dysuria, dysmenorrhoea, bed-wetting, polydipsia, polyuria, a poor appetite, indigestion and peptic ulcer, obesity, dirt eating, headache and limb or chest pains. There is a psychological component to several skin conditions, such as eczema, urticaria, lichen planus and pruritus. Many other somatic symptoms can be caused by psychological problems.

It has been suggested that psychological factors may influence the resistance to infectious disease (Friedman & Glasgow, 1966).

Reference

Friedman SB, Glasgow LA. Psychological factors and resistance to infectious disease. *Pediatr Clin North Am* 1966; **13**: 315.

Some Symptoms of Importance

At the risk of repetition, I propose in this section to enumerate some symptoms of special importance in children, because failure to take note of them may have disastrous results.

Jaundice on the first day, because it requires urgent treatment: it is due to haemolytic disease until proved otherwise. Severe jaundice in the newborn period calls for urgent investigation.

Vomitus containing bile in the newborn period, or vomiting with abdominal distension, suggests intestinal obstruction.

Blood in a baby's vomitus after the newborn period, suggests hiatus hernia or reflux, and calls for investigation.

Diarrhoea in an infant or young child is important because of the rapidity with which dehydration may occur.

Stridor of acute onset is important because of the rapidity with which it may get worse and cause complete obstruction.

Cough of really sudden onset, without an upper respiratory infection, suggests an inhaled foreign body.

Ear pain, due to otitis media, requires immediate antibiotic treatment (and *not* drops in the ear).

Neck stiffness (in flexion) suggests meningitis. It is essential to have a lumbar puncture carried out before any antibiotic is given, so that if it is due to pyogenic meningitis the organism can be isolated and the appropriate treatment can be given.

Fits with fever in the child are important because although febrile convulsions are the most likely diagnosis, they may be due to pyogenic meningitis. Hence a lumbar puncture must be performed.

The onset of drowsiness with an infection may represent pyogenic meningitis.

Loss of weight is important because of the many serious causes which could be responsible.

A severe attack of asthma, not responding to the usual treatment.

Poisoning of any kind is important because hospital investigation and treatment are needed. The dangerous latent period, between the time of ingestion of the poison and the onset of symptoms, after salicylates, especially enteric coated or sustained release tablets, or after iron or diphenoxylate, is a particular hazard. Unexplained abnormal excitement, drowsiness, convulsions or vomiting may be due to an overdose of drugs or poisoning.

Some Popular Fallacies

In this section are listed some common errors made when diagnosing the cause of some of the symptoms mentioned in this book.

Vomiting, crying, green stools or diarrhoea are *not* due to breast milk not suiting the baby. The only exceptions to this are the exceedingly rare conditions galactosaemia or lactose intolerance. If these are suspected the child should be referred to a paediatrician for the appropriate tests. Green stools in fully breast fed babies are normal. Green stools passed by a bottle fed baby are normal unless there is diarrhoea.

Vomiting, crying or diarrhoea are *not* due to the breast milk being too strong for the baby—or not strong enough.

Vomiting, crying or diarrhoea in a full term breast fed or bottle fed baby are *not* due to overfeeding.

Vomiting, crying or diarrhoea are *not* due to the particular dried food or other properly constituted feed not suiting the baby. Nothing will be achieved by changing from one dried food to another. The child may, however, be intolerant of certain carbohydrates. The child with coeliac disease is probably intolerant of gluten. The child with hypercalcaemia is intolerant of ordinary foods and requires a special low calcium milk. A very occasional baby is sensitive to milk protein.

Infrequent stools in a well breast fed baby are *not* due to constipation. They are normal.

True constipation in an artificially fed baby is *not* due to insufficiency of roughage in the diet. It may be due to inadequate fluid or other factors.

Crying at night by the older baby is *not* due to indigestion or wind. It is almost certainly due to mismanagement and habit formation.

A poor appetite in a well child is almost certainly *not* due to disease—though routine physical and urine examination should be carried out; it is almost certainly due to food forcing.

Bed-wetting after the age of three, when it has always occurred, is almost certainly *not* merely psychological in origin, or due to jealousy or faulty management—though psychological problems can readily be added to the basic problem of delayed maturation.

Constant dribbling incontinence is *not* due to delayed maturation; in the boy it is usually due to urethral valves, and in the girl to an ectopic ureter in the vagina, or a ureterocele.

Teething does *not* cause bronchitis, convulsions, fever, rash or diarrhoea.

Delayed walking is *not* a problem for the orthopaedic specialist. It is *not* due to congenital dislocation of the hip.

Delayed talking is *not* due to tongue-tie, laziness, 'everything being done for him', and almost certainly not due to jealousy. If the child is mentally normal, it is usually a familial feature, but may be due to deafness.

Obesity is almost certainly *not* due to the excessively rare condition of Fröhlich's syndrome. I have not yet seen a case.

If a child has convulsions and is not well between fits, the diagnosis is almost certainly *not* uncomplicated epilepsy. The unwellness could be a side effect of drugs or other cause of convulsions.

Drowsiness following a head injury is often due to something unconnected with the head injury—such as acute otitis media or urinary tract infection. There may (or may not) have been a change in the symptoms, or the development of new symptoms which would point to a diagnosis different from that of a complication of the head injury.

Symptoms and signs suggestive of encephalitis may be due not to encephalitis, but a metabolic disease.

It is wrong to expect typical symptoms if a child has inhaled a foreign body. A foreign body may not show in an X-ray of the chest, the X-ray of the chest may be normal, and there may be no cough (for a time).

Although one is much more likely to be right if one ascribes all a child's symptoms to *one* disease, the occasional coexistence of two diseases is liable to cause confusion. For instance, a child with asthma may inhale a foreign body: a child with typical asthma may have fibrocystic disease of the pancreas.

The diagnosis that a child's symptoms are merely due to the mother's overanxiety and 'fussing' is an extremely dangerous one. On innumerable occasions I have seen this diagnosis cause a tragic error, and often medico-legal consequences.

The Paediatric Diagnostic Problem— Elementary Principles of Diagnosis

For those faced with a baffling diagnostic problem, the following is a summary of points made in the text of this book.

1   Non-disease is more common than disease. Common conditions, and variations of those common conditions, are more likely than rare diseases.

2   A full history is essential

    (a)   In the case of an infant, the history must include all possible relevant prenatal factors, including drugs taken, infections, nutrition and other socio-economic factors and metabolic disease. Nearly all women take drugs in pregnancy—many of them not considering tablets or other medicine to be drugs. Some are addicts—to alcohol, nicotine or other drugs—and are likely to deny that they are taking those drugs.

    (b)   In the case of an infant or young child, the history must include all perinatal factors—and in many cases (e.g. when there was anoxia at birth, an abnormal delivery or convulsions) these factors have to be related to prenatal factors, which are commonly much more important.

(c) In all cases a full history of drugs taken must be known. One can never assume that the mother will provide a full list, including those obtained from the chemist without prescription. In this book, in which I have attempted to cover all common symptoms of disease, more than 90 per cent of the symptoms discussed could be side effects of drugs.

(d) The possibility of poisoning or overdose has to be remembered, even though the parents stoutly deny its possibility, claiming that the child could not have had access to drugs (or could have taken only a very small quantity). The true diagnosis may be non-accidental injury.

Drug addiction, including solvent sniffing, may cause much confusion because of the wide variety of drugs or solvents available, and because their use is liable to be denied.

(e) The mother may be fabricating the child's symptoms as in the reverse Munchausen syndrome, or deliberately giving the child drugs when she visits him in hospital.

(f) The mother's real anxiety may be concealed. She complains that the child has innumerable symptoms, none suggesting disease: they may be symptoms which a neighbour's or friend's child had when suffering from leukaemia or other serious disease.

3   The examination should be re-checked, and signs of non-accidental injury should be sought.

4   The physical findings are checked against the history, and discrepancies should be noted. I recommend the doctor at this stage to sit and think.

5   If the diagnosis is still unknown, the appropriate books should be referred to. Below I have included the titles of books which I think would be helpful. For instance, when faced with a rare syndrome, the reader is advised to refer to the books by Bergsma or Warkany.

6   Only at this stage should relevant or possibly relevant special investigations be performed.

I recommend the following books:

Useful Books

Alagille D, Odievre M. *Liver and biliary tract disease in childhood*. New York: Wiley, 1979.

Anderson CM, Burke V. *Paediatric gastroenterology*. Oxford: Blackwell Scientific Publications, 1975.

Bakwin H, Bakwin RM. *Clinical management of behaviour disorders in children*. Philadelphia: Saunders, 1972.

Bean WB. *Rare diseases and lesions*. Springfield: Charles Thomas, 1967.

Bergsma D. *Birth defects compendium*. London: Macmillan Press, 1979.

Caffey J. *Pediatric X-ray diagnosis*. Chicago: Year Book Publications, 1978.

Davies DM. *Textbook of adverse drug reactions*. Oxford: Oxford University Press, 1981.

Dewhurst CJ. *Gynaecological disorders of infants and children*. London: Cassell, 1974.

Drillien CM, Drummond MB. *Neurodevelopmental problems in early childhood*. Oxford: Blackwell Scientific Publications, 1977.

Dubowitz V. *Muscle disorders in childhood*. Philadelphia: Saunders, 1978.

Dukes MNG (Ed). *Meyler's side effects of drugs*. Amsterdam: Excerpta Medica, 1979.

El Shafie M, Klippel CH. *Associated congenital anomalies*. Baltimore: Williams Wilkins, 1981.

Fitzpatrick TB, Eisen AZ, Wolff K, Freedberg IM, Austen KF. *Dermatology in general medicine*. New York: McGraw Hill, 1979.

Ford FR. *Disease of the nervous system in infancy, childhood and adolescence*. Springfield: Charles C. Thomas, 1973.

Forfar JO, Arneil GC. *Textbook of paediatrics*. Edinburgh: Churchill Livingstone, 1982.

Gardner LI. *Endocrine and genetic diseases of childhood*. Philadelphia: Saunders 1977.

Harries JT. *Essentials of paediatric gastroenterology*. London: Churchill Livingstone, 1977.

Illingworth RS. *The normal child*, 8th Edn. London: Churchill Livingstone, 1982.

Illingworth RS. *Development of the infant and young child, normal and abnormal*, 7th Edn. London: Churchill Livingstone, 1980.

Innes Williams D. *Paediatric urology*. London: Butterworths, 1968.

Jelliffe DB, Stanfield JP. *Diseases of children in the subtropics and tropics*. London: Edward Arnold, 1978.

Jones PG. *Clinical paediatric surgery*. Bristol: Wright, 1978.

Krugman S, Katz SL. *Infectious diseases of children*. St Louis: Mosby, 1981.

Lagos JC. *Differential diagnosis in paediatric neurology*. Boston: Little, Brown & Co, 1971.

Menkes JH. *Textbook of child neurology*. Philadelphia: Lea & Febiger, 1974.

Nelson WE, Vaughan VC, McKay RJ, Behrman RE. *Textbook of pediatrics*. Philadelphia: Saunders, 1979.

Raffensperger JG. *Swenson's pediatric surgery*. New York: Appleton Century Crofts, 1980.

Rook A, Wilkinson DS. Ebling FJG. *Textbook of dermatology*, 3rd Edn. Oxford: Blackwell Scientific Publications, 1979.

Rosenberg RN. *Neurology*. New York: Grune and Stratton, 1980.

Schaffer AJ, Avery ME. *Diseases of the newborn*. Philadelphia: Saunders, 1977.

Sharrard WJW. *Paediatric orthopaedics and fractures*, 2nd Edn. Oxford: Blackwell Scientific Publications, 1979.

Sherlock S. *Diseases of the liver and biliary system*, 6th Edn. Oxford: Blackwell Scientific Publications, 1981.

Smyth GDL. *Diagnostic ENT*. Oxford: Oxford University Press, 1978.

Stanbury JB, Wyngaarden JB, Frederickson DS. *The metabolic basis of inherited disease*. New York: McGraw Hill, 1978.

Swaiman KF, Wright PS. *Pediatric neuromuscular diseases*. St Louis: Mosby, 1979.

Tampion J. *Dangerous plants*. London: David & Charles, 1977.

Verbov J. *Paediatric dermatology*. London: Heinemann, 1979.

Wade OL. *Adverse reactions to drugs*. London: Heinemann 1975.

Walsh FB, Hoyt WF. *Clinical ophthalmology*. Baltimore: Williams and Wilkins, 1969.

Warkany J. *Congenital malformations*. Chicago: Year Book Publications, 1971.

Willoughby MLN. *Paediatric haematology*. London: Churchill Livingstone, 1977.

Index

Principal references are given in bold type.